Everyman, I will go with thee,
and be thy guide

THE EVERYMAN
LIBRARY

The Everyman Library was founded by J. M. Dent in 1906. He chose the name Everyman because he wanted to make available the best books ever written in every field to the greatest number of people at the cheapest possible price. He began with Boswell's 'Life of Johnson'; his one-thousandth title was Aristotle's 'Metaphysics', by which time sales exceeded forty million.

Today Everyman paperbacks remain true to J. M. Dent's aims and high standards, with a wide range of titles at affordable prices in editions which address the needs of today's readers. Each new text is reset to give a clear, elegant page and to incorporate the latest thinking and scholarship. Each book carries the pilgrim logo, the character in 'Everyman', a medieval morality play, a proud link between Everyman past and present.

Christina Rossetti

POEMS AND PROSE

Edited by
JAN MARSH

EVERYMAN
J. M. DENT · LONDON
CHARLES E. TUTTLE
VERMONT

This edition first published in Everyman
in 1994
Reprinted 1996, 1998

J. M. Dent
Orion Publishing Group
Orion House, 5 Upper St Martin's Lane,
London WC2H 9EA
and
Charles E. Tuttle Co. Inc.
28 South Main Street,
Rutland, Vermont 05701, USA

Typeset in Sabon by Deltatype Ltd, Ellesmere Port, Cheshire

Printed in Great Britain by
The Guernsey Press Company Ltd, Guernsey, C.I.

British Library Cataloguing-in-Publication Data
is available upon request.

ISBN 0 460 87536 1

CONTENTS

NOTE ON THE AUTHOR AND EDITOR

CHRISTINA G. ROSSETTI (1830–94) was among the finest poets writing in English in the Victorian era, whose work remains popular with general readers and scholars alike. It ranges from simple-seeming lyrics and carols such as 'In the bleak mid-winter', through dramatic fantasy poems like 'Goblin Market' to devotional and mystical meditations on the human and divine. Her work displays a teasing sense of humour, and a Gothic imagination. Born into a largely Italian family in London, she was sister to two members of the Pre-Raphaelite Brotherhood, and in her own right worked at the London Penitentiary for Fallen Women, helping to reclaim prostitutes from a life of sin. She published four volumes of poetry, two books for children, and a collection of sparkling stories, some of which are reprinted here for the first time. In later life she became renowned as a religious writer in an age of doubt, and as a sonneteer to rival Petrarch and Shakespeare.

JAN MARSH is a biographer and critic, whose books include *Christina Rossetti: A Literary Biography* (1994); *The Legend of Elizabeth Siddal* (1989); *Pre-Raphaelite Sisterhood* (1985); and *Edward Thomas: Poet for his Country* (1978). Educated at the universities of Cambridge and Sussex, she has lectured widely in Britain and North America on women in the Pre-Raphaelite circle and issues of gender in Victorian art and literature.

CHRONOLOGY OF ROSSETTI'S LIFE

Year	*Age*	*Life*
1826		Marriage of Gabriele Rossetti and Frances Mary Lavinia Polidori (FLR)
1827		Birth of Maria Francesca Rossetti (MFR)
1828		Birth of Gabriel Charles Dante Rossetti (DGR)
1829		Birth of William Michael Rossetti (WMR)
1830		Birth of Christina Georgina Rossetti (CGR) on 5 December
1842	11	First surviving poem 'To My Mother'
1843	12	FLR and her daughters attend Christ Church Albany Street, under Rev. William Dodsworth. Gabriele Rossetti suffers breakdown and loss of income
1844	13	MFR leaves home to become a governess
1845	14	CGR suffers nervous breakdown. WMR joins Civil Service as junior clerk. DGR at art school. MFR returns home to be daily governess and language teacher. Park Village Sisterhood founded in Christ Church parish
c. 1846		CGR becomes confirmed member of the Church of England
1847	16	*Verses* by Christina G. Rossetti issued by grandfather
1848	17	First commercially published poems, in *Athenaeum* (October). Engagement to James Collinson, member of Pre-Raphaelite Brotherhood.

CHRONOLOGY OF HER TIMES

Year	Artistic Events	Historical Events
1820–1		Uprising by and suppression of Carbonari and other patriots in Naples
1824	Death of Byron at Missilonghi	
1832		First Reform Act in Britain
1837		Accession of Queen Victoria
1838–9		Chartist Movement
1842	Tennyson, *Poems*	
1843	Dickens, *A Christmas Carol* Carlyle, *Past and Present*	
1844	Elizabeth Barrett, *Poems*	
1845		J. H. Newman joins Church of Rome
1846	Elopement and marriage of Elizabeth Barrett and Robert Browning	
1846–7		Famine in Ireland
1847	Charlotte Brontë, *Jane Eyre* Anne Brontë, *Agnes Grey* Emily Brontë, *Wuthering Heights* Tennyson, *The Princess*	
1848	Pre-Raphaelite Brotherhood	Democratic revolutions in France, Germany, Austria, Poland and parts of Italy

Year	*Age*	*Life*
1850	19	Seven poems in the *Germ*. Visit to Longleat House, Wiltshire. Writes *Maude: A Story for Girls*. End of engagement to James Collinson
1851	20	Rossetti family move to Camden Town, where CGR assists her mother with a school for young children
1852	21	CGR contributes verses in Italian and epistolary novel *Corrispondenzia Famigliare* (unfinished) to *The Bouquet from Marylebone Gardens*
1853	22–3	CGR resident with mother and father in Frome, Somerset. Grandfather Polidori dies
1854	23	Gabriele Rossetti dies in London (April). CGR meets Mary Howitt, author and editor, and has poems published in anthologies. Other contributions rejected by *Blackwood's* and *Fraser's*. Aunt Eliza Polidori joins Florence Nightingale's nursing team at the Barrack Hospital, Scutari
1855	24	CGR meets Bessie Rayner Parkes, Barbara Leigh Smith (Bodichon), Adelaide Proctor and other women writers
1856	25	*The Lost Titian* published in *The Crayon* (New York)
1857	26	*Nick* published in the *National Magazine*. CGR visits Warlingham, Surrey
1857–8	26–7	Acquaintance and possible proposal from John Brett. Visit to Letitia and William Bell Scott in Newcastle
1859	28	CGR joins staff of Diocesan Penitentiary for Fallen Women at Highgate. Writes 'Goblin Market'. 'In the Round Tower at Jhansi' and 'Maude Clare' published in *Once a Week*
1860	29	MFR begins attachment to All Saints Sisterhood, Marylebone. DGR marries Elizabeth Siddal
1861	30	'Up-hill' published in *Macmillan's Magazine* (February), followed by other poems. CGR prepares her first collection. Contributes to *English Woman's Journal*
1862	31	Death of Elizabeth Siddal Rossetti (February); DGR moves to Chelsea. *Goblin Market and Other Poems* published (April) to critical acclaim. CGR's first foreign trip, to Paris and Normandy (June)

Year	*Artistic Events*	*Historical Events*
1850	Death of Wordsworth Tennyson, *In Memoriam*; becomes Poet Laureate	Roman Catholic hierarchy established in Britain
1851		Napoleon III assumes power in France The Great Exhibition
1852	Harriet Beecher Stowe, *Uncle Tom's Cabin* (British publication)	
1853	Elizabeth Gaskell, *Ruth* Charlotte Yonge, *Heir of Redclyffe*	
1854	Tennyson, *The Charge of the Light Brigade*	Crimean War declared by Britain and France against Russia; Florence Nightingale leads nursing team to Scutari; Gold Rush in Australia
1856	William Morris and Edward Burne-Jones, *Oxford & Cambridge Magazine*	Feminist campaign for Married Women's Property Act
1857	Elizabeth Barrett Browning, *Aurora Leigh* Baudelaire, *Les Fleurs du Mal*	Indian Mutiny
1859	Charles Darwin, *The Origin of Species* Mill, *On Liberty* Tennyson, *Idylls of the King*	
1859–60		Liberation and eventual unification of Italy
1860	Ruskin, *Unto this Last*	Society for the Employment of Women
1861	Death of Elizabeth Barrett Browning	American Civil War begins Death of Prince Albert
1862		Emancipation Proclamation by President Lincoln Formation of Morris & Co

Year	*Age*	*Life*
1862–4	31–3	Meets fellow poets Jean Ingelow and Dora Greenwell. Joins Portfolio Society, informal writers and artists' group founded by Barbara Bodichon. Contributes to *Victoria Magazine* and to religious anthologies
1864–5	33–4	Probable end of work at Highgate, owing to bronchial cough. Spends winter at Hastings, working on new collection. Begins poem sequence in Italian inspired by love for Charles Cayley
1865	35	Travels to Switzerland and northern Italy with FLR and WMR
1866	36	*Poems* published by Roberts Bros, Boston. *The Prince's Progress and Other Poems* published by Macmillan. CGR visits William Bell Scott and Alice Boyd at Penkill Castle, Ayrshire. Declines proposal from Charles Cayley
1867	37	Three religious stories in the *Churchman's Shilling Magazine*, followed by article on translations of Dante. Rossetti Household moves to Euston Square, Bloomsbury
1870	40	Publication of *Poems* by DGR. Publication of *Commonplace and Other Short Stories*, issued by Ellis & Co
1870–2	40–2	CGR suffers serious illness (Graves' disease)
1871	41	Publication of *SingSong* by Dalziels for Routledge, with illustrations by Arthur Hughes
1872	42	DGR suffers nervous collapse and suicidal paranoia
1873	43	WMR becomes engaged to Lucy Madox Brown. MFR begins novitiate at All Saints' Sisterhood
1874	44	WMR's marriage. Publication of *Annus Domini: A Prayer for Each Day of the Year* (James Parker & Co). Publication of *Speaking Likenesses* by Macmillan
1875	45	Collected edition of *Poems* published by Macmillan. Birth of CGR's niece Olive Rossetti
1876	46	CGR, FLR and aunts move to Torrington Square, Bloomsbury. Death of MFR

Year	Artistic Events	Historical Events
1865	Carroll, *Alice in Wonderland*	American Civil War ends Foundation of Vassar College, USA
1866	Swinburne, *Poems and Ballads*	
1867		Second British Reform Act Women's suffrage societies launched in Britain and USA
1868	William Morris, *The Earthly Paradise* Robert Browning, *The Ring and the Book* Mill, *The Subjection of Women*	Gladstone, PM
1869	Arnold, *Culture and Anarchy*	Foundation of Girton College; Suez Canal opened
1870	Death of Dickens	Franco-Prussian War; Elementary Education Act
1871		Paris Commune
1872	George Eliot, *Middlemarch*	
1873	Pater, *Studies in the History of the Renaissance*	
1874		Annexation of Gold Coast (Ghana) by Britain
1876	Ibsen, *A Doll's House* Alice Meynell, *Preludes*	Queen Victoria proclaimed Empress of India; university entrance and medical education opened to British women

Year	*Age*	*Life*
1877	47	CGR and FLR visit DGR near Herne Bay, Kent
1878–80	48–50	CGR attends lectures on *Divine Comedy* at University College, London. Corresponds with Augusta Webster on subject of women's franchise
1879	49	Publication of *Harmony on 1 Corinthians XII* in *New and Old* church magazine. Publication of *Seek and Find: Short Studies of the Benedicite* by SPCK
1880	50	Major sonnet sequences in progress. CGR involved in anti-vivisection campaign
1881	51	Death of James Collinson. Publication of *A Pageant and Other Poems* by Macmillan. Publication of *Called to be Saints: the Minor Festivals devotionally studied* by SPCK
1882	52	Death of DGR at Birchington, Kent, attended by CGR and FLR. Publication of *Poems, New Series* by Roberts Bros, Boston. CGR considers writing biographies of Adelaide Proctor, Elizabeth Barrett Browning and Ann Radcliffe for *Eminent Women* series, but all projects fall through
1883	53	Publication of *Letter and Spirit: Notes on the Commandments* by SPCK. Death of Charles Cayley. CGR involved in child protection campaign
1885	55	Publication of *Time Flies, A Reading Diary* by SPCK. Start of friendships with Katharine Tynan and Lisa Wilson
1886	56	Death of FLR
1887–92	57–62	CGR nurses Aunts Charlotte and Eliza Polidori till their deaths
1890	60	Publication of enlarged edition of *Poems* by Macmillan
1892	62	Publication of *The Face of the Deep: a commentary on the Apolcalypse* by SPCK. Surgery for cancer
1893	63	Publication of *Verses* by SPCK
1894	63–4	Death of Lucy Brown Rossetti (April). CGR dies (29 December)

Year	*Artistic Events*	*Historical Events*
1881	James, *Portrait of a Lady* Wilde, *Poems*	Married Women's Property Act
1882		British occupation of Egypt
1883	Olive Schreiner, *Story of an African Farm*	
1885	W. T. Stead, *The Maiden Tribute of Modern Babylon*	Age of sexual consent raised to 16; British war against Sudan Death of Gen. Gordon at Khartoum; foundation of Socialist League Demonstrations against unemployment in London
1886		Irish Home Rule Bill defeated
1889	Death of Browning Yeats, *Wanderings of Oisin*	
1890	Death of Tennyson and Newman Morris, *News from Nowhere* Emily Dickinson, *Poems*	
1894		Woman Suffrage Act in New Zealand

INTRODUCTION

On the death of Lord Tennyson in 1892, many in Britain regarded Christina Rossetti as the finest living poet. Lewis Carroll declared: 'If only the Queen would consult *me* as to whom to make Poet Laureate! I would say "For once, Madam, take a *lady*!" '[1]

Christina Rossetti's reputation slumped during the anti-Victorian reaction in the first half of the twentieth century, and was slow to recover alongside those of her contemporaries amongst the 'great Victorians'. But her work has always been admired by poets, and by the general public familiar with her carol 'In the bleak mid-winter', with her sonnet 'Remember', read at so many funerals, and with the gist if not the whole of 'Up-hill' and 'Goblin Market'.

Since 1980 Rossetti has been regaining her critical stature too. According to Isobel Armstrong, in 'Re-Reading Victorian Poetry', 'In the depth and range of their projects, and in the beauty and boldness of their experiments with language, Tennyson, Browning and Christina Rossetti stand pre-eminent.'[2]

But while Rossetti has always been well represented in anthologies, and now increasingly in scholarly journals, there are as yet few satisfactory and available editions of her work, and few full-length critical studies. Until recently, too, it was possible for her name to be ignored in general works on Victorian poetry. Readers by and large have therefore had to rely on their own responses – a process this volume hopes to encourage by providing a wider range of texts than has hitherto been available, with brief notes, contextual information and suggestions for further reading. Studies of Rossetti are growing apace: in a few years her critical significance in English literature will be transformed. It is nevertheless easy to enjoy her writing without any specialist knowledge, for her words spring off the page with irresistible grace and spirit.

As well as poetry, Christina Rossetti wrote and published fiction and prose – satirical, devotional, critical and visionary.

This Selection includes several examples, together with extracts from her lively letters. The republication of both fiction and prose adds a dimension to our understanding of her career and contemporary reputation. The poetry, however, is her claim to fame, and to critical attention. She wrote over a thousand individual pieces, of which 226 are included here. They are, for the most part, deftly simple and astoundingly subtle.

Christina Georgina Rossetti was the youngest child of Gabriele Rossetti, Italian poet and exiled patriot, and his wife Frances, née Polidori, herself the daughter of an English mother and an Italian father, a translator and teacher who had settled in Britain. Christina was reared on tales of how Papa had escaped from Naples with a price on his head, and on memories of Uncle John Polidori, Byron's physician and the author of *The Vampyre*. The four children – Maria Francesca, born 1827, Dante Gabriel, born 1828, William Michael, born 1829, and Christina, born 5 December 1830 – were accustomed to hearing both English and Italian; though in time their maternal inheritance largely prevailed, all four studied, translated and sometimes wrote in Italian, whose musicality is one key to Christina's versification.

Politically, the family was aligned with the liberal forces that brought about the European 'year of revolutions' in 1848. Their father, who at the time of Christina's birth held the chair of Italian at the newly founded Kings College, London, as a Dante scholar, lived in hope of returning home in triumph. Meanwhile, he was acting doyen of the exile community in London, and a warm, expansive host. In old age, William recreated the scene in the family parlour, seeing

> my father and three or four foreigners engaged in animated talk on the affairs of Europe, from the point of patriotic aspiration and hope long deferred . . . with frequent and fervent recitations of poetry . . .
>
> My mother quiet but interested, and sometimes taking her mild womanly part in the conversation; and we four children . . . drinking it all in as a sort of necessary atmosphere of the daily life, yet with our own little interests and occupations – reading, colouring prints, looking into illustrated books, nursing a cat . . .[3]

When their father's hopes of 'name and fame' in Britain faded, Frances Rossetti silently transferred her intellectual ambitions, encouraging all four children to excellence in the liberal arts and keeping a precious 'maternal store' of their productions (and later, of their reviews).[4] Christina's first poem, written at age eleven, was a birthday gift to her mother, carefully preserved. Some few months afterwards she was hailed as the 'poet of the family'[5] – just as Gabriel was predicted to become a world-famous painter.

Christina described her parents as 'clever and cultivated'. But the never-wealthy family was plunged into poverty in the early 1840s when their father's mental and physical health collapsed, inaugurating a dark time that none wished to remember. At the age of fourteen Christina suffered a serious breakdown herself, and subsequently experienced regular bouts of depression and related illness; much of her teenage verse expresses a Keatsian wish for death and oblivion, in which the poet is imaged as lying in her grave, emotionally frozen and estranged.

In this period, together with her sister, mother and maternal aunts, she came under the powerful influence of the nascent Anglo-Catholic movement in the Church of England led by Edward Pusey, a frequent preacher at the church where the Rossetti women worshipped under incumbent William Dodsworth. In the same parish, in 1845, the first Anglican conventual order for women since the Reformation was founded, inspiring in Maria Rossetti a lifelong desire for the religious life, finally achieved in 1874, and in Christina a lifelong commitment to High Anglican beliefs, together with a deep fear of unworthiness and damnation. This was augmented, somewhat unusually, with a strong strain of Adventism (belief in the imminence of the Final Judgment) derived from Dodsworth, and a firm Protestant resistance to Papal jurisdiction, Mariolatry and sacerdotal intercession, which led in time to her own contributions to religious thought. In Christina's theology, every believer had a direct relation to her God, and a duty to speak. Doctrinally, she was aligned with the Anglican Divines of the seventeenth century and writers like Herbert, Donne, Vaughan and Bunyan.

She was educated entirely at home by her mother, with some tuition in Italian from her grandfather. She always regarded herself as the family dunce, but her reading in literature and history was wide, if lacking – like most girls of her time – in maths, science and classics. In 1847 her first small selection of poems was privately printed by her grandfather. Intended mainly for domestic consumption, this was also her poetic debut, within a tradition of juvenile achievement that included Felicia Hemans's first collection at age fourteen, and Elizabeth Barrett's *The Battle of Marathon* at the same age. The most notable poem in Rossetti's collection was 'The Dead City', which blends a Sleeping Beauty theme with that of spiritual atrophy following sensual indulgence.

The following year Christina had two poems accepted by the *Athenaeum*, the most prestigious literary weekly of the era. She seemed well-set on a 'brilliant career', but the proscriptions of Victorian femininity – the cultural ban on 'publicity' and the devotional promotion of humility – made literary ambition difficult for women to negotiate. As Sara Coleridge, daughter of the poet and fellow writer, remarked approvingly: 'all the women of first-rate genius I have known have been and are diffident, feminine and submissive in habits and temper.'[6]

By temperament Christina Rossetti was far from submissive. She identified her prevalent faults as pride and anger, which she strove to conquer, changing in the process from a lively, mischievous girl into a painfully self-controlled young woman, retreating behind a mask of excessive and sometimes offensive politeness, hardly able to unbend even with close friends. As a child she had been aligned with Maria by gender, with William by age and with Gabriel by a shared spiritedness that developed into a mutual sense of artistic endeavour as Gabriel became his sister's greatest admirer and most acute critic, which she warmly acknowledged. Together, Christina, Gabriel and William competed at *bouts-rimés*, racing to complete a sonnet to each other's rhymes in the shortest time. Invited to join her brothers' proposed 'literary club', however, she declined on the grounds that it would seem like 'display, the sort of thing she abhors'.[7]

This is one of the problems explored in *Maude*, Christina's first surviving story, whose heroine struggles with the conflicting demands of religion, poetry and submissive femininity, articulated in the figures of Magdalen, who becomes a nun; the eponymous heroine, who suffers from ambition and spiritual distress; and her cousin Mary, who follows the conventional path of courtship and marriage. This was followed by the unfinished *Corrispondenzia Famigliare*, an epistolary tale in Italian, again with three main characters: Angela-Maria, daughter of an Italian patriot; fashionable Emma; and pious Clorinda, engaged to a curate.

At the end of 1848 Christina was drawn into the excitement of the Pre-Raphaelite Brotherhood or 'PRB', founded by her brothers and their friends William Holman Hunt, John Everett Millais, James Collinson, Thomas Woolner and Frederick Stephens. Her verse featured prominently, albeit anonymously, in their short-lived magazine the *Germ* (1850, four issues only). By this date she had been engaged to James Collinson for some fifteen months – a decorous and somewhat distant affair, according to the conventions of the time; owing to their youth, there was no prospect of marriage for several years. According to William, Christina accepted James without being 'in love', but then fully bestowed her affections upon him, so that his decision around May 1850 to dedicate himself to a life of celibate service in the Catholic Church struck a devastating blow at her immature heart. But it is a mistake to attribute her many poems of unhappy love entirely to James's defection: several of the most memorable were written at earlier dates, and the strain of melancholy heartbreak that runs though her work has origins not only in her experiences but also in her emotional formation and in the nineteenth-century tradition of mourning verse, particularly popular among women poets but given supreme expression in Tennyson's *In Memoriam* (1850) – a work of immense and inescapable influence over later writers.

Contrary to many assumptions, Christina seldom posed for the PRB painters, but she did sit to Collinson for her portrait and to Gabriel for the head of the Virgin in *The Girlhood of Mary* (1849) and *Ecce Ancilla Domini* (1850). Despite some instruction in drawing, she retained a naive childlike hand, and showed very little 'eye' in respect of visual art, confessing herself easily fatigued by trudging round exhibitions. But much of her writing is akin to Pre-Raphaelite painting in its infusion of brilliance and feeling:

> I deck myself with silks and jewelry,
> I plume myself like any mated dove;
> They praise my rustling show, and never see
> My heart is breaking for a little love.
> While sprouts green lavender
> With rosemary and myrrh,
> For in quick spring my sap is all astir.

From the outset, humour, satire and subversion coexisted alongside sadness in Rossetti's natural poetic voice. Overall, the mournful mode predominates, yet the sprightly, mocking, colloquial tone is equally characteristic, and some of the finest moments in her verse are those where cool irony blends piquantly with sorrow. Her sensibility was seldom sentimental. During the 1850s, when her poems met rejection from editors, she wrote several sparkling tales, *Nick*, *Hero*, and *The Lost Titian*, wittily exploring anger, envy, ambition and artistic rivalry – themes and emotions that women were not supposed to express. *The Lost Titian* draws with particular brilliance on her dual linguistic inheritance and intimacy with the PRB.

In 1853–4 Christina spent twelve months in Frome, Somerset, assisting her mother in a small school and caring for her invalid father. In this period both her grandparents died, as did her father soon after the return to London. Thereafter she lived with mother, sister, brother William and one or more aunts, first on the eastern side of Regents Park (where the zoo was a favourite haunt) and then in Bloomsbury. She always considered herself a 'town bird', disclaiming any detailed knowledge of nature, despite her many poems on the seasons – which are indeed expressive of inner feelings rather than the climate or countryside. Over her lifetime, nature poetry came to be overwhelmingly popular in verse, while to Rossetti the natural world was increasingly seen as an intimation or image of the mystery at the heart of creation, the work of the Creator.

She had a wide circle of friends, both artistic and religious, and in 1857–8 briefly attracted the affections of painter John Brett, who is thought to have come close to proposing. In all matters of the heart, however, Christina was extremely reticent. It appears that Brett's ardour coincided with James Collinson's marriage, and an episode in Christina's novella *Commonplace* suggests she first saw this in a newspaper announcement.

'Is the eye waxen dim, is the dark hair changing to grey that hath won neither laurel nor bay?' she wrote mournfully at the end of 1860, soon after her thirtieth birthday. Commenting on this poem, William wrote, in his wordy manner:

> It is quite possible that Christina – the most modest of poets but by no means wanting in the self-consciousness of poetic faculty – thought in 1860 that the bay [wreath of fame] had been kept waiting quite long enough.[8]

Ironically, however, the failure of her career to take off during the 1850s enabled Rossetti to develop a distinctive and original poetic voice, free from the conventions that shaped and softened most women's verse, and also helped her emerge from the shadow of Tennyson. Though she often claimed not to be well-read, her work reveals many intertextual echoes and references, linking it to Barrett Browning, Keats and the Spasmodics, as well as showing earlier influences from L.E.L., Hemans, Crabbe, Scott, Blake and Pope. Favourite Gothic authors included Maturin, Beddoes and Edgar Allan Poe. She was also familiar with neo-classical Italian writers from Tasso onwards, and like the other members of her family had an intimate knowledge of Dante, and also of Petrarch, on whom she wrote an extended entry for the Universal Dictionary of Biography, in which she referred to family documents showing herself to be descended from Laura.[9]

In 1854 she applied unsuccessfully to join her aunt Eliza Polidori as a Nightingale nurse in the Crimean War. She took a number of short governessing posts, but disliked the work and was similarly ill-suited to the welfare visiting undertaken by many women in her position. In 1859, however, she became a professional voluntary worker or Associate Sister at the St Mary Magdalene Home for Fallen Women at Highgate, carrying out residential and supervisory duties in the reformation of young prostitutes. This occupation (which probably continued for four or five years) coincided with the composition of Rossetti's masterpiece 'Goblin Market', a moral fantasy and many-layered text of multiple meanings. Not least of these is the indirect depiction of erotic arousal and female desire, conveyed in Laura's frenzied sucking of the goblin fruits and her final orgasmic epiphany as she tastes the juice again on her sister's lips:

Like the watchtower of a town
Which an earthquake shatters down,
Like a lightning-stricken mast,
Like a wind-uprooted tree
Spun about,
Like a foam-topped waterspout
Cast down headlong in the sea,
She fell at last;
Pleasure past and anguish past

'Goblin Market' is the subject of more critical essays than all the rest of Rossetti's work: a perennial text with new value for each generation and especially fruitful in its multivalent imagery. In terms of authorial intent, it is a fairy-tale fantasy derived from folkloric sources about traffic between humans and elves – the eating of fairy food leads to dangerous enchantment – and a simultaneous fable of temptation, remorse and redemption, in which Laura's soul sickens unto death as the result of her transgression, only redeemed by the Christ-like action of Lizzie, who offers herself as in the Eucharist. But its power – and its staying power as a text – comes from less conscious elements, or rather from the interaction of intentional, concealed and unconscious strands; as Armstrong notes in relation to Victorian verse in general, there is 'a way of reading which gives equal weight to a text's stated project and to the polysemic and possibly wayward meanings it generates'.[10] Do not be intimidated by this poem, however: 'Goblin Market' is a joy to read – especially aloud.

It furnished the title poem of Rossetti's first collection, published by Macmillan in April 1862. The reviews were enthusiastic, with 'An Apple-Gathering,' 'Echo' and 'Up-hill' being singled out for especial praise. Elizabeth Barrett Browning's death two months later led to Rossetti being hailed as her natural successor as 'female laureate'. The two women never met, nor is Barrett Browning known to have seen any of Rossetti's work, but some months afterwards Browning himself called to pay his respects, and in later life Rossetti often expressed her admiration for 'EBB'. There are curious similarities between 'The Lowest Room' and 'Aurora Leigh', though the dates of composition make any direct influence impossible.

Thereafter, part of Rossetti's problem was the high expectations aroused by the *Goblin Market* volume. Never again, in fact, did she attain what she herself called the 'special felicity' of her goblins, but she refused the temptation to write more in the same vein. To Macmillan, in 1863, she wrote: 'I am yet more firmly convinced that my system of not writing against the grain is the right one.'[11]

She preferred to wait and to 'take what came when it came'. This statement, together with the fact that she rarely re-worked poems once complete (apart from minor alterations or excisions) and William's assertion that 'her habits of composition were entirely of the casual and spontaneous kind . . . if something came into her head which she found suggestive of verse, she put it into verse',[12] has led to the misleading idea that her poems were more or less involuntary, artless effusions, springing fully formed from her pen, rather than crafted works of art. As Angela Leighton has shown, this illusion of spontaneity was part of the female poet's persona, strategically obscuring the entry into public speech.[13] In the context of highly gendered writing and reading, women's words were frequently presented as flowing direct from the heart not the head, as if writing on, or from, the body. In fact, though Rossetti did not struggle over her verses nor make subsequent alterations (unlike Gabriel, who tattooed his proofs with changes), her habits of composition were careful, technically challenging and self-consciously aware of the poetic mask. She was always a writer of exact meaning, just as she was never a poet of false metre, however free and varied her verse lines.

On an early occasion she warned William against circulating some of her poems among friends, lest they be construed as 'love personals', and this is in part what makes her work so exciting: the poems sound, but are not, confessional. She herself valued the 'genuine lyric cry' above other forms of poetic labour,[14] relishing the delicate construction of simple surfaces over complexities of expression; some of her own have the gossamer strength of spiders' webs. Between 1862 and 1864 Rossetti was involved with the Portfolio Society, a group of women (and the occasional man) who circulated poems and drawings on themes set each month, for mutual criticism. The group was conceived by Barbara Bodichon and her sister, and Rossetti described herself as 'a corresponding member' who submitted work but did not attend meetings.

'The Prince's Progress' is a second moral fantasy, based in her own words on a 'reverse of the Sleeping Beauty', but also on Bunyan. The Princess, who stands perhaps for the Prince's immortal soul, is not awakened but lost by his dalliance with the delights of the world. 'Of course I don't expect the general public to catch these refined clues, but there they are for such minds as mine,' she told Gabriel in regard to certain symbolic details.[15] Gabriel played a major role in selecting the contents for this, vetoing some of the more intensely religious pieces and also 'The Lowest Room', which he felt was infected with a 'falsetto muscularity' borrowed from Barrett Browning. This gendered assessment shows how clearly women were expected to stick to 'feminine' themes, and not stray into argumentative or philosophical verse. Christina respected Gabriel's judgement, however – he had, in general, high standards and a good ear – and welcomed his suggestions, up to a point. When he continued to delay the volume with further criticisms, she responded with 'six well-defined and several paroxysms of stamping, foaming, hair-uprooting', to signify her impatience.[16] And in her third collection she silently inserted 'The Lowest Room', much to his dismay.

Published in 1866, *The Prince's Progress and Other Poems* was rather eclipsed by the commotion that surrounded the appearance and suppression of Swinburne's *Poems and Ballads*, for which William Rossetti drafted a defence, linking its poetics with her own. Swinburne numbered himself among Christina's warmest admirers, though his praise was more extravagant than purposeful, and while few poets could be further apart in terms of content and intent, both share a similar stylistic predilection for circularity, assonance, feminine rhymes and anaphora that places them in rhetorical affinity – with each other and with *écriture feminine*. In some respects Swinburne borrowed as much from Rossetti as from Baudelaire, and by the same token Rossetti may be placed in the ranks of developing Aestheticism and English Symbolism, with the qualification that in her case the religiosity was genuine.

Another younger poet deeply influenced by Christina Rossetti was Gerard Manley Hopkins. Both poets wrestled with guilty desire, and had a troubled relationship with their God, if not their faith. Though Rossetti is often held to be an unproblematically (even banal) religious writer, her verse is also wracked by doubt and fear. As Angela Leighton notes, far from being 'a simple and pious woman', whose poems reveal few questionings, Rossetti 'seems to have suffered from some profound underlying doubt and distrust'.[17] When she prayed, God did not often answer. When he called, she could not always respond. She related almost exclusively to Christ, intensely invoking Jesus's suffering and torture, as if drawn to identification, and in middle life she confessed to being literally afraid of God the Father, having felt 'towards the Divine Son as if He alone were our Friend, the Divine Father being our foe; as if Christ had not only to rescue us from the righteous wrath of His Father, but to shelter us from His enmity.'[18]

Patriarchy, in personal, religious and literary terms, was certainly an oppressive and restrictive force in Rossetti's life, and in recent years readers have often deplored her internalized acceptance of gender inferiority in such poems as 'The Lowest Room' and 'The Lowest Place', whose titles seem to offer a keynote to her self-image. It is, however, important to distinguish religious self-abasement here (even if the grovelling sinner is scarcely attractive to today's tastes), for in secular respects her articulation of gender issues in verse and prose should be seen as sites of struggle rather than submission. Christina had a lifelong argument with feminism, shaped by her assertive temper, egalitarian upbringing and friendship with leading members of the women's movement in the 1850s and '60s such as Mary Howitt, Barbara Bodichon, Emily Davies, and oppositionally by the edicts of Puseyite religion, her sister Maria's self-denying example and her own choice of financial dependence (she was first supported by William, and later inherited investments). In veiled shape, gender issues inform a great deal of her work, but it is impossible to reconcile her statements on sexual inequality. She refused requests to support university education and votes for women, and even signed the notorious women's anti-suffrage petition circulated in 1889. At around the same time (that of Jack the Ripper) she also noted, however, that 'we women claim no more than equality with our brethren in head and heart', while in terms of physical strength the fact that women were 'far more liable to undergo than to inflict hurt, to be cut (for instance) than to cut'[19] was in her view a powerful argument against male assumptions of supremacy.

Her second serious 'affair of the heart' was with a timid, unworldly and (in the eyes of the world) somewhat ridiculous linguist named Charles Bagot Cayley, a friend of the family, to whom she was attracted in 1864, and to or for whom she composed a sequence of love poems in Italian, which were discovered after her death. Cayley was so shy that he did not immediately perceive her feelings and when in 1866 he finally asked her to marry him, she declined, on the grounds of religious (and, one suspects, personal) incompatibility, despite maintaining a devoted friendship until his death. Her brother Gabriel married in 1860 and was widowed two years later; Maria, whose heart was briefly warmed by John Ruskin, remained single; and William married late, being the only sibling to produce children. The family was thus close and loving, but repeatedly struck by tragedy.

In the late 1860s, Christina turned to prose, writing a sequence of religiously motivated tales on the topics of pew-rent, adherence to the Anglican communion and the dangers of materialism, greed and godlessness. These were succeeded by satirical fiction, in the sharp social observation of *Commonplace*, which traces the fortunes of three sisters who respectively marry for wealth, marry for love and remain single. This, as Gabriel remarked with surprise, was rather in the Jane Austen mode, with comparable wit and insight, but a plot that owes more to Maria Edgeworth. In 1870 her small stock of eight stories was published by Ellis & Co; they sank virtually without trace and have never been reprinted.

Around the same time, she wrote a collection of poems for children, published as *SingSong* (1872) with attractive illustrations by Arthur Hughes. It has long been regarded as a gem of the genre, though perhaps more by adults than by the children for whom it was intended, for the little poems, many half-glancingly based on traditional rhymes, cover a full range of topics, including infant death and sorrow, now deemed inappropriate for the nursery. In this book may be glimpsed memories from Christina's own childhood, with its joys and tears – and a profound understanding of how the world appears to the young. *SingSong*, well-received, was followed in 1874 by *Speaking Likenesses*, three linked stories for slightly older children. This is more astringent in tone and has indeed been described as 'a peculiarly revolting' text for children.[20] As it has long been out of print, its republication here may allow this judgement to be tested, but it may be noted that many of the episodes in *Alice in Wonderland* are equally unpleasant. Christina Rossetti was more of a moralist than Lewis Carroll (who incidentally began *Alice* shortly after reading 'Goblin Market', and the following year photographed all the Rossetti family to their great satisfaction) and, as her nieces and nephew discovered, was ever-anxious to curb wilfulness in children, lest self prevail. Read correctly, however, *Speaking Likenesses* is both an instructional and healing narrative, with a happy ending, as the heroines undergo various painful trials before earning the final reward.

In 1870–2 Christina suffered a long illness caused by a thyroid condition, which kept her house-bound and often bed-ridden. At times life-threatening, it left her permanently weakened, and not surprisingly with a renewed sense of religious obligation, immediately expressed in a little day-book of prayers. As was customary at the time, the Rossetti women read the Bible daily, and in later life Christina's writing often seems composed in a sort of scriptural dialect of biblical phrases and imagery, somewhat in the Anabaptist manner. Issued by a religious publishing firm,

Annus Domini was followed by *Called to be Saints* (written 1875–6 but published in 1881), a dense Anglican hagiography designed for boys and girls in their teens. This was succeeded by a Harmony, forming an indirect commentary on 1 Corinthians XII ('And now abideth faith, hope, charity, these three: but the greatest of these is charity'), which was in part a response to contemporary war-mongering, and by a longer meditation on the Benedicite or praise poem of the Three Holy Children from the Book of Daniel. Then came *Letter and Spirit* (1883), on the Ten Commandments, and in 1885 Rossetti's favourite among her prose writings, the 'reading diary' *Time Flies*, with both prose and verse entries, ranging from the absurd to the profound – all intended to be rather like 'Thought for the Day'. This is the most personal of her devotional books, containing many specific memories and observations available nowhere else in her writing. It is the closest we have to a spiritual autobiography, offering the careful reader an insight into how Rossetti saw and understood her life. By this date she had lost nearly all those dear to her: Maria died of cancer in 1876, unexpectedly young; Gabriel died in 1882, after a wretched decade of schizophrenic distress and paranoia; Charles Cayley in 1883; and Frances Rossetti, peacefully, in 1885. Thereafter, Christina devoted herself to the care of two ageing aunts.

Her devotional books have received virtually no critical study, but they shaped her second career as a spiritual guide; this became increasingly important as she strove to bear contemplative witness in an age of unbelief, imperial aggression, social unrest and intermittent horror. It is now commonplace to identify a team of Victorian 'sages' declaiming against the evils of the age – Carlyle, Mill, Arnold, Ruskin – to which Christina Rossetti also belongs, although her distinctive contribution is undoubtedly occluded for present readers by the exclusively Christian cast of her testimony.

'If I were bringing a case against God, Christina Rossetti is one of the first witnesses I should call,' wrote Virginia Woolf in 1918,[21] in reaction against those aspects of Victorian religion that turned the age into an adjective for all that is narrow, prudish, self-denying. William Rossetti, who shared Woolf's view, described his sister's 'over-scrupulosity' as a severe defect,

> more befitting for a nunnery than for London streets. It weakens

> the mind, straitens the temperament and character, chills the impulse and the influence. Over-scrupulosity made Christina Rossetti shut up her mind to almost all things save the Bible, and the admonitions and ministrations of priests. To ponder for herself whether a thing was true or not ceased to be a part of her intellect. The only question was whether or not it conformed to the Bible, as viewed by Anglo-Catholicism. Her temperament and character, naturally warm and free, became 'a fountain sealed' . . . Impulse and *élan* were checked, both in acts and writing.[22]

This is a harsh judgement. Readers must decide for themselves whether it is a true valuation of the effect of Christianity on her work, or whether the contemplation of all matters *sub specie aeternitatis* is a proper one for poets and for readers, even not sharing the same doctrinal beliefs.

Though always obedient to her Church, Rossetti was far from willing to accept the admonitions of priests in all respects. Her devotional writing was a covert challenge to the sermons and studies that poured from clerical pens at this period. 'But Bishops should write for me, not I for Bishops!' she joked in *Time Flies*. Women's ministry was not on the Anglican agenda, of course (and no one would have been more horrified than Rossetti had it been), but it was certainly a topic she pondered. 'The fact of the priesthood being exclusively man's leaves me in no doubt that the highest functions are not in this world open to both sexes,' she wrote in 1878.[23] But, she added, in *Seek and Find*:

> In many points the feminine lot copies very closely the voluntarily assumed position of our Lord . . . Woman must obey, and Christ 'learned obedience'. She must be fruitful but in sorrow, and He . . . had not brought forth much fruit except He had died . . . He came not to be ministered unto, but to minister . . .

and, she concluded:

> One final consolation yet remains to careful and troubled hearts: in Christ there is neither male nor female, for we are all one.[24]

Which brings us to the question of Christina Rossetti's ongoing obsession with Heaven. So many of her poems invoke the Christian notion of paradise as a solace for earthly sufferings and a site of loving reunion. All her life Rossetti believed fervently in life after death and the reunion of souls (she was adamantly opposed to all forms of spiritualism, however, as spurious claims to posthumous communication), but her ideas on heaven underwent a continuous refinement, deeply influenced by her reading of Plato. This led her to conceive of Heaven as an ideal realm, metaphorically figuring the perfection of earthly states. As such, it represented the goal that should govern life. The best may be forever out of reach, but the aim abides. Such Christian Platonism has a long history, and cannot be dismissed as babyish, or wished away. Rossetti was, incidentally, not as prudish as is sometimes thought: though she pasted strips of paper over indecent passages in Swinburne's *Atalanta*, she read the whole of Plato, writing only to warn a friend that some parts were unsuitable for reading aloud.

'Christina had no politics,' said William, adding that her mind was 'much more conservative' than anything else.[25] But this must be read in the context of his hostility towards her religion. Where Christina's views can be discerned, they were more Liberal than Tory (she had of course no vote to bestow on any party). Like the rest of the family she opposed Austro-Hungarian hegemony in Italy and supported liberty and democracy throughout Europe. Politically, she opposed war, slavery (in the American South), cruelty to animals (in the prevalent practice of vivisection), the exploitation of girls in under-age prostitution and all forms of military aggression. How gladly would she incur income tax for the sake of not killing Egyptians! she told William when British gunboats were shelling Alexandria.

In the late 1870s Rossetti attended lecture courses on Dante's *Divine Comedy* at University College, London, and assisted with research for a scholarly edition of Spenser's *Faerie Queene*. In her own writing she turned increasingly to the sonnet form, influenced by her reading of Petrarch and others, and by the revival of interest in the form. *Monna Innominata*, her first sonnet sequence, is founded on the conceit of a 'lady troubadour' writing to her beloved, in a gender reversal of the usual sonnet convention.

Christina Rossetti's reputation grew steadily, especially in North America, and by the 1880s she was regularly receiving visits and volumes of verse from admirers. Younger writers influenced by her work include Alice Meynell, Amy Levy, Mary Coleridge, Katharine Tynan and, one suspects, W. B. Yeats. Her last devotional book, *The Face of the Deep* (1892), returned to the Adventism of her youth with a contemplative commentary on the Apocalypse. This was followed by a collection of devotional poems, *Verses* (1894), whose title echoed that of her first book.

In 1893 she contracted cancer. After a painful mastectomy, several months of suffering and some weeks of distressing fear as to the prospect of eternal damnation despite her blameless life, she died on 29 December 1894. Among her most faithful and affectionate friends at the end was one Lisa Wilson, who left a sequence of 'Love Songs to my Lady' addressed to Christina.

In his Memoir prefacing the first complete collection of Rossetti's poems in 1904, William provided a scrupulous but carefully censored version of his sister's life that has formed the basis of all subsequent biographical accounts. Read attentively, it is full of observation, but the overall effect is oddly muted, contributing to the image of Rossetti as a pious recluse. Of her temperament, William wrote: 'She was replete with the spirit of self-postponement, which passed into self-sacrifice whenever that quality was in demand.' But, he went on:

> A small point she was the first to concede; but, as soon as a jot of duty seemed involved in it, tenacity was in the very essence of her being.

Of her own assessment of her talent, he wrote:

> Did Christina Rossetti consider herself truly a poetess, and a good one? Truly a poetess, most decidedly yes; and, within the range of her subject and thought, a good one. This did not make her in the least conceited or arrogant as regards herself, nor captious as to the work of others; but it did render her very resolute in setting a line of demarcation between a person who is a poet and another person who is a versifier. Pleadings *in misericordiam* were of no use with her, and she never could see any good reason why one who is not a poet should write in metre.[26]

As her correspondence shows, she had indeed a keen eye and ear for the distinction between true poetry and mere versification, and it is not surprising that when, in December 1890, she received a copy of *Poems* by the as-yet unknown Emily Dickinson (issued by her own American publisher Roberts Bros) she responded with admiration and awe – for the 'wonderfully Blakean gift' and 'startling recklessness of poetic ways and means'.[27]

A quarter of a century earlier, Rossetti had told her brother Gabriel that there were few other contemporary writers with whose powers she felt it vain to compare her own – an oblique acknowledgement of literary self-knowledge and aspiration to set against the more characteristic expressions of self-disparagement. Christina Rossetti was truly a poet, and a good one.

JAN MARSH

REFERENCES

1 *The Letters of Lewis Carroll*, ed. M. C. Cohen, 1979, vol. 2, p. 986.
2 Isobel Armstrong, *Victorian Poetry: Poetry, Poetics and Politics*, 1993, p.8.
3 *Dante Gabriel Rossetti: Family Letters, with a Memoir*, ed. W. M. Rossetti, 1895 vol. 1, p. 54.
4 *Family Letters of Christina Rossetti*, ed. W. M. Rossetti, 1908, p. 105.
5 William Sharp, *Papers Critical and Reminiscent*, 1912, p. 73.
6 *Letters of Sara Coleridge*, ed. Edith Coleridge, 1873, p. 218.
7 *Letters of Dante Gabriel Rossetti*, ed. O. Doughty and J. R. Wahl, 1965, vol. 1, p. 45.
8 *Poetical Works of Christina Rossetti*, ed. W. M. Rossetti, 1904, p. 472.
9 No evidence of these documents has been discovered.
10 Isobel Armstrong, *Victorian Poetry*, p. 10.
11 *The Rossetti-Macmillan Letters*, ed. L. M. Packer, 1963, p. 19.
12 *The Poetical Works of Christina Rossetti*, p. xviii.
13 Angela Leighton, *Victorian Women Poets: Writing against the Heart*, 1993, pp. 33, 59ff.
14 *Family Letters of Christina Rossetti*, p. 65.
15 *Rossetti Papers 1862 to 1870*, compiled by W. M. Rossetti, 1899, p. 93.
16 Angela Leighton, *Victorian Women Poets*, p. 375, quoting Stuart Curran in *Victorian Poetry*, vol. 9, p. 298.
17 Christina Rossetti, *Letter and Spirit*, 1883, p. 12.
18 Christina Rossetti, *The Face of the Deep*, 1892, p. 410.
19 *Times Literary Supplement*, 29 May 1959, p. xi.
20 *The Diary of Virginia Woolf*, ed. A. O. Bell, 1977, vol. 1, p. 178.
21 *Poetical Works of Christina Rossetti*, p. lxviii.
22 See Mackenzie Bell, *Christina Rossetti*, 1898, p. 124.
23 *Seek and Find*, 1879, pp. 30–32.
24 *Poetical Works of Christina Rossetti*, p. lxx.
25 ibid., pp. lxvii and lxix.
26 *Family Letters of Christina Rossetti*, p. 176.
27 *Rossetti Papers 1862 to 1870*, p. 89.

NOTE ON THE TEXTS

The texts in this edition are taken from those published by Christina Rossetti in her lifetime or by William Rossetti when editing her previously unpublished poems in 1904. There are no doubtful and few variant readings and in general the published versions follow the manuscript texts closely, although in certain cases Christina Rossetti omitted or re-arranged stanzas when preparing poems for publication. All available versions are documented in *The Complete Poems of Christina Rossetti: A Variorum Edition*, edited by R. W. Crump in three volumes (1979–90). The fiction and prose texts are those published by Christina Rossetti or (in the case of *Maude*) by William Rossetti shortly after her death. Correspondence comes from *The Family Letters of Christina Rossetti*, edited by William Rossetti in 1908. A comprehensive edition of *The Collected Letters of Christina Rossetti*, edited by Antony H. Harrison, is currently being published by the University Press of Virginia (1995–).

Dates of composition are given for each item. Texts are arranged according to genre, and chronologically within each genre.

NOTE ON THE TEXTS

[illegible]

The texts in this edition are taken from those published by Christina Rossetti in her lifetime or by William Rossetti when editing her previously unpublished poems in 1896. There are minor [illegible] and the Italian poems and in general the published versions follow the manuscript texts closely, although in certain cases Christina Rossetti omitted or rearranged stanzas when preparing poems for publication. Alternative variants are documented in *The Complete Poems of Christina Rossetti: A Variorum Edition*, edited by R. W. Crump in three volumes (1979–90). The fiction and prose texts are those published by Christina Rossetti or, in the case of *Maude*, by William Rossetti shortly after her death. Correspondence extracts from *The Family Letters of Christina Rossetti*, edited by William Rossetti in 1908. A comprehensive edition of *The Collected Letters of Christina Rossetti*, edited by Antony H. Harrison, is currently being published by the University Press of Virginia (1997).

Dates of composition are given where known. Texts are arranged according to genre, and chronologically within each genre.

SELECTED POETRY

LYRICS, BALLADS AND SHORTER POEMS

*Heaven**

I

What is heaven? 'tis a country
Far away from mortal ken;
'Tis a land, where, by God's bounty,
After death live righteous men.

2

That that blest land I may enter
Is my humble, earnest cry;
Lord! admit me to Thy presence,
Lord! admit me, or I die.

1842

On Albina

The roses lingered in her cheeks,
When fair Albina fainted;
Oh! gentle Reader, could it be
That fair Albina painted?

1844

Forget me Not

I

'Forget me not! Forget me not!'
The maiden once did say,
When to some far-off battle-field
Her lover sped away.

2

'Forget me not! Forget me not!'
Says now the chamber-maid
When the traveller on his journey
No more will be delayed.

1844

*Charity**

I praised the myrtle and the rose,
At sunrise in their beauty vying;
I passed them at the short day's close,
And both were dying.

The summer sun his rays was throwing
Brightly; yet ere I sought my rest,
His last cold ray, more deeply glowing,
Died in the west.

After this bleak world's stormy weather,
All, all, save Love alone, shall die;
For Faith and Hope shall merge together
In Charity.

1844

*Lines to my Grandfather**

Dear Grandpapa,
To be obedient,
I'll try and write a letter;
Which (as I hope you'll deem expedient)
Must serve for lack of better.

My muse of late was not prolific,
And sometimes I must feel
To make a verse a task terrific
Rather of woe than weal.

As I have met with no adventure
Of wonder and refulgence,
I must write plain things at a venture
And trust to your indulgence.

The apple-tree is showing
  Its blossom of bright red
With a soft colour glowing
  Upon its leafy bed.

The pear-tree's pure white blossom
  Like stainless snow is seen;
And all earth's genial bosom
  Is clothed with varied green.

The fragrant may is blooming,
  The yellow cowslip blows;
Among its leaves entombing
  Peeps forth the pale primrose.

The kingcup flowers and daisies
  Are opening hard by;
And many another raises
  Its head, to please and die.

I love the gay wild flowers
  Waving in fresh spring air;
Give me uncultured bowers
  Before the bright parterre!

And now my letter is concluded,
  To do well I have striven;
And though news is well-nigh excluded,
  I hope to be forgiven.

With love to all the beautiful,
  And those who cannot slaughter,
I sign myself,
          your dutiful,
      Affectionate Granddaughter.

1845

*Hope in Grief**

Tell me not that death of grief
Is the only sure relief.
Tell me not that hope when dead
Leaves a void that nought can fill,
Gnawings that may not be fed.

Tell me not there is no skill
That can bind the breaking heart,
That can soothe the bitter smart,
When we find ourselves betrayed,
When we find ourselves forsaken,
By those for whom we would have laid
Our young lives down, nor wished to waken.
Say not that life is to all
But a gaily coloured pall,
Hiding with its deceitful glow
The hearts that break beneath it,
Engulphing as they anguished flow
The scalding tears that seethe it.
Say not, vain this world's turmoil,
Vain its trouble and its toil,
All its hopes and fears are vain,
Long, unmitigated pain.
What though we should be deceived
By the friend that we love best?
All in this world have been grieved,
Yet many have found rest.
Our present life is as the night,
Our future as the morning light:
Surely the night will pass away,
And surely will uprise the day.

1845

On the Death of a Cat,

A FRIEND OF MINE, AGED TEN YEARS AND A HALF*

Who shall tell the lady's grief
When her Cat was past relief?
Who shall number the hot tears
Shed o'er her, beloved for years?
Who shall say the dark dismay
Which her dying caused that day?

Come, ye Muses, one and all,
Come obedient to my call.
Come and mourn, with tuneful breath,

Each one for a separate death;
And while you in numbers sigh,
I will sing her elegy.

Of a noble race she came,
And Grimalkin was her name.
Young and old full many a mouse
Felt the prowess of her house:
Weak and strong full many a rat
Cowered beneath her crushing pat:
And the birds around the place
Shrank from her too close embrace.
But one night, reft of her strength,
She laid down and died at length:
Lay a kitten by her side,
In whose life the mother died.
Spare her line and lineage,
Guard her kitten's tender age,
And that kitten's name as wide
Shall be known as her's that died.

And whoever passes by
The poor grave where Puss doth lie,
Softly, softly let him tread,
Nor disturb her narrow bed.

1846

The Ruined Cross

She wreathed bright flower-wreaths in her hair,
  And all men smiled as she passed by:
And she smiled too, for now she knew
    That her last hour was nigh.

Soft radiance shone upon her path,
  Her step was fearless, free and light;
Her cheek was flushed with burning red,
    Her azure eye was bright.

On, on, still on, she hurried on,
  For in the wind she heard a knell,

And to her ear the water's splash
    Was as a dying bell.

And in the flowers she saw decay,
  And saw decay in every tree;
And change was written on the sun,
    And change upon the sea.

She might not pause upon the road,
  Lest Death should claim his promised bride
Ere yet her longing was fulfilled,
    Her young heart satisfied.

The sun arose, the sun went down,
  The moonbeams on the waters shone
How many times! yet paused she not,
    But ever journeyed on.

And still, tho' toilsome was the way,
  The colour flushed her sunken cheek;
Nor dimmed the azure of her eye,
    Nor waxed her purpose weak.

At length she reached a lonely spot, . . .
  Why trembled she? why turned she pale?
A ruined Cross stood in the midst
    Of a most quiet vale.

A Cross o'ergrown with moss and flowers,
  A cross fast sinking to decay;
The Cross she knew, the Cross she loved
    In childhood's happy day.

And she had journeyed many miles,
  Morning and eve untiringly,
To look again upon that Cross,
    To look again and die.

She knelt within its sacred shade,
  And hung her garland on the stone;
Her azure eyes were bright with tears
    Of love and joy unknown.

And there she knelt, and there she prayed
Until her heart was satisfied;—
The ancient Cross is standing yet,
The youthful wanderer died.

1846

*Sappho**

I sigh at day-dawn, and I sigh
When the dull day is passing by.
I sigh at evening, and again
I sigh when night brings sleep to men.
Oh! it were better far to die
Than thus for ever mourn and sigh,
And in death's dreamless sleep to be
Unconscious that none weep for me;
Eased from my weight of heaviness,
Forgetful of forgetfulness,
Resting from pain and care and sorrow
Thro' the long night that knows no morrow;
Living unloved, to die unknown,
Unwept, unattended and alone.

1846

*Will These Hands Ne'er be Clean?**

And who is this lies prostrate at thy feet?
And is he dead, thou man of wrath and pride?
Yes, now thy vengeance is complete,
Thy hate is satisfied.
What had he done to merit this of thee?
Who gave thee power to take away his life?
Oh deeply-rooted direful enmity
That ended in long strife!
See where he grasped thy mantle as he fell,
Staining it with his blood; how terrible
Must be the payment due for this in hell!

And dost thou think to go and see no more
Thy bleeding victim, now the struggle's o'er?
To find out peace in other lands,

And wash the red mark from thy hands?
It shall not be; for everywhere
He shall be with thee; and the air
Shall smell of blood, and on the wind
His groans pursue thee close behind.
When waking he shall stand before thee;
And when at length sleep shall come o'er thee,
Powerless to move, alive to dream,
So dreadful shall thy visions seem
That thou shalt own them even to be
More hateful than reality.
What time thou stoopest down to drink
Of limpid waters, thou shalt think
It is thy foe's blood bubbles up
From the polluted fountain's cup,
That stains thy lip, that cries to Heaven
For vengeance – and it shall be given.

And when thy friends shall question thee,
'Why art thou changed so heavily?'
Trembling and fearful thou shalt say
'I am not changed,' and turn away;
For such an outcast shalt thou be
Thou wilt not dare ask sympathy.

And so thy life will pass, and day by day
The current of existence flow away;
And though to thee earth shall be hell, and breath
Vengeance, yet thou shalt tremble more at death.
And one by one thy friends will learn to fear thee,
And thou shalt live without a hope to cheer thee;
Lonely amid a thousand, chained though free,
The curse of memory shall cling to thee:
Ages may pass away, worlds rise and set—
But thou shalt not forget.

1846

*Spring Quiet**

Gone were but the Winter,
Come were but the Spring,
I would go to a covert
Where the birds sing;

Where in the whitethorn
  Singeth a thrush,
And a robin sings
  In the holly-bush.

Full of fresh scents
  Are the budding boughs
Arching high over
  A cool green house:

Full of sweet scents,
  And whispering air
Which sayeth softly:
  'We spread no snare;

'Here dwell in safety,
  Here dwell alone,
With a clear stream
  And a mossy stone.

'Here the sun shineth
  Most shadily;
Here is heard an echo
  Of the far sea,
  Tho' far off it be.'

1847

*Immalee**

I gather thyme upon the sunny hills,
  And its pure fragrance ever gladdens me,
  And in my mind having tranquillity
I smile to see how my green basket fills.
And by clear streams I gather daffodils;
  And in dim woods find out the cherry-tree,
  And take its fruit, and the wild strawberry,
And nuts, and honey; and live free from ills.
I dwell on the green earth, 'neath the blue sky,
  Birds are my friends, and leaves my rustling roof;

The deer are not afraid of me, and I
  Hear the wild goat, and hail its hastening hoof;
The squirrels sit perked as I pass them by,
  And even the watchful hare stands not aloof.

1847

*Death's Chill Between**

Chide not: let me breathe a little,
  For I shall not mourn him long;
Though the life-cord was so brittle,
  The love-cord was very strong.
I would take little space
Till I find a sleeping-place.

You can go, – I shall not weep;
  You can go unto your rest.
My heart-ache is all too deep,
  And too sore my throbbing breast.
Can sobs be, or angry tears,
Where are neither hopes nor fears?

Though with you I am alone
  And must be so everywhere,
I will make no useless moan—
  None shall say, 'She could not bear.'
While life lasts I will be strong,—
But I shall not struggle long.

Listen, listen! – everywhere
  A low voice is calling me,
And a step is on the stair,
  And one comes you do not see.
Listen, listen! – Evermore
A dim hand knocks at the door.

Hear me! He is come again,
  My own dearest is come back.
Bring him in from the cold rain;
  Bring wine, and let nothing lack.
Thou and I will rest together,
Love, until the sunny weather.

I will shelter thee from harm,
  Hide thee from all heaviness;
Come to me, and keep thee warm
  By my side in quietness.
I will lull thee to thy sleep
With sweet songs; we will not weep.

Who hath talked of weeping? yet
  There is something at my heart
Gnawing, I would fain forget,
  And an aching and a smart—
Ah my Mother, 'tis in vain,
For he is not come again.

1847

*Heart's Chill Between**

I did not chide him, tho' I knew
  That he was false to me:
Chide the exhaling of the dew,
  The ebbing of the sea,
The fading of a rosy hue,
  But not inconstancy.

Why strive for love when love is o'er?
  Why bind a restive heart?
He never knew the pain I bore
  In saying: 'We must part;
Let us be friends, and nothing more':—
  Oh woman's shallow art!

But it is over, it is done;
  I hardly heed it now;
So many weary years have run
  Since then, I think not how
Things might have been; but greet each one
  With an unruffled brow.

What time I am where others be
  My heart seems very calm,
Stone calm; but if all go from me
  There comes a vague alarm.

A shrinking in the memory
  From some forgotten harm.

And often thro' the long long night
  Waking when none are near.
I feel my heart beat fast with fright,*
  Yet know not what I fear.
Oh how I long to see the light
  And the sweet birds to hear!

To have the sun upon my face,
  To look up through the trees,
To walk forth in the open space,
  And listen to the breeze,
And not to dream the burial place
  Is clogging my weak knees.

Sometimes I can nor weep nor pray,
  But am half stupefied;
And then all those who see me say
  Mine eyes are opened wide,
And that my wits seem gone away:—
  Ah would that I had died!

Would I could die and be at peace,
  Or living could forget;
My grief nor grows nor doth decrease,
  But ever is: – and yet
Methinks now that all this shall cease
  Before the sun shall set.

1847

*Lines given with a Penwiper**

I have compassion on the carpeting,
  And on your back I have compassion too.
The splendid Brussels web is suffering
  In the dimmed lustre of each glowing hue;
And you the everlasting altering
  Of your position with strange aches must rue.
Behold, I come the carpet to preserve,
And save your spine from a continual curve.

1847

*Undine**

She did not answer him again
  But walked straight to the door;
Her hand nor trembled on the lock,
  Nor her foot on the floor,
But as she stood up steadily
  She turned, and looked once more.

She turned, and looked on him once more:
  Her face was very pale;
And from her forehead her long hair
  Fell back like a thick veil;
But, though her lips grew white, the fire
  Of her eyes did not fail.

Then as she fixed her eyes on him
  Old thoughts came back again
Of the dear rambles long ago
  Through meadow-land and lane,
When all the woods were full of flowers,
  And all the fields of grain.

When all the birds were full of song
  Except the turtle dove;
And that sat cooing tenderly
  In the green boughs above;
When they hoped the same hopes, and when
  He told her of his love.

Old memories came back to her
  Of what once made her glad,
Till her heart seemed to stand quite still,
  And every pulse she had:
Then the blood rose up to her brain
  And she was almost mad.

Yet still she stood there steadily
  And looked him in the face;
There was no tear upon her cheek;
  Upon her brow no trace

Of the agonizing strife within,
  The shame and the disgrace.

And so she stayed a little while
  Until she turned once more,
Without a single sob or sigh;
  But her heart felt quite sore:
The spirit had been broken, and
  The hope of life was o'er.

1848

Sonnets Written to Bouts-rimés*

I seek among the living & I seek
Among the dead for some to love; but few
I find at last & these have quite run through
Their store of love & friendship is too weak
And cold for me; yet will I never speak
Telling my heart want to cold listeners who
Will wonder smiling; I can bear & do.
No tears shall sully my unfurrowed cheek.
So when my dust shall mix with other dust,
When I shall have found quiet in decay
And lie at ease & cease to be & rot,
Those whom I love thinking of me shall not
Grieve with a measure, saying: Now we must
Weep for a little ere we go & play.

1848

And is this August weather? nay not so
With the long rain the cornfield waxeth dark.
How the cold rain comes pouring down & hark
To the chill wind whose measured pace & slow
Seems still to linger being loth to go.
I cannot stand beside the sea and mark
Its grandeur; it's too wet for that: no lark
In this drear season cares to sing or show.
And since its name is August all men find

Fire not allowable; Winter foregone
Had more of sunlight & of glad warmth more.
I shall be fain to run upon the shore
And mark the rain. Hath the sun ever shone?
Cheer up! there can be nothing worse to mind.

1848

So I grew half delirious and quite sick,
And thro' the darkness saw strange faces grin
Of monsters at me. One put forth a fin,
And touched me clammily: I could not pick
A quarrel with it: it began to lick
My hand, making meanwhile a piteous din
And shedding human tears: it would begin
To near me, then retreat. I heard the quick
Pulsation of my heart, I marked the fight
Of life and death within me; then sleep threw
Her veil around me; but this thing is true.
When I awoke the sun was at his height,
And I wept sadly, knowing that one new
Creature had love for me, and others spite.

1849

Song

She sat and sang alway
By the green margin of a stream,
Watching the fishes leap and play
Beneath the glad sunbeam.

I sat and wept away
Beneath the moon's most shadowy beam,
Watching the blossoms of the May
Weep leaves into the stream.

I wept for memory;
She sang for hope that is so fair:
My tears were swallowed by the sea;
Her songs died on the air.

1848

Song

When I am dead, my dearest,
  Sing no sad songs for me;
Plant thou no roses at my head,
  Nor shady cypress* tree:
Be the green grass above me
  With showers and dewdrops wet;
And if thou wilt, remember,
  And if thou wilt, forget.

I shall not see the shadows,
  I shall not feel the rain;
I shall not hear the nightingale
  Sing on, as if in pain:
And dreaming through the twilight
  That doth not rise nor set,
Haply* I may remember,
  And haply may forget.

1848

*Song**

Oh roses for the flush of youth,
  And laurel for the perfect prime;
But pluck an ivy branch for me
  Grown old before my time.

Oh violets for the grave of youth,
  And bay for those dead in their prime;
Give me the withered leaves I chose
  Before in the old time.

1849

Symbols

I watched a rosebud very long
  Brought on by dew and sun and shower,
  Waiting to see the perfect flower:
Then, when I thought it should be strong,
  It opened at the matin* hour
  And fell at evensong.*

I watched a nest from day to day,
  A green nest full of pleasant shade,
  Wherein three speckled eggs were laid:
But when they should have hatched in May,
  The two old birds had grown afraid
    Or tired, and flew away.

Then in my wrath I broke the bough
  That I had tended so with care,
  Hoping its scent should fill the air;
I crushed the eggs, not heeding how
  Their ancient promise had been fair:
    I would have vengeance now.

But the dead branch spoke from the sod,
  And the eggs answered me again:
  Because we failed dost thou complain?
Is thy wrath just? And what if God,
  Who waiteth for thy fruits in vain,
    Should also take the rod?

1849

*To Lalla, reading my verses topsy-turvy**

Darling little Cousin,
  With your thoughtful look
Reading topsy-turvy
  From a printed book

English hieroglyphics,
  More mysterious
To you, than Egyptian
  Ones would be to us;—

Leave off for a minute
  Studying, and say
What is the impression
  That those marks convey?

Only solemn silence,
   And a wondering smile:
But your eyes are lifted
   Unto mine the while.

In their gaze so steady
   I can surely trace
That a happy spirit
   Lighteth up your face.

Tender, happy spirit,
   Innocent and pure;
Teaching more than science,
   And than learning more.

How should I give answer
   To that asking look?
Darling little Cousin
   Go back to your book.

Read on: if you knew it,
   You have cause to boast:—
You are much the wisest,
   Though I know the most.

1849

*An End**

Love, strong as Death, is dead.
Come, let us make his bed
Among the dying flowers:
A green turf at his head;
And a stone at his feet,
Whereon we may sit
In the quiet evening hours.

He was born in the Spring,
And died before the harvesting:
On the last warm Summer day
He left us; he would not stay
For Autumn twilight cold and gray.

Sit we by his grave, and sing
He is gone away.

To few chords and sad and low
Sing we so:
Be our eyes fixed on the grass
Shadow-veiled as the years pass,
While we think of all that was
In the long ago.

1849

*Dream-Land**

Where sunless rivers weep
Their waves into the deep,
She sleeps a charmèd sleep:
  Awake her not.
Led by a single star,
She came from very far
To seek where shadows are
  Her pleasant lot.

She left the rosy morn,
She left the fields of corn,
For twilight cold and lorn
  And water springs.
Thro' sleep, as thro' a veil,
She sees the sky look pale,
And hears the nightingale
  That sadly sings.

Rest, rest, a perfect rest
Shed over brow and breast;
Her face is toward the west,
  The purple land.
She cannot see the grain
Ripening on hill and plain;
She cannot feel the rain
  Upon her hand.

Rest, rest, for evermore
Upon a mossy shore;
Rest, rest at the heart's core
  Till time shall cease:
Sleep that no pain shall wake;
Night that no morn shall break,
Till joy shall overtake
  Her perfect peace.

1849

After Death

The curtains were half drawn, the floor was swept
  And strewn with rushes, rosemary and may
  Lay thick upon the bed on which I lay,
Where thro' the lattice ivy-shadows crept.
He leaned above me, thinking that I slept
  And could not hear him; but I heard him say:
  'Poor child, poor child:' and as he turned away
Came a deep silence, and I knew he wept.
He did not touch the shroud, or raise the fold
  That hid my face, or take my hand in his,
    Or ruffle the smooth pillows for my head:
    He did not love me living; but once dead
  He pitied me; and very sweet it is
To know he still is warm tho' I am cold.

1849

*Remember**

Remember me when I am gone away,
  Gone far away into the silent land;
  When you can no more hold me by the hand,
Nor I half turn to go yet turning stay.
Remember me when no more day by day
  You tell me of our future that you planned:
  Only remember me; you understand
It will be late to counsel then or pray.
Yet if you should forget me for a while
  And afterwards remember, do not grieve:
  For if the darkness and corruption leave

A vestige of the thoughts that once I had,
Better by far you should forget and smile
Than you should remember and be sad.

1849

Three Moments

The Child said: 'Pretty bird
'Come back and play with me.'
The bird said: 'It is in vain,
'For I am free.
'I am free, I will not stay,
'But will fly far away,
'In the woods to sing and play,
'Far away, far away.'
The Child sought her Mother:
'I have lost my bird;' said she
Weeping bitterly:
But the Mother made her answer,
Half sighing pityingly,
Half smiling cheerily:
'Tho' thy bird come nevermore
'Do not weep;
'Find another playfellow
'Child, and keep
'Tears for future pain more deep.'

'Sweet rose do not wither,'
The Girl said.
But a blight had touched its heart
And it drooped its crimson head.
In the morning it had opened
Full of life and bloom,
But the leaves fell off one by one
Till the twilight gloom.
One by one the leaves fell
By summer winds blown from their stem;
They fell upon the dewy earth
Which nourished once now tainted them.
Again the young Girl wept
And sought her Mother's ear:

'My rose is dead so full of grace,
'The very rose I meant to place
'In the wreath that I wear.'
'Nay, never weep for such as this;'
The Mother answered her:
'But weave another crown, less fair
'Perhaps, but fitter for thy hair.
'And keep thy tears,' the Mother said:
'For something heavier.'

The Woman knelt; but did not pray
Nor weep nor cry; she only said:
'Not this, not this:' and clasped her hands
Against her heart and bowed her head
While the great struggle shook the bed.
'Not this, not this:' tears did not fall:
'Not this:' it was all
She could say; no sobs would come;
The mortal grief was almost dumb.—
At length when it was over, when
She knew it was and would be so,
She cried: 'Oh Mother, where are they,
'The tears that used to flow
'So easily? one single drop
'Might save my reason now, or stop
'My heart from breaking. Blessed tears
'Wasted in former years!'
Then the grave Mother made reply:
'Oh Daughter mine be of good cheer,
'Rejoicing thou canst shed no tear.
'Thy pain is almost over now.
'Once more thy heart shall throb with pain,
'But then shall never throb again.
'Oh happy thou who canst not weep,
'Oh happy thou!'

1850

*The Three Enemies**

THE FLESH

'Sweet, thou art pale.'
'More pale to see,
Christ hung upon the cruel tree
And bore His Father's wrath for me.'

'Sweet, thou art sad.'
'Beneath a rod
More heavy, Christ for my sake trod
The winepress of the wrath of God.'

'Sweet, thou art weary.'
'Not so Christ:
Whose mighty love of me sufficed
For Strength, Salvation, Eucharist.'

'Sweet, thou art footsore.'
'If I bleed,
His feet have bled: yea, in my need
His Heart once bled for mine indeed.'

THE WORLD

'Sweet, thou art young.'
'So He was young
Who for my sake in silence hung
Upon the Cross with Passion wrung.'

'Look, thou art fair.'
'He was more fair
Than men, Who deigned for me to wear
A visage marred beyond compare.'

'And thou hast riches.'
'Daily bread:
All else is His; Who living, dead,
For me lacked where to lay His Head.'

'And life is sweet.'
'It was not so

To Him, Whose Cup did overflow
With mine unutterable woe.'

THE DEVIL

'Thou drinkest deep.'
'When Christ would sup
He drained the dregs from out my cup:
So how should I be lifted up?'

'Thou shalt win Glory.'
'In the skies,
Lord Jesus, cover up mine eyes
Lest they should look on vanities.'

'Thou shalt have Knowledge.'
'Helpless dust,
In Thee, O Lord, I put my trust:
Answer Thou for me, Wise and Just.'

'And Might.'—
'Get thee behind me. Lord,
Who hast redeemed and not abhorred
My soul, oh keep it by Thy Word.'

1851

'A fair World tho' a fallen'——

You tell me that the world is fair, in spite
Of the old fall; and that I should not turn
So to the grave, and let my spirit yearn
After the quiet of the long last night.
Have I then shut mine eyes against the light,
Grief-deafened lest my spirit should discern?
Yet how could I keep silence when I burn?
And who can give me comfort? – hear the right.
Have patience with the weak and sick at heart:
Bind up the wounded with a tender touch.
Comfort the sad, tear-blinded as they go:—
For tho' I failed to choose the better part,
Were it a less unutterable woe
If we should come to love this world too much?—

1851

*'Behold, I stand at the door and knock'**

Who standeth at the gate? – A woman old,
  A widow from the husband of her love:
'O Lady, stay; this wind is piercing cold,
  Oh look at the keen frosty moon above;
I have no home, am hungry, feeble, poor:'—
  'I'm really very sorry, but I can
  Do nothing for you, there's the clergyman,'—
The Lady said, and shivering closed the door.

Who standeth at the gate? – Way-worn and pale,
  A grey-haired man asks charity again:
'Kind Lady, I have journeyed far, and fail
  Thro' weariness; for I have begged in vain
Some shelter, and can find no lodging-place:'—
  She answered: 'There's the Workhouse very near,
  Go, for they'll certainly receive you there:'—
Then shut the door against his pleading face.

Who standeth at the gate? – A stunted child,
  Her sunk eyes sharpened with precocious care:
'O Lady, save me from a home defiled,
  From shameful sights and sounds that taint the air.
Take pity on me, teach me something good;'—
  'For shame, why don't you work instead of cry?—
  I keep no young impostors here, not I;'—
She slammed the door, indignant where she stood.

Who standeth at the gate, and will be heard?—
  Arise, O woman, from thy comforts now:
Go forth again to speak the careless word,
  The cruel word unjust, with hardened brow.
But Who is This, That standeth not to pray
  As once, but terrible to judge thy sin?
  This, Whom thou wouldst not succour, nor take in,
Nor teach, but leave to perish by the way?—

'Thou didst it not unto the least of these,
  And in them hast not done it unto Me.
Thou wast as a princess, rich and at ease,

Now sit in dust and howl for poverty.
Three times I stood beseeching at thy gate,
Three times I came to bless thy soul and save:
But now I come to judge for what I gave,
And now at length thy sorrow is too late.'*

1851

Moonshine

Fair the sun riseth,
Bright as bright can be,
Fair the sun shineth
On a fair fair sea.

'Across the water
'Wilt thou come with me,
'Miles and long miles, love,
'Over the salt sea?'—

'If thou wilt hold me
'Truly by the hand,
'I will go with thee
'Over sea and sand.

'If thou wilt hold me
'That I shall not fall,
'I will go with thee,
'Love, in spite of all.'

Fair the moon riseth
On her heavenly way
Making the waters
Fairer than by day.

A little vessel
Rocks up the sea,
Where stands a maiden
Fair as fair can be.

Her smile rejoices
Though her mouth is mute,

She treads the vessel
With her little foot.

Truly he holds her
Faithful to his pledge
Guiding the vessel
From the water's edge.

Fair the moon saileth
With her pale fair light,
Fair the girl gazeth
Out into the night.

Saith she: 'Like silver
'Shines thy hair, not gold;'—
Saith she: 'I shiver
'In thy steady hold.

'Love,' she saith weeping,
'Loose thy hold awhile,
'My heart is freezing
'In thy freezing smile.'

The moon is hidden
By a silver cloud,
Fair as a halo
Or a maiden's shroud.

No more beseeching,
Ever on they go:
The vessel rocketh
Softly to and fro;

And still he holds her
That she shall not fall,
Till pale mists whiten
Dimly over all.

Onward and onward,
Far across the sea;
Onward and onward,
Pale as pale can be;

Onward and onward,
 Ever hand in hand,
From sun and moon light
 To another land.

1852

*Books in the Running Brooks**

'It is enough, enough,' one said,
 At play among the flowers:
'I spy a rose upon the thorn,
 A rainbow in the showers;
I hear a merry chime of bells
 Ring out the passing hours.'—
  Soft springs the fountain
   From the daisied ground:
  Softly falling on the moss
   Without a sound.

'It is enough,' she said, and fixed
 Calm eyes upon the sky:
'I watch a flitting tender cloud
 Just like a dove go by;
A lark is rising from the grass;
 A wren is building nigh.'—
  Softly the fountain
   Threads its silver way,
  Screened by the scented bloom
   Of whitest may.

'Enough?' she whispered to herself,
 As doubting: 'Is it so?'
 Enough to wear the roses fair?
 Oh sweetest flowers that blow:—
Oh yes, it surely is enough,
 My happy home below.'—
  A shadow stretcheth
   From the hither shore:
  Those waters darken
   More and more and more.

'It is enough,' she says; but with
  A listless, weary moan:
'Enough,' if mixing with her friends;
  'Enough,' if left alone.
But to herself: 'Not yet enough,
  This suffering, to atone?'—
    The cold black waters
      Seem to stagnate there;
    Without a single wave,
      Or breath of air.

And now she says: 'It is enough,'
  Half languid and half stirred:
'Enough,' to silence and to sound,
  Thorn, blossom, soaring bird:
'Enough,' she says; but with a lack
  Of something in the word.—
    Defiled and turbid
      See the waters pass;
    Half light, half shadow,
      Struggling thro' the grass.

Ah, will it ever dawn, that day*
  When calm for good or ill
Her heart shall say: 'It is enough,
  For Thou art with me still;
It is enough, O Lord my God,
  Thine only blessed Will.'—
    Then shall the fountain sing
      And flow to rest;
    Clear as the sun track
      To the purple West.

1852

*To what purpose is this waste?'**

A windy shell singing upon the shore:
A lily budding in a desert place;
Blooming alone
With no companion
To praise its perfect perfume and its grace:

A rose crimson and blushing at the core,
Hedged in with thorns behind it and before:
A fountain in the grass,
Whose shadowy waters pass
Only to nourish birds and furnish food
For squirrels of the wood:
An oak deep in the forest's heart, the house
Of black-eyed tiny mouse;
Its strong roots fit for fuel roofing in
The hoarded nuts, acorns and grains of wheat;
Shutting them from the wind and scorching heat,
And sheltering them when the rains begin:

A precious pearl deep buried in the sea
Where none save fishes be:
The fullest merriest note
For which the skylark strains his silver throat,
Heard only in the sky
By other birds that fitfully
Chase one another as they fly:
The ripest plum down tumbled to the ground
By southern winds most musical of sound.
But by no thirsty traveller found:
Honey of wild bees in their ordered cells
Stored, not for human mouths to taste:—
I said, smiling superior down: What waste
Of good, where no man dwells.

This I said on a pleasant day in June
Before the sun had set, tho' a white moon
Already flaked the quiet blue
Which not a star looked thro'.
But still the air was warm, and drowsily
It blew into my face:
So since that same day I had wandered deep
Into the country, I sought out a place
For rest beneath a tree,
And very soon forgot myself in sleep:
Not so mine own words had forgotten me.
Mine eyes were opened to behold
All hidden things,

And mine ears heard all secret whisperings:
So my proud tongue that had been bold
To carp and to reprove,
Was silenced by the force of utter Love.

All voices of all things inanimate
Join with the song of Angels and the song
Of blessed Spirits, chiming with
Their Hallelujahs. One wind wakeneth
Across the sleeping sea, crisping along
The waves, and brushes thro' the great
Forests and tangled hedges, and calls out
Of rivers a clear sound,
And makes the ripe corn rustle on the ground,
And murmurs in a shell;
Till all their voices swell
Above the clouds in one loud hymn
Joining the song of Seraphim,
Or like pure incense circle round about
The walls of Heaven, or like a well-spring rise
In shady Paradise.

A lily blossoming unseen
Holds honey in its silver cup
Whereon a bee may sup,
Till being full she takes the rest
And stores it in her waxen nest:
While the fair blossom lifted up
On its one stately stem of green
Is type of her, the Undefiled,*
Arrayed in white, whose eyes are mild
As a white dove's, whose garment is
Blood-cleansed from all impurities
And earthly taints,
Her robe the righteousness of Saints.

And other eyes than our's
Were made to look on flowers,
Eyes of small birds and insects small:
The deep sun-blushing rose
Round which the prickles close
Opens her bosom to them all.

The tiniest living thing
That soars on feathered wing,
Or crawls among the long grass out of sight,
Has just as good a right
To its appointed portion of delight
As any King.

Why should we grudge a hidden water stream
To birds and squirrels while we have enough?
As if a nightingale should cease to sing
Lest we should hear, or finch leafed out of sight
Warbling its fill in summer light;
As if sweet violets in the spring
Should cease to blow, for fear our path should seem
Less weary or less rough.

So every oak that stands a house
For skilful mouse,
And year by year renews its strength,
Shakes acorns from a hundred boughs
Which shall be oaks at length.

Who hath weighed the waters and shall say
What is hidden in the depths from day?
Pearls and precious stones and golden sands,
Wondrous weeds and blossoms rare,
Kept back from human hands,
But good and fair,
A silent praise as pain is silent prayer.
A hymn, an incense rising toward the skies,
As our whole life should rise;
An offering without stint from earth below,
Which Love accepteth so.

Thus is it with a warbling bird,
With fruit bloom-ripe and full of seed,
With honey which the wild bees draw
From flowers, and store for future need
By a perpetual law.
We want the faith that hath not seen
Indeed, but hath believed His truth

Who witnessed that His work was good:
So we pass cold to age from youth.
Alas for us: for we have heard
And known, but have not understood.

O earth, earth, earth, thou yet shalt bow
Who art so fair and lifted up,
Thou yet shalt drain the bitter cup.
Men's eyes that wait upon thee now,
All eyes shall see thee lost and mean,
Exposed and valued at thy worth,
While thou shalt stand ashamed and dumb.—
Ah, when the Son of Man shall come,
Shall He find faith upon the earth?—

1853

*The P.R.B.**

I

The two Rossettis (brothers they)
And Holman Hunt and John Millais,
With Stephens chilvalrous and bland,
And Woolner in a distant land,*
In these six men I awestruck see
Embodied the great P.R.B.
D. G. Rossetti offered two
Good pictures* to the public view:
Unnumbered ones great John Millais,
And Holman more than I can say
* * * * * * *
William Rossetti calm and solemn
Cuts up his brethren by the column.*

2

The P.R.B. is in its decadence:—
For Woolner in Australia cooks his chops;
And Hunt is yearning for the land of Cheops;*
D. G. Rossetti shuns the vulgar optic;*
While William M. Rossetti merely lops
His B.s* in English disesteemed as Coptic;*

Calm Stephens in the twilight smokes his pipe
But long the dawning of his public day;
And he at last, the champion, great Millais
Attaining academic opulence
Winds up his signature with A.R.A.:—*
So rivers merge in the perpetual sea,
So luscious fruit must fall when over ripe,
And so the consummated P.R.B.

1853

(Untitled)

All night I dream you love me well,
All day I dream that you are cold:
Which is the dream? ah, who can tell,
Ah would that it were told.

So I should know my certain doom,
Know all the gladness or the pain;
So pass into the dreamless tomb,
Or never doubt again.

1853

*The World**

But day she wooes me, soft, exceeding fair:
But all night as the moon so changeth she;
Loathsome and foul with hideous leprosy
And subtle serpents gliding in her hair.
By day she wooes me to the outer air,
Ripe fruits, sweet flowers, and full satiety:
But thro' the night, a beast she grins at me,
A very monster void of love and prayer.
By day she stands a lie: by night she stands
In all the naked horror of the truth
With pushing horns and clawed and clutching hands.
Is this a friend indeed; that I should sell
My soul to her, give her my life and youth,
Till my feet, cloven too, take hold on hell?

1854

*From the Antique**

It's a weary life, it is; she said:—
  Doubly blank in a woman's lot:
I wish and I wish I were a man;
  Or, better than any being, were not:

Were nothing at all in all the world,
  Not a body and not a soul;
Not so much as a grain of dust
  Or drop of water from pole to pole.

Still the world would wag on the same,
  Still the seasons go and come;
Blossoms bloom as in days of old,
  Cherries ripen and wild bees hum.

None would miss me in all the world,
  How much less would care or weep:
I should be nothing; while all the rest
  Would wake and weary and fall asleep.

1854

*Three Stages**

I

I looked for that which is not, nor can be,
  And hope deferred* made my heart sick in truth;
  But years must pass before a hope of youth
    Is resigned utterly.

I watched and waited with a steadfast will:
  And though the object* seemed to flee away
  That I so longed for, ever, day by day,
    I watched and waited still.

Sometimes I said: This thing shall be no more:
  My expectation wearies and shall cease;*
  I will resign it now and be at peace:—
    Yet never gave it o'er.

Sometimes I said: It is an empty name
  I long for; to a name why should I give
  The peace of all the days I have to live?—
    Yet gave it all the same.

Alas, thou foolish one! alike unfit
  For healthy joy and salutary pain;
  Thou knowest the chase useless, and again
    Turnest to follow it.

2

My happy happy dream is finished with,
  My dream in which alone I lived so long.
My heart slept – woe is me, it wakeneth;
    Was weak – I thought it strong.

Oh weary wakening from a life-true dream:
  Oh pleasant dream from which I wake in pain:
I rested all my trust on things that seem,
    And all my trust is vain.

I must pull down my palace that I built,
  Dig up the pleasure-gardens of my soul;
Must change my laughter to sad tears for guilt,
    My freedom to control.

Now all the cherished secrets of my heart,
  Now all my hidden hopes are turned to sin:
Part of my life is dead, part sick, and part
    Is all on fire within.

The fruitless thought of what I might have been
  Haunting me ever will not let me rest:
A cold north wind has withered all my green,
    My sun is in the west.

But where my palace stood, with the same stone,
  I will uprear a shady hermitage;
And there my spirit shall keep house alone,
    Accomplishing its age:

There other garden beds shall lie around
   Full of sweet-briar and incense-bearing thyme;
There I will sit, and listen for the sound
      Of the last lingering chime.

3

I thought to deal the death-stroke at a blow,
   To give all, once for all, but nevermore;—
Then sit to hear the low waves fret the shore,
      Or watch the silent snow.

'Oh rest,' I thought, 'in silence and the dark;
   Oh rest, if nothing else, from head to feet:
   Though I may see no more the poppied wheat,
      Or sunny soaring lark.

'These chimes are slow, but surely strike at last;
   This sand is slow, but surely droppeth thro';*
   And much there is to suffer, much to do,
      Before the time be past.

'So will I labour, but will not rejoice:
   Will do and bear, but will not hope again;
   Gone dead alike to pulses of quick pain,
      And pleasure's counterpoise:'

I said so in my heart, and so I thought
   My life would lapse, a tedious monotone:
I thought to shut myself, and dwell alone
      Unseeking and unsought.

But first I tired, and then my care grew slack;
   Till my heart slumbered, maybe wandered too:—
I felt the sunshine glow again, and knew
      The swallow on its track;

All birds awoke to building in the leaves,
   All buds awoke to fulness and sweet scent,
   Ah, too, my heart woke unawares, intent
      On fruitful harvest sheaves.

Full pulse of life, that I had deemed was dead,
  Full throb of youth, that I had deemed at rest,—
  Alas, I cannot build myself a nest,
    I cannot crown my head

With royal purple blossoms for the feast,
  Nor flush with laughter, nor exult in song;—
  These joys may drift, as time now drifts along;
    And cease, as once they ceased.

I may pursue, and yet may not attain,
  Athirst and panting all the days I live:
  Or seem to hold, yet nerve myself to give
    What once I gave, again.

1854

*Listening**

She listened like a cushat dove
  That listens to its mate alone;
She listened like a cushat dove
  That loves but only one.

Not fair as men would reckon fair,
  Nor noble as they count the line;
Only as graceful as a bough
  And tendrils of the vine;
Only as noble as sweet Eve
  Your ancestress and mine.

And downcast were her dovelike eyes,
  And downcast was her tender cheek,
Her pulses fluttered like a dove
  To hear him speak.

1854

Echo

Come to me in the silence of the night;
Come in the speaking silence of a dream;
Come with soft rounded cheeks and eyes as bright
As sunlight on a stream;
Come back in tears,
O memory, hope, love of finished years.

Oh dream how sweet, too sweet, too bitter sweet,
Whose wakening should have been in Paradise,
Where souls brimfull of love abide and meet;
Where thirsting longing eyes
Watch the slow door
That opening, letting in, lets out no more.

Yet come to me in dreams, that I may live
My very life again tho' cold in death:
Come back to me in dreams, that I may give
Pulse for pulse, breath for breath:
Speak low, lean low,
As long ago, my love, how long ago.

1854

*My Dream**

Hear now a curious dream I dreamed last night,
Each word whereof is weighed and sifted truth.

I stood beside Euphrates while it swelled
Like overflowing Jordan in its youth:
It waxed and coloured sensibly to sight,
Till out of myriad pregnant waves there welled
Young crocodiles, a gaunt blunt-featured crew;
Fresh-hatched perhaps and daubed with birthday dew.
The rest if I should tell, I fear my friend,
My closest friend would deem the facts untrue;
And therefore it were wisely left untold;
Yet if you will, why, hear it to the end.

Each crocodile was girt with massive gold
And polished stones that with their wearers grew:
But one there was who waxed beyond the rest,
Wore kinglier girdle and a kingly crown,
Whilst crowns and orbs and sceptres starred his breast.
All gleamed compact and green with scale on scale,
But special burnishment adorned his mail
And special terror weighed upon his frown;
His punier brethren quaked before his tail,
Broad as a rafter, potent as a flail.
So he grew lord and master of his kin:
But who shall tell the tale of all their woes?
An execrable appetite arose,
He battened on them, crunched, and sucked them in.
He knew no law, he feared no binding law,
But ground them with inexorable jaw:
The luscious fat distilled upon his chin,
Exuded from his nostrils and his eyes,
While still like hungry death he fed his maw;
Till every minor crocodile being dead
And buried too, himself gorged to the full,
He slept with breath oppressed and unstrung claw.
Oh marvel passing strange which next I saw:
In sleep he dwindled to the common size,
And all the empire faded from his coat.
Then from far off a wingèd vessel came,
Swift as a swallow, subtle as a flame:
I know not what it bore of freight or host,
But white it was as an avenging ghost.
It levelled strong Euphrates in its course;
Supreme yet weightless as an idle mote
It seemed to tame the waters without force
Till not a murmur swelled or billow beat:
Lo, as the purple shadow swept the sands,
The prudent crocodile rose on his feet
And shed appropriate* tears and wrung his hands.

What can it mean? you ask. I answer not
For meaning, but myself must echo, What?
And tell it as I saw it on the spot.

1855

Cobwebs

It is a land with neither night nor day,
  Nor heat nor cold, nor any wind, nor rain,
  Nor hills nor valleys; but one even plain
Stretches thro' long unbroken miles away,
While thro' the sluggish air a twilight grey
  Broodeth; no moons or seasons wax and wane,
  No ebb and flow are there along the main,
No bud-time no leaf-falling there for aye,
No ripple on the sea, no shifting sand,
  No beat of wings to stir the stagnant space,
No pulse of life thro' all the loveless land
And loveless sea; no trace of days before,
  No guarded home, no toil-won restingplace
No future hope, no fear for evermore.

1855

*An Afterthought**

Oh lost garden Paradise:—
  Were the roses redder there
  Than they blossom otherwhere?
  Was the night's delicious shade
  More intensely star inlaid?
Who can tell what memories
Of lost beloved Paradise
Saddened Eve with sleepless eyes?—

Fair first mother lulled to rest
In a choicer garden nest,
Curtained with a softer shading
Than thy tenderest child is laid in,
Was the sundawn brighter far
Than our daily sundawns are?
Was that love, first love of all
  Warmer, deeper, better worth
  Than has warmed poor hearts of earth
Since the utter ruinous fall?—

Ah supremely happy once,
  Ah supremely broken hearted
  When her tender feet departed
  From the accustomed paths of peace:
Catching Angel orisons
For the last last time of all,
Shedding tears that would not cease
For the bitter bitter fall.

Yet the accustomed hand for leading,
Yet the accustomed heart for love;
Sure she kept one part of Eden
Angels could not strip her of.
Sure the fiery messenger*
Kindling for his outraged Lord,
Willing with the perfect Will,
Yet rejoiced the flaming sword*
Chastening sore but sparing still
Shut her treasure out with her.

What became of Paradise?
  Did the cedars droop at all
  (Springtide hastening to the fall)
  Missing the beloved hand—
  Or did their green perfection stand
Unmoved beneath the perfect skies?—
Paradise was rapt on high,
It lies before the gate of Heaven:—
  Even now slumbers there forgiven,
  Slumbers Rachel* comforted,
  Slumber all the blessed dead
Of days and months and years gone by,
A solemn swelling company.

They wait for us beneath the trees
Of Paradise that lap of ease:
They wait for us, till God shall please.
Oh come the day of death, that day
Of rest which cannot pass away:
When the last work is wrought, the last
Pang of pain is felt and past
And the blessed door made fast.

1855

*Shut Out**

The door was shut. I looked between
  Its iron bars; and saw it lie,
  My garden, mine, beneath the sky,
Pied with all flowers bedewed and green:

From bough to bough the song-birds crossed,
  From flower to flower the moths and bees;
  With all its nests and stately trees
It had been mine, and it was lost.

A shadowless spirit kept the gate,
  Blank and unchanging like the grave.
  I peering thro' said: 'Let me have
Some buds to cheer my outcast state.'

He answered not. 'Or give me, then,
  But one small twig from shrub or tree;
  And bid my home remember me
Until I come to it again.'

The spirit was silent; but he took
  Mortar and stone to build a wall;
  He left no loophole great or small
Thro' which my straining eyes might look:

So now I sit here quite alone
  Blinded with tears; nor grieve for that,
  For nought is left worth looking at
Since my delightful land is gone.

A violet bed is budding near,
  Wherein a lark has made her nest:
  And good they are, but not the best;
And dear they are, but not so dear.

1856

*By the Water**

There are rivers lapsing down
    Lily-laden to the sea;
Every lily is a boat
    For bees, one, two, or three:
I wish there were a fairy boat
    For you, my friend, and me.

We would rock upon the river,
    Scarcely floating by;
Rocking rocking like the lilies,
    You, my friend, and I;
Rocking like the stately lilies
    Beneath the statelier sky.

But ah, where is that river
    Whose hyacinth banks descend
Down to the sweeter lilies,
    Till soft their shadows blend
Into a watery twilight?—
    And ah, where is my friend?—

1856

*A Chilly Night**

I rose at the dead of night
    And went to the lattice alone
To look for my Mother's ghost
    Where the ghostly moonlight shone.

My friends had failed one by one,
    Middleaged, young, and old,
Till the ghosts were warmer to me
    Than my friends that had grown cold.

I looked and I saw the ghosts
    Dotting plain and mound:
They stood in the blank moonlight
    But no shadow lay on the ground;
They spoke without a voice
    And they leapt without a sound.

I called: 'O my Mother dear,'—
  I sobbed: 'O my Mother kind,
Make a lonely bed for me
  And shelter it from the wind:

'Tell the others not to come
  To see me night or day;
But I need not tell my friends
  To be sure to keep away.'

My Mother raised her eyes,
  They were blank and could not see;
Yet they held me with their stare
  While they seemed to look at me.

She opened her mouth and spoke,
  I could not hear a word
While my flesh crept on my bones
  And every hair was stirred.

She knew that I could not hear
  The message that she told
Whether I had long to wait
  Or soon should sleep in the mould:
I saw her toss her shadowless hair
  And wring her hands in the cold.

I strained to catch her words
  And she strained to make me hear,
But never a sound of words
  Fell on my straining ear.

From midnight to the cockcrow
  I kept my watch in pain
While the subtle ghosts grew subtler
  In the sad night on the wane.

From midnight to the cockcrow
  I watched till all were gone,
Some to sleep in the shifting sea
  And some under turf and stone:

Living had failed and dead had failed
And I was indeed alone.

1856

Amen

It is over. What is over?
Nay, how much is over truly:
Harvest days we toiled to sow for;
Now the sheaves are gathered newly,
Now the wheat is garnered duly.

It is finished. What is finished?
Much is finished known or unknown:
Lives are finished; time diminished;
Was the fallow field left unsown?
Will these buds be always unblown?

It suffices. What suffices?
All suffices reckoned rightly:
Spring shall bloom where now the ice is,
Roses make the bramble sightly,
And the quickening sun shine brightly,
And the latter wind blow lightly,
And my garden teem with spices.

1856

*The Hour and the Ghost**

BRIDE

O love, love, hold me fast,
He draws me away from thee;
I cannot stem the blast,
Nor the cold strong sea:
Far away a light shines
Beyond the hills and pines;
It is lit for me.

BRIDEGROOM

I have thee close, my dear,
No terror can come near;
Only far off the northern light shines clear.

GHOST

Come with me, fair and false,
To our home, come home.
It is my voice that calls:
Once thou wast not afraid
When I woo'd, and said,
'Come, our nest is newly made'—
Now cross the tossing foam.

BRIDE

Hold me one moment longer,
He taunts me with the past,
His clutch is waxing stronger,
Hold me fast, hold me fast.
He draws me from thy heart,
And I cannot withhold:
He bids my spirit depart
With him into the cold:—
Oh bitter vows of old!

BRIDEGROOM

Lean on me, hide thine eyes:
Only ourselves, earth and skies,
Are present here: be wise.

GHOST

Lean on me, come away,
I will guide and steady:
Come, for I will not stay:
Come, for house and bed are ready.
Ah, sure bed and house,
For better and worse, for life and death:
Goal won with shortened breath:
Come, crown our vows.

BRIDE

One moment, one more word,
While my heart beats still,
While my breath is stirred
By my fainting will.
O friend forsake me not,
Forget not as I forgot:
But keep thy heart for me,
Keep thy faith true and bright;
Thro' the lone cold winter night
Perhaps I may come to thee.

BRIDEGROOM

Nay peace, my darling, peace:
Let these dreams and terrors cease:
Who spoke of death or change or aught but ease?

GHOST

O fair frail sin,
O poor harvest gathered in!
Thou shalt visit him again
To watch his heart grow cold;
To know the gnawing pain
I know of old;
To see one much more fair
Fill up the vacant chair,
Fill his heart, his children bear:—
While thou and I together
In the outcast weather
Toss and howl and spin.*

1856

*A Triad**

Three sang of love together: one with lips
  Crimson, with cheeks and bosom in a glow,
Flushed to the yellow hair and finger tips;
  And one there sang who soft and smooth as snow
  Bloomed like a tinted hyacinth at a show;
And one was blue with famine after love,
  Who like a harpstring snapped rang harsh and low

The burden of what those were singing of.
One shamed herself in love; one temperately
  Grew gross in soulless love, a sluggish wife;
One famished died for love. Thus two of three
  Took death for love and won him after strife;
One droned in sweetness like a fattened bee:
  All on the threshold, yet all short of life.

1856

*Love from the North**

I had a love in soft south land,
  Beloved thro' April far in May;
He waited on my lightest breath,
  And never dared to say me nay.

He saddened if my cheer was sad,
  But gay he grew if I was gay;
We never differed on a hair,
  My yes his yes, my nay his nay.

The wedding hour was come, the aisles
  Were flushed with sun and flowers that day;
I pacing balanced in my thoughts:
'It's quite too late to think of nay.'—

My bridegroom answered in his turn,
  Myself had almost answered 'yea:'
When thro' the flashing nave I heard
  A struggle and resounding 'nay'.

Bridemaids and bridegroom shrank in fear,
  But I stood high who stood at bay:
'And if I answer yea, fair Sir,
  What man art thou to bar with nay?'

He was a strong man from the north,
  Light-locked, with eyes of dangerous grey:
'Put yea by for another time
  In which I will not say thee nay.'

He took me in his strong white arms,
  He bore me on his horse away
O'er crag, morass, and hairbreadth pass,
  But never asked me yea or nay.

He made me fast with book and bell,
 With links of love he makes me stay;
Till now I've neither heart nor power
 Nor will nor wish to say him nay.

1856

*In an Artist's Studio**

One face looks out from all his canvasses,
 One selfsame figure sits or walks or leans;
 We found her hidden just behind those screens,
That mirror gave back all her loveliness.
A queen in opal or in ruby dress,
 A nameless girl in freshest summer greens,
 A saint, an angel;—every canvas means
The same one meaning, neither more nor less.
He feeds upon her face by day and night,
 And she with true kind eyes looks back on him
Fair as the moon and joyful as the light:
 Not wan with waiting, not with sorrow dim;
Not as she is, but was when hope shone bright;
 Not as she is, but as she fills his dream.

1856

A Better Resurrection

I have no wit, no words, no tears;
 My heart within me like a stone
Is numbed too much for hopes or fears;
 Look right, look left, I dwell alone;
I lift mine eyes, but dimmed with grief
 No everlasting hills* I see;
My life is in the falling leaf:
 O Jesus, quicken me.

My life is like a faded leaf,
 My harvest dwindled to a husk;
Truly my life is void and brief
 And tedious in the barren dusk;
My life is like a frozen thing,
 No bud nor greenness can I see:
Yet rise it shall—the sap of Spring;
 O Jesus, rise in me.

My life is like a broken bowl,
A broken bowl that cannot hold
One drop of water for my soul
Or cordial in the searching cold;
Cast in the fire the perished thing,
Melt and remould it, till it be
A royal cup for Him my King:
O Jesus, drink of me.

1857

Introspective

I wish it were over the terrible pain,
Pang after pang again and again;
First the shattering ruining blow,
Then the probing steady and slow.

Did I wince? I did not faint:
My soul broke but was not bent;
Up I stand like a blasted tree
By the shore of the shivering sea.

On my boughs neither leaf nor fruit,
No sap in my uttermost root,
Brooding in an anguish dumb
On the short past and the long to come.

Dumb I was when the rain fell,
Dumb I remain and will never tell:
O my soul I talk with thee
But not another the sight must see.

I did not start when the torture stung,
I did not faint when the torture wrung;
Let it come tenfold if come it must
But I will not groan when I bite the dust.

1857

*'The heart knoweth its own bitterness'**

When all the over-work of life
Is finished once, and fast asleep
We swerve no more beneath the knife
But taste that silence cool and deep;

Forgetful of the highways rough,
  Forgetful of the thorny scourge,
  Forgetful of the tossing surge,
Then shall we find it is enough?—

How can we say 'enough' on earth;
  'Enough' with such a craving heart:
I have not found it since my birth
  But still have bartered part for part.
I have not held and hugged the whole,
  But paid the old to gain the new;
  Much have I paid, yet much is due,
Till I am beggared sense and soul.

I used to labour, used to strive
  For pleasure with a restless will:
Now if I save my soul alive
  All else what matters, good or ill?
I used to dream alone, to plan
  Unspoken hopes and days to come:—
  Of all my past this is the sum:
I will not lean on child of man.

To give, to give, not to receive,
  I long to pour myself, my soul,
Not to keep back or count or leave
  But king with king to give the whole:
I long for one to stir my deep—
  I have had enough of help and gift—
  I long for one to search and sift
Myself, to take myself and keep.

You* scratch my surface with your pin;
  You stroke me smooth with hushing breath;—
Nay pierce, nay probe, nay dig within,
  Probe my quick core and sound my depth.
You call me with a puny call,
  You talk, you smile, you nothing do;
  How should I spend my heart on you,
My heart that so outweighs you all?

Your vessels are by much too strait;
  Were I to pour you could not hold,
Bear with me: I must bear to wait

A fountain sealed* thro' heat and cold.
Bear with me days or months or years;
Deep must call deep until the end
When friend shall no more envy friend
Nor vex his friend at unawares.

Not in this world of hope deferred,
This world of perishable stuff;—
Eye hath not seen,* nor ear hath heard,
Nor heart conceived that full 'enough':
Here moans the separating sea,
Here harvests fail, here breaks the heart;
There God shall join and no man part,
I full of Christ and Christ of me.

1857

*Day-Dreams**

Gazing through her chamber window
Sits my soul's dear soul:
Looking northward, looking southward,
Looking to the goal,
Looking back without control.

I have strewn thy path, beloved,
With plumed meadowsweet,
Iris and pale perfumed lilies,
Roses most complete:
Wherefore pause on listless feet?

But she sits and never answers,
Gazing, gazing still
On swift fountain, shadowed valley,
Cedared sunlit hill:
Who can guess or read her will?

Who can guess or read the spirit
Shrined within her eyes,
Part a longing, part a languor,
Part a mere surprise,
While slow mists do rise and rise?

Is it love she looks and longs for,
Is it rest or peace,

Is it slumber self-forgetful
  In its utter ease,
Is it one or all of these?

So she sits and doth not answer
  With her dreaming eyes,
With her languid look delicious
  Almost paradise,
Less than happy, over-wise.

Answer me, O self-forgetful—
  Or of what beside?—
Is it day-dream of a maiden,
  Vision of a bride,
Is it knowledge, love, or pride?

Cold she sits through all my kindling,
  Deaf to all I pray:
I have wasted might and wisdom,
  Wasted night and day:
Deaf she dreams to all I say.

Now if I could guess her secret,
  Were it worth the guess?—
Time is lessening, hope is lessening,
  Love grows less and less:
What care I for no or yes?

I will give her stately burial,
  Though, when she lies dead:
For dear memory of the past time,
  Of her royal head,
Of the much I strove and said.

I will give her stately burial,
  Stately willow-branches bent:
Have her carved in alabaster,*
  As she dreamed and leant
While I wondered what she meant.

1857

*In the Round Tower at Jhansi**

A hundred, a thousand to one; even so;
  Not a hope in the world remained:
The swarming howling wretches below
  Gained and gained and gained.

Skene looked at his pale young wife:—
  'Is the time come?' – 'The time is come!'—
Young, strong, and so full of life:
  The agony struck them dumb.

Close his arm about her now,
  Close her cheek to his,
Close the pistol to her brow—
  God forgive them this!

'Will it hurt much?' – 'No, mine own:
  I wish I could bear the pang for both.'
'I wish I could bear the pang alone:
  Courage, dear, I am not loth.'

Kiss and kiss: 'It is not pain
  Thus to kiss and die.
One kiss more.' – 'And yet one again.'—
  'Good bye.' – 'Good bye.'

1857

*A Nightmare**

I have a love in ghostland—
  Early found, ah me, how early lost!—
Blood-red seaweeds drip along that coastland
  By the strong sea wrenched and tossed.
In every creek there slopes a dead man's islet,
  And such an one in every bay;
All unripened in the unended twilight:
  For there comes neither night nor day.

Unripe harvest there hath none to reap it
  From the watery misty place;
Unripe vineyard there hath none to keep it
  In unprofitable space.

Living flocks and herds are nowhere found there;
  Only ghosts in flocks and shoals:
Indistinguished hazy ghosts surround there
  Meteors whirling on their poles;
Indistinguished hazy ghosts abound there;
  Troops, yea swarms, of dead men's souls.—

Have they towns to live in?—
  They have towers and towns from sea to sea;
Of each town the gates are seven;
  Of one of these each ghost is free.
Civilians, soldiers, seamen,
  Of one town each ghost is free:
They are ghastly men those ghostly freemen:
  Such a sight may you not see.—

How know you that your lover
  Of death's tideless waters stoops to drink?—
Me by night doth mouldy darkness cover,
  It makes me quake to think:
All night long I feel his presence hover
  Thro' the darkness black as ink.

Without a voice he tells me
  The wordless secrets of death's deep:
If I sleep, he like a trump compels me
  To stalk forth in my sleep:
If I wake, he rides me like a nightmare;
  I feel my hair stand up, my body creep:
Without light I see a blasting sight there,
  See a secret I must keep.

1857

Another Spring

If I might see another Spring
  I'd not plant summer flowers and wait:
I'd have my crocuses at once,
My leafless pink mezereons,
  My chill-veined snowdrops, choicer yet
  My white or azure violet,
Leaf-nested primrose; anything
    To blow at once, not late.

If I might see another Spring
  I'd listen to the daylight birds
That build their nests and pair and sing,
Nor wait for mateless nightingale;
  I'd listen to the lusty herds,
  The ewes with lambs as white as snow,
I'd find out music in the hail
    And all the winds that blow.

If I might see another Spring—
  Oh stinging comment on my past
That all my past results in 'if'—
  If I might see another Spring
I'd laugh today, today is brief;
I would not wait for anything:
  I'd use today that cannot last,
    Be glad today and sing.

1857

Memory

I

I nursed it in my bosom while it lived,
  I hid it in my heart when it was dead;
In joy I sat alone, even so I grieved
    Alone and nothing said.

I shut the door to face the naked truth,
  I stood alone – I faced the truth alone,
Stripped bare of self-regard or forms or ruth
    Till first and last were shown.

I took the perfect balances and weighed;
  No shaking of my hand disturbed the poise;
Weighed, found it wanting: not a word I said,
    But silent made my choice.

None know the choice I made; I make it still.
  None know the choice I made and broke my heart,
Breaking mine idol: I have braced my will
    Once, chosen for once my part.

I broke it at a blow, I laid it cold,
  Crushed in my deep heart where it used to live.
My heart dies inch by inch; the time grows old,
    Grows old in which I grieve.

2

I have a room whereinto no one enters
  Save I myself alone:
  There sits a blessed memory on a throne,
There my life centres;

While winter comes and goes—oh tedious comer!—
  And while its nip-wind blows;
  While bloom the bloodless lily and warm rose
Of lavish summer.

If any should force entrance he might see there
  One buried yet not dead,
  Before whose face I no more bow my head
Or bend my knee there;

But often in my worn life's autumn weather
  I watch there with clear eyes,
  And think how it will be in Paradise
When we're together.

1857

A Birthday

My heart is like a singing bird
  Whose nest is in a watered shoot;
My heart is like an apple tree
  Whose boughs are bent with thickset fruit;
My heart is like a rainbow shell
  That paddles in a halcyon sea;
My heart is gladder than all these
  Because my love is come to me.

Raise me a dais of silk and down;
  Hang it with vair and purple dyes;
Carve it in doves and pomegranates,
  And peacocks with a hundred eyes;

Work it in gold and silver grapes,
In leaves and silver fleurs-de-lys;
Because the birthday of my life
Is come, my love is come to me.

1857

*An Apple-Gathering**

I plucked pink blossoms from mine apple tree
And wore them all that evening in my hair:
Then in due season when I went to see
I found no apples there.

With dangling basket all along the grass
As I had come I went the selfsame track:
My neighbours mocked me while they saw me pass
So empty-handed back.

Lilian and Lilias smiled in trudging by,
Their heaped-up basket teazed me like a jeer;
Sweet-voiced they sang beneath the sunset sky,
Their mother's home was near.

Plump Gertrude passed me with her basket full,
A stronger hand than hers helped it along;
A voice talked with her thro' the shadows cool
More sweet to me than song.

Ah Willie, Willie, was my love less worth
Than apples with their green leaves piled above?
I counted rosiest apples on the earth
Of far less worth than love.

So once it was with me you stooped to talk
Laughing and listening in this very lane:
To think that by this way we used to walk
We shall not walk again!

I let my neighbours pass me, ones and twos
And groups; the latest said the night grew chill,
And hastened: but I loitered, while the dews
Fell fast I loitered still.

1857

*Winter: My Secret**

I tell my secret? No indeed, not I!
Perhaps some day, who knows?
But not today; it froze, and blows, and snows,
And you're too curious: fie!
You want to hear it? well:
Only, my secret's mine, and I won't tell.

Or, after all, perhaps there's none:
Suppose there is no secret after all,
But only just my fun.
Today's a nipping day, a biting day;
In which one wants a shawl,
A veil, a cloak, and other wraps:
I cannot ope to every one who taps,
And let the draughts come whistling thro' my hall;
Come bounding and surrounding me,
Come buffeting, astounding me,
Nipping and clipping thro' my wraps and all.
I wear my mask for warmth: who ever shows
His nose to Russian snows
To be pecked at by every wind that blows?
You would not peck? I thank you for good will,
Believe, but leave that truth untested still.

Spring's an expansive time: yet I don't trust
March with its peck of dust,
Nor April with its rainbow-crowned brief showers,
Nor even May, whose flowers
One frost may wither thro' the sunless hours.

Perhaps some languid summer day,
When drowsy birds sing less and less,
And golden fruit is ripening to excess,
If there's not too much sun nor too much cloud,
And the warm wind is neither still nor loud,
Perhaps my secret I may say,
Or you may guess.

1857

*Maude Clare**

Out of the church she followed them
   With a lofty step and mein:
His bride was like a village maid,
   Maude Clare was like a queen.

'Son Thomas,' his lady mother said,
   With smiles, almost with tears:
'May Nell and you but live as true
   As we have done for years;

'Your father thirty years ago
   Had just your tale to tell;
But he was not so pale as you,
   Nor I so pale as Nell.'

My lord was pale with inward strife,
   And Nell was pale with pride;
My lord gazed long on pale Maude Clare
   Or ever he kissed the bride.

'Lo, I have brought my gift, my lord,
   Have brought my gift,' she said:
'To bless the hearth, to bless the board,
   To bless the marriage-bed.

'Here's my half of the golden chain
   You wore about your neck,
That day we waded ankle-deep
   For lilies in the beck:*

'Here's my half of the faded leaves
   We plucked from budding bough,
With feet amongst the lily leaves,—
   The lilies are budding now.'

He strove to match her scorn with scorn,
   He faltered in his place:
'Lady,' he said, – 'Maude Clare,' he said,—
   'Maude Clare:' – and hid his face.

She turn'd to Nell: 'My Lady Nell,
   I have a gift for you;

Tho' were it fruit, the bloom were gone,
  Or, were it flowers, the dew.

'Take my share of a fickle heart,
  Mine of a paltry love:
Take it or leave it as you will,
  I wash my hands thereof.'

'And what you leave,' said Nell, 'I'll take,
  And what you spurn, I'll wear;
For he's my lord for better and worse,
  And him I love, Maude Clare.

'Yea, tho' you're taller by the head,
  More wise, and much more fair;
I'll love him till he loves me best,
  Me best of all, Maude Clare.'

1858

At Home

When I was dead, my spirit turned
  To seek the much frequented house:
I passed the door, and saw my friends
  Feasting beneath green orange boughs;
From hand to hand they pushed the wine,
  They sucked the pulp of plum and peach;
They sang, they jested, and they laughed.
    For each was loved of each.

I listened to their honest chat:
  Said one: 'Tomorrow we shall be
Plod plod along the featureless sands
  And coasting miles and miles of sea.'
Said one: 'Before the turn of tide
  We will achieve the eyrie-seat.'
Said one: 'Tomorrow shall be like
    Today, but much more sweet.'

'Tomorrow,' said they, strong with hope,
  And dwelt upon the pleasant way:
'Tomorrow,' cried they one and all,
  While no one spoke of yesterday.

Their life stood full at blessed noon;
  I, only I, had passed away:
'Tomorrow and today,' they cried;
    I was of yesterday.

I shivered comfortless, but cast
  No chill across the tablecloth;
I all-forgotten shivered, sad
  To stay and yet to part how loth:
I passed from the familiar room,
  I who from love had passed away,
Like the remembrance of a guest
    That tarrieth but a day.

1858

*Up-hill**

Does the road wind up-hill all the way?
  Yes, to the very end.
Will the day's journey take the whole long day?
  From morn to night, my friend.

But is there for the night a resting-place?
  A roof for when the slow dark hours begin.
May not the darkness hide it from my face?
  You cannot miss that inn.

Shall I meet other wayfarers at night?
  Those who have gone before.
Then must I knock, or call when just in sight?
  They will not keep you standing at that door.

Shall I find comfort, travel-sore and weak?
  Of labour you shall find the sum.
Will there be beds for me and all who seek?
  Yea, beds for all who come.

1858

*Old and New Year Ditties**

1

New Year met me somewhat sad:
  Old Year leaves me tired,
Stripped of favourite things I had,
  Baulked of much desired:
Yet farther on my road today
God willing, farther on my way.

New Year coming on apace
  What have you to give me?
Bring you scathe, or bring you grace,
Face me with an honest face;
  You shall not deceive me:
Be it good or ill, be it what you will,
It needs shall help me on my road,
My rugged way to heaven, please God.

1856

2

Watch with me, men, women, and children dear,
You whom I love, for whom I hope and fear,
Watch with me this last vigil of the year.
Some hug their business, some their pleasure scheme;
Some seize the vacant hour to sleep or dream;
Heart locked in heart some kneel and watch apart.

Watch with me, blessed spirits, who delight
All thro' the holy night to walk in white,
Or take your ease after the long-drawn fight.
I know not if they watch with me: I know
They count this eve of resurrection slow,
And cry, 'How long?' with urgent utterance strong.

Watch with me, Jesus, in my loneliness:
Tho' others say me nay, yet say Thou yes;
Tho' others pass me by, stop Thou to bless.
Yea, Thou dost stop with me this vigil night;
Tonight of pain, tomorrow of delight:
I, Love, am Thine; Thou, my God, art mine.

1858

3

Passing away, saith the World, passing away:
Chances, beauty and youth sapped day by day:
Thy life never continueth in one stay.
Is the eye waxen dim, is the dark hair changing to grey
That hath won neither laurel nor bay?*
I shall clothe myself in Spring and bud in May:
Thou, root-stricken, shalt not rebuild thy decay
On my bosom for aye.
Then I answered: Yea.

Passing away, saith my Soul, passing away:
With its burden of fear and hope, of labour and play;
Hearken what the past doth witness and say:
Rust in thy gold, a moth is in thine array,
A canker is in thy bud, thy leaf must decay.
At midnight, at cockcrow, at morning, one certain day
Lo the bridegroom shall come and shall not delay:
Watch thou and pray.
Then I answered: Yea.

Passing away, saith my God, passing away:
Winter passeth after the long delay:
New grapes on the vine, new figs on the tender spray,
Turtle calleth turtle in Heaven's May.
Tho' I tarry, wait for Me, trust Me, watch and pray.
Arise, come away, night is past and lo it is day,
My love, My sister, My spouse, thou shalt hear Me say.
Then I answered: Yea.

1860

Winter Rain

Every valley drinks,
Every dell and hollow:
Where the kind rain sinks and sinks,
Green of Spring will follow.

Yet a lapse of weeks
Buds will burst their edges,
Strip their wool-coats, glue-coats, streaks,
In the woods and hedges;

Weave a bower of love
  For birds to meet each other,
Weave a canopy above
  Nest and egg and mother.

But for fattening rain
  We should have no flowers,
Never a bud or leaf again
  But for soaking showers;

Never a mated bird
  In the rocking tree-tops,
Never indeed a flock or herd
  To graze upon the lea-crops.

Lambs so woolly white,
  Sheep the sun-bright leas on,
They could have no grass to bite
  But for rain in season.

We should find no moss
  In the shadiest places,
Find no waving meadow grass
  Pied with broad-eyed daisies:

But miles of barren sand,
  With never a son or daughter,
Not a lily on the land,
  Or lily on the water.

1859

*L.E.L.**

'Whose heart was breaking for a little love.'

Downstairs I laugh, I sport and jest with all:*
  But in my solitary room above
I turn my face in silence to the wall;
  My heart is breaking for a little love.
    Tho' winter frosts are done,
    And birds pair every one,
And leaves peep out, for springtide is begun.

I feel no spring, while spring is wellnigh blown,
  I find no nest, while nests are in the grove:

Woe's me for mine own heart that dwells alone,
  My heart that breaketh for a little love.
    While golden in the sun
    Rivulets rise and run,
While lilies bud, for springtide is begun.

All love, are loved, save only I; their hearts
  Beat warm with love and joy, beat full thereof:
They cannot guess, who play the pleasant parts,
  My heart is breaking for a little love.
    While beehives wake and whirr,
    And rabbit thins his fur,
In living spring that sets the world astir.

I deck myself with silks and jewelry,
  I plume myself like any mated dove:
They praise my rustling show, and never see
  My heart is breaking for a little love.
    While sprouts green lavender
    With rosemary and myrrh,
For in quick spring the sap is all astir.

Perhaps some saints in glory guess the truth,
  Perhaps some angels read it as they move,
And cry one to another full of ruth,
'Her heart is breaking for a little love.'
    Tho' other things have birth,
    And leap and sing for mirth,
When springtime wakes and clothes and feeds the earth.

Yet saith a saint: 'Take patience for thy scathe;'*
  Yet saith an angel: 'Wait, for thou shalt prove
True best is last, true life is born of death,
  O thou, heart-broken for a little love.
    Then love shall fill thy girth,
    And love make fat thy dearth,
When new spring builds new heaven and clean new earth.'

1859

*'Then they that feared the Lord spake often one to another'**

Friend I commend to thee the narrow way:
Not because I, please God, will walk therein,
But rather for the love-feast of that day
The exceeding prize which whoso will may win.
This world is old and rotting at the core
Here death's heads mock us with a toothless grin
Here heartiest laughter leaves us spent and sore.
We heap up treasures for the fretting moth,
Our children heap, our fathers heaped before,
But what shall profit us the cumbrous growth?
It cannot journey with us, cannot save,
Stripped in that darkness be we lief or loth
Stripped bare to what we are from all we have,
Naked we came, naked we must return
To one obscure inevitable grave.
If this the lesson is which we must learn
Taught by God's discipline of love or wrath
(To brand or purify His fire must burn)—
Friend I commend to thee the narrow path
That thou and I, please God, may walk therein,
May taste and see how good is God Who hath
Loved us while hating even to death our sin.

1859

*Cousin Kate**

I was a cottage maiden
Hardened by sun and air,
Contented with my cottage mates,
Not mindful I was fair.
Why did a great lord find me out,
And praise my flaxen hair?
Why did a great lord find me out
To fill my heart with care?

He lured me to his palace home—
Woe's me for joy thereof—
To lead a shameless shameful life,

His plaything and his love.
He wore me like a silken knot,
He changed me like a glove;
So now I moan, an unclean thing,
Who might have been a dove.

O Lady Kate, my cousin Kate,
You grew more fair than I:
He saw you at your father's gate,
Chose you, and cast me by.
He watched your steps along the lane,
Your work among the rye;
He lifted you from mean estate
To sit with him on high.

Because you were so good and pure
He bound you with his ring:
The neighbours call you good and pure,
Call me an outcast thing.
Even so I sit and howl in dust,
You sit in gold and sing:
Now which of us has tenderer heart?
You had the stronger wing.

O cousin Kate, my love was true,
Your love was writ in sand:
If he had fooled not me but you,
If you stood where I stand,
He'd not have won me with his love
Nor bought me with his land;
I would have spit into his face
And not have taken his hand.

Yet I've a gift you have not got,
And seem not like to get:
For all your clothes and wedding-ring
I've little doubt you fret.
My fair-haired son, my shame, my pride,
Cling closer, closer yet:
Your father would give lands for one
To wear his coronet.

1859

Noble Sisters

'Now did you mark a falcon,
  Sister dear, sister dear,
Flying toward my window
  In the morning cool and clear?
With jingling bells about her neck,
  But what beneath her wing?
It may have been a ribbon,
  Or it may have been a ring.'—
    'I marked a falcon swooping
      At the break of day:
    And for your love, my sister dove,
      I 'frayed the thief away.'—

'Or did you spy a ruddy hound,
  Sister fair and tall,
Went snuffing round my garden bound,
  Or crouched by my bower wall?
With a silken leash about his neck;
  But in his mouth may be
A chain of gold and silver links,
  Or a letter writ to me.'—
    'I heard a hound, highborn sister,
      Stood baying at the moon:
    I rose and drove him from your wall
      Lest you should wake too soon.'—

'Or did you meet a pretty page
  Sat swinging on the gate;
Sat whistling like a bird,
  Or may be slept too late:
With eaglets broidered on his cap,
  And eaglets on his glove?
If you had turned his pockets out,
  You had found some pledge of love.'—
    'I met him at this daybreak,
      Scarce the east was red:
    Lest the creaking gate should anger you,
      I packed him home to bed.'—

'Oh patience, sister. Did you see
  A young man tall and strong,

Swift-footed to uphold the right
And to uproot the wrong,
Come home across the desolate sea
To woo me for his wife?
And in his heart my heart is locked,
And in his life my life.'—
'I met a nameless man, sister,
Who loitered round our door:
I said: Her husband loves her much,
And yet she loves him more.'—

'Fie, sister, fie, a wicked lie,
A lie, a wicked lie,
I have none other love but him,
Nor will have till I die.
And you have turned him from our door,
And stabbed him with a lie:
I will go seek him thro' the world
In sorrow till I die.'—
'Go seek in sorrow, sister,
And find in sorrow too:
If thus you shame* our father's name
My curse go forth with you.'

1860

*Sister Maude**

Who told my mother of my shame,
Who told my father of my dear?
Oh who but Maude, my sister Maude,
Who lurked to spy and peer.

Cold he lies, as cold as stone,
With his clotted curls about his face:
The comeliest corpse in all the world
And worthy of a queen's embrace.

You might have spared his soul, sister,
Have spared my soul, your own soul too:
Though I had not been born at all,
He'd never have looked at you.

My father may sleep in Paradise,
  My mother at Heaven-gate:
But sister Maude shall get no sleep
  Either early or late.

My father may wear a golden gown,
  My mother a crown may win;
If my dear and I knocked at Heaven-gate
  Perhaps they'd let us in:
But sister Maude, oh sister Maude,
Bide *you* with death and sin.

1860

*'No, Thank You, John'**

I never said I loved you, John:
  Why will you teaze me day by day,
And wax a weariness to think upon
    With always 'do' and 'pray'?

You know I never loved you, John;
  No fault of mine made me your toast:
Why will you haunt me with a face as wan
    As shows an hour-old ghost?

I dare say Meg or Moll would take
  Pity upon you, if you'd ask:
And pray don't remain single for my sake
    Who can't perform that task.

I have no heart? – Perhaps I have not;
  But then you're mad to take offence
That I don't give you what I have not got:
    Use your own common sense.

Let bygones be bygones:
  Don't call me false, who owed not to be true:
I'd rather answer 'No' to fifty Johns
    Than answer 'Yes' to you.

Let's mar our pleasant days no more,
  Song-birds of passage, days of youth:
Catch at today, forget the days before:
    I'll wink at your untruth.

Let us strike hands as hearty friends;
No more, no less; and friendship's good:
Only don't keep in view ulterior ends,
And points not understood

In open treaty. Rise above
Quibbles and shuffling off and on:
Here's friendship for you if you like; but love,—
No, thank you, John.

1860

Mirage

The hope I dreamed of was a dream,
Was but a dream; and now I wake
Exceeding comfortless, and worn, and old,
For a dream's sake.

I hang my harp upon a tree,
A weeping willow in a lake;*
I hang my silenced harp there, wrung and snapt
For a dream's sake.

Lie still, lie still, my breaking heart;
My silent heart, lie still and break:
Life, and the world, and mine own self, are changed
For a dream's sake.

1860

*Promises like Piecrust**

Promise me no promises,
So will I not promise you;
Keep we both our liberties,
Never false and never true:
Let us hold the die uncast,
Free to come as free to go;
For I cannot know your past,
And of mine what can you know?

You, so warm, may once have been
Warmer towards another one;
I, so cold, may once have seen

Sunlight, once have felt the sun:
Who shall show us if it was
Thus indeed in time of old?
Fades the image from the glass
And the fortune is not told.

If you promised, you might grieve
For lost liberty again;
If I promised, I believe
I should fret to break the chain:
Let us be the friends we were,
Nothing more but nothing less;
Many thrive on frugal fare
Who would perish of excess.

1861

Wife to Husband

Pardon the faults in me,
For the love of years ago:
Good bye.
I must drift across the sea,
I must sink into the snow,
I must die.

You can bask in this sun,
You can drink wine, and eat:
Good bye.
I must gird myself and run,
Tho' with unready feet:
I must die.

Blank sea to sail upon,
Cold bed to sleep in:
Good bye.
While you clasp, I must be gone
For all your weeping:
I must die.

A kiss for one friend,
And a word for two,—
Good bye:—
A lock that you must send,

A kindness you must do:
I must die.

Not a word for you,
Not a lock or kiss,
Good bye.
We, one, must part in two;
Verily death is this:
I must die.

1861

*Good Friday**

Am I a stone and not a sheep
That I can stand, O Christ, beneath Thy Cross,
To number drop by drop Thy Blood's slow loss,
And yet not weep?

Not so those women* loved
Who with exceeding grief lamented Thee;
Not so fallen Peter weeping bitterly;
Not so the thief was moved;

Not so the Sun and Moon
Which hid their faces in a starless sky,
A horror of great darkness at broad noon—*
I, only I.

Yet give not o'er,
But seek Thy sheep, true Shepherd of the flock;
Greater than Moses, turn and look once more
And smite a rock.

1862

*On the Wing**

Once in a dream (for once I dreamed of you)
We stood together in an open field;
Above our heads two swift-winged pigeons wheeled,
Sporting at ease and courting full in view.
When loftier still a broadening darkness flew,
Down-swooping, and a ravenous hawk revealed;
Too weak to fight, too fond to fly, they yield;
So farewell life and love and pleasures new.

Then as their plumes fell fluttering to the ground,
Their snow-white plumage flecked with crimson drops,
I wept, and thought I turned towards you to weep:
But you were gone; while rustling hedgerow tops
Bent in a wind which bore to me a sound
Of far-off piteous bleat of lambs and sheep.

1862

*The Queen of Hearts**

How comes it, Flora, that, whenever we
Play cards together, you invariably,
However the pack parts,
Still hold the Queen of Hearts?

I've scanned you with a scrutinizing gaze,
Resolved to fathom these your secret ways:
But, sift them as I will,
Your ways are secret still.

I cut and shuffle; shuffle, cut, again;
But all my cutting, shuffling, proves in vain:
Vain hope, vain forethought too;
That Queen still falls to you.

I dropped her once, prepense; but, ere the deal
Was dealt, your instinct seemed her loss to feel:
'There should be one card more,'
You said, and searched the floor.

I cheated once; I made a private notch
In Heart-Queen's back, and kept a lynx-eyed watch;
Yet such another back
Deceived me in the pack:

The Queen of Clubs assumed by arts unknown
An imitative dint that seemed my own;
This notch, not of my doing,
Misled me to my ruin.

It baffles me to puzzle out the clue,
Which must be skill, or craft, or luck in you:
Unless, indeed, it be
Natural affinity.

1863

*Helen Grey**

Because one loves you, Helen Grey,
  Is that a reason you should pout
  And like a March wind veer about
And frown and say your shrewish say?
Don't strain the cord until it snaps,
  Don't split the sound heart with your wedge,
  Don't cut your fingers with the edge
Of your keen wit: you may perhaps.

Because you're handsome, Helen Grey,
  Is that a reason to be proud?
  Your eyes are bold, your laugh is loud,
Your steps go mincing on their way:
But so you miss that modest charm
  Which is the surest charm of all;
  Take heed; you yet may trip and fall,
And no man care to stretch his arm.

Stoop from your cold height, Helen Grey,
  Come down and take a lowlier place;
  Come down to fill it now with grace;
Come down you must perforce some day:
For years cannot be kept at bay,
  And fading years will make you old;
  Then in their turn will men seem cold,
When you yourself are nipped and grey.

1863

*A Bird's-Eye View**

'Croak, croak, croak,'
Thus the Raven spoke,
Perched on his crooked tree
As hoarse as hoarse could be.
Shun him and fear him,
Lest the Bridegroom hear him;
Scout him and rout him
With his ominous eye about him.

Yet, 'Croak, croak, croak,'
Still tolled from the oak;

From that fatal black bird,
Whether heard or unheard:
'O ship upon the high seas,
Freighted with lives and spices,
Sink, O ship,' croaked the Raven:
'Let the Bride mount to heaven.'

In a far foreign land
Upon the wave-edged sand,
Some friends gaze wistfully
Across the glittering sea.
'If we could clasp our sister,'
Three say, 'now we have missed her!'
'If we could kiss our daughter!'
Two sigh across the water.

Oh the ship sails fast
With silken flags at the mast,
And the home-wind blows soft;
But a Raven sits aloft,
Chuckling and choking,
Croaking, croaking, croaking:—
Let the beacon-fire blaze higher;
Bridegroom, watch; the Bride draws nigher.

On a sloped sandy beach,
Which the spring-tide billows reach,
Stand a watchful throng
Who have hoped and waited long:
'Fie on this ship, that tarries
With the priceless freight it carries.
The time seems long and longer:
O languid wind, wax stronger;'—

Whilst the Raven perched at ease
Still croaks and does not cease,
One monotonous note
Tolled from his iron throat:
'No father, no mother,
But I have a sable brother:
He sees where ocean flows to,
And he knows what he knows too.'

A day and a night
They kept watch worn and white;
A night and a day
For the swift ship on its way:
For the Bride and her maidens
—Clear chimes the bridal cadence—
For the tall ship that never
Hove in sight for ever.

On either shore, some
Stand in grief loud or dumb
As the dreadful dread
Grows certain tho' unsaid.
For laughter there is weeping,
And waking instead of sleeping,
And a desperate sorrow
Morrow after morrow.

Oh who knows the truth,
How she perished in her youth,
And like a queen went down
Pale in her royal crown:
How she went up to glory
From the sea-foam chill and hoary,
From the sea-depth black and riven
To the calm that is in Heaven?

They went down, all the crew,
The silks and spices too,
The great ones and the small,
One and all, one and all.
Was it thro' stress of weather,
Quicksands, rocks, or all together?
Only the Raven knows this,
And he will not disclose this.—

After a day and a year
The bridal bells chime clear;
After a year and a day
The Bridegroom is brave and gay:
Love is sound, faith is rotten;
The old Bride is forgotten:—

Two ominous Ravens only
Remember, black and lonely.

1863

*A Dumb Friend**

I planted a young tree when I was young;
  But now the tree is grown and I am old:
  There wintry robin shelters from the cold
    And tunes his silver tongue.

A green and living tree I planted it,
  A glossy-foliaged tree of evergreen:
  All thro' the noontide heat it spread a screen
    Whereunder I might sit.

But now I only watch it where it towers:
  I, sitting at my window, watch it tossed
  By rattling gale, or silvered by the frost;
    Or, when sweet summer flowers,

Wagging its round green head with stately grace
  In tender winds that kiss it and go by:
  It shows a green full age; and what show I?
    A faded wrinkled face.

So often have I watched it, till mine eyes
  Have filled with tears and I have ceased to see,
  That now it seems a very friend to me
    In all my secrets wise.

A faithful pleasant friend who year by year
  Grew with my growth and strengthened with my strength,
  But whose green lifetime shows a longer length:
    When I shall not sit here

It still will bud in spring, and shed rare leaves
  In autumn, and in summer heat give shade,
  And warmth in winter; when my bed is made
    In shade the cypress weaves.

1863

*Consider**

Consider
The lilies of the field whose bloom is brief:—
We are as they;
Like them we fade away,
As doth a leaf.

Consider
The sparrows of the air of small account:
Our God doth view
Whether they fall or mount,—
He guards us too.

Consider
The lilies that do neither spin nor toil,
Yet are most fair:—
What profits all this care
And all this coil?

Consider
The birds that have no barn nor harvest-weeks;
God gives them food:—
Much more our Father seeks
To do us good.

1863

*The Lowest Place**

Give me the lowest place: not that I dare
Ask for that lowest place, but Thou hast died
That I might live and share
Thy glory by Thy side.

Give me the lowest place: or if for me
That lowest place too high, make one more low
Where I may sit and see
My God and love Thee so.

1863

Somewhere or Other

Somewhere or other there must surely be
The face not seen, the voice not heard,
The heart that not yet – never yet – ah me!
Made answer to my word.

Somewhere or other, may be near or far;
Past land and sea, clean out of sight;
Beyond the wandering moon, beyond the star
That tracks her night by night.

Somewhere or other, may be far or near;
With just a wall, a hedge, between;
With just the last leaves of the dying year
Fallen on a turf grown green.

1863

What Would I Give?

What would I give for a heart of flesh to warm me thro',
Instead of this heart of stone ice-cold whatever I do;
Hard and cold and small, of all hearts the worst of all.

What would I give for words, if only words would come;
But now in its misery my spirit has fallen dumb:
O merry friends, go your way, I have never a word to say.

What would I give for tears, not smiles but scalding tears,
To wash the black mark clean, and to thaw the frost of years,
To wash the stain ingrain and to make me clean again.

1864

Who Shall Deliver Me?

God strengthen me to bear myself;
That heaviest weight of all to bear,
Inalienable weight of care.

All others are outside myself;
I lock my door and bar them out,
The turmoil, tedium, gad-about.

I lock my door upon myself,
And bar them out; but who shall wall
Self from myself, most loathed of all?

If I could once lay down myself,
And start self-purged upon the race
That all must run! Death runs apace.

If I could set aside myself,
And start with lightened heart upon
The road by all men overgone!

God harden me against myself,
This coward with pathetic voice
Who craves for ease, and rest, and joys:

Myself, arch-traitor to myself;
My hollowest friend, my deadliest foe,
My clog whatever road I go.

Yet One there is can curb myself,
Can roll the strangling load from me,
Break off the yoke and set me free.

1864

*The Ghost's Petition**

'There's a footstep coming; look out and see.'—
  'The leaves are falling, the wind is calling;
No one cometh across the lea.'—

'There's a footstep coming; O sister, look.'—
  'The ripple flashes, the white foam dashes;
No one cometh across the brook.'—

'But he promised that he would come:
  Tonight, tomorrow, in joy or sorrow,
He must keep his word, and must come home.

'For he promised that he would come:
  His word was given; from earth or heaven,
He must keep his word, and must come home.

'Go to sleep, my sweet sister Jane;
  You can slumber, who need not number
Hour after hour, in doubt and pain.

'I shall sit here awhile, and watch;
  Listening, hoping, for one hand groping
In deep shadow to find the latch.'

After the dark, and before the light,
  One lay sleeping; and one sat weeping,
Who had watched and wept the weary night.

After the night, and before the day,
  One lay sleeping; and one sat weeping—
Watching, weeping for one away.

There came a footstep climbing the stair;
  Some one standing out on the landing
Shook the door like a puff of air—

Shook the door and in he passed.
  Did he enter? In the room centre
Stood her husband: the door shut fast.

'O Robin,* but you are cold—
  Chilled with the night-dew: so lily-white you
Look like a stray lamb from our fold.

'O Robin, but you are late:
  Come and sit near me – sit here and cheer me.'—
(Blue the flame burnt in the grate.)

'Lay not down your head on my breast:
  I cannot hold you, kind wife, nor fold you
In the shelter that you love best.

'Feel not after my clasping hand:
  I am but a shadow, come from the meadow
Where many lie, but no tree can stand.

'We are trees which have shed their leaves:
  Our heads lie low there, but no tears flow there;
Only I grieve for my wife who grieves.

'I could rest if you would not moan
  Hour after hour; I have no power
To shut my ears where I lie alone.

'I could rest if you would not cry;
  But there's no sleeping while you sit weeping—
Watching, weeping so bitterly.'—

'Woe's me! woe's me! for this I have heard.
  Oh night of sorrow! – oh black tomorrow!
Is it thus that you keep your word?

'O you who used so to shelter me
  Warm from the least wind – why, now the east wind
Is warmer than you, whom I quake to see.

'O my husband of flesh and blood,
  For whom my mother I left, and brother,
And all I had, accounting it good,

'What do you do there, underground,
  In the dark hollow? I'm fain to follow.
What do you do there? – what have you found?'—

'What I do there I must not tell:
  But I have plenty: kind wife, content ye:
It is well with us – it is well.

'Tender hand hath made our nest;
  Our fear is ended, our hope is blended
With present pleasure, and we have rest.'—

'Oh, but Robin, I'm fain to come,
  If your present days are so pleasant;
For my days are so wearisome.

'Yet I'll dry my tears for your sake:
  Why should I tease you, who cannot please you
Any more with the pains I take?'

1864

Twice

I took my heart in my hand
  (O my love, O my love),
I said: Let me fall or stand,
  Let me live or die,
But this once hear me speak—
  (O my love, O my love)—
Yet a woman's words are weak;
  You should speak, not I.

You took my heart in your hand
  With a friendly smile,

With a critical eye you scanned,
  Then set it down,
And said: It is still unripe,
  Better wait awhile;
Wait while the skylarks pipe,
  Till the corn grows brown.

As you set it down it broke—
  Broke, but I did not wince;
I smiled at the speech you spoke,
  At your judgment that I heard:
But I have not often smiled
  Since then, nor questioned since,
Nor cared for corn-flowers wild,
  Nor sung with the singing bird.

I take my heart in my hand,
  O my God, O my God,
My broken heart in my hand:
  Thou hast seen, judge Thou.
My hope was written on sand,
  O my God, O my God;
Now let Thy judgment stand—
  Yea, judge me now.

This contemned of a man,
  This marred one heedless day,
This heart take Thou to scan
  Both within and without:
Refine with fire its gold,
  Purge Thou its dross away—
Yea hold it in Thy hold,
  Whence none can pluck it out.

I take my heart in my hand—
  I shall not die, but live—
Before Thy face I stand;
  I, for Thou callest such:
All that I have I bring,
  All that I am I give,
Smile Thou and I shall sing,
  But shall not question much.

1864

*Bird or Beast?**

Did any bird come flying
  After Adam and Eve,
When the door was shut against them
  And they sat down to grieve?

I think not Eve's peacock
  Splendid to see
And I think not Adam's eagle,
  But a dove may be.

Did any beast come pushing
  Thro' the thorny hedge
Into the thorny thistly world
  Out from Eden's edge?

I think not a lion
  Tho' his strength is such;
But an innocent loving lamb
  May have done as much.

If the dove preached from her bough
  And the lamb from his sod,
The lamb and the dove
  Were preachers sent from God.

1864

*Eve**

'While I sit at the door
Sick to gaze within
Mine eye weepeth sore
For sorrow and sin:
As a tree my sin stands
To darken all lands;
Death is the fruit it bore.

'How have Eden bowers grown
Without Adam to bend them!
How have Eden flowers blown
Squandering their sweet breath
Without me to tend them!
The Tree of Life was ours,
Tree twelvefold-fruited,
Most lofty tree that flowers,

Most deeply rooted:
I chose the tree of death.

'Hadst thou but said me nay,
Adam, my brother,
I might have pined away;
I, but none other:
God might have let thee stay
Safe in our garden,
By putting me away
Beyond all pardon.

'I, Eve, sad mother
Of all who must live,
I, not another,
Plucked bitterest fruit to give
My friend, husband, lover;—
O wanton eyes, run over;
Who but I should grieve?—
Cain hath slain his brother:
Of all who must die mother,
Miserable Eve!'

Thus she sat weeping,
Thus Eve our mother,
Where one lay sleeping
Slain by his brother.
Greatest and least
Each piteous beast
To hear her voice
Forgot his joys
And set aside his feast.

The mouse paused in his walk
And dropped his wheaten stalk;
Grave cattle wagged their heads
In rumination;
The eagle gave a cry
From his cloud station;
Larks on thyme beds
Forbore to mount or sing;
Bees drooped upon the wing;
The raven perched on high
Forgot his ration;
The conies in their rock,

A feeble nation,
Quaked sympathetical;
The mocking-bird left off to mock;
Huge camels knelt as if
In deprecation;
The kind hart's tears were falling;
Chattered the wistful stork;
Dove-voices with a dying fall
Cooed desolation
Answering grief by grief.

Only the serpent in the dust
Wriggling and crawling,
Grinned an evil grin and thrust
His tongue out with its fork.

1865

*A Sketch**

The blindest buzzard that I know
  Does not wear wings to spread and stir,
  Nor does my special mole wear fur
And grub among the roots below;
  He sports a tail indeed, but then
  It's to a coat; he's man with men;
    His quill is cut to a pen.

In other points our friend's a mole,
  A buzzard, beyond scope of speech:
  He sees not what's within his reach,
Misreads the part, ignores the whole.
  Misreads the part so reads in vain,
  Ignores the whole tho' patent plain,
    Misreads both parts again.

My blindest buzzard that I know,
  My special mole, when will you see?
  Oh no, you must not look at me,
There's nothing hid for me to show.
  I might show facts as plain as day;
  But since your eyes are blind, you'd say:
    Where? What? and turn away.

1864

If I had Words

If I had words, if I had words
  At least to vent my misery:—
But muter than the speechless herds*
  I have no voice wherewith to cry.
I have no strength to lift my hands,
  I have no heart to lift mine eye,
My soul is bound with brazen* bands,
  My soul is crushed and like to die.
My thoughts that wander here and there,
  That wander wander listlessly,
Bring nothing back to cheer my care,
  Nothing that I may live thereby.
My heart is broken in my breast,
  My breath is but a broken sigh—
Oh if there be a land of rest
  It is far off, it is not nigh.
If I had wings as hath a dove,
  If I had wings that I might fly,
I yet would seek the land of love
  Where fountains run which run not dry;
Tho' there be none that road to tell,
  And long that road is verily:
Then if I lived I should do well,
  And if I died I should but die.
If I had wings as hath a dove
  I would not sift the what and why,
I would make haste to find out love,
  If not to find at least to try.
I would make haste to love, my rest;
  To love, my truth that doth not lie:
Then if I lived it might be best,
  Or if I died I could but die.

1864

*Amor si sveglia?**

In nuova primavera
  Rinasce il genio antico;
Amor t'insinua 'Spera'—
  Pur io nol dico.

S' 'Ama' – ti dice Amore;
  S'ei t'incoraggia, amico,
Giurando 'È tuo quel core'—
  Pur io nol dico.

Anzi, quel cor davvero
  Chi sa se valga un fico?
Lo credo, almen lo spero;
  Ma pur nol dico.

1863

*'Lassu fia caro il rivederci'—**

Dolce cor mio perduto e non perduto,
  Dolce mia vita che mi lasci in morte,
  Amico e più che amico, ti saluto.
Ricordati di me; che cieche e corte
  Fur speranze mie, ma furon tue:
  Non disprezzar questa mia dura sorte.
Lascia ch'io dica 'Le speranze sue
  'Come le mie languiro in questo inverno'—
  Pur mi rassegnerò quel che fue fue.
Lascia ch'io dica ancor 'Con lui discerno
  'Giorno che spunta da gelata sera,
  'Lungo cielo al di là di breve inferno,
'Al di là dell'inverno primavera.'

1867

Jessie Cameron

'Jessie, Jessie Cameron,
  Hear me but this once,' quoth he.
'Good luck go with you, neighbour's son,
  But I'm no mate for you,' quoth she.
Day was verging toward the night
  There beside the moaning sea,

Dimness overtook the light
  There where the breakers be.
'O Jessie, Jessie Cameron,
  I have loved you long and true.'—
'Good luck go with you, neighbour's son,
  But I'm no mate for you.'

She was a careless fearless girl,
  And made her answer plain,
Outspoken she to earl or churl,
  Kindhearted in the main,
But somewhat heedless with her tongue
  And apt at causing pain;
A mirthful maiden she and young,
  Most fair for bliss or bane.
'Oh long ago I told you so,
  I tell you so today:
Go you your way, and let me go
  Just my own free way.'

The sea swept in with moan and foam
  Quickening the stretch of sand;
They stood almost in sight of home;
  He strove to take her hand.
'Oh can't you take your answer then,
  And won't you understand?
For me you're not the man of men,
  I've other plans are planned.
You're good for Madge, or good for Cis,
  Or good for Kate, may be:
But what's to me the good of this
  While you're not good for me?'

They stood together on the beach,
  They two alone,
And louder waxed his urgent speech,
  His patience almost gone:
'Oh say but one kind word to me,
  Jessie, Jessie Cameron.'—
'I'd be too proud to beg,' quoth she,
  And pride was in her tone.
And pride was in her lifted head,
  And in her angry eye,
And in her foot, which might have fled,
  But would not fly.

Some say that he had gipsy blood,
  That in his heart was guile:
Yet he had gone thro' fire and flood
  Only to win her smile.
Some say his grandam* was a witch,
  A black witch from beyond the Nile,
Who kept an image in a niche
  And talked with it the while.
And by her hut far down the lane
  Some say they would not pass at night,
Lest they should hear an unked strain
  Or see an unked* sight.

Alas for Jessie Cameron!—
  The sea crept moaning, moaning nigher:
She should have hastened to begone,—
  The sea swept higher, breaking by her:
She should have hastened to her home
  While yet the west was flushed with fire,
But now her feet are in the foam,
  The sea-foam sweeping higher.
O mother, linger at your door,
  And light your lamp to make it plain;
But Jessie she comes home no more,
  No more again.

They stood together on the strand,
  They only each by each;
Home, her home, was close at hand,
  Utterly out of reach.
Her mother in the chimney nook
  Heard a startled sea-gull screech,
But never turned her head to look
  Towards the darkening beach:
Neighbours here and neighbours there
  Heard one scream, as if a bird
Shrilly screaming cleft the air:—
  That was all they heard.

Jessie she comes home no more,
  Comes home never;
Her lover's step sounds at his door
  No more for ever.

And boats may search upon the sea
  And search along the river,
But none know where the bodies be:
  Sea-winds that shiver,
Sea-birds that breast the blast,
  Sea-waves swelling,
Keep the secret first and last
  Of their dwelling.

Whether the tide so hemmed them round
  With its pitiless flow,
That when they would have gone they found
  No way to go;
Whether she scorned him to the last
  With words flung to and fro,
Or clung to him when hope was past,
  None will ever know:
Whether he helped or hindered her,
  Threw up his life or lost it well,
The troubled sea for all its stir
  Finds no voice to tell.

Only watchers by the dying
  Have thought they heard one pray
Wordless, urgent; and replying
  One seem to say him nay:
And watchers by the dead have heard
  A windy swell from miles away,
With sobs and screams, but not a word
  Distinct for them to say:
And watchers out at sea have caught
  Glimpse of a pale gleam here or there,
Come and gone as quick as thought,
  Which might be hand or hair.

1864

Despised and Rejected

My sun has set, I dwell
In darkness as a dead man out of sight;
And none remains, not one, that I should tell
To him mine evil plight

This bitter night.
I will make fast my door
That hollow friends may trouble me no more.

'Friend, open to Me.' —Who is this that calls?
Nay, I am deaf as are my walls:
Cease crying, for I will not hear
Thy cry of hope or fear.
Others were dear,
Others forsook me: what art thou indeed
That I should heed
Thy lamentable need?
Hungry should feed,
Or stranger lodge thee here?

'Friend, My Feet bleed.
Open thy door to Me and comfort Me.'
I will not open, trouble me no more.
Go on thy way footsore,
I will not rise and open unto thee.

'Then is it nothing to thee? Open, see
Who stands to plead with thee.
Open, lest I should pass thee by, and thou
One day entreat My Face
And howl for grace,
And I be deaf as thou art now.
Open to Me.'

Then I cried out upon him: Cease,
Leave me in peace:
Fear not that I should crave
Aught thou mayst have.
Leave me in peace, yea trouble me no more,
Lest I arise and chase thee from my door.
What, shall I not be let
Alone, that thou dost vex me yet?

But all night long that voice spake urgently:
'Open to Me.'
Still harping in mine ears:
'Rise, let Me in.'
Pleading with tears:
'Open to Me that I may come to thee.'

While the dew dropped, while the dark hours were cold
'My Feet bleed, see My Face,
See My Hands bleed that bring thee grace,
My Heart doth bleed for thee,
Open to Me.'

So till the break of day:
Then died away
That voice, in silence as of sorrow;
Then footsteps echoing like a sigh
Passed me by,
Lingering footsteps slow to pass.
On the morrow
I saw upon the grass
Each footprint marked in blood, and on my door
The mark of blood for evermore.

1864

Weary in Well-Doing

I would have gone; God bade me to stay:
  I would have worked; God bade me rest.
He broke my will from day to day,
  He read my yearnings unexpressed
    And said them nay.

Now I would stay; God bids me go:
  Now I would rest; God bids me work.
He breaks my heart tossed to and fro,
  My soul is wrung with doubts that lurk
    And vex it so.

I go, Lord, where Thou sendest me;
  Day after day I plod and moil:
But, Christ my God, when will it be
  That I may let alone my toil
    And rest with Thee?

1864

*Amor Mundi**

'Oh where are you going with your love-locks flowing
On the west wind blowing along this valley track?'
'The downhill path is easy, come with me an it please ye,
We shall escape the uphill by never turning back.'

So they two went together in glowing August weather,
The honey-breathing heather lay to their left and right;
And dear she was to doat on, her swift feet seemed to float on
The air like soft twin pigeons too sportive to alight.

'Oh what is that in heaven where grey cloud-flakes are seven,
Where blackest clouds hang riven just at the rainy skirt?'
'Oh that's a meteor sent us, a message dumb, portentous,
An undeciphered solemn signal of help or hurt.'

'Oh what is that glides quickly where velvet flowers grow thickly,
Their scent comes rich and sickly?'—'A scaled and hooded worm.'
'Oh what's that in the hollow, so pale I quake to follow?'
'Oh, that's a thin dead body which waits the eternal term.'

'Turn again, O my sweetest, – turn again, false and fleetest:
This beaten way thou beatest I fear is hell's own track.'
'Nay, too steep for hill-mounting; nay, too late for cost-counting:
This downhill path is easy, but there's no turning back.'

1865

*Maggie A Lady**

You must not call me Maggie, you must not call me Dear,
For I'm Lady of the Manor now stately to see;
And if there comes a babe, as there may some happy year,
'Twill be little lord or lady at my knee.

Oh but what ails you, my sailor cousin Phil,
That you shake and turn white like a cockcrow ghost?
You're as white as I turned once down by the mill,
When one told me you and ship and crew were lost:
Philip my playfellow, when we were boy and girl.
(It was the Miller's Nancy told it to me),

Philip with the merry life in lip and curl,
  Philip my playfellow drowned in the sea!

I thought I should have fainted, but I did not faint;
  I stood stunned at the moment, scarcely sad,
Till I raised my wail of desolate complaint
  For you, my cousin, brother, all I had.

They said I looked so pale – some say so fair—
  My lord stopped in passing to soothe me back to life:
I know I missed a ringlet from my hair
  Next morning; and now I am his wife.

Look at my gown, Philip, and look at my ring,
  I'm all crimson and gold from top to toe:
All day long I sit in the sun and sing,
  Where in the sun red roses blush and blow.

And I'm the rose of roses, says my lord;
  And to him I'm more than the sun in the sky,
While I hold him fast with the golden cord
  Of a curl, with the eyelash of an eye.

His mother said 'fie,' and his sisters cried 'shame,'
  His highborn ladies cried 'shame' from their place:
They said 'fie' when they only heard my name,
  But fell silent when they saw my face.

Am I so fair, Philip? Philip, did you think
  I was so fair when we played boy and girl,
Where blue forget-me-nots bloomed on the brink
  Of our stream which the mill-wheel sent awhirl?

If I was fair then sure I'm fairer now,
  Sitting where a score of servants stand,
With a coronet on high days for my brow
  And almost a sceptre for my hand.

You're but a sailor, Philip, weatherbeaten brown,
  A stranger on land and at home on the sea,
Coasting as best you may from town to town:
  Coasting along do you often think of me?

I'm a great lady in a sheltered bower,
  With hands grown white thro' having nought to do:
Yet sometimes I think of you hour after hour
  Till I nigh wish myself a child with you.

1865

*En Route**

Wherefore art thou strange, and not my mother?
Thou hast stolen my heart and broken it:
Would that I might call thy sons 'My brother,'
Call thy daughters 'Sister sweet':
Lying in thy lap, not in another,
Dying at thy feet.

Farewell, land of love, Italy,
Sister-land of Paradise:
With mine own feet I have trodden thee,
Have seen with mine own eyes:
I remember, thou forgettest me,
I remember thee.

Blessed be the land that warms my heart,
And the kindly clime that cheers,
And the cordial faces clear from art,
And the tongue sweet in mine ears:
Take my heart, its truest tenderest part,
Dear land, take my tears.

1865

*Enrica**

She came among us from the South
And made the North her home awhile;
Our dimness brightened in her smile,
Our tongue grew sweeter in her mouth.

We chilled beside her liberal glow,
She dwarfed us by her ampler scale,
Her full-blown blossom made us pale,
She summer-like and we like snow.

We Englishwomen, trim, correct,
All minted in the selfsame mould,
Warm-hearted but of semblance cold,
All-courteous out of self-respect.

She woman in her natural grace,
Less trammelled she by lore of school,
Courteous by nature not by rule,
Warm-hearted and of cordial face.

So for awhile she made her home
  Among us in the rigid North,
  She who from Italy came forth
And scaled the Alps and crossed the foam.

But if she found us like our sea,
  Of aspect colourless and chill,
  Rock-girt; like it she found us still
Deep at our deepest, strong and free.

1865

*A Daughter of Eve**

A fool I was to sleep at noon,
  And wake when night is chilly
Beneath the comfortless cold moon;
A fool to pluck my rose too soon,
  A fool to snap my lily.

My garden-plot I have not kept;
  Faded and all-forsaken,
I weep as I have never wept:
Oh it was summer when I slept,
  It's winter now I waken.

Talk what you please of future Spring
  And sun-warmed sweet tomorrow:—
Stripped bare of hope and everything,
No more to laugh, no more to sing,
  I sit alone with sorrow.

1865

*Mother Country**

Oh what is that country
  And where can it be,
Not mine own country,
  But dearer far to me?
Yet mine own country,
  If I one day may see
Its spices and cedars,
  Its gold and ivory.

As I lie dreaming
  It rises, that land;
There rises before me
  Its green golden strand,
With the bowing cedars
  And the shining sand;
It sparkles and flashes
  Like a shaken brand.

Do angels lean nearer
  While I lie and long?
I see their soft plumage
  And catch their windy song,
Like the rise of a high tide
  Sweeping full and strong;
I mark the outskirts
  Of their reverend throng.

Oh what is a king here,
  Or what is a boor?
Here all starve together,
  All dwarfed and poor;
Here Death's hand knocketh
  At door after door,
He thins the dancers
  From the festal floor.

Oh what is a handmaid,
  Or what is a queen?
All must lie down together
  Where the turf is green,
The foulest face hidden,
  The fairest not seen;
Gone as if never
  They had breathed or been.

Gone from sweet sunshine
  Underneath the sod,
Turned from warm flesh and blood
  To senseless clod,

Gone as if never
   They had toiled or trod,
Gone out of sight of all
   Except our God.

Shut into silence
   From the accustomed song,
Shut into solitude
   From all earth's throng,
Run down tho' swift of foot,
   Thrust down tho' strong;
Life made an end of
   Seemed it short or long.

Life made an end of,
   Life but just begun,
Life finished yesterday,
   Its last sand run;
Life new-born with the morrow,
   Fresh as the sun:
While done is done for ever;
Undone, undone.

And if that life is life,
   This is but a breath,
The passage of a dream
   And the shadow of death;
But a vain shadow
   If one considereth;
Vanity of vanities,
   As the Preacher saith.

1866

*'Cannot sweeten'**

If that's water you wash your hands in
   Why is it black as ink is black?—
Because my hands are foul with my folly:
   Oh the lost time that comes not back!—

If that's water you bathe your feet in
   Why is it red as wine is red?—

Because my feet sought blood in their goings;
  Red red is the track they tread.—

Slew you mother or slew you father
  That your foulness passeth not by?—
Not father and oh not mother:
  I slew my love with an evil eye.—

Slew you sister or slew you brother
  That in peace you have not a part?—
Not brother and oh not sister:
  I slew my love with a hardened heart.

He loved me because he loved me,
  Not for grace or beauty I had;
He loved me because he loved me;
  For his loving me I was glad.

Yet I loved him not for his loving
  While I played with his love and truth,
Not loving him for his loving,
  Wasting his joy, wasting his youth.

I ate his life as a banquet,
  I drank his life as new wine,
I fattened upon his leanness,
  Mine to flourish and his to pine.

So his life fled as running water,
  So it perished as water spilt:
If black my hands and my feet as scarlet,
  Blacker redder my heart of guilt.

Cold as a stone, as hard, as heavy;
  All my sighs ease it no whit,
All my tears make it no cleaner
  Dropping dropping dropping on it.

1866

*An Echo from Willowwood**

'O ye, all ye that walk in Willowwood.'
D. G. ROSSETTI

Two gazed into a pool, he gazed and she,
  Not hand in hand, yet heart in heart, I think,
  Pale and reluctant on the water's brink.
As on the brink of parting which must be.
Each eyed the other's aspect, she and he,
  Each felt one hungering heart leap up and sink,
  Each tasted bitterness which both must drink,
There on the brink of life's dividing sea.
Lilies upon the surface, deep below
  Two wistful faces craving each for each,
  Resolute and reluctant without speech:—
A sudden ripple made the faces flow
  One moment joined, to vanish out of reach:
  So those hearts joined, and ah! were parted so.

c. 1870

*The German-French Campaign**

These two pieces, written during the suspense of a great nation's agony, aim at expressing human sympathy, not political bias.

I

'THY BROTHER'S BLOOD CRIETH.'*

All her corn-fields rippled in the sunshine,
  All her lovely vines, sweets-laden, bowed;
Yet some weeks to harvest and to vintage:
  When, as one man's hand, a cloud
Rose and spread, and, blackening, burst asunder
    In rain and fire and thunder.

Is there nought to reap in the day of harvest?
  Hath the vine in her day no fruit to yield?
Yea, men tread the press, but not for sweetness,
  And they reap a red crop from the field.
Build barns, ye reapers, garner all aright,
    Tho' your souls be called tonight.

A cry of tears goes up from blackened homesteads,
  A cry of blood goes up from reeking earth:
Tears and blood have a cry that pierces Heaven
  Thro' all its Hallelujah swells of mirth;
God hears their cry, and tho' He tarry, yet
    He doth not forget.

Mournful Mother, prone in dust weeping
  Who shall comfort thee for those who are not?
As thou didst, men do to thee; and heap the measure,
  And heat the furnace sevenfold hot:
As thou once, now these to thee — who pitieth thee
    From sea to sea?

O thou King,* terrible in strength, and building
  Thy strong future on thy past!
Tho' he drink the last, the King of Sheshach,*
  Yet he shall drink at the last.
Art thou greater than great Babylon,
    Which lies overthrown?

Take heed, ye unwise among the people;
  O ye fools, when will ye understand?—
He that planted the ear shall He not hear,
  Nor He smite who formed the hand?
'Vengeance is Mine, is Mine,' thus saith the Lord:—
    O Man, put up thy sword.

2

'Today for me.'

  She sitteth still who used to dance,
She weepeth sore and more and more:—
Let us sit with thee weeping sore,
    O fair France.

  She trembleth as the days advance
Who used to be so light of heart:—
We in thy trembling bear a part,
    Sister France.

  Her eyes shine tearful as they glance:
'Who shall give back my slaughtered sons?

'Bind up,' she saith, 'my wounded ones.'—
Alas, France!

She struggles in a deathly trance,
As in a dream her pulses stir,
She hears the nations calling her,
'France, France, France.'

Thou people of the lifted lance,
Forbear her tears, forbear her blood:
Roll back, roll back, thy whelming flood,
Back from France.

Eye not her loveliness askance,
Forge not for her a galling chain;
Leave her at peace to bloom again,
Vine-clad France.

A time there is for change and chance,
A time for passing of the cup:
And One abides* can yet bind up
Broken France.

A time there is for change and chance:
Who next shall drink the trembling cup,
Wring out its dregs and suck them up
After France?

1871

*A Christmas Carol**

In the bleak mid-winter
Frosty wind made moan,
Earth stood hard as iron,
Water like a stone;
Snow has fallen, snow on snow,
Snow on snow,
In the bleak mid-winter
Long ago.

Our God, Heaven cannot hold Him
Nor earth sustain;

Heaven and earth shall flee away
  When He comes to reign:
In the bleak mid-winter
  A stable-place sufficed
The Lord God Almighty
  Jesus Christ.

Enough for Him whom cherubim
  Worship night and day,
A breastful of milk
  And a mangerful of hay;
Enough for Him whom angels
  Fall down before,
The ox and ass and camel
  Which adore.

Angels and archangels
  May have gathered there,
Cherubim and seraphim
  Throng'd the air,
But only His mother
  In her maiden bliss
Worshipped the Beloved
  With a kiss.

What can I give Him,
  Poor as I am?
If I were a shepherd
  I would bring a lamb,
If I were a wise man
  I would do my part,—
Yet what I can I give Him,
  Give my heart.

1871

*A Rose Plant in Jericho**

At morn I plucked a rose and gave it Thee,
  A rose of joy and happy love and peace,
    A rose with scarce a thorn:
    But in the chillness of a second morn

   My rose bush drooped, and all its gay increase
Was but one thorn that wounded me.

I plucked the thorn and offered it to Thee;
   And for my thorn Thou gavest love and peace,
      Not joy this mortal morn:
      If Thou hast given much treasure for a thorn,
   Wilt Thou not give me for my rose increase
Of gladness, and all sweets to me?

My thorny rose, my love and pain, to Thee
   I offer; and I set my heart in peace,
      And rest upon my thorn:
      For verily I think tomorrow morn
   Shall bring me Paradise, my gift's increase,
Yea, give Thy very Self to me.

c. 1873

*'Italia, Io Ti Saluto!'**

To come back from the sweet South, to the North
   Where I was born, bred, look to die;
Come back to do my day's work in its day,
      Play out my play—
   Amen, amen, say I.

To see no more the country half my own,
   Nor hear the half familiar speech,
Amen, I say; I turn to that bleak North
      Whence I came forth—
   The South lies out of reach.

But when our swallows fly back to the South,
   To the sweet South, to the sweet South,
The tears may come again into my eyes
      On the old wise,
   And the sweet name to my mouth.

mid-1870s

Confluents

As rivers seek the sea,
   Much more deep than they,
So my soul seeks thee
   Far away:
As running rivers moan
On their course alone,
   So I moan
   Left alone.

As the delicate rose
   To the sun's sweet strength
Doth herself unclose,
   Breadth and length;
So spreads my heart to thee
Unveiled utterly,
   I to thee
   Utterly.

As morning dew exhales
   Sunwards pure and free,
So my spirit fails
   After thee:
As dew leaves not a trace
On the green earth's face;
   I, no trace
   On thy face.

Its goal the river knows,
   Dewdrops find a way,
Sunlight cheers the rose
   In her day:
Shall I, lone sorrow past,
Find thee at the last?
   Sorrow past,
   Thee at last?

c. 1875

(*Untitled*)

Sooner or later: yet at last*
The Jordan* must be past;

It may be he will overflow
His banks the day we go;

It may be that his cloven deep
Will stand up* on a heap.

Sooner or later: yet one day
We all must pass that way;

Each man, each woman, humbled, pale,
Pass veiled within the veil;

Child, parent, bride, companion,
Alone, alone, alone.

For none a ransom can be paid,
A suretyship be made:

I, bent by mine own burden, must
Enter my house of dust;

I, rated to the full amount,
Must render mine account.

When earth and sea shall empty all
Their graves of great and small;

When earth wrapped in a fiery flood
Shall no more hide her blood;

When mysteries shall be revealed;
All secrets be unsealed;

When things of night, when things of shame,
Shall find at last a name,

Pealed for a hissing and a curse
Throughout the universe:

Then Awful Judge, most Awful God,
Then cause to bud Thy rod,

To bloom with blossoms, and to give
Almonds; yea, bid us live.*

I plead Thyself with Thee, I plead
Thee in our utter need:

Jesus, most Merciful of Men,
Show mercy on us then;

Lord God of Mercy and of men,
Show mercy on us then.

1876

*A Life's Parallels**

Never on this side of the grave again,
On this side of the river,
On this side of the garner of the grain,
Never,—

Ever while time flows on and on and on,
That narrow noiseless river,
Ever while corn bows heavy-headed, wan,
Ever,—

Never despairing, often fainting, rueing,
But looking back, ah never!
Faint yet pursuing, faint yet still pursuing
Ever.

c. 1877

*De Profundis**

Oh why is heaven built so far,
Oh why is earth set so remote?
I cannot reach the nearest star
That hangs afloat.

I would not care to reach the moon,
  One round monotonous of change;
Yet even she repeats her tune
    Beyond my range.

I never watch the scattered fire
  Of stars, or sun's far-trailing train,
But all my heart is one desire,
    And all in vain:

For I am bound with fleshly bands,
  Joy, beauty, lie beyond my scope;
I strain my heart, I stretch my hands,
    And catch at hope.

c. 1877

*An October Garden**

In my Autumn garden I was fain
  To mourn among my scattered roses;
  Alas for that last rosebud which uncloses
To Autumn's languid sun and rain
When all the world is on the wane!
  Which has not felt the sweet constraint of June,
  Nor heard the nightingale in tune.

Broad-faced asters by my garden walk,
  You are but coarse compared with roses:
  More choice, more dear that rosebud which uncloses
Faint-scented, pinched, upon its stalk,
That least and last which cold winds balk;
  A rose it is tho' least and last of all,
  A rose to me tho' at the fall.

1877

*'Summer is Ended'**

To think that this meaningless thing was ever a rose,
    Scentless, colourless, *this*!
  Will it ever be thus (who knows?)
      Thus with our bliss,
  If we wait till the close?

Tho' we care not to wait for the end, there comes the end
Sooner, later, at last,
Which nothing can mar, nothing mend:
An end locked fast,
Bent we cannot re-bend.

1877

*Soeur Louise de la Miséricorde (1674)**

I have desired, and I have been desired;
But now the days are over of desire,
Now dust and dying embers mock my fire;
Where is the hire for which my life was hired?
Oh vanity of vanities, desire!

Longing and love, pangs of a perished pleasure,
Longing and love, a disenkindled fire,
And memory a bottomless gulf of mire,
And love a fount of tears outrunning measure;
Oh vanity of vanities, desire!

Now from my heart, love's deathbed, trickles, trickles,
Drop by drop slowly, drop by drop of fire,
The dross of life, of love, of spent desire;
Alas, my rose of life gone all to prickles,—
Oh vanity of vanities, desire!

Oh vanity of vanities, desire;
Stunting my hope which might have strained up higher,
Turning my garden plot to barren mire;
Oh death-struck love, oh disenkindled fire,
Oh vanity of vanities, desire!

1877

Yet a Little While

I dreamed and did not seek: today I seek
Who can no longer dream;
But now am all behindhand, waxen weak,
And dazed amid so many things that gleam
Yet are not what they seem.

I dreamed and did not work: today I work
Kept wide awake by care
And loss, and perils, dimly guessed to lurk;
I work and reap not, while my life goes bare
And void in wintry air.

I hope indeed; but hope itself is fear
Viewed on the sunny side;
I hope, and disregard the world that's here,
The prizes drawn, the sweet things that betide;
I hope, and I abide.

c. 1878–9

He and She

'Should one of us remember,
And one of us forget,
I wish I knew what each will do—
But who can tell as yet?'

'Should one of us remember,
And one of us forget,
I promise you what I will do—
And I'm content to wait for you,
And not be sure as yet.'

c. 1878–9

'One Foot on Sea, and One on Shore.'

'Oh tell me once and tell me twice
And tell me thrice to make it plain,
When we who part this weary day,
When we who part shall meet again.'

'When windflowers blossom on the sea
And fishes skim along the plain,
Then we who part this weary day,
Then you and I shall meet again.'

'Yet tell me once before we part,
Why need we part who part in pain?

If flowers must blossom on the sea,
  Why, we shall never meet again.

'My cheeks are paler than a rose,
  My tears are salter than the main,
My heart is like a lump of ice
  If we must never meet again.'

'Oh weep or laugh, but let me be,
  And live or die, for all's in vain;
For life's in vain since we must part,
  And parting must not meet again

'Till windflowers blossom on the sea
  And fishes skim along the plain;
Pale rose of roses let me be,
  Your breaking heart breaks mine again.'

c. 1878–9

*An 'Immurata' Sister**

Life flows down to death; we cannot bind
  That current that it should not flee:
Life flows down to death, as rivers find
  The inevitable sea.

Men work and think, but women feel;
  And so (for I'm a woman, I)
  And so I should be glad to die
And cease from impotence of zeal,
And cease from hope, and cease from dread,
  And cease from yearnings without gain,
  And cease from all this world of pain,
And be at peace among the dead.

Hearts that die, by death renew their youth,
  Lightened of this life that doubts and dies;
Silent and contented, while the Truth
  Unveiled makes them wise.

Why should I seek and never find
  That something which I have not had?

Fair and unutterably sad
The world hath sought time out of mind;
The world hath sought and I have sought,—
Ah, empty world and empty I!
For we have spent our strength for nought,
And soon it will be time to die.

Sparks fly upward toward their fount of fire,
Kindling, flashing, hovering:—
Kindle, flash, my soul; mount higher and higher,
Thou whole burnt-offering!

1865/80

*Freaks of Fashion**

Such a hubbub in the nests,
Such a bustle and squeak!
Nestlings, guiltless of a feather,
Learning just to speak,
Ask –'And how about the fashions?'
From a cavernous beak.

Perched on bushes, perched on hedges,
Perched on firm hahas,
Perched on anything that holds them,
Gay papas and grave mammas
Teach the knowledge-thirsty nestlings:
Hear the gay papas.

Robin says: 'A scarlet waistcoat
Will be all the wear,
Snug, and also cheerful-looking
For the frostiest air,
Comfortable for the chest too
When one comes to plume and pair.'

'Neat gray hoods will be in vogue,'
Quoth a Jackdaw: 'Glossy gray,
Setting close, yet setting easy,
Nothing fly-away;
Suited to our misty mornings,
À la negligée.'

Flushing salmon, flushing sulphur,
  Haughty Cockatoos
Answer – 'Hoods may do for mornings,
  But for evenings choose
High head-dresses, curved like crescents,
  Such as well-bred persons use.'

'Top-knots, yes; yet more essential
  Still, a train or tail,'
Screamed the Peacock: 'Gemmed and lustrous,
  Not too stiff, and not too frail;
Those are best which rearrange as
  Fans, and spread or trail.'

Spoke the Swan, entrenched behind
  An inimitable neck:
'After all, there's nothing sweeter
  For the lawn or lake
Then simple white, if fine and flaky
  And absolutely free from speck.'

'Yellow,' hinted a Canary,
  'Warmer, not less *distingué*.'
'Peach colour,' put in a Lory,
  'Cannot look *outré*.'
'All the colours are in fashion,
  And are right,' the Parrots say.

'Very well. But do contrast
  Tints harmonious,'
Piped a Blackbird, justly proud
  Of bill aurigerous;
'Half the world may learn a lesson
  As to that from us.'

Then a Stork took up the word:
  'Aim at height and *chic*:
Not high heels, they're common; somehow,
  Stilted legs, not thick,
Not yet thin:' he just glanced downward
  And snapped to his beak.

Here a rustling and a whirring,
  As of fans outspread,
Hinted that mammas felt anxious
  Lest the next thing said
Might prove less than quite judicious,
  Or even underbred.

So a mother Auk resumed
  The broken thread of speech:
'Let colours sort themselves, my dears,
  Yellow, or red, or peach;
The main points, as it seems to me,
  We mothers have to teach,

'Are form and texture, elegance,
  An air reserved, sublime;
The mode of wearing what we wear
  With due regard to month and clime.
But now, let's all compose ourselves,
  It's almost breakfast-time.'

A hubbub, a squeak, a bustle!
  Who cares to chatter or sing
With delightful breakfast coming?
  Yet they whisper under the wing:
'So we may wear whatever we like,
  Anything, everything!'

1879

*Brother Bruin**

A dancing Bear grotesque and funny
Earned for his master heaps of money,
Gruff yet good-natured, fond of honey,
And cheerful if the day was sunny.
Past hedge and ditch, past pond and wood
He tramped, and on some common stood;
There cottage children circling gaily,
He in their midmost footed daily.
Pandean pipes and drum and muzzle
Were quite enough his brain to puzzle:
But like a philosophic bear

He let alone extraneous care
And danced contented anywhere.

Still, year on year, and wear and tear,
Age even the gruffest bluffest bear.
A day came when he scarce could prance,
And when his master looked askance
On dancing Bear who would not dance.
To looks succeeded blows; hard blows
Battered his ears and poor old nose.
From bluff and gruff he waxed curmudgeon;
He danced indeed, but danced in dudgeon,
Capered in fury fast and faster:—
Ah, could he once but hug his master
And perish in one joint disaster!
But deafness, blindness, weakness growing,
Not fury's self could keep him going.
One dark day when the snow was snowing
His cup was brimmed to overflowing:
He tottered, toppled on one side,
Growled once, and shook his head, and died.
The master kicked and struck in vain,
The weary drudge had distanced pain
And never now would wince again.
The master growled: he might have howled
Or coaxed – that slave's last growl was growled.
So gnawed by rancour and chagrin
One thing remained: he sold the skin.

What next the man did is not worth
Your notice or my setting forth,
But hearken what befell at last.
His idle working days gone past,
And not one friend and not one penny
Stored up (if ever he had any
Friends: but his coppers had been many),
All doors stood shut against him, but
The workhouse door which cannot shut.
There he droned on – a grim old sinner
Toothless and grumbling for his dinner,
Unpitied quite, uncared for much

(The ratepayers not favouring such),
Hungry and gaunt, with time to spare:
Perhaps the hungry gaunt old Bear
Danced back, a haunting memory.
Indeed I hope so: for you see
If once the hard old heart relented
The hard old man may have repented.

1880s?

(Untitled)

A handy Mole who plied no shovel*
To excavate his vaulted hovel,
While hard at work met in mid-furrow
An Earthworm boring out his burrow.
Our Mole had dined and must grow thinner
Before he gulped a second dinner,
And on no other terms cared he
To meet a worm of low degree.
The Mole turned on his blindest eye
Passing the base mechanic by;
The Worm entrenched in actual blindness
Ignored or kindness or* unkindness;
Each wrought his own exclusive tunnel
To reach his own exclusive funnel.

A plough its flawless track pursuing
Involved them in one common ruin.
Where now the mine and countermine,
The dined-on and the one to dine?
The impartial ploughshare of extinction
Annulled them all without distinction.

1884

Advent

Earth grown old, yet still so green,
Deep beneath her crust of cold
Nurses fire unfelt, unseen:
Earth grown old.

We who live are quickly told:
Millions more lie hid between
Inner swathings of her fold.

When will fire break up her screen?
When will life burst thro' her mould?
Earth, earth, earth, thy cold is keen,
Earth grown old.

1884/5

*Rogationtide**

Who scatters tares shall reap no wheat,
But go hungry while others eat.

Who sows the wind shall not reap grain;
The sown wind whirleth back again.

What God opens must open be,
Tho' man pile the sand of the sea.

What God shuts is opened no more,
Tho' man weary himself to find the door.

1884/5

'When I was in trouble I called upon the Lord'

A burdened heart that bleeds and bears
And hopes and waits in pain,
And faints beneath its fears and cares,
Yet hopes again:

Wilt Thou accept the heart I bring,
O gracious Lord and kind,
To ease it of a torturing sting,
And staunch and bind?

Alas, if Thou wilt none of this,
None else have I to give:
Look Thou upon it as it is,
Accept, relieve.

Or if Thou wilt not yet relieve,
  Be not extreme to sift:
Accept a faltering will to give,
  Itself Thy gift.

1884/5

*(Untitled)**

Where shall I find a white rose blowing?—
  Out in the garden where all sweets be.—
But out in my garden the snow was snowing
  And never a white rose opened for me.
Nought but snow and a wind were blowing
    And snowing.

Where shall I find a blush rose blushing?—
  On the garden wall or the garden bed.—
But out in my garden the rain was rushing
  And never a blush rose raised its head.
Nothing glowing, flushing or blushing:
    Rain rushing.

Where shall I find a red rose budding?—
  Out in the garden where all things grow.—
But out in my garden a flood was flooding
  And never a red rose began to blow.
Out in a flooding what should be budding?
    All flooding!

Now is winter and now is sorrow,
  No roses but only thorns today:
Thorns will put on roses tomorrow,
  Winter and sorrow scudding away.
No more winter and no more sorrow
    Tomorrow.

1884

(Untitled)

Roses on a brier,
  Pearls from out the bitter sea,
Such is earth's desire
  However pure it be.

Neither bud nor brier,
  Neither pearl nor brine for me:
Be stilled, my long desire;
  There shall be no more sea.*

Be stilled, my passionate heart;
  Old earth shall end, new earth shall be:
Be still, and earn thy part
  Where shall be no more sea.

1884/5

'Endure hardness'

A cold wind stirs the blackthorn
  To burgeon and to blow,
Besprinkling half-green hedges
  With flakes and sprays of snow.

Thro' coldness and thro' keenness,
  Dear hearts, take comfort so:
Somewhere or other doubtless
  These make the blackthorn blow.

1884/5

'When my heart is vexed I will complain'

'The fields are white to harvest, look and see,
Are white abundantly.
The full-orbed harvest moon shines clear,
The harvest time draws near,
Be of good cheer.'

'Ah, woe is me!
I have no heart for harvest time,
Grown sick with hope deferred from chime to chime.'

'But Christ can give thee heart Who loveth thee:
Can set thee in the eternal ecstasy
Of His great jubilee:
Can give thee dancing heart and shining face,
And lips filled full of grace,

And pleasures as the rivers and the sea.
Who knocketh at His door
He welcomes evermore:

Kneel down before
That ever-open door
(The time is short) and smite
Thy breast, and pray with all thy might.'

'What shall I say?'
'Nay, pray.
Tho' one but say "Thy Will be done,"
He hath not lost his day
At set of sun.'

1884/5

(Untitled)

If love is not worth loving, then life is not worth living,
Nor aught is worth remembering but well forgot;
For store is not worth storing and gifts are not worth giving,
If love is not;

And idly cold is death-cold, and life-heat idly hot,
And vain is any offering and vainer our receiving,
And vanity of vanities is all our lot.

Better than life's heaving heart is death's heart unheaving,
Better than the opening leaves are the leaves that rot,
For there is nothing left worth achieving or retrieving,
If love is not.

1884/5

*'Doeth well . . . doeth better'**

My love whose heart is tender said to me,
'A moon lacks light except her sun befriend her.
Let us keep tryst in heaven, dear Friend,' said she,
My love whose heart is tender.

From such a loftiness no words could bend her:
Yet still she spoke of 'us' and spoke as 'we,'
Her hope substantial, while my hope grew slender.

Now keeps she tryst beyond earth's utmost sea,
Wholly at rest, tho' storms should toss and rend her;
And still she keeps my heart and keeps its key,
My love whose heart is tender.

1884/5

(Untitled)

All heaven is blazing yet
With the meridian sun:
Make haste, unshadowing sun, make haste to set;
O lifeless life, have done.
I choose what once I chose;
What once I willed, I will:
Only the heart its own bereavement knows;
O clamorous heart, lie still.

That which I chose, I choose;
That which I willed, I will;
That which I once refused, I still refuse:
O hope deferred, be still.
That which I chose and choose
And will is Jesus' Will:
He hath not lost his life who seems to lose:
O hope deferred, hope still.

1884/5

*'Son, remember'**

I laid beside thy gate, am Lazarus;
See me or see me not I still am there,
Hungry and thirsty, sore and sick and bare,
Dog-comforted and crumbs-solicitous:
While thou in all thy ways art sumptuous,
Daintily clothed, with dainties for thy fare:
Thus a world's wonder thou art quit of care,
And be I seen or not seen I am thus.

One day a worm for thee, a worm for me:
With my worm angel songs and trumpet burst
And plenitude an end of all desire:
But what for thee, alas! but what for thee?
Fire and an unextinguished thirst,
Thirst in an unextinguishable fire.

c. 1890

'Heaviness may endure for a night, but Joy cometh in the morning'

No thing is great on this side of the grave,
Nor any thing of any stable worth:
Whatso is born from earth returns to earth:
No thing we grasp proves half the thing we crave:
The tidal wave shrinks to the ebbing wave:
Laughter is folly, madness lurks in mirth:
Mankind sets off a-dying from the birth:
Life is a losing game, with what to save?
Thus I sat mourning like a mournful owl,
And like a doleful dragon made ado,
Companion of all monsters of the dark:
When lo! the light cast off its nightly cowl,
And up to heaven flashed a carolling lark,
And all creation sang its hymn anew.

While all creation sang its hymn anew
What could I do but sing a stave in tune?
Spectral on high hung pale the vanishing moon
Where a last gleam of stars hung paling too.
Lark's lay – a cockcrow – with a scattered few
Soft early chirpings – with a tender croon
Of doves – a hundred thousand calls, and soon
A hundred thousand answers sweet and true.
These set me singing too at unawares:
One note for all delights and charities,
One note for hope reviving with the light,
One note for every lovely thing that is;
Till while I sang my heart shook off its cares
And revelled in the land of no more night.

1884/5

*'A Helpmeet for Him'**

Woman was made for man's delight;
  Charm, O woman, be not afraid!
His shadow by day, his moon by night,
  Woman was made.

Her strength with weakness is overlaid;
  Meek compliances veil her might;
Him she stays, by whom she is stayed.

World-wide champion of truth and right,
  Hope in gloom and in danger aid,
Tender and faithful, ruddy and white,
  Woman was made.

c. 1887

'There is a budding morrow in midnight'

Wintry boughs against a wintry sky;
    Yet the sky is partly blue
      And the clouds are partly bright:—
Who can tell but sap is mounting high
      Out of sight,
Ready to burst through?

Winter is the mother-nurse of Spring,
    Lovely for her daughter's sake,
      Not unlovely for her own:
For a future buds in everything;
      Grown, or blown,
Or about to break.

c. 1887

(Untitled)

Lord, I am here. – But, child, I look for thee
  Elsewhere and nearer Me.—
Lord, that way moans a wide insatiate sea:
  How can I come to Thee?—

Set foot upon the water, test and see
    If thou canst come to Me.—
Couldst Thou not send a boat to carry me,
    Or dolphin swimming free?—
Nay, boat nor fish if thy will faileth thee:
    For My Will too is free.—
O Lord, I am afraid. – Take hold on Me:
    I am stronger than the sea.—
Save, Lord, I perish. – I have hold of thee,
    I made and rule the sea,
I bring thee to the haven where thou wouldst be.

c. 1890

'Judge not according to the appearance'

Lord, purge our eyes to see
Within the seed a tree,
    Within the glowing egg a bird,
        Within the shroud a butterfly:

Till taught by such, we see
Beyond all creatures Thee,
    And hearken for Thy tender word,
    And hear it, 'Fear not: it is I.'

c. 1890

(Untitled)

The half moon shows a face of plaintive sweetness
    Ready and poised to wax or wane;
A fire of pale desire in incompleteness,
    Tending to pleasure or to pain:—
Lo, while we gaze she rolleth on in fleetness
    To perfect loss or perfect gain.

Half bitterness we know, we know half sweetness;
    This world is all on wax, on wane:
When shall completeness round time's incompleteness,
    Fulfilling joy, fulfilling pain?—
Lo, while we ask, life rolleth on in fleetness
    To finished loss or finished gain.

c. 1890

(Untitled)

Can I know it? – Nay.—*
Shall I know it? – Yea,
When all mists have cleared away
For ever and aye.—

Why not then today?—
Who hath said thee nay?
Life a hopeful heart and pray
In a humble way.—

Other hearts are gay.—
Ask not joy today:
Toil today along the way
Keeping grudge at bay.—

On a past May-day
Flowers pranked all the way;
Nightingales sang out their say
On a night of May.—

Dost thou covet May
On an Autumn day?
Foolish memory saith its say
Of sweets past away.—

Gone the bloom of May,
Autumn beareth bay:
Flowerless wreath for head grown grey
Seemly were today.—

Dost thou covet bay?
Ask it not today:
Rather for a palm-branch pray;
None will say thee nay.

c. 1890

*For Each**

My harvest is done, its promise is ended,
  Weak and watery sets the sun,
Day and night in one mist are blended,
  My harvest is done.

  Long while running, how short when run,
Time to eternity has descended,
  Timeless eternity has begun.

Was it the narrow way that I wended?
  Snares and pits was it mine to shun?
The scythe has fallen, so long suspended,
  My harvest is done.

c. 1890

(Untitled)

Looking back along life's trodden way
  Gleams and greenness linger on the track;
Distance melts and mellows all today,
    Looking back.

Rose and purple and a silvery grey,
  Is that cloud the cloud we called so black?
Evening harmonizes all today,
    Looking back.

Foolish feet so prone to halt or stray,
  Foolish heart so restive on the rack!
Yesterday we sighed, but not today
    Looking back.

1884/5

POEMS FOR CHILDREN, FROM *SINGSONG**

Love me, – I love you,
  Love me, my baby;
Sing it high, sing it low,
  Sing it as may be.

Mother's arms under you,
  Her eyes above you;
Sing it high, sing it low,
  Love me, – I love you.

1869

'Kookoorookoo! kookoorookoo!'
  Crows the cock before the morn;
'Kikirikee! kikirikee!'
  Roses in the east are born.

'Kookoorookoo! kookoorookoo!'
  Early birds begin their singing;
'Kikirikee! Kikirikee!'
  The day, the day, the day is springing.

1869

Dead in the cold, a song-singing thrush,
Dead at the foot of a snowberry bush,—
Weave him a coffin of rush,
Dig him a grave where the soft mosses grow,
Raise him a tombstone of snow.

1869

I dug and dug amongst the snow,
And thought the flowers would never grow;
I dug and dug amongst the sand,
And still no green thing came to hand.

Melt, O snow! the warm winds blow
To thaw the flowers and melt the snow;
But all the winds from every land
Will rear no blossom from the sand.

1869

What are heavy? sea-sand and sorrow:
What are brief? today and tomorrow:
What are frail? Spring blossoms and youth:
What are deep? the ocean and truth.

1869

Twist me a crown of wind-flowers;
  That I may fly away
To hear the singers at their song,
  And players at their play.

Put on your crown of wind-flowers:
  But whither would you go?
Beyond the surging of the sea
  And the storms that blow.

Alas! your crown of wind-flowers
  Can never make you fly:
I twist them in a crown today
  And tonight they die.

1869

If a pig wore a wig,
  What could we say?
Treat him as a gentleman,
  And say 'Good day.'

If his tail chanced to fail,
  What could we do?—
Send him to the tailoress
  To get one new.

1869

The peacock has a score of eyes,
  With which he cannot see;
The cod-fish has a silent sound,
  However that may be;

No dandelions tell the time,
  Although they turn to clocks;
Cat's-cradle does not hold the cat,
  Nor foxglove fit the fox.

1869

If hope grew on a bush,
  And joy grew on a tree,
What a nosegay for the plucking
  There would be!

But oh! in windy autumn,
  When frail flowers wither,
What should we do for hope and joy,
  Fading together?

1869

I planted a hand
  And there came up a palm,
I planted a heart
  And there came up balm.

Then I planted a wish,
  But there sprang a thorn,
While heaven frowned with thunder
  And earth sighed forlorn.

1869

If a mouse could fly,
  Or if a crow could swim,
Or if a sprat could walk and talk,
  I'd like to be like him.

If a mouse could fly,
  He might fly away;
Or if a crow could swim,
  It might turn him grey;
Or if a sprat could walk and talk,
  What would he find to say?

1869

A white hen sitting
  On white eggs three:
Next, three speckled chickens
  As plump as plump can be.

An owl, and a hawk,
  And a bat come to see:
But chicks beneath their mother's wing
  Squat safe as safe can be.

1869

Who has seen the wind?
  Neither I nor you:
But when the leaves hang trembling
  The wind is passing thro'.

Who has seen the wind?
  Neither you nor I:
But when the trees bow down their heads
  The wind is passing by.

1869

I caught a little ladybird
  That flies far away;
I caught a little lady wife
  That is both staid and gay.

Come back, my scarlet ladybird,
  Back from far away;
I weary of my dolly wife,
  My wife that cannot play.

She's such a senseless wooden thing
  She stares the livelong day;
Her wig of gold is stiff and cold
  And cannot change to grey.

1869

'I dreamt I caught a little owl
  And the bird was blue—'

'But you may hunt for ever
And not find such an one.'

'I dreamt I set a sunflower,
  And red as blood it grew—'

'But such a sunflower never
Bloomed beneath the sun.'

1869

NARRATIVE AND LONGER POEMS

*The Dead City**

Once I rambled in a wood
With a careless hardihood,
Heeding not the tangled way;
Labyrinths around me lay,
But for them I never stood.

On, still on, I wandered on,
And the sun above me shone;
And the birds around me winging
With their everlasting singing
Made me feel not quite alone.

In the branches of the trees,
Murmured like the hum of bees
The low sound of happy breezes,
Whose sweet voice that never ceases
Lulls the heart to perfect ease.

Streamlets bubbled all around
On the green and fertile ground,
Thro' the rushes and the grass,
Like a sheet of liquid glass,
With a soft and trickling sound.

And I went, I went on faster,
Contemplating no disaster;
And I plucked ripe blackberries,
But the birds with envious eyes
Came and stole them from their master:

For the birds here were all tame;
Some with bodies like a flame,

Some that glanced the branches thro'
Pure and colourless as dew;
Fearlessly to me they came.

Before me no mortal stood
In the mazes of that wood;
Before me the birds had never
Seen a man, but dwelt for ever
In a happy solitude;

Happy solitude, and blest
With beatitude of rest;
Where the woods are ever vernal,
And the life and joy eternal,
Without Death's or Sorrow's test.

Oh most blessed solitude!
Oh most full beatitude!
Where are quiet without strife,
And imperishable life,
Nothing marred, and all things good.

And the bright sun, life begetting,
Never rising, never setting,
Shining warmly overhead,
Nor too pallid, nor too red,
Lulled me to a sweet forgetting,

Sweet forgetting of the time:
And I listened for no chime
Which might warn me to begone;
But I wandered on, still on,
'Neath the boughs of oak and lime.

Know I not how long I strayed
In the pleasant leafy shade;
But the trees had gradually
Grown more rare, the air more free,
The sun hotter overhead.

Soon the birds no more were seen
Glancing thro' the living green;
And a blight had passed upon
All the trees; and the pale sun
Shone with a strange lurid sheen.

Then a darkness spread around:
I saw nought, I heard no sound;
Solid darkness overhead,
With a trembling cautious tread
Passed I o'er the unseen ground.

But at length a pallid light
Broke upon my searching sight;
A pale solitary ray,
Like a star at dawn of day
Ere the sun is hot and bright.

Towards its faintly glimmering beam
I went on as in a dream;
A strange dream of hope and fear!
And I saw as I drew near
'Twas in truth no planet's gleam;

But a lamp above a gate
Shone in solitary state
O'er a desert drear and cold,
O'er a heap of ruins old,
O'er a scene most desolate.

By that gate I entered lone
A fair city of white stone;
And a lovely light to see
Dawned, and spread most gradually
Till the air grew warm and shone.

Thro' the splendid streets I strayed
In that radiance without shade,
Yet I heard no human sound;
All was still and silent round
As a city of the dead.

All the doors were open wide;
Lattices on every side
In the wind swung to and fro;
Wind that whispered very low;
Go and see the end of pride.

With a fixed determination
Entered I each habitation,
But they all were tenantless;
All was utter loneliness,
All was deathless desolation.

In the noiseless market-place
Was no care-worn busy face;
There were none to buy or sell,
None to listen or to tell,
In this silent emptiness.

Thro' the city on I went
Full of awe and wonderment;
Still the light around me shone,
And I wandered on, still on,
In my great astonishment,

Till at length I reached a place
Where amid an ample space
Rose a palace for a king;
Golden was the turreting,
And of solid gold the base.

The great porch was ivory,
And the steps were ebony;
Diamond and chrysoprase
Set the pillars in a blaze,
Capitalled with jewelry.

None was there to bar my way—
And the breezes seemed to say:
Touch not these, but pass them by,
Pressing onwards: therefore I
Entered in and made no stay.

All around was desolate:
I went on; a silent state
Reigned in each deserted room,
And I hastened thro' the gloom
Till I reached an outer gate.

Soon a shady avenue
Blossom-perfumed, met my view.
Here and there the sun-beams fell
On pure founts, whose sudden swell
Up from marble basins flew.

Every tree was fresh and green;
Not a withered leaf was seen
Thro' the veil of flowers and fruit;
Strong and sapful were the root,
The top boughs, and all between.

Vines were climbing everywhere
Full of purple grapes and fair:
And far off I saw the corn
With its heavy head down borne,
By the odour-laden air.

Who shall strip the bending vine?
Who shall tread the press for wine?
Who shall bring the harvest in
When the pallid ears begin
In the sun to glow and shine?

On I went, alone, alone,
Till I saw a tent that shone
With each bright and lustrous hue;
It was trimmed with jewels too,
And with flowers; not one was gone.

Then the breezes whispered me:
Enter in, and look, and see
How for luxury and pride
A great multitude have died:—
And I entered tremblingly.

Lo, a splendid banquet laid
In the cool and pleasant shade.
Mighty tables, every thing
Of sweet Nature's furnishing
That was rich and rare, displayed;

And each strange and luscious cate
Practised Art makes delicate;
With a thousand fair devices
Full of odours and of spices;
And a warm voluptuous state.

All the vessels were of gold
Set with gems of worth untold.
In the midst a fountain rose
Of pure milk, whose rippling flows
In a silver basin rolled.

In a green emerald baskets were
Sun-red apples, streaked, and fair;
Here the nectarine and peach
And ripe plum lay, and on each
The bloom rested every where.

Grapes were hanging overhead,
Purple, pale, and ruby-red;
And in panniers all around
Yellow melons shone, fresh found,
With the dew upon them spread.

And the apricot and pear
And the pulpy fig were there;
Cherries and dark mulberries,
Bunchy currants, strawberries,
And the lemon wan and fair.

And unnumbered others too,
Fruits of every size and hue,
Juicy in their ripe perfection,
Cool beneath the cool reflection
Of the curtains' skyey blue.

All the floor was strewn with flowers
Fresh from sunshine and from showers,
Roses, lilies, jessamine;
And the ivy ran between
Like a thought in happy hours.

And this feast too lacked no guest
With its warm delicious rest;
With its couches softly sinking,
And its glow, not made for thinking,
But for careless joy at best.

Many banquetters were there,
Wrinkled age, the young, the fair;
In the splendid revelry
Flushing cheek and kindling eye
Told of gladness without care.

Yet no laughter rang around,
Yet they uttered forth no sound;
With the smile upon his face
Each sat moveless in his place,
Silently, as if spell-bound.

The low whispering voice was gone,
And I felt awed and alone.
In my great astonishment
To the feasters up I went—
Lo, they all were turned to stone.

Yea they all were statue-cold,
Men and women, young and old;
With the life-like look and smile
And the flush; and all the while
The hard fingers kept their hold.

Here a little child was sitting
With a merry glance, befitting
Happy age and heedless heart;
There a young man sat apart
With a forward look unweeting.

Nigh them was a maiden fair;
And the ringlets of her hair
Round her slender fingers twined;
And she blushed as she reclined,
Knowing that her love was there.

Here a dead man sat to sup,
In his hand a drinking cup;
Wine cup of the heavy gold,
Human hand stony and cold,
And no life-breath struggling up.

There a mother lay, and smiled
Down upon her infant child;
Happy child and happy mother
Laughing back to one another
With a gladness undefiled.

Here an old man slept, worn out
With the revelry and rout;
Here a strong man sat and gazed
On a girl, whose eyes unraised
No more wandered round about.

And none broke the stillness, none;
I was the sole living one.
And methought that silently
Many seemed to look on me
With strange stedfast eyes that shone.

Full of fear I would have fled;
Full of fear I bent my head,
Shutting out each stony guest:—
When I looked again the feast
And the tent had vanished.

Yes, once more I stood alone
Where the happy sunlight shone
And a gentle wind was sighing,
And the little birds were flying,
And the dreariness was gone.

All these things that I have said
Awed me, and made me afraid.
What was I that I should see
So much hidden mystery?
And I straightway knelt and prayed.

1847

*'Look on this picture and on this'**

I wish we once were wedded, – then I must be true;
You should hold my will in yours to do or to undo:
But now I hate myself Eva when I look at you.

You have seen her hazel eyes, her warm dark skin,
Dark hair – but oh those hazel eyes a devil is dancing in:—
You my saint lead up to heaven, she lures down to sin.

Listen Eva I repent, indeed I do my love:
How should I choose a peacock and leave and grieve a dove?—
If I could turn my back on her and follow you above.

No it's not her beauty bloomed like an autumn peach,
Not her pomp of beauty too high for me to reach;
It's her eyes, her witching manner – ah the lore they teach.

You are winning, well I know it, who should know but I?
You constrain me, I must yield or else must hasten by:—
But she, she fascinates me, I can neither fight nor fly.

She's so redundant, stately; – in truth now have you seen
Ever anywhere such beauty, such a stature, such a mien?
She may be queen of devils but she's every inch a queen.

If you sing to me, I hear her subtler sweeter still
Whispering in each tender cadence strangely sweet to fill
All that lacks in music all my soul and sense and will.

If you dance, tho' mine eyes follow where my hand I gave
I only see her presence like a sunny wave
I only feel her presence like a wind too strong to rave.

If we talk: I love you, do you love me again?—
Tho' your lips speak it's her voice I flush to hear so plain
Say: Love you? yes I love you, love can neither change nor
    wane.

But, you ask, 'why struggle? I have given you up:
Take again your pledges, snap the cord and break the cup:
Feast you with your temptation for I in heaven will sup.'—

Can I bear to think upon you strong to break not bend,*
Pale with inner intense passion silent to the end,
Bear to leave you, bear to grieve you, O my dove my friend?

One short pang and you would rise a light in heaven
While we grovelled in the darkness mean and unforgiven
Tho' our cup of love brimmed sevenfold crowns of love were
    seven.

What shall I choose, what can I for you and her and me;
With you the haven of rest, with her the tossing miry sea;
Time's love with her, or choose with you love's all eternity.—

Nay, you answer coldly yet with a quivering voice:
That is over, doubt and struggle, we have sealed our choice;
Leave me to my contentment vivid with fresh hopes and joys.

Listening so, I hide mine eyes and fancy years to come:
You cherished in another home with no cares burdensome;
You straitened in a windingsheet pulseless at peace and dumb.

So I fancy – The new love has driven the old away;
She has found a dearer shelter, a dearer stronger stay;
Perhaps now she would thank me for the freedom of that day.

Open house and heart barred to me alone the door;
Children bound to meet her, babies crow before;—
Blessed wife and blessed mother whom I may see no more.

Or I fancy – In the grave her comely body lies;
She is 'tiring* for the Bridegroom* till the morning star shall
    rise,
Then to shine a glory in the nuptials of the skies.

No more yearning tenderness, no more pale regret,
She will not look for me when the marriage guests are set,
She joys with joy eternal as we had never met.

I would that one of us were dead, were gone no more to meet,
Or she and I were dead together stretched here at your feet,
That she and I were strained together in one windingsheet:

Hidden away from all the world upon this bitter morn;
Hidden from all the scornful world, from all your keener scorn;
Secure and secret in the dark as blessed babe unborn.

A pitiless fiend is in your eyes to tempt me and to taunt:
If you were dead I verily believe that you would haunt
The home you loved, the man you loved, you said you loved – avaunt.

Why do you face me with those eyes so calm they drive me mad,
Too proud to droop before me and own that you are sad?
Why have you a lofty angel made me mean and cursed and bad?

How have you the heart to face me with that passion in your stare
Deathly silent? weep before me, rave at me in your despair—
If you keep patience wings will spring and a halo from your hair.

Yet what matters – yea what matters? your frenzy can but mock:
You do not hold my heart's life key to lock and to unlock,
The door will not unclose to you tho' long you wait and knock.

Have I wronged you? nay not I nor she in deed or will:
You it is alone that mingle the venomous cup and fill;
Why are you so little lovely that I cannot love you still?—

One pulse, one tone, one ringlet of her's outweighs the whole
Of you, your puny graces puny body puny soul:
You but a taste of sweetness, she an overrunning bowl.

Did I make you, that you blame me because you are not the
best?
Not so, be wise, take patience, turn away and be at rest:
Shall I not know her lovelier who is far loveliest?—

See now how proud you are, like us after all, no saint;
Not so upright but that you are bowed with the old bent;
White at white-heat, tainted with the devil's special taint.

Sit you still and wring the cup drop after loathsome drop:
You have let loose a torrent it is not you can stop;
You have sowed a noisome field-ful, now reap the stinging
crop.

Did you think to sit in safety, to watch me torn and tost
Struggling like a mad dog, watch her tempting doubly lost?
Howl you, you wretched woman, for your flimsy hopes are
crost.

Be still, tho' you may writhe you shall hear the branding truth:
You who thought to sit in judgment on our souls forsooth,
To sit in frigid judgment on our ripe luxuriant youth.

Did I love you? never from the first cold day to this;
You are not sufficient for my aim of life, my bliss;
You are not sufficient, but I found the one that is.

The wine of love that warms me from this life's mortal
chill:
Drunk with love I drink again, a thirst I drink my fill;
Lapped in love I care not doth it make alive or kill.*

Then did I never love you? – ah the sting struck home at last;
You are drooping, fainting, dying – the worst of death is past;
A light is on your face from the nearing heaven forecast.

Never? – yes I loved you then; I loved: the word still charms:—
For the first time last time lie here in my heart my arms,
For the first last time as if I shielded you from harms.

I trampled you, poor dove, to death; you clung to me, I
spurned;
I taunted you, I tortured you, while you sat still and
yearned:—
Oh lesson taught in anguish but in double anguish learned.

For after all I loved you, loved you then, I love you yet.
Listen love I love you: see, the seal of truth is set
On my face in tears – you cannot see? then feel them wet.

Pause at heaven's dear gate, look back, one moment back to
grieve;
You go home thro' death to life; but I, I still must live:
On the threshold of heaven's love, O love can you forgive?—

Fully freely fondly, with heart truth above an oath,
With eager utter pardon given unasked and nothing loth,
Heaping coals of fire upon our heads forgiving both.

One word more – not one: one look more – too late too late:—
Lapped in love she sleeps who was lashed with scorn and hate;
Nestling in the lap of love the dove has found a mate.

Night has come, the night of rest; day will come, that day:
To her glad dawn of glory kindled from the deathless ray;
To us a searching fire and strict balances to weigh.

The tearless tender eyes are closed, the tender lips are dumb:
I shall not see or hear them more until that day shall come:
Then they must speak, what will they say – what then will be
the sum?—

Shall we stand upon the left and she upon the right—
We smirched with endless death and shame, she glorified in
white:
Will she sound our accusation in intolerable light?

Be open-armed to us in love – type of another Love—
As she forgave us once below will she forgive above,
Enthroned to all eternity our sister friend and dove?—

1856

*The Lowest Room**

Like flowers sequestered from the sun
And wind of summer, day by day
I dwindled paler, whilst my hair
Showed the first tinge of grey.

'Oh what is life, that we should live?
 Or what is death, that we must die?
A bursting bubble is our life:
  I also, what am I?'

'What is your grief? now tell me, sweet,
 That I may grieve,' my sister said;
And stayed a white embroidering hand
  And raised a golden head:

Her tresses showed a richer mass,
 Her eyes looked softer than my own,
Her figure had a statelier height,
  Her voice a tenderer tone.

'Some must be second and not first;
 All cannot be the first of all:
Is not this, too, but vanity?
  I stumble like to fall.

'So yesterday I read the acts
 Of Hector and each clangorous king
With wrathful great Æacides:—*
  Old Homer leaves a sting.'

The comely face looked up again,
 The deft hand lingered on the thread:
'Sweet, tell me what is Homer's sting,
  Old Homer's sting?' she said.

'He stirs my sluggish pulse like wine,
 He melts me like the wind of spice,
Strong as strong Ajax' red right hand,
  And grand like Juno's eyes.

'I cannot melt the sons of men,
 I cannot fire and tempest-toss:—
Besides, those days were golden days,
  Whilst these are days of dross.'

She laughed a feminine low laugh,
 Yet did not stay her dexterous hand:
'Now tell me of those days,' she said,
  'When time ran golden sand.'

'Then men were men of might and right,
  Sheer might, at least, and weighty swords;
Then men in open blood and fire
    Bore witness to their words,

'Crest-rearing kings with whistling spears;
  But if these shivered up in the shock
They wrenched up hundred-rooted trees,
    Or hurled the effacing rock.

'Then hand to hand, then foot to foot,
  Stern to the death-grip grappling then,
Who ever thought of gunpowder
    Amongst these men of men?

'They knew whose hand struck home the death,
  They knew who broke but would not bend,*
Could venerate an equal foe
    And scorn a laggard friend.

'Calm in the utmost stress of doom,
  Devout toward adverse powers above,
They hated with intenser hate
    And loved with fuller love.

'Then heavenly beauty could allay
  As heavenly beauty stirred the strife:
By them a slave* was worshipped more
    Than is by us a wife.'

She laughed again, my sister laughed;
  Made answer o'er the laboured cloth:
'I rather would be one of us
    Than wife, or slave, or both.'

'Oh better then be slave or wife
  Than fritter now blank life away:
Then night had holiness of night,
    And day was sacred day.

'The princess laboured at her loom,
  Mistress and handmaiden alike;
Beneath their needles grew the field
    With warriors armed to strike.

'Or, look again, dim Dian's* face
Gleamed perfect thro' the attendant night;
Were such not better than those holes
Amid that waste of white?*

'A shame it is, our aimless life:
I rather from my heart would feed
From silver dish in gilded stall
With wheat and wine the steed—

'The faithful steed that bore my lord
In safety thro' the hostile land,
The faithful steed that arched his neck
To fondle with my hand.'

Her needle erred; a moment's pause,
A moment's patience, all was well.
Then she: 'But just suppose the horse,
Suppose the rider fell?

'Then captive in an alien house,
Hungering on exile's bitter bread,—
They happy, they who won the lot
Of sacrifice,' she said.

Speaking she faltered, while her look
Showed forth her passion like a glass:
With hand suspended, kindling eye,
Flushed cheek, how fair she was!

'Ah well, be those the days of dross;*
This, if you will, the age of gold:
Yet had those days a spark of warmth,
While these are somewhat cold—

'Are somewhat mean and cold and slow,
Are stunted from heroic growth:
We gain but little when we prove
The worthlessness of both.'

'But life is in our hands,' she said:
'In our own hands for gain or loss:
Shall not the Sevenfold Sacred Fire
Suffice to purge our dross?

'Too short a century of dreams,
 One day of work sufficient length:
Why should not you, why should not I
 Attain heroic strength?

'Our life is given us as a blank;
 Ourselves must make it blest or curst:
Who dooms me I shall only be
 The second, not the first?

'Learn from old Homer, if you will,
 Such wisdom as his books have said:
In one of the acts of Ajax shine,
 In one of Diomed.*

'Honoured all heroes whose high deeds
 Thro' life, thro' death, enlarge their span:
Only Achilles in his rage
 And sloth is less than man.'

'Achilles only less than man?
 He less than man who, half a god,
Discomfited all Greece with rest,
 Cowed Ilion with a nod?

'He offered vengeance, lifelong grief
 To one dear ghost, uncounted price:
Beasts, Trojans, adverse gods, himself,
 Heaped up the sacrifice.

'Self-immolated to his friend,
 Shrined in world's wonder, Homer's page,
Is this the man, the less than men
 Of this degenerate age?'

'Gross from his acorns, tusky boar
 Does memorable acts like his;
So for her snared offended young
 Bleeds the swart lioness.'

But here she paused; our eyes had met,
 And I was whitening with the jeer;
She rose: 'I went too far,' she said;
 Spoke low: 'Forgive me, dear.

'To me our days seem pleasant days,
Our home a haven of pure content;
Forgive me if I said too much,
So much more than I meant.

'Homer, tho' greater than his gods,
With rough-hewn virtues was sufficed
And rough-hewn men: but what are such
To us who learn of Christ?'

The much-loved pathos of her voice,
Her almost tearful eyes, her cheek
Grown pale, confessed the strength of love
Which only made her speak:

For mild she was, of few soft words,
Most gentle, easy to be led,
Content to listen when I spoke
And reverence what I said;

I elder sister by six years;
Not half so glad, or wise, or good:
Her words rebuked my secret self
And shamed me where I stood.

She never guessed her words reproved
A silent envy nursed within,
A selfish, souring discontent
Pride-born, the devil's sin.

I smiled, half bitter, half in jest:
'The wisest man* of all the wise
Left for his summary of life
"Vanity of vanities."

'Beneath the sun there's nothing new:
Men flow, men ebb, mankind flows on:
If I am wearied of my life,
Why so was Solomon.

'Vanity of vanities he preached
Of all he found, of all he sought:
Vanity of vanities, the gist
Of all the words he taught.

'This in the wisdom of the world,
In Homer's page, in all, we find:
As the sea is not filled, so yearns
Man's universal mind.

'This Homer felt, who gave his men
With glory but a transient state:
His very Jove could not reverse
Irrevocable fate.

'Uncertain all their lot save this—
Who wins must lose, who lives must die:
All trodden out into the dark
Alike, all vanity.'

She scarcely answered when I paused,
But rather to herself said: 'One
Is here,' low-voiced and loving, 'Yea,
Greater than Solomon.'

So both were silent, she and I:
She laid her work aside, and went
Into the garden-walks, like spring.
All gracious with content;

A little graver than her wont,
Because her words had fretted me;
Not warbling quite her merriest tune
Bird-like from tree to tree.

I chose a book to read and dream:
Yet half the while with furtive eyes
Marked how she made her choice of flowers
Intuitively wise,

And ranged them with instinctive taste
Which all my books had failed to teach;
Fresh rose herself, and daintier
Than blossom of the peach.

By birthright higher than myself,
Tho' nestling of the selfsame nest:
No fault of hers, no fault of mine,
But stubborn to digest.

I watched her, till my book unmarked
  Slid noiseless to the velvet floor;
Till all the opulent summer-world
    Looked poorer than before.

Just then her busy fingers ceased,
  Her fluttered colour went and came;
I knew whose step was on the walk,
    Whose voice would name her name.

* * *

Well, twenty years have passed since then:
  My sister now, a stately wife
Still fair, looks back in peace and sees
    The longer half of life—

The longer half of prosperous life,
  With little grief, or fear, or fret:
She, loved and loving long ago,
    Is loved and loving yet.

A husband honourable, brave,
  Is her main wealth in all the world:
And next to him one like herself,
    One daughter golden-curled;

Fair image of her own fair youth,
  As beautiful and as serene,
With almost such another love
    As her own love has been.

Yet, tho' of world-wide charity,
  And in her home most tender dove,
Her treasure and her heart are stored
    In the home-land of love:

She thrives, God's blessed husbandry;
Most like a vine* which full of fruit
Doth cling and lean and climb toward heaven
    While earth still binds its root.

I sit and watch my sister's face:
  How little altered since the hours

When she, a kind, light-hearted girl,
Gathered her garden flowers;

Her song just mellowed by regret
For having teased me with her talk;
Then all-forgetful as she heard
One step upon the walk.

While I? I sat alone and watched;
My lot in life, to live alone
In mine own world of interests,
Much felt but little shown.

Not to be first: how hard to learn
That lifelong lesson of the past;
Line graven on line and stroke on stroke;
But, thank God, learned at last.

So now in patience I possess
My soul year after tedious year,
Content to take the lowest place,
The place assigned me here.

Yet sometimes, when I feel my strength
Most weak, and life most burdensome,
I lift mine eyes up to the hills
From whence my help shall come:

Yea, sometimes still I lift my heart
To the Archangelic trumpet-burst,
When all deep secrets shall be shown,
And many last be first.*

1856

*The Convent Threshold**

There's blood between us, love, my love,
There's father's blood, there's brother's blood;
And blood's a bar I cannot pass:
I choose the stairs that mount above,
Stair after golden skyward stair,
To city and to sea of glass.
My lily feet are soiled with mud,
With scarlet mud which tells a tale

Of hope that was, of guilt that was,
Of love that shall not yet avail;
Alas, my heart, if I could bare
My heart, this selfsame stain is there:
I seek the sea of glass and fire*
To wash the spot, to burn the snare;
Lo, stairs are meant to lift us higher:
Mount with me, mount the kindled stair.

Your eyes look earthward, mine look up.
I see the far-off city grand,
Beyond the hills a watered land,
Beyond the gulf a gleaming strand
Of mansions where the righteous sup;
Who sleep at ease among their trees,
Or wake to sing a cadenced hymn
With Cherubim and Seraphim;
They bore the Cross, they drained the cup,
Racked, roasted, crushed, wrenched limb from limb,
They the offscouring of the world:
The heaven of starry heavens unfurled,
The sun before their face is dim.

You looking earthward, what see you?
Milk-white, wine-flushed among the vines,
Up and down leaping, to and fro,
Most glad, most full, made strong with wines,
Blooming as peaches pearled with dew,
Their golden windy hair afloat,
Love-music warbling in their throat,
Young men and women come and go.

You linger, yet the time is short:
Flee for your life, gird up your strength
To flee; the shadows stretched at length
Show that day wanes; that night draws nigh;
Flee to the mountain, tarry not.
Is this a time for smile and sigh,
For songs among the secret trees
Where sudden blue birds nest and sport?
The time is short and yet you stay:
Today while it is called today
Kneel, wrestle, knock, do violence, pray;

Today is short, tomorrow nigh:
Why will you die? why will you die?

You sinned with me a pleasant sin:
Repent with me, for I repent.
Woe's me the lore I must unlearn!
Woe's me that easy way we went,
So rugged when I would return!
How long until my sleep begin,
How long shall stretch these nights and days?
Surely, clean Angels cry, she prays;
She laves her soul with tedious tears:
How long must stretch these years and years?

I turn from you my cheeks and eyes,
My hair which you shall see no more—
Alas for joy that went before,
For joy that dies, for love that dies.
Only my lips still turn to you,
My livid lips that cry, Repent.
Oh weary life, Oh weary Lent,
Oh weary time whose stars are few.

How should I rest in Paradise,
Or sit on steps of heaven alone?
If Saints and Angels spoke of love
Should I not answer from my throne:
Have pity upon me, ye my friends,
For I have heard the sound thereof:
Should I not turn with yearning eyes,
Turn earthwards with a pitiful pang?
Oh save me from a pang in heaven.
By all the gifts we took and gave,
Repent, repent, and be forgiven:
This life is long, but yet it ends;
Repent and purge your soul and save:
No gladder song the morning stars
Upon their birthday morning sang
Than Angels sing when one repents.

I tell you what I dreamed last night:
A spirit with transfigured face
Fire-footed clomb an infinite space.

I heard his hundred pinions clang,
Heaven-bells rejoicing rang and rang,
Heaven-air was thrilled with subtle scents,
Worlds spun upon their rushing cars:
He mounted shrieking: 'Give me light.'
Still light was poured on him, more light!
Angels, Archangels he outstripped
Exultant in exceeding might,
And trod the skirts of Cherubim.
Still 'Give me light,' he shrieked; and dipped
His thirsty face, and drank a sea,
Athirst with thirst it could not slake.
I saw him, drunk with knowledge, take
From aching brows the aureole crown—
His locks writhed like a cloven snake—
He left his throne to grovel down
And lick the dust of Seraphs' feet:
For what is knowledge duly weighed?
Knowledge is strong, but love is sweet;
Yea all the progress he had made
Was but to learn that all is small
Save love, for love is all in all.

I tell you what I dreamed last night:
It was not dark, it was not light,
Cold dews had drenched my plenteous hair
Thro' clay; you came to seek me there.
And 'Do you dream of me?' you said.
My heart was dust that used to leap
To you; I answered half asleep:
'My pillow is damp, my sheets are red,
There's a leaden tester to my bed:
Find you a warmer playfellow,
A warmer pillow for your head,
A kinder love to love than mine.'
You wrung your hands; while I like lead
Crushed downwards thro' the sodden earth:
You smote your hands but not in mirth,
And reeled but were not drunk with wine.

For all night long I dreamed of you:
I woke and prayed against my will,

Then slept to dream of you again.
At length I rose and knelt and prayed:
I cannot write the words I said,
My words were slow, my tears were few;
But thro' the dark my silence spoke
Like thunder. When this morning broke,
My face was pinched, my hair was grey,
And frozen blood was on the sill
Where stifling in my struggle I lay.

If now you saw me you would say:
Where is the face I used to love?
And I would answer: Gone before;
It tarries veiled in paradise.
When once the morning star shall rise,
When earth with shadow flees away
And we stand safe within the door,
Then you shall lift the veil thereof.
Look up, rise up: for far above
Our palms are grown, our place is set;
There we shall meet as once we met
And love with old familiar love.

1858

*Goblin Market**

Morning and evening
Maids heard the goblins cry:
'Come buy our orchard fruits,
Come buy, come buy:
Apples and quinces,
Lemons and oranges,
Plump unpecked cherries,
Melons and raspberries,
Bloom-down-cheeked peaches,
Swart-headed mulberries,
Wild free-born cranberries,
Crab-apples, dewberries,
Pine-apples, blackberries,
Apricots, strawberries;—
All ripe together
In summer weather,—

Morns that pass by,
Fair eves that fly;
Come buy, come buy;
Our grapes fresh from the vine,
Pomegranates full and fine,
Dates and sharp bullaces,
Rare pears and greengages,
Damsons and bilberries,
Taste them and try:
Currants and gooseberries,
Bright-fire-like barberries,*
Figs to fill your mouth,
Citrons from the South,
Sweet to tongue and sound to eye;
Come buy, come buy.'

Evening by evening
Among the brookside rushes,
Laura bowed her head to hear,
Lizzie veiled her blushes:
Crouching close together
In the cooling weather,
With clasping arms and cautioning lips,
With tingling cheeks and finger tips.
'Lie close,' Laura said,
Pricking up her golden head:
'We must not look at goblin men,
We must not buy their fruits:
Who knows upon what soil they fed
Their hungry thirsty roots?'
'Come buy,' call the goblins
Hobbling down the glen.
'Oh,' cried Lizzie, 'Laura, Laura,
You should not peep at goblin men.'
Lizzie covered up her eyes,
Covered close lest they should look;
Laura reared her glossy head,
And whispered like the restless brook:
'Look, Lizzie, look, Lizzie,
Down the glen tramp little men.
One hauls a basket,

One bears a plate,
One lugs a golden dish
Of many pounds weight.
How fair the vine must grow
Whose grapes are so luscious;
How warm the wind must blow
Thro' those fruit bushes.'
'No,' said Lizzie: 'No, no, no;
Their offers should not charm us,
Their evil gifts would harm us.'
She thrust a dimpled finger
In each ear, shut eyes and ran:
Curious Laura chose to linger
Wondering at each merchant man.
One had a cat's face,
One whisked a tail,
One tramped at a rat's pace,
One crawled like a snail,
One like a wombat prowled obtuse and furry,
One like a ratel* tumbled hurry skurry.
She heard a voice like voice of doves
Cooing all together:
They sounded kind and full of loves
In the pleasant weather.

Laura stretched her gleaming neck
Like a rush-imbedded swan,
Like a lily from the beck,
Like a moonlit poplar branch,
Like a vessel at the launch
When its last restraint is gone.

Backwards up the mossy glen
Turned and trooped the goblin men,
With their shrill repeated cry,
'Come buy, come buy.'
When they reached where Laura was
They stood stock still upon the moss,
Leering at each other,
Brother and queer brother;
Signalling each other,
Brother with sly brother.

One set his basket down,
One reared his plate;
One began to weave a crown
Of tendrils, leaves and rough nuts brown
(Men sell not such in any town);
One heaved the golden weight
Of dish and fruit to offer her:
'Come buy, come buy,' was still their cry.
Laura stared but did not stir,
Longed but had no money:
The whisk-tailed merchant bade her taste
In tones as smooth as honey,
The cat-faced purr'd,
The rat-paced spoke a word
Of welcome, and the snail-paced even was heard;
One parrot-voiced and jolly
Cried 'Pretty Goblin' still for 'Pretty Polly;'—
One whistled like a bird.

But sweet-tooth Laura spoke in haste:
'Good folk, I have no coin;
To take were to purloin:
I have no copper in my purse,
I have no silver either,
And all my gold is on the furze*
That shakes in windy weather
Above the rusty heather.'
'You have much gold upon your head,'
They answered all together:
'Buy from us with a golden curl.'*
She clipped a precious golden lock,
She dropped a tear more rare than pearl,
Then sucked their fruit globes fair or red:
Sweeter than honey from the rock.
Stronger than man-rejoicing wine,
Clearer than water flowed that juice;
She never tasted such before,
How should it cloy with length of use?
She sucked and sucked and sucked the more
Fruits which that unknown orchard bore;
She sucked until her lips were sore;

Then flung the emptied rinds away
But gathered up one kernel-stone,
And knew not was it night or day
As she turned home alone.

Lizzie met her at the gate
Full of wise upbraidings:
'Dear, you should not stay so late,
Twilight is not good for maidens;
Should not loiter in the glen
In the haunts of goblin men.
Do you not remember Jeanie,*
How she met them in the moonlight,
Took their gifts both choice and many,
Ate their fruits and wore their flowers
Plucked from bowers
Where summer ripens at all hours?
But ever in the noonlight
She pined and pined away;
Sought them by night and day,
Found them no more but dwindled and grew grey;
Then fell with the first snow,
While to this day no grass will grow
Where she lies now:
I planted daisies there a year ago
That never blow.
You should not loiter so.'
'Nay, hush,' said Laura:
'Nay, hush, my sister:
I ate and ate my fill,
Yet my mouth waters still;
Tomorrow night I will
Buy more:' and kissed her:
'Have done with sorrow;
I'll bring you plums tomorrow
Fresh on their mother twigs,
Cherries worth getting;
You cannot think what figs
My teeth have met in,
What melons icy-cold
Piled on a dish of gold

Too huge for me to hold,
What peaches with a velvet nap,
Pellucid grapes without one seed:
Odorous indeed must be the mead
Whereon they grow, and pure the wave they drink
With lilies at the brink,
And sugar-sweet their sap.'

Golden head by golden head,
Like two pigeons in one nest
Folded in each other's wings,
They lay down in their curtained bed:
Like two blossoms on one stem,
Like two flakes of new-fall'n snow,
Like two wands of ivory
Tipped with gold for awful kings.
Moon and stars gazed in at them,
Wind sang to them lullaby,
Lumbering owls forbore to fly,
Not a bat flapped to and fro
Round their rest:
Cheek to cheek and breast to breast
Locked together in one nest.

Early in the morning
When the first cock crowed his warning,
Neat like bees, as sweet and busy,
Laura rose with Lizzie:
Fetched in honey, milked the cows,
Aired and set to rights the house,
Kneaded cakes of whitest wheat,
Cakes for dainty mouths to eat,
Next churned butter, whipped up cream,
Fed their poultry, sat and sewed;
Talked as modest maidens should:
Lizzie with an open heart,
Laura in an absent dream,
One content, one sick in part;
One warbling for the mere bright day's delight,
One longing for the night.

At length slow evening came:
They went with pitchers to the reedy brook;

Lizzie most placid in her look,
Laura most like a leaping flame.
They drew the gurgling water from its deep;
Lizzie plucked purple and rich golden flags,
Then turning homewards said: 'The sunset flushes
Those furthest loftiest crags;
Come, Laura, not another maiden lags,
No wilful squirrel wags,
The beasts and birds are fast asleep.'
But Laura loitered still among the rushes
And said the bank was steep.

And said the hour was early still,
The dew not fall'n, the wind not chill:
Listening ever, but not catching
The customary cry,
'Come buy, come buy,'
With its iterated jingle
Of sugar-baited words:
Not for all her watching
Once discerning even one goblin
Racing, whisking, tumbling, hobbling;
Let alone the herds
That used to tramp along the glen,
In groups or single,
Of brisk fruit-merchant men.
Till Lizzie urged, 'O Laura, come;
I hear the fruit-call but I dare not look:
You should not loiter longer at this brook:
Come with me home.
The stars rise, the moon bends her arc,
Each glowworm winks her spark,
Let us get home before the night grows dark:
For clouds may gather
Tho' this is summer weather,
Put out the lights and drench us thro';
Then if we lost our way what should we do?'

Laura turned cold as stone
To find her sister heard that cry alone,
That goblin cry,
'Come buy our fruits, come buy.'

Must she then buy no more such dainty fruit?
Must she no more such succous pasture find,
Gone deaf and blind?
Her tree of life drooped from the root:
She said not one word in her heart's sore ache;
But peering thro' the dimness, nought discerning,
Trudged home, her pitcher dripping all the way;
So crept to bed, and lay
Silent till Lizzie slept;
Then sat up in a passionate yearning,
And gnashed her teeth for baulked desire, and wept
As if her heart would break.

Day after day, night after night,
Laura kept watch in vain
In sullen silence of exceeding pain.
She never caught again the goblin cry:
'Come buy, come buy;'—
She never spied the goblin men
Hawking their fruits along the glen:
But when the noon waxed bright
Her hair grew thin and grey;
She dwindled, as the fair full moon doth turn
To swift decay and burn
Her fire away.

One day remembering her kernel-stone
She set it by a wall that faced the south;
Dewed it with tears, hoped for a root,
Watched for a waxing shoot,
But there came none;
It never saw the sun,
It never felt the trickling moisture run:
While with sunk eyes and faded mouth
She dreamed of melons, as a traveller sees
False waves in desert drouth
With shade of leaf-crowned trees,
And burns the thirstier in the sandful breeze.

She no more swept the house,
Tended the fowls or cows,
Fetched honey, kneaded cakes of wheat,
Brought water from the brook:

But sat down listless in the chimney-nook
And would not eat.

Tender Lizzie could not bear
To watch her sister's cankerous care
Yet not to share.
She night and morning
Caught the goblins' cry:
'Come buy our orchard fruits,
Come buy, come buy:'—
Beside the brook, along the glen,
She heard the tramp of goblin men,
The voice and stir
Poor Laura could not hear;
Longed to buy fruit to comfort her,
But feared to pay too dear.
She thought of Jeanie in her grave,
Who should have been a bride;
But who for joys brides hope to have
Fell sick and died
In her gay prime,
In earliest Winter time,
With the first glazing rime,
With the first snow-fall of crisp Winter time.

Till Laura dwindling
Seemed knocking at Death's door:
Then Lizzie weighed no more
Better and worse;
But put a silver penny in her purse,
Kissed Laura, crossed the heath with clumps of furze
At twilight, halted by the brook:
And for the first time in her life
Began to listen and look.

Laughed every goblin
When they spied her peeping:
Came towards her hobbling,
Flying, running, leaping,
Puffing and blowing,
Chuckling, clapping, crowing,
Clucking and gobbling,
Mopping and mowing,

Full of airs and graces,
Pulling wry faces,
Demure grimaces,
Cat-like and rat-like,
Ratel- and wombat-like,
Snail-paced in a hurry,
Parrot-voiced and whistler,
Helter skelter, hurry skurry,
Chattering like magpies,
Fluttering like pigeons,
Gliding like fishes,—
Hugged her and kissed her,
Squeezed and caressed her:
Stretched up their dishes,
Panniers, and plates:
'Look at our apples
Russet and dun,
Bob at our cherries,
Bite at our peaches,
Citrons and dates,
Grapes for the asking,
Pears red with basking
Out in the sun,
Plums on their twigs;
Pluck them and suck them,
Pomegranates, figs.'—

'Good folk,' said Lizzie,
Mindful of Jeanie:
'Give me much and many:'—
Held out her apron,
Tossed them her penny.
'Nay, take a seat with us,
Honour and eat with us,'
They answered grinning:
'Our feast is but beginning.
Night yet is early,
Warm and dew-pearly,
Wakeful and starry:
Such fruits as these
No man can carry;
Half their bloom would fly,

Half their dew would dry,
Half their flavour would pass by.
Sit down and feast with us,
Be welcome guest with us,
Cheer you and rest with us.'—
'Thank you,' said Lizzie: 'But one waits
At home alone for me:
So without further parleying,
If you will not sell me any
Of your fruits tho' much and many,
Give me back my silver penny
I tossed you for a fee.'—
They began to scratch their pates,
No longer wagging, purring,
But visibly demurring,
Grunting and snarling.
One called her proud,
Cross-grained, uncivil;
Their tones waxed loud,
Their looks were evil.
Lashing their tails
They trod and hustled her,
Elbowed and jostled her,
Clawed with their nails,
Barking, mewing, hissing, mocking,
Tore her gown and soiled her stocking,
Twitched her hair out by the roots,
Stamped upon her tender feet,
Held her hands and squeezed their fruits
Against her mouth to make her eat.
White and golden* Lizzie stood,
Like a lily in a flood,—
Like a rock of blue-veined stone
Lashed by tides obstreperously,—
Like a beacon left alone
In a hoary roaring sea,
Sending up a golden fire,—
Like a fruit-crowned orange-tree
White with blossoms honey-sweet
Sore beset by wasp and bee,—
Like a royal virgin town

Topped with gilded dome and spire
Close beleaguered by a fleet
Mad to tug her standard down.

One may lead a horse to water,
Twenty cannot make him drink.
Tho' the goblins cuffed and caught her,
Coaxed and fought her,
Bullied and besought her,
Scratched her, pinched her black as ink,
Kicked and knocked her,
Mauled and mocked her,
Lizzie uttered not a word;
Would not open lip from lip
Lest they should cram a mouthful in:
But laughed in heart to feel the drip
Of juice that syrupped all her face,
And lodged in dimples of her chin,
And streaked her neck which quaked like curd.
At last the evil people
Worn out by her resistance
Flung back her penny, kicked their fruit
Along whichever road they took,
Not leaving root or stone or shoot;
Some writhed into the ground,
Some dived into the brook
With ring and ripple,
Some scudded on the gale without a sound,
Some vanished in the distance.

In a smart, ache, tingle,
Lizzie went her way;
Knew not was it night or day;
Sprang up the bank, tore thro' the furze,
Threaded copse and dingle,
And heard her penny jingle
Bouncing in her purse,
Its bounce was music to her ear.
She ran and ran
As if she feared some goblin man
Dogged her with gibe or curse
Or something worse:
But not one goblin skurried after,

Nor was she pricked by fear;
The kind heart made her windy-paced
That urged her home quite out of breath with haste
And inward laughter.

She cried 'Laura,' up the garden,
'Did you miss me?
Come and kiss me.
Never mind my bruises,
Hug me, kiss me, suck my juices
Squeezed from goblin fruits for you,
Goblin pulp and goblin dew.
Eat me, drink me,* love me;
Laura, make much of me:
For your sake I have braved the glen
And had to do with goblin merchant men.'

Laura started from her chair,
Flung her arms up in the air,
Clutched her hair:
'Lizzie, Lizzie, have you tasted
For my sake the fruit forbidden?
Must your light like mine be hidden,
Your young life like mine be wasted,
Undone in mine undoing
And ruined in my ruin,
Thirsty, cankered, goblin-ridden?'—
She clung about her sister,
Kissed and kissed and kissed her:
Tears once again
Refreshed her shrunken eyes,
Dropping like rain
After long sultry drouth;
Shaking with aguish fear, and pain,
She kissed and kissed her with a hungry mouth.

Her lips began to scorch,
That juice was wormwood to her tongue,
She loathed the feast:
Writhing as one possessed she leaped and sung,
Rent all her robe, and wrung
Her hands in lamentable haste,
And beat her breast.

Her locks streamed like the torch
Borne by a racer at full speed,
Or like the mane of horses in their flight,
Or like an eagle when she stems the light
Straight toward the sun,
Or like a caged thing freed,
Or like a flying flag when armies run.

Swift fire spread thro' her veins, knocked at her heart,
Met the fire smouldering there
And overbore its lesser flame;
She gorged on bitterness without a name:
Ah! fool, to choose such part
Of soul-consuming care!
Sense failed in the mortal strife:
Like the watch-tower of a town
Which an earthquake shatters down,
Like a lightning-stricken mast,
Like a wind-uprooted tree
Spun about,
Like a foam-topped waterspout
Cast down headlong in the sea,
She fell at last;
Pleasure past and anguish past,
Is it death or is it life?

Life out of death.
That night long Lizzie watched by her,
Counted her pulse's flagging stir,
Felt for her breath,
Held water to her lips, and cooled her face
With tears and fanning leaves:
But when the first birds chirped about their eaves,
And early reapers plodded to the place
Of golden sheaves,
And dew-wet grass
Bowed in the morning winds so brisk to pass,
And new buds with new day
Opened of cup-like lilies on the stream,
Laura awoke as from a dream,
Laughed in the innocent old way,
Hugged Lizzie but not twice or thrice;

Her gleaming locks showed not one thread of grey,
Her breath was sweet as May
And light danced in her eyes.

Days, weeks, months, years
Afterwards, when both were wives
With children of their own;
Their mother-hearts beset with fears,
Their lives bound up in tender lives;
Laura would call the little ones
And tell them of her early prime,
Those pleasant days long gone
Of not-returning time:
Would talk about the haunted glen,
The wicked, quaint fruit-merchant men,
Their fruits like honey to the throat
But poison in the blood;
(Men sell not such in any town:)
Would tell them how her sister stood,
In deadly peril to do her good,
And win the fiery antidote:
Then joining hands to little hands
Would bid them cling together,
'For there is no friend like a sister
In calm or stormy weather;
To cheer one on the tedious way,
To fetch one if one goes astray,
To lift one if one totters down,
To strengthen whilst one stands.'

1859

*A Royal Princess**

I, a princess, king-descended, decked with jewels, gilded, drest,
Would rather be a peasant with her baby at her breast,
For all I shine so like the sun, and am purple like the west.

Two and two my guards behind, two and two before,
Two and two on either hand, they guard me evermore;
Me, poor dove that must not coo – eagle that must not soar.

All my fountains cast up perfumes, all my gardens grow
Scented woods and foreign spices, with all flowers in blow
That are costly, out of season as the seasons go.

All my walls are lost in mirrors, whereupon I trace
Self to right hand, self to left hand, self in every place,
Self-same solitary figure, self-same seeking face.

Then I have an ivory chair high to sit upon,
Almost like my father's chair, which is an ivory throne;
There I sit uplift and upright, there I sit alone.

Alone by day, alone by night, alone days without end;
My father and my mother give me treasures, search and
spend—
O my father! O my mother! have you ne'er a friend?

As I am a lofty princess, so my father is
A lofty king, accomplished in all kingly subtleties,
Holding in his strong right hand world-kingdoms' balances.

He has quarrelled with his neighbours, he has scourged his
foes;
Vassal counts and princes follow where his pennon goes,
Long-descended valiant lords whom the vulture knows,

On whose track the vulture swoops, when they ride in state
To break the strength of armies and topple down the great:
Each of these my courteous servant, none of these my mate.

My father counting up his strength sets down with equal pen
So many head of cattle, head of horses, head of men;
These for slaughter, these for labour, with the how and
when.

Some to work* on roads, canals; some to man his ships;
Some to smart in mines beneath sharp overseers' whips;
Some to trap fur-beasts in lands where utmost winter nips.

Once it came into my heart and whelmed me like a flood,
That these too are men and women, human flesh and blood;
Men with hearts and men with souls, tho' trodden down like
mud.

Our feasting was not glad that night, our music was not gay;
On my mother's graceful head I marked a thread of grey,
My father frowning at the fare seemed every dish to weigh.

I sat beside them sole princess in my exalted place,
My ladies and my gentlemen stood by me on the dais:
A mirror showed me I look old and haggard in the face;

It showed me that my ladies all are fair to gaze upon,
Plump, plenteous-haired, to every one love's secret lore is
known,
They laugh by day, they sleep by night; ah, me, what is a
throne?

The singing men and women sang that night as usual,
The dancers danced in pairs and sets, but music had a fall,
A melancholy windy fall as at a funeral.

Amid the toss of torches to my chamber back we swept;
My ladies loosed my golden chain; meantime I could have
wept
To think of some in galling chains whether they waked or
slept.

I took my bath of scented milk, delicately waited on,
They burned sweet things for my delight, cedar and
cinnamon.
They lit my shaded silver lamp, and left me there alone.

A day went by, a week went by. One day I heard it said:
'Men are clamouring, women, children, clamouring to be fed;
Men like famished dogs are howling in the streets for bread.'

So two whispered by my door, not thinking I could hear,
Vulgar naked truth, ungarnished for a royal ear;
Fit for cooping in the background, not to stalk so near.

But I strained my utmost sense to catch this truth, and mark:
'There are families out grazing* like cattle in the park.'
'A pair of peasants must be saved, even if we build an ark.'

A merry jest, a merry laugh, each strolled upon his way;
One was my page, a lad I reared and bore with day by day;
One was my youngest maid, as sweet and white as cream in
May.

Other footsteps followed softly with a weightier tramp;
Voices said: 'Picked soldiers have been summoned from the
camp,
To quell these base-born ruffians who make free to howl and
stamp.'

'Howl and stamp?' one answered: 'they made free to hurl a
stone
At the minister's state coach, well aimed and stoutly thrown.'

'There's work then for the soldiers, for this rank crop must be mown.'

'One I saw, a poor old fool with ashes on his head,
Whimpering because a girl had snatched his crust of bread:
Then he dropped; when some one raised him, it turned out he was dead.'

'After us the deluge,'* was retorted with a laugh:
'If bread's the staff of life, they must walk without a staff.'
'While I've a loaf they're welcome to my blessing and the chaff.'

These passed. 'The king:' stand up. Said my father with a smile:
'Daughter mine, your mother comes to sit with you awhile,
She's sad today, and who but you her sadness can beguile?'

He too left me. Shall I touch my harp now while I wait,—
(I hear them doubling guard below before our palace gate) —
Or shall I work the last gold stitch into my veil of state;

Or shall my woman stand and read some unimpassioned scene,
There's music of a lulling sort in words that pause between;
Or shall she merely fan me while I wait here for the queen?

Again I caught my father's voice in sharp word of command:
'Charge!' a clash of steel: 'Charge again, the rebels stand.
Smite and spare not, hand to hand; smite and spare not, hand to hand.'

There swelled a tumult at the gate, high voices waxing higher;
A flash of red reflected light lit the cathedral spire;
I heard a cry for faggots, then I heard a yell for fire.*

'Sit and roast there with your meat, sit and bake there with your bread,
You who sat to see us starve,' one shrieking woman said:
'Sit on your throne and roast with your crown upon your head.'

Nay, this thing will I do, while my mother tarrieth,
I will take my fine spun gold, but not to sew therewith,
I will take my gold and gems, and rainbow fan and wreath;

With a ransom in my lap, a king's ransom in my hand,
I will go down to this people, will stand face to face, will stand
Where they curse king, queen, and princess of this cursed land.

They shall take all to buy them bread, take all I have to give;
I, if I perish,* perish; they today shall eat and live;
I, if I perish, perish; that's the goal I half conceive:

Once to speak before the world, rend bare my heart and show
The lesson I have learned, which is death, is life, to know.
I, if I perish, perish; in the name of God I go.

1861

*Maiden-Song**

Long ago and long ago,
  And long ago still,
There dwelt three merry maidens
  Upon a distant hill.
One was tall Meggan,
  And one was dainty May,
But one was fair Margaret,
  More fair than I can say,
Long ago and long ago.

When Meggan plucked the thorny rose,
  And when May pulled the brier,
Half the birds would swoop to see,
  Half the beasts draw nigher;
Half the fishes of the streams
  Would dart up to admire:
But when Margaret plucked a flag-flower,
  Or poppy hot aflame,
All the beasts and all the birds
  And all the fishes came
To her hand more soft than snow.

Strawberry leaves and May-dew
  In brisk morning air,
Strawberry leaves and May-dew
  Make maidens fair.

'I go for strawberry leaves,'
  Meggan said one day:
'Fair Margaret can bide at home,
  But you come with me, May;
Up the hill and down the hill,
  Along the winding way
You and I are used to go.'

So these two fair sisters
  Went with innocent will
Up the hill and down again,
  And round the homestead hill:
While the fairest sat at home,
  Margaret like a queen,
Like a blush-rose, like the moon
  In her heavenly sheen,
Fragrant-breathed as milky cow
  Or field of blossoming bean,
Graceful as an ivy bough
  Born to cling and lean;
Thus she sat to sing and sew.

When she raised her lustrous eyes
  A beast peeped at the door;
When she downward cast her eyes
  A fish gasped on the floor;
When she turned away her eyes
  A bird perched on the sill,
Warbling out its heart of love,
  Warbling warbling still,
With pathetic pleadings low.

Light-foot May with Meggan
  Sought the choicest spot,
Clothed with thyme-alternate grass:
  Then, while day waxed hot,
Sat at ease to play and rest,
  A gracious rest and play;
The loveliest maidens near or far,
  When Margaret was away,
Who sat at home to sing and sew.

Sun-glow flushed their comely cheeks,
  Wind-play tossed their hair,
Creeping things among the grass
  Stroked them here and there;
Meggan piped a merry note,
  A fitful wayward lay,
While shrill as bird on topmost twig
  Piped merry May;
Honey-smooth the double flow.

Sped a herdsman from the vale,
  Mounting like a flame,
All on fire to hear and see,
  With floating locks he came,
Looked neither north nor south,
  Neither east nor west,
But sat him down at Meggan's feet
  As love-bird on his nest,
And wooed her with a silent awe,
  With trouble not expressed;
She sang the tears into his eyes,
  The heart out of his breast:
So he loved her, listening so.

She sang the heart out of his breast,
  The words out of his tongue;
Hand and foot and pulse he paused
  Till her song was sung.
Then he spoke up from his place
  Simple words and true:
'Scanty goods have I to give,
  Scanty skill to woo;
But I have a will to work,
  And a heart for you:
Bid me stay or bid me go.'

Then Meggan mused within herself:
  'Better be first with him,
Than dwell where fairer Margaret sits,
  Who shines my brightness dim,
For ever second where she sits,
  However fair I be:

I will be lady of his love,
  And he shall worship me;
I will be lady of his herds
  And stoop to his degree,
At home where kids and fatlings grow.'

Sped a shepherd from the height
  Headlong down to look,
(White lambs followed, lured by love
  Of their shepherd's crook):
He turned neither east nor west,
  Neither north nor south,
But knelt right down to May, for love
  Of her sweet-singing mouth;
Forgot his flocks, his panting flocks
  In parching hill-side drouth;
Forgot himself for weal or woe.

Trilled her song and swelled her song
  With maiden coy caprice
In a labyrinth of throbs,
  Pauses, cadences;
Clear-noted as a dropping brook,
  Soft-noted like the bees,
Wild-noted as the shivering wind
  Forlorn thro' forest trees:
Love-noted like the wood-pigeon
  Who hides herself for love,
Yet cannot keep her secret safe,
  But cooes and cooes thereof:
Thus the notes rang loud or low.

He hung breathless on her breath;
  Speechless, who listened well;
Could not speak or think or wish
  Till silence broke the spell.
Then he spoke, and spread his hands,
  Pointing here and there:
'See my sheep and see the lambs,
  Twin lambs which they bare.
All myself I offer you,
  All my flocks and care,
Your sweet song hath moved me so.'

In her fluttered heart young May
  Mused a dubious while:
'If he loves me as he says'—
  Her lips curved with a smile:
'Where Margaret shines like the sun
  I shine but like a moon;
If sister Meggan makes her choice
  I can make mine as soon;
At cockcrow we were sister-maids,
  We may be brides at noon.'
Said Meggan, 'Yes;' May said not 'No.'

Fair Margaret stayed alone at home,
  Awhile she sang her song,
Awhile sat silent, then she thought:
  'My sisters loiter long.'
That sultry noon had waned away,
  Shadows had waxen great:
'Surely,' she thought within herself,
  'My sisters loiter late.'
She rose, and peered out at the door,
  With patient heart to wait,
And heard a distant nightingale
  Complaining of its mate;
Then down the garden slope she walked,
  Down to the garden gate,
Leaned on the rail and waited so.

The slope was lightened by her eyes
  Like summer lightning fair,
Like rising of the haloed moon
  Lightened her glimmering hair,
While her face lightened like the sun
  Whose dawn is rosy white.
Thus crowned with maiden majesty
  She peered into the night,
Looked up the hill and down the hill,
  To left hand and to right,
Flashing like fire-flies to and fro.

Waiting thus in weariness
  She marked the nightingale

Telling, if any one would heed,
  Its old complaining tale.
Then lifted she her voice and sang,
  Answering the bird:
Then lifted she her voice and sang,
  Such notes were never heard
From any bird where Spring's in blow.

The king of all that country
  Coursing far, coursing near,
Curbed his amber-bitted steed,
  Coursed amain to hear;
All his princes in his train,
  Squire, and knight, and peer,
With his crown upon his head,
  His sceptre in his hand,
Down he fell at Margaret's knees
  Lord king of all that land,
To her highness bending low.

Every beast and bird and fish
  Came mustering to the sound,
Every man and every maid
  From miles of country round:
Meggan on her herdsman's arm,
  With her shepherd May,
Flocks and herds trooped at their heels
  Along the hill-side way;
No foot too feeble for the ascent,
  Not any head too grey;
Some were swift and none were slow.

So Margaret sang her sisters home
  In their marriage mirth;
Sang free birds out of the sky,
  Beasts along the earth,
Sang up fishes of the deep—
  All breathing things that move
Sang from far and sang from near
  To her lovely love;
Sang together friend and foe;

Sang a golden-bearded king
 Straightway to her feet,
Sang him silent where he knelt
 In eager anguish sweet.
But when the clear voice died away,
 When longest echoes died,
He stood up like a royal man
 And claimed her for his bride.
So three maids were wooed and won
 In a brief May-tide,
Long ago and long ago.

1863

*The Prince's Progress**

Till all sweet gums and juices flow,
Till the blossom of blossoms blow,
The long hours go and come and go,
 The bride she sleepeth, waketh, sleepeth,
Waiting for one whose coming is slow:—
 Hark! the bride weepeth.

'How long shall I wait, come heat come rime?'—
'Till the strong Prince comes, who must come in time'
(Her women say), 'there's a mountain to climb,
 A river to ford. Sleep, dream and sleep:
Sleep' (they say): 'we've muffled the chime,
 Better dream than weep.'

In his world-end palace the strong Prince sat,
Taking his ease on cushion and mat,
Close at hand lay his staff and his hat.*
 'When wilt thou start? the bride waits, O youth.'—
'Now the moon's at full;* I tarried for that,
 Now I start in truth.

'But tell me first, true voice of my doom,
Of my veiled bride in her maiden bloom;
Keeps she watch thro' glare and thro' gloom,
 Watch for me asleep and awake?'—
 'Spell-bound she watches in one white room,
 And is patient for thy sake.

'By her head lilies and rosebuds grow;
The lilies droop, will the rosebuds blow?
The silver slim lilies hang the head low;
Their stream is scanty, their sunshine rare;
Let the sun blaze out, and let the stream flow,
They will blossom and wax fair.

'Red and white poppies grow at her feet,
The blood-red wait for sweet summer heat,
Wrapped in bud-coats hairy* and neat;
But the white buds swell, one day they will burst,
Will open their death-cups drowsy and sweet—
Which will open the first?'

Then a hundred sad voices lifted a wail,
And a hundred glad voices piped on the gale:
'Time is short, life is short,' they took up the tale:
'Life is sweet, love is sweet, use today while you may;
Love is sweet, and tomorrow may fail;
Love is sweet, use today.'

While the song swept by, beseeching and meek,
Up rose the Prince with a flush on his cheek,
Up he rose to stir and to seek,
Going forth in the joy of his strength;
Strong of limb* if of purpose weak,
Starting at length.

Forth he set in the breezy morn,
Across green fields of nodding corn,
As goodly a Prince as ever was born,
Carolling with the carolling lark;—
Sure his bride will be won and worn,
Ere fall of the dark.

So light his step, so merry his smile,
A milkmaid loitered beside a stile,
Set down her pail and rested awhile,
A wave-haired milkmaid, rosy and white;
The Prince, who had journeyed at least a mile,
Grew athirst at the sight.

'Will you give me a morning draught?'—
'You're kindly welcome,' she said, and laughed.

He lifted the pail, new milk he quaffed;
  Then wiping his curly black beard like silk:
'Whitest cow that ever was calved
    Surely gave you this milk.'

Was it milk now, or was it cream?
Was she a maid, or an evil dream?
Her eyes began to glitter and gleam;
  He would have gone, but he stayed instead;
Green they gleamed as he looked in them:
    'Give me my fee,' she said.—

'I will give you a jewel of gold.'—
'Not so; gold is heavy and cold.'—
'I will give you a velvet fold
  Of foreign work your beauty to deck.'—
'Better I like my kerchief rolled
    Light and white round my neck.'—

'Nay,' cried he, 'but fix your own fee.'—
She laughed, 'You may give the full moon to me;
Or else sit under this apple-tree
  Here for one idle day by my side;
After that I'll let you go free,
    And the world is wide.'

Loth to stay, yet to leave her slack,
He half turned away, then he quite turned back:
For courtesy's sake he could not lack
  To redeem his own royal pledge;
Ahead too the windy heaven lowered black
    With a fire-cloven edge.

So he stretched his length in the apple-tree shade,
Lay and laughed and talked to the maid,
Who twisted her hair in a cunning braid
  And writhed it in shining serpent-coils,*
And held him a day and night fast laid
    In her subtle toils.

At the death of night and birth of day,
When the owl left off his sober play,
And the bat hung himself out of the way,
  Woke the song of mavis and merle,*

And heaven put off its hodden grey
    For mother-o'-pearl.

Peeped up daisies here and there,
Here, there, and everywhere;
Rose a hopeful lark in the air,
  Spreading out towards the sun his breast;
While the moon set solemn and fair
    Away in the West.

'Up, up, up,' called the watchman lark,
In his clear réveillée: 'Hearken, oh hark!
Press to the high goal, fly to the mark.
  Up, O sluggard, new morn is born;
If still asleep when the night falls dark,
    Thou must wait a second morn.'

'Up, up, up,' sad glad voices swelled:
'So the tree falls and lies as it's felled.
Be thy bands loosed, O sleeper, long held
  In sweet sleep whose end is not sweet.
Be the slackness girt and the softness quelled
    And the slowness fleet.'

Off he set. The grass grew rare,
A blight lurked in the darkening air,
The very moss grew hueless and spare,
  The last daisy stood all astunt;
Behind his back the soil lay bare,
    But barer in front.

A land of chasm and rent, a land
Of rugged blackness on either hand:
If water trickled its track was tanned
  With an edge of rust to the chink;
If one stamped on stone or on sand
    It returned a clink.

A lifeless land, a loveless land,
Without lair or nest on either hand:
Only scorpions jerked in the sand,
  Black as black iron, or dusty pale;
From point to point sheer rock was manned
    By scorpions in mail.

A land of neither life nor death,
Where no man buildeth or fashioneth,
Where none draws living or dying breath;
No man cometh or goeth there,
No man doeth, seeketh, saith,
In the stagnant air.

Some old volcanic upset must
Have rent the crust and blackened the crust;
Wrenched and ribbed it beneath its dust
Above earth's molten centre at seethe,
Heaved and heaped it by huge upthrust
Of fire beneath.

Untrodden before, untrodden since:
Tedious land for a social Prince;
Halting, he scanned the outs and ins,
Endless, labyrinthine, grim,
Of the solitude that made him wince,
Laying wait for him.

By bulging rock and gaping cleft,
Even of half mere daylight reft,
Rueful he peered to right and left,
Muttering in his altered mood:
'The fate is hard that weaves my weft,
Tho' my lot be good.'

Dim the changes of day to night,
Of night scarce dark to day not bright.
Still his road wound towards the right,
Still he went, and still he went,
Till one night he spied a light,
In his discontent.

Out it flashed from a yawn-mouthed cave,
Like a red-hot eye from a grave.
No man stood there of whom to crave
Rest for wayfarer plodding by:
Tho' the tenant were churl or knave
The Prince might try.

In he passed and tarried not,
Groping his way from spot to spot,

Towards where the cavern flare glowed hot:—
  An old, old mortal, cramped and double,
Was peering into a seething-pot,
    In a world of trouble.

The veriest atomy* he looked,
With grimy fingers clutching and crooked,
Tight skin, a nose all bony and hooked,
  And a shaking, sharp, suspicious way;
Blinking, his eyes had scarcely brooked
    The light of day.

Stared the Prince, for the sight was new;
Stared, but asked without more ado:
'May a weary traveller lodge with you,
    Old father, here in your lair?
In your country the inns seem few,
    And scanty the fare.'

The head turned not to hear him speak;
The old voice whistled as thro' a leak
(Out it came in a quavering squeak):
  'Work for wage is a bargain fit:
If there's aught of mine that you seek
    You must work for it.

'Buried alive from light and air
This year is the hundredth year,
I feed my fire with a sleepless care,
  Watching my potion wane or wax:
Elixir of Life* is simmering there,
    And but one thing lacks.

'If you're fain to lodge here with me,
Take that pair of bellows you see—
Too heavy for my old hands they be—
  Take the bellows and puff and puff:
When the steam curls rosy and free
    The broth's boiled enough.

'Then take your choice of all I have;
I will give you life if you crave.
Already I'm mildewed for the grave,
  So first myself I must drink my fill:

But all the rest may be yours, to save
 Whomever you will.'

'Done,' quoth the Prince, and the bargain stood.
First he piled on resinous wood,
Next plied the bellows in hopeful mood;
 Thinking, 'My love and I will live.
If I tarry, why life is good,
 And she may forgive.'

The pot began to bubble and boil;
The old man cast in essence and oil,
He stirred all up with a triple coil
 Of gold and silver and iron wire,
Dredged in a pinch of virgin soil,
 And fed the fire.

But still the steam curled watery white;
Night turned to day and day to night;
One thing lacked, by his feeble sight
 Unseen, unguessed by his feeble mind:
Life might miss him, but Death the blight
 Was sure to find.

So when the hundredth year was full
The thread was cut and finished the school.
Death snapped the old worn-out tool,
 Snapped him short while he stood and stirred
(Tho' stiff he stood as a stiff-necked mule)
 With never a word.

Thus at length the old crab was nipped.
The dead hand slipped, the dead finger dipped
In the broth as the dead man slipped,—
 That same instant, a rosy red
Flushed the stream, and quivered and clipped
 Round the dead old head.

The last ingredient was supplied
(Unless the dead man mistook or lied).
Up started the Prince, he cast aside
 The bellows plied thro' the tedious trial,
Made sure that his host had died,
 And filled a phial.

'One night's rest,' thought the Prince: 'This done,
Forth I speed with the rising sun:
With the morrow I rise and run,
  Come what will of wind or of weather.
This draught of Life when my Bride is won
    We'll drink together.'

Thus the dead man stayed in his grave,
Self-chosen, the dead man in his cave;
There he stayed, were he fool or knave,
  Or honest seeker who had not found:
While the Prince outside was prompt to crave
    Sleep on the ground.

'If she watches, go bid her sleep;
Bid her sleep, for the road is steep;
He can sleep who holdeth her cheap,
  Sleep and wake and sleep again.
Let him sow, one day he shall reap,
    Let him sow the grain.

'When there blows a sweet garden rose,
Let it bloom and wither if no man knows;
But if one knows when the sweet thing blows,
  Knows, and lets it open and drop,
If but a nettle his garden grows
    He hath earned the crop.'

Thro' his sleep the summons rang,
Into his ears it sobbed and it sang.
Slow he woke with a drowsy pang,
  Shook himself without much debate,
Turned where he saw green branches hang,
    Started tho' late.

For the black land was travelled o'er,
He should see the grim land no more.
A flowering country stretched before
  His face when the lovely day came back:
He hugged the phial of Life he bore,
    And resumed his track.

By willow courses he took his path,
Spied what a nest the kingfisher hath,

Marked the fields green to aftermath,*
  Marked where the red-brown field-mouse ran,
Loitered awhile for a deep-stream bath,
    Yawned for a fellow-man.

Up on the hills not a soul in view,
In the vale not many nor few;
Leaves, still leaves, and nothing new.
  It's oh for a second maiden, at least,
To bear the flagon, and taste it too,
    And flavour the feast.

Lagging he moved, and apt to swerve;
Lazy of limb, but quick of nerve.
At length the water-bed took a curve,
  The deep river swept its bankside bare;
Waters streamed from the hill-reserve—
    Waters here, waters there.

High above, and deep below,
Bursting, bubbling, swelling the flow,
Like hill-torrents after the snow,—
  Bubbling, gurgling, in whirling strife,
Swaying, sweeping, to and fro,—
    He must swim for his life.

Which way? – which way? – his eyes grew dim
With the dizzying whirl – which way to swim?
The thunderous downshoot deafened him;
  Half he choked in the lashing spray:
Life is sweet, and the grave is grim—
    Which way? – which way?

A flash of light, a shout from the strand:
'This way – this way; here lies the land!'
His phial clutched in one drowning hand;
  He catches – misses – catches a rope;
His feet slip on the slipping sand:
    Is there life? – is there hope?

Just saved, without pulse or breath,—
Scarcely saved from the gulp of death;
Laid where a willow shadoweth—
  Laid where a swelling turf is smooth.

(O Bride! but the Bridegroom lingereth
For all thy sweet youth.)

Kind hands do and undo,
Kind voices whisper and coo:
'I will chafe his hands' – 'And I' – 'And you
Raise his head, put his hair aside.'
(If many laugh, one well may rue:
Sleep on, thou Bride.)

So the Prince was tended with care:
One wrung foul ooze from his clustered hair;
Two chafed his hands, and did not spare;
But one propped his head that dropped awry:
Till his eyes oped, and at unaware
They met eye to eye.

Oh a moon face in a shadowy place,
And a light touch and a winsome grace,
And a thrilling tender voice which says:
'Safe from waters that seek the sea—
Cold waters by rugged ways—
Safe with me.'

While overhead bird whistles to bird,
And round about plays gamesome herd:
'Safe with us' – some take up the word—
'Safe with us, dear lord and friend:
All the sweeter if long deferred
Is rest in the end.'

Had he stayed to weigh and to scan,
He had been more or less than a man:
He did what a young man can,
Spoke of toil and an arduous way—
Toil tomorrow, while golden ran
The sands of today.

Slip past, slip fast.
Uncounted hours from first to last,
Many hours till the last is past,
Many hours dwindling to one—
One hour whose die is cast,
One last hour gone.

Come, gone – gone for ever—
Gone as an unreturning river—
Gone as to death the merriest liver—
  Gone as the year at the dying fall—
Tomorrow, today, yesterday, never—
    Gone once for all.

Came at length the starting-day,
With last words, and last, last words to say,
With bodiless cries from far away—
  Chiding wailing voices that rang
Like a trumpet-call to the tug and fray;
    And thus they sang:

'Is there life? – the lamp burns low;
Is there hope? – the coming is slow:
The promise promised so long ago,
  The long promise, has not been kept.
Does she live? – does she die? she slumbers so
  Who so oft has wept.

'Does she live? – does she die? – she languisheth
As a lily drooping to death,
As a drought-worn bird with failing breath,
  As a lovely vine without a stay,
As a tree whereof the owner saith,
    "Hew it down today." '

Stung by that word the Prince was fain
To start with his tedious road again.
He crossed the stream where a ford was plain,
  He clomb the opposite bank tho' steep,
And swore to himself to strain and attain
    Ere he tasted sleep.

Huge before him a mountain frowned
With foot of rock on the valley ground,
And head with snows incessant crowned,
  And a cloud mantle about its strength,
And a path which the wild goat hath not found
    In its breadth and length.

But he was strong to do and dare:
If a host had withstood him there,

He had braved a host with little care
  In his lusty youth and his pride,
Tough to grapple tho' weak to snare.
    He comes, O Bride.

Up he went where the goat scarce clings,
Up where the eagle folds her wings,
Past the green line of living things,
  Where the sun cannot warm the cold,—
Up he went as a flame enrings
    Where there seems no hold.

Up a fissure barren and black,
Till the eagles tired upon his track,
And the clouds were left behind his back,
  Up till the utmost peak was past.
Then he gasped for breath and his strength fell slack;
    He paused at last.

Before his face a valley spread
Where fatness laughed, wine, oil, and bread,
Where all fruit-trees their sweetness shed,
  Where all birds make love to their kind,
Where jewels twinkled, and gold lay red
    And not hard to find.

Midway down the mountain side
(On its green slope the path was wide)
Stood a house for a royal bride,
  Built all of changing opal stone,*
The royal palace, till now descried
    In his dreams alone.

Less bold than in days of yore,
Doubting now tho' never before,
Doubting he goes and lags the more:
  Is the time late? does the day grow dim?
Rose, will she open the crimson core
    Of her heart to him?

Above his head a tangle glows
Of wine-red roses, blushes, snows,
Closed buds and buds that unclose,
  Leaves, and moss, and prickles too;

His hand shook as he plucked a rose,
And the rose dropped dew.

Take heart of grace! the potion of Life
May go far to woo him a wife:
If she frown, yet a lover's strife
Lightly raised can be laid again:
A hasty word is never the knife
To cut love in twain.

Far away stretched the royal land,
Fed by dew, by a spice-wind fanned:
Light labour more, and his foot would stand
On the threshold, all labour done;
Easy pleasure laid at his hand,
And the dear Bride won.

His slackening steps pause at the gate—
Does she wake or sleep? – the time is late—
Does she sleep now, or watch and wait?
She has watched, she has waited long,
Watching athwart the golden grate
With a patient song.

Fling the golden portals wide,
The Bridegroom comes to his promised Bride;
Draw the gold-stiff curtains aside,
Let them look on each other's face,
She in her meekness, he in his pride—
Day wears apace.

Day is over, the day that wore.
What is this that comes thro' the door,
The face covered, the feet before?
This that coming takes his breath;
This Bride not seen, to be seen no more
Save of Bridegroom Death?

Veiled figures carrying her
Sweep by yet make no stir;
There is a smell of spice and myrrh,
A bride-chant burdened with one name;
The bride-song rises steadier
Than the torches' flame:

'Too late for love, too late for joy,
  Too late, too late!
You loitered on the road too long,
  You trifled at the gate:
The enchanted dove upon her branch
  Died without a mate;
The enchanted princess in her tower
  Slept, died, behind the grate;
Her heart was starving all this while
  You made it wait.

'Ten years ago, five years ago,
  One year ago,
Even then you had arrived in time,
  Tho' somewhat slow;
Then you had known her living face
  Which now you cannot know:
The frozen fountain would have leaped,
  The buds gone on to blow,
The warm south wind would have awaked
  To melt the snow.

'Is she fair now as she lies?
  Once she was fair;
Meet queen for any kingly king,
  With gold-dust on her hair.
Now these are poppies in her locks,
  White poppies she must wear;
Must wear a veil to shroud her face
  And the want graven there:
Or is the hunger fed at length,
  Cast off the care?

'We never saw her with a smile
  Or with a frown;
Her bed seemed never soft to her,
  Tho' tossed of down;
She little heeded what she wore,
  Kirtle, or wreath, or gown;
We think her white brows often ached
  Beneath her crown,
Till silvery hairs showed in her locks

That used to be so brown.

'We never heard her speak in haste:
Her tones were sweet,
And modulated just so much
As it was meet:
Her heart sat silent thro' the noise
And concourse of the street.
There was no hurry in her hands,
No hurry in her feet;
There was no bliss drew nigh to her,
That she might run to greet.

'You should have wept her yesterday,
Wasting upon her bed:
But wherefore should you weep today
That she is dead?
Lo, we who love weep not today,
But crown her royal head.
Let be these poppies that we strew,
Your roses are too red:
Let be these poppies, not for you
Cut down and spread.'

1864–5

*'The Iniquity of the Fathers upon the Children'**

Oh the rose of keenest thorn!
One hidden summer morn
Under the rose I was born.

I do not guess his name
Who wrought my Mother's shame,
And gave me life forlorn,
But my Mother, Mother, Mother,
I know her from all other.
My Mother pale and mild,
Fair as ever was seen,
She was but scarce sixteen,
Little more than a child,
When I was born
To work her scorn.
With secret bitter throes,

In a passion of secret woes,
She bore me under the rose.

One who my Mother nursed
Took me from the first:—
'O nurse, let me look upon
This babe that costs so dear;

Tomorrow she will be gone;
Other mothers may keep
Their babes awake and asleep,
But I must not keep her here.'—
Whether I know or guess,
I know this not the less.

So I was sent away
That none might spy the truth:
And my childhood waxed to youth
And I left off childish play.
I never cared to play
With the village boys and girls;
And I think they thought me proud,
I found so little to say
And kept so from the crowd:
But I had the longest curls
And I had the largest eyes,
And my teeth were small like pearls;
The girls might flout and scout me,
But the boys would hang about me
In sheepish mooning wise.

Our one-street village stood
A long mile from the town,
A mile of windy down
And bleak one-sided wood,
With not a single house.
Our town itself was small,
With just the common shops,
And throve in its small way.
Our neighbouring gentry reared
The good old-fashioned crops,
And made old-fashioned boasts
Of what John Bull would do
If Frenchman Frog appeared,

And drank old-fashioned toasts,
And made old-fashioned bows
To my Lady at the Hall.

My Lady at the Hall
Is grander than they all:
Hers is the oldest name
In all the neighbourhood;
But the race must die with her
Tho' she's lofty dame,
For she's unmarried still.
Poor people say she's good
And has an open hand
As any in the land,
And she's the comforter
Of many sick and sad;
My nurse once said to me
That everything she had
Came of my Lady's bounty:
'Tho' she's greatest in the county
She's humble to the poor,
No beggar seeks her door
But finds help presently.
I pray both night and day
For her, and you must pray:
But she'll never feel distress
If needy folk can bless.'

I was a little maid
When here we came to live
From somewhere by the sea.
Men spoke a foreign tongue
There where we used to be
When I was merry and young,
Too young to feel afraid;
The fisher-folk would give
A kind strange word to me,
There by the foreign sea:
I don't know where it was,
But I remember still
Our cottage on a hill,
And fields of flowering grass

On that fair foreign shore.

I liked my old home best,
But this was pleasant too:
So here we made our nest
And here I grew.
And now and then my Lady

In riding past our door
Would nod to Nurse and speak,
Or stoop and pat my cheek;
And I was always ready
To hold the field-gate wide
For my Lady to go thro';
My Lady in her veil
So seldom put aside,
My Lady grave and pale.

I often sat to wonder
Who might my parents be,
For I knew of something under
My simple-seeming state.
Nurse never talked to me
Of mother or of father,
But watched me early and late
With kind suspicious cares:
Or not suspicious, rather
Anxious, as if she knew
Some secret I might gather
And smart for unawares.
Thus I grew.

But Nurse waxed old and grey,
Bent and weak with years.
There came a certain day
That she lay upon her bed
Shaking her palsied head,
With words she gasped to say
Which had to stay unsaid.
Then with a jerking hand
Held out so piteously
She gave a ring to me
Of gold wrought curiously,

A ring which she had worn
Since the day that I was born,
She once had said to me:
I slipped it on my finger;
Her eyes were keen to linger
On my hand that slipped it on;
Then she sighed one rattling sigh

And stared on with sightless eyes:—
The one who loved me was gone.

How long I stayed alone
With the corpse, I never knew,
For I fainted dead as stone:
When I came to life once more
I was down upon the floor,
With neighbours making ado
To bring me back to life.
I heard the sexton's wife
Say: 'Up, my lad, and run
To tell it at the Hall;
She was my Lady's nurse,
And done can't be undone.
I'll watch by this poor lamb.
I guess my Lady's purse
Is always open to such:
I'd run up on my crutch
A cripple as I am,'
(For cramps had vexed her much)
'Rather than this dear heart
Lack one to take her part.'

For days day after day
On my weary bed I lay
Wishing the time would pass;
Oh, so wishing that I was
Likely to pass away:
For the one friend whom I knew
Was dead, I knew no other,
Neither father nor mother;
And I, what should I do?

One day the sexton's wife

Said: 'Rouse yourself, my dear:
My Lady has driven down
From the Hall into the town,
And we think she's coming here.
Cheer up, for life is life.'

But I would not look or speak,
Would not cheer up at all.
My tears were like to fall,
So I turned round to the wall
And hid my hollow cheek
Making as if I slept,
As silent as a stone,
And no one knew I wept.
What was my Lady to me,
The grand lady from the Hall?
She might come, or stay away,
I was sick at heart that day:
The whole world seemed to be
Nothing, just nothing to me,
For aught that I could see.

Yet I listened where I lay:
A bustle came below,
A clear voice said: 'I know;
I will see her first alone,
It may be less of a shock
If she's so weak today:'—
A light hand turned the lock,
A light step crossed the floor,
One sat beside my bed:
But never a word she said:

For me, my shyness grew
Each moment more and more:
So I said never a word
And neither looked nor stirred;
I think she must have heard
My heart go pit-a-pat:
Thus I lay, my Lady sat,
More than a mortal hour—
(I counted one and two
By the house-clock while I lay):
I seemed to have no power

To think of a thing to say,
Or do what I ought to do,
Or rouse myself to a choice.

At last she said: 'Margaret,
Won't you even look at me?'
A something in her voice
Forced my tears to fall at last,
Forced sobs from me thick and fast;
Something not of the past,
Yet stirring memory;
A something new, and yet
Not new, too sweet to last,
Which I never can forget.

I turned and stared at her:
Her cheek showed hollow-pale;
Her hair like mine was fair,
A wonderful fall of hair
That screened her like a veil;
But her height was statelier,
Her eyes had depth more deep;
I think they must have had
Always a something sad,
Unless they were asleep.

While I stared, my Lady took
My hand in her spare hand
Jewelled and soft and grand,
And looked with a long long look
Of hunger in my face;
As if she tried to trace
Features she ought to know,
And half hoped, half feared, to find.
Whatever was in her mind
She heaved a sigh at last,
And began to talk to me.

'Your nurse was my dear nurse,
And her nursling's dear,' said she:
'No one told me a word
Of her getting worse and worse,
Till her poor life was past'

(Here my Lady's tears dropped fast):
'I might have been with her,
I might have promised and heard,
But she had no comforter.
She might have told me much
Which now I shall never know,
Never never shall know.'
She sat by me sobbing so,
And seemed so woe-begone,
That I laid one hand upon
Hers with a timid touch,
Scarce thinking what I did,
Not knowing what to say:
That moment her face was hid
In the pillow close to mine,
Her arm was flung over me,
She hugged me, sobbing so
As if her heart would break,
And kissed me where I lay.

After this she often came
To bring me fruit or wine,
Or sometimes hothouse flowers.
And at nights I lay awake
Often and often thinking
What to do for her sake.
Wet or dry it was the same:
She would come in at all hours,
Set me eating and drinking
And say I must grow strong;
At last the day seemed long
And home seemed scarcely home
If she did not come.

Well, I grew strong again:
In time of primroses,
I went to pluck them in the lane;
In time of nestling birds,
I heard them chirping round the house;
And all the herds
Were out at grass when I grew strong,
And days were waxen long,

And there was work for bees
Among the May-bush boughs,
And I had shot up tall,
And life felt after all
Pleasant, and not so long
When I grew strong.

I was going to the Hall
To be my Lady's maid:
'Her little friend,' she said to me,
'Almost her child,'
She said and smiled
Sighing painfully;
Blushing, with a second flush
As if she blushed to blush.

Friend, servant, child: just this
My standing at the Hall;
The other servants calls me 'Miss,'
My Lady calls me 'Margaret,'
With her clear voice musical.
She never chides when I forget
This or that; she never chides.
Except when people come to stay,
(And that's not often) at the Hall,
I sit with her all day
And ride out when she rides.
She sings to me and makes me sing;
Sometimes I read to her,
Sometimes we merely sit and talk.
She noticed once my ring
And made me tell its history:
That evening in our garden walk
She said she should infer
The ring had been my father's first,
Then my mother's, given for me
To the nurse who nursed
My mother in her misery,
That so quite certainly
Some one might know me, who . . .
Then she was silent, and I too.

I hate when people come:
The women speak and stare
And mean to be so civil.
This one will stroke my hair,
That one will pat my cheek
And praise my Lady's kindness,
Expecting me to speak;
I like the proud ones best
Who sit as struck with blindness,
As if I wasn't there.
But if any gentleman
Is staying at the Hall
(Tho' few come prying here),
My Lady seems to fear
Some downright dreadful evil,
And makes me keep my room
As closely as she can:
So I hate when people come,
It is so troublesome.
In spite of all her care,
Sometimes to keep alive
I sometimes do contrive
To get out in the grounds
For a whiff of wholesome air,
Under the rose you know:
It's charming to break bounds,
Stolen waters are sweet,
And what's the good of feet
If for days they mustn't go?
Give me a longer tether,
Or I may break from it.

Now I have eyes and ears
And just some little wit:
'Almost my Lady's child;'
I recollect she smiled,
Sighed and blushed together;
Then her story of the ring
Sounds not improbable,
She told it me so well
It seemed the actual thing:—

Oh, keep your counsel close,
But I guess under the rose,
In long past summer weather
When the world was blossoming,
And the rose upon its thorn:
I guess not who he was
Flawed honour like a glass
And made my life forlorn,
But my Mother, Mother, Mother,
Oh, I know her from all other.

My Lady, you might trust
Your daughter with your fame.
Trust me, I would not shame
Our honourable name,
For I have noble blood
Tho' I was bred in dust
And brought up in the mud.
I will not press my claim,
Just leave me where you will:
But you might trust your daughter,
For blood is thicker than water
And you're my mother still.

So my Lady holds her own
With condescending grace,
And fills her lofty place
With an untroubled face
As a queen may fill a throne.
While I could hint a tale—
(But then I am her child)—
Would make her quail;
Would set her in the dust,
Lorn with no comforter,
Her glorious hair defiled
And ashes on her cheek:
The decent world would thrust
Its finger out at her,
Not much displeased I think
To make a nine days' stir;
The decent world would sink
Its voice to speak of her.

Now this is what I mean
To do, no more, no less:
Never to speak, or show
Bare sign of what I know.
Let the plot pass unseen;
Yea, let her never guess
I hold the tangled clue
She huddles out of view.

Friend, servant, almost child,
So be it and nothing more
On this side of the grave.
Mother, in Paradise,
You'll see with clearer eyes;
Perhaps in this world even
When you are like to die
And face to face with Heaven
You'll drop for once the lie:
But you must drop the mask, not I.

My Lady promises
Two hundred pounds with me
Whenever I may wed
A man she can approve:
And since besides her bounty
I'm fairest in the county
(For so I've heard it said,
Tho' I don't vouch for this),
Her promised pounds may move
Some honest man to see
My virtues and my beauties;
Perhaps the rising grazier,
Or temperance publican,
May claim my wifely duties.
Meanwhile I wait their leisure
And grace-bestowing pleasure,
I wait the happy man;
But if I hold my head
And pitch my expectations
Just higher than their level,
They must fall back on patience;
I may not mean to wed,

Yet I'll be civil.

Now sometimes in a dream
My heart goes out of me
To build and scheme,
Till I sob after things that seem
So pleasant in a dream:
A home such as I see
My blessed neighbours live in
With father and with mother,
All proud of one another,
Named by one common name
From baby in the bud
To full-blown workman father;
It's little short of Heaven.
I'd give my gentle blood
To wash my special shame
And drown my private grudge;
I'd toil and moil much rather
The dingiest cottage drudge
Whose mother need not blush,
Than live here like a lady
And see my Mother flush
And hear her voice unsteady
Sometimes, yet never dare
Ask to share her care.

Of course the servants sneer
Behind my back at me;
Of course the village girls,
Who envy me my curls
And gowns and idleness,
Take comfort in a jeer;
Of course the ladies guess
Just so much of my history
As points the emphatic stress
With which they laud my Lady;
The gentlemen who catch
A casual glimpse of me
And turn again to see,
Their valets on the watch
To speak a word with me,

All know and sting me wild;
Till I am almost ready
To wish that I were dead,
No faces more to see,
No more words to be said,
My Mother safe at last
Disburdened of her child,
And the past past.

'All equal before God'—
Our Rector has it so,
And sundry sleepers nod:
It may be so; I know
All are not equal here,
And when the sleepers wake
They make a difference.
'All equal in the grave'—
That shows an obvious sense:
Yet something which I crave
Not death itself brings near;
How should death half atone
For all my past; or make
The name I bear my own?

I love my dear old Nurse
Who loved me without gains;
I love my mistress even,
Friend, Mother, what you will:
But I could almost curse
My Father for his pains;
And sometimes at my prayer
Kneeling in sight of Heaven
I almost curse him still:
Why did he set his snare
To catch at unaware
My Mother's foolish youth;
Load me with shame that's hers,
And her with something worse,
A lifelong lie for truth?

I think my mind is fixed
On one point and made up:

To accept my lot unmixed;
Never to drug the cup
But drink it by myself.
I'll not be wooed for pelf;
I'll not blot out my shame
With any man's good name;
But nameless as I stand,
My hand is my own hand,
And nameless as I came
I go to the dark land.

'All equal in the grave'—
I bide my time till then:
'All equal before God'—
Today I feel His rod,
Tomorrow He may save: Amen.

1865

*A Ballad of Boding**

There are sleeping dreams and waking dreams;
What seems is not always as it seems.

I looked out of my window* in the sweet new morning,
And there I saw three barges of manifold adorning
Went sailing toward the East:
The first had sails like fire,
The next like glittering wire,
But sackcloth were the sails of the least;
And all the crews made music, and two had spread a feast.

The first choir breathed in flutes,
And fingered soft guitars;
The second won from lutes
Harmonious chords and jars,
With drums for stormy bars:
But the third was all of harpers and scarlet trumpeters;
Notes of triumph, then
An alarm again,
As for onset, as for victory, rallies, stirs,
Peace at last and glory to the vanquishers.

The first barge showed for figurehead a Love with wings;*

The second showed for figurehead a Worm* with stings;
The third, a Lily tangled to a Rose* which clings.
The first bore for freight gold and spice and down;
The second bore a sword, a sceptre, and a crown;
The third, a heap of earth gone to dust and brown.
Winged Love meseemed like Folly in the face;
Stinged Worm meseemed loathly in his place;
Lily and Rose were flowers of grace.

Merry went the revel of the fire-sailed crew,
Singing, feasting, dancing to and fro:
Pleasures ever changing, ever graceful, ever new;
Sighs, but scarce of woe;
All the sighing
Wooed such sweet replying;
All the sighing, sweet and low,
Used to come and go
For more pleasure, merely so.
Yet at intervals some one grew tired
Of everything desired,
And sank, I knew not whither, in sorry plight,
Out of sight.

The second crew seemed ever
Wider-visioned, graver,
More distinct of purpose, more sustained of will;
With heads erect and proud,
And voices sometimes loud;
With endless tacking, counter-tacking,
All things grasping, all things lacking,
It would seem;
Ever shifting helm, or sail, or shroud,
Drifting on as in a dream.
Hoarding to their utmost bent,
Feasting to their fill,
Yet gnawed by discontent,
Envy, hatred, malice, on their road they went.
Their freight was not a treasure,
Their music not a pleasure;
The sword flashed, cleaving thro' their bands,
Sceptre and crown changed hands.

The third crew as they went
Seemed mostly different;
They toiled in rowing, for to them the wind was contrary,
As all the world might see.
They laboured at the oar,
While on their heads they bore
The fiery stress of sunshine more and more.
They laboured at the oar hand-sore,
Till rain went splashing,
And spray went dashing,
Down on them, and up on them, more and more.

Their sails were patched and rent,
Their masts were bent,
In peril of their lives they worked and went.
For them no feast was spread,
No soft luxurious bed
Scented and white,
No crown or sceptre hung in sight;
In weariness and painfulness,
In thirst and sore distress,
They rowed and steered from left to right
With all their might.
Their trumpeters and harpers round about
Incessantly played out,
And sometimes they made answer with a shout;
But oftener they groaned or wept,
And seldom paused to eat, and seldom slept.
I wept for pity watching them, but more
I wept heart-sore
Once and again to see
Some weary man plunge overboard, and swim
To Love or Worm ship floating buoyantly:
And there all welcomed him.

The ships steered each other apart and seemed to scorn each other,
Yet all the crews were interchangeable;
Now one man, now another,
—Like bloodless spectres some, some flushed by health,—
Changed openly, or changed by stealth,
Scaling a slippery side, and scaled it well.

The most left Love ship, hauling wealth
Up Worm ship's side;
While some few hollow-eyed
Left either for the sack-sailed boat;
But this, tho' not remote,
Was worst to mount, and whoso left it once
Scarce ever came again,
But seemed to loathe his erst companions,
And wish and work them bane.

Then I knew (I know not how) there lurked quicksands full of dread,
Rocks and reefs and whirlpools in the water bed,
Whence a waterspout
Instantaneously leaped out,
Roaring as it reared its head.
Soon I spied a something dim,
Many-handed, grim,
That went flitting to and fro the first and second ship;
It puffed their sails full out
With puffs of smoky breath
From a smouldering lip,
And cleared the waterspout
Which reeled roaring round about
Threatening death.
With a horny hand it steered,
And a horn appeared
On its sneering head upreared
Haughty and high
Against the blackening lowering sky.
With a hoof it swayed the waves;
They opened here and there,
Till I spied deep ocean graves
Full of skeletons
That were men and women once
Foul or fair;
Full of things that creep
And fester in the deep
And never breathe the clean life-nurturing air.

The third bark held aloof
From the Monster with the hoof,

Despite his urgent beck,
And fraught with guile
Abominable his smile;
Till I saw him take a flying leap on to that deck.
Then full of awe,
With these same eyes I saw
His head incredible retract its horn
Rounding like babe's new born,
While silvery phosphorescence played
About his dis-horned head.
The sneer smoothed from his lip.
He beamed blandly on the ship;
All winds sank to a moan,
All waves to a monotone
(For all these seemed his realm),
While he laid a strong caressing hand upon the helm.

Then a cry well nigh of despair
Shrieked to heaven, a clamour of desperate prayer.
The harpers harped no more,
While the trumpeters sounded sore,
An alarm to wake the dead from their bed:
To the rescue, to the rescue, now or never,
To the rescue, O ye living, O ye dead,
Or no more help or hope for ever!—
The planks strained as tho' they must part asunder,
The masts bent as tho' they must dip under,
And the winds and the waves at length
Girt up their strength,
And the depths were laid bare,
And heaven flashed fire and volleyed thunder
Thro' the rain-choked air,
And sea and sky seemed to kiss
In the horror and the hiss
Of the whole world shuddering everywhere.

Lo! a Flyer swooping down
With wings to span the globe,
And splendour for his robe
And splendour for his crown.
He lighted on the helm with a foot of fire,
And spun the Monster overboard:
And that monstrous thing abhorred,
Gnashing with balked desire,

Wriggled like a worm infirm
Up the Worm
Of the loathly figurehead.
There he crouched and gnashed;
And his head re-horned, and gashed
From the other's grapple, dripped bloody red.

I saw that thing accurst
Wreak his worst
On the first and second crew:
Some with baited hook
He angled for and took,
Some dragged overboard in a net he threw,
Some he did to death
With hoof or horn or blasting breath.

I heard a voice of wailing
Where the ships went sailing,
A sorrowful voice prevailing
Above the sound of the sea,
Above the singers' voices,
And musical merry noises;
All songs had turned to sighing,
The light was failing,
The day was dying—
Ah me,
That such a sorrow should be!

There was sorrow on the sea and sorrow on the land
When Love ship went down by the bottomless quicksand
To its grave in the bitter wave.
There was sorrow on the sea and sorrow on the land
When Worm ship went to pieces on the rock-bound strand,
And the bitter wave was its grave.
But land and sea waxed hoary
In whiteness of a glory
Never told in story
Nor seen by mortal eye,
When the third ship crossed the bar
Where whirls and breakers are,
And steered into the splendours of the sky;
That third bark and that least
Which had never seemed to feast,
Yet kept high festival above sun and moon and star.

1878/9

*An Old-World Thicket**

*. . . 'Una selva oscura'**

DANTE

Awake or sleeping (for I know not which)
  I was or was not mazed within a wood
Where every mother-bird brought up her brood
  Safe in some leafy niche
Of oak or ash, of cypress or of beech,

Of silvery aspen trembling delicately,
  Of plane or warmer-tinted sycamore,
  Of elm that dies in secret from the core,
    Of ivy weak and free,
Of pines, of all green lofty things that be.

Such birds they seemed as challenged each desire;
  Like spots of azure heaven upon the wing,
  Like downy emeralds that alight and sing,
    Like actual coals on fire,
Like anything they seemed, and everything.

Such mirth they made, such warblings and such chat
  With tongue of music in a well-tuned beak,
  They seemed to speak more wisdom than we speak,
    To make our music flat
And all our subtlest reasonings wild or weak.

Their meat was nought but flowers like butterflies,
  With berries coral-coloured or like gold;
  Their drink was only dew, which blossoms hold
    Deep where the honey lies;
Their wings and tails were lit by sparkling eyes.

The shade wherein they revelled was a shade
  That danced and twinkled to the unseen sun;
  Branches and leaves cast shadows one by one,
    And all their shadows swayed
In breaths of air that rustled and that played.

A sound of waters neither rose nor sank,
  And spread a sense of freshness through the air;
  It seemed not here or there, but everywhere,
    As if the whole earth drank,
Root fathom deep and strawberry on its bank.

But I who saw such things as I have said,
  Was overdone with utter weariness;
  And walked in care, as one whom fears oppress
    Because above his head
Death hangs, or damage, or the dearth of bread.

Each sore defeat of my defeated life
  Faced and outfaced me in that bitter hour;
  And turned to yearning palsy all my power,
    And all my peace to strife,
Self stabbing self with keen lack-pity knife.

Sweetness of beauty moved me to despair,
  Stung me to anger by its mere content,
  Made me all lonely on that way I went,
    Piled care upon my care,
Brimmed full my cup, and stripped me empty and bare:

For all that was but showed what all was not,
  But gave clear proof of what might never be;
  Making more destitute my poverty,
    And yet more blank my lot,
  And me much sadder by its jubilee.*

Therefore I sat me down: for wherefore walk?
  And closed mine eyes: for wherefore see or hear?
  Alas, I had no shutter to mine ear,
    And could not shun the talk
  Of all rejoicing creatures far or near.

Without my will I hearkened and I heard
  (Asleep or waking, for I know not which),
  Till note by note the music changed its pitch;
    Bird ceased to answer bird,
And every wind sighed softly if it stirred.

The drip of widening waters seemed to weep,
  All fountains sobbed and gurgled as they sprang,
Somewhere a cataract cried out in its leap
    Sheer down a headlong steep;
  High over all cloud-thunders gave a clang.

Such universal sound of lamentation
  I heard and felt, fain not to feel or hear;
  Nought else there seemed but anguish far and near;

Nought else but all creation
Moaning and groaning wrung by pain or fear,*

Shuddering in the misery of its doom:
My heart then rose a rebel against light,
Scouring all earth and heaven and depth and height,
Ingathering wrath and gloom,
Ingathering wrath to wrath and night to night.

Ah me, the bitterness of such revolt,
All impotent, all hateful, and all hate,
That kicks and breaks itself against the bolt
Of an imprisoning fate,
And vainly shakes, and cannot shake the gate.

Agony to agony, deep called to deep,
Out of the deep I called of my desire;
My strength was weakness and my heart was fire;
Mine eyes that would not weep
Or sleep, scaled height and depth, and could not sleep;

The eyes, I mean, of my rebellious soul,
For still my bodily eyes were closed and dark:
A random thing I seemed without a mark,
Racing without a goal,
Adrift upon life's sea without an ark.*

More leaden than the actual self of lead
Outer and inner darkness weighed on me.
The tide of anger ebbed. Then fierce and free
Surged full above my head
The moaning tide of helpless misery.

Why should I breathe, whose breath was but a sigh?
Why should I live, who drew such painful breath?
Oh weary work, the unanswerable why!—
Yet I, why should I die,
Who had no hope in life, no hope in death?

Grasses and mosses and the fallen leaf
Make peaceful bed for an indefinite term;
But underneath the grass there gnaws a worm—
Haply,* there gnaws a grief—
Both, haply always; not, as now, so brief.

The pleasure I remember, it is past;
The pain I feel, is passing passing by;
Thus all the world is passing, and thus I:
All things that cannot last
Have grown familiar, and are born to die.

And being familiar, have so long been borne
That habit trains us not to break but bend:
Mourning grows natural to us who mourn
In foresight of an end,
But that which ends not who shall brave or mend?

Surely the ripe fruits tremble on their bough,
They cling and linger trembling till they drop:
I, trembling, cling to dying life; for how
Face the perpetual Now?
Birthless and deathless, void of start or stop,

Void of repentance, void of hope and fear,
Of possibility, alternative,
Of all that ever made us bear to live
From night to morning here,
Of promise even which has no gift to give.

The wood, and every creature of the wood,*
Seemed mourning with me in an undertone;
Soft scattered chirpings and a windy moan,
Trees rustling where they stood
And shivered, showed compassion for my mood.

Rage to despair; and now despair had turned
Back to self-pity and mere weariness,
With yearnings like a smouldering fire that burned,
And might grow more or less,
And might die out or wax to white excess.

Without, within me, music seemed to be;
Something not music, yet most musical,
Silence and sound in heavenly harmony;
At length a pattering fall
Of feet, a bell, and bleatings, broke through all.

Then I looked up. The wood lay in a glow
From golden sunset and from ruddy sky;
The sun had stooped to earth though once so high;

Had stooped to earth, in slow
Warm dying loveliness brought near and low.

Each water drop made answer to the light,
Lit up a spark and showed the sun his face;
Soft purple shadows paved the grassy space
And crept from height to height,
From height to loftier height crept up apace.

While opposite the sun a gazing moon
Put on his glory for her coronet,
Kindling her luminous coldness to its noon,
As his great splendour set;
One only star made up her train as yet.

Each twig was tipped with gold, each leaf was edged
And veined with gold from the gold-flooded west;
Each mother-bird, and mate-bird, and unfledged
Nestling, and curious nest,
Displayed a gilded moss or beak or breast.

And filing peacefully between the trees,
Having the moon behind them, and the sun
Full in their meek mild faces, walked at ease
A homeward flock, at peace
With one another and with every one.

A patriarchal ram with tinkling bell
Led all his kin; sometimes one browsing sheep
Hung back a moment, or one lamb would leap
And frolic in a dell;
Yet still they kept together, journeying well,

And bleating, one or other, many or few,
Journeying together toward the sunlit west;
Mild face by face, and woolly breast by breast,
Patient, sun-brightened too,
Still journeying toward the sunset and their rest.

1879

SONNET SEQUENCES

*'They desire a better country'**

I

I would not if I could undo my past,
  Tho' for its sake my future is a blank;
  My past for which I have myself to thank,
For all its faults and follies first and last.
I would not cast anew the lot once cast,
  Or launch a second ship for one that sank,
  Or drug with sweets the bitterness I drank,
Or break by feasting my perpetual fast.
I would not if I could: for much more dear
  Is one remembrance than a hundred joys,
    More than a thousand hopes in jubilee;
  Dearer the music of one tearful voice
    That unforgotten calls and calls to me,
'Follow me* here, rise up, and follow here.'

II

What seekest thou, far in the unknown land?
  In hope I follow joy gone on before;
  In hope and fear persistent more and more,
As the dry desert lengthens out its sand.
Whilst day and night I carry in my hand
  The golden key to ope the golden door
  Of golden home; yet mine eye weepeth sore,
For long the journey is that makes no stand.
And who is this that veiled doth walk with thee?
  Lo, this is Love that walketh at my right;
    One exile holds us both, and we are bound
  To selfsame home-joys in the land of light.
Weeping thou walkest with him; weepeth he?—
    Some sobbing weep, some weep and make no sound.

III

A dimness of a glory glimmers here
  Thro' veils and distance from the space remote,
  A faintest far vibration of a note
Reaches to us and seems to bring us near;
Causing our face to glow with braver cheer,
  Making the serried mist to stand afloat,
  Subduing languor with an antidote,
And strengthening love almost to cast out fear:
Till for one moment golden city walls
  Rise looming on us, golden walls of home,
Light of our eyes until the darkness falls;
  Then thro' the outer darkness burdensome
I hear again the tender voice that calls,
  'Follow me hither, follow, rise and come.'

c. 1867/8

*By Way of Remembrance**

Remember, if I claim too much of you,
  I claim it of my brother and my friend:
  Have patience with me till the hidden end,
Bitter or sweet, in mercy shut from view.
Pay me my due; though I to pay your due
  Am all too poor and past what will can mend:
  Thus of your bounty you must give and lend
Still unrepaid by aught I look to do.
Still unrepaid by aught of mine on earth:
  But overpaid, please God, when recompense
Beyond the mystic Jordan and new birth
  Is dealt to virtue as to innocence;
When Angels singing praises in their mirth
  Have borne you in their arms and fetched you hence.

Will you be there?* my yearning heart has cried:
  Ah me, my love, my love, shall I be there,
  To sit down in your glory and to share
Your gladness, glowing as a virgin bride?
Or will another dearer, fairer-eyed,
  Sit nigher to you in your jubilee;
  And mindful one of other will you be

Borne higher and higher on joy's ebbless tide?
—Yea, if I love I will not grudge you this:
I too shall float upon that heavenly sea
And sing my joyful praises without ache;
Your overflow of joy shall gladden me,
My whole heart shall sing praises for your sake
And find its own fulfilment in your bliss.

In resurrection is it awfuller
That rising of the All or of the Each:
Of all kins of all nations of all speech,
Or one by one of him and him and her?
When dust reanimate begins to stir
Here, there, beyond, beyond, reach beyond reach;
While every wave disgorges on its beach
Alive or dead-in-life some seafarer.
In resurrection, on the day of days,
That day of mourning throughout all the earth,
In resurrection may we meet again:
No more with stricken hearts to part in twain;
As once in sorrow one, now one in mirth,
One in our resurrection songs of praise.

I love you and you know it – this at least,
This comfort is mine own in all my pain:
You know it and can never doubt again,
And love's mere self is a continual feast.
Not oath of mine nor blessing-word of priest
Could make my love more certain or more plain:—
Life as a rolling moon doth wax and wane
O weary moon, still rounding, still decreased!
Life wanes: and when love folds his wings above
Tired joy, and less we feel his conscious pulse,
Let us go fall asleep, dear Friend, in peace:—
A little while, and age and sorrow cease;
A little while, the love reborn annuls
Loss and decay and death – and all is love.

1870

*The Thread of Life**

1

The irresponsive silence of the land,
  The irresponsive sounding of the sea,
  Speak both one message of one sense to me:—
Aloof, aloof, we stand aloof, so stand
Thou too aloof bound with the flawless band
  Of inner solitude; we bind not thee;
  But who from thy self-chain shall set thee free?
What heart shall touch thy heart? what hand thy hand?—
And I am sometimes proud and sometimes meek,
  And sometimes I remember days of old
When fellowship seemed not so far to seek
  And all the world and I seemed much less cold,
  And at the rainbow's foot lay surely gold,
And hope fell strong and life itself not weak.

2

Thus am I mine own prison. Everything
  Around me free and sunny and at ease:
  Or if in shadow, in a shade of trees
Which the sun kisses, where the gay birds sing
And where all winds make various murmuring;
  Where bees are found, with honey for the bees;
  Where sounds are music, and where silences
Are music of an unlike fashioning.
Then gaze I at the merrymaking crew,
  And smile a moment and a moment sigh
Thinking: Why can I not rejoice with you?
  But soon I put the foolish fancy by:
I am not what I have nor what I do;
  But what I was I am, I am even I.

3

Therefore myself is that one only thing
  I hold to use or waste, to keep or give;
  My sole possession every day I live,

And still mine own despite Time's winnowing.
Ever mine own, while moons and seasons bring
From crudeness ripeness mellow and sanative;
Ever mine own, till Death shall ply his sieve;
And still mine own, when saints break grave and sing.
And this myself as king unto my King
I give, to Him Who gave Himself for me;
Who gives Himself to me, and bids me sing
A sweet new song of His redeemed set free;
He bids me sing: O death, where is thy sting?
And sing: O grave, where is thy victory?

c. 1878/9

*Monna innominata**

A SONNET OF SONNETS

Beatrice, immortalized by 'altissimo poeta . . . cotanto amante';* Laura, celebrated by a great tho' an inferior bard, – * have alike paid the exceptional penalty of exceptional honour, and have come down to us resplendent with charms, but (at least, to my apprehension) scant of attractiveness.

These heroines of world-wide fame were preceded by a bevy of unnamed ladies 'donne innominate'* sung by a school of less conspicuous poets;* and in that land and that period* which gave simultaneous birth to Catholics, to Albigenses, and to Troubadours, one can imagine many a lady as sharing her lover's poetic aptitude, while the barrier between them might be one held sacred by both, yet not such as to render mutual love incompatible with mutual honour.

Had such a lady spoken for herself, the portrait left us might have appeared more tender, if less dignified, than any drawn even by a devoted friend. Or had the Great Poetess of our own day* and nation only been unhappy instead of happy, her circumstances would have invited her to bequeath to us, in lieu of the 'Portuguese Sonnets', an inimitable 'donna innominata' drawn not from fancy but from feeling, and worthy to occupy a niche beside Beatrice and Laura.

1

*'Lo dì che han detto a' dolci amici addio.'**

DANTE

*'Amor, con quanto sforzo oggi mi vinci!'!'**

PETRARCA

Come back to me, who wait and watch for you:—
  Or come not yet, for it is over then,
  And long it is before you come again,
So far between my pleasures are and few.
While, when you come not, what I do I do
  Thinking 'Now when he comes,' my sweetest 'when:'
  For one man is my world of all the men
This wide world holds; O love, my world is you.
Howbeit, to meet you grows almost a pang
  Because the pang of parting comes so soon;
My hope hangs waning, waxing, like a moon
  Between the heavenly days on which we meet:
Ah me, but where are now the songs I sang
  When life was sweet because you called them sweet?

2

*'Era già l'ora che volge il desio.'**

DANTE

*'Ricorro al tempo ch'io vi vidi prima.'**

PETRARCA

I wish I could remember that first day,
  First hour, first moment of your meeting me,
  If bright or dim the season, it might be
Summer or Winter for aught I can say;
So unrecorded did it slip away,
  So blind was I to see and to foresee,
  So dull to mark the budding of my tree
That would not blossom yet for many a May.
If only I could recollect it, such
  A day of days! I let it come and go
  As traceless as a thaw of bygone snow;
It seemed to mean so little, meant so much;
If only now I could recall that touch,
  First touch of hand in hand – Did one but know!

3

*'O ombre vane, fuor che ne l'aspetto!'**

DANTE

*'Immaginata guida la conduce.'**

PETRARCA

I dream of you to wake: would that I might
  Dream of you and not wake but slumber on;
  Nor find with dreams the dear companion gone,
As Summer ended Summer birds take flight.
In happy dreams I hold you full in sight,
  I blush again who waking look so wan;
  Brighter than sunniest day that ever shone,
In happy dreams your smile makes day of night.
Thus only in a dream we are at one,
  Thus only in a dream we give and take
    The faith that maketh rich who take or give;
  If thus to sleep is sweeter than to wake,
    To die were surely sweeter than to live,
Tho' there be nothing new beneath the sun.

4

*'Poca favilla gran fiamma seconda.'**

DANTE

'Ogni altra cosa, ogni pensier va fore,
*E sol ivi con voi rimansi amore.'**

PETRARCA

I loved you first: but afterwards your love
  Outsoaring mine, sang such a loftier song
As drowned the friendly cooings of my dove.
  Which owes the other most? my love was long,
  And yours one moment seemed to wax more strong;
I loved and guessed at you, you construed me
And loved me for what might or might not be—
  Nay, weights and measures do us both a wrong.
For verily love knows not 'mine' or 'thine;'
  With separate 'I' and 'thou' free love has done,
    For one is both and both are one in love:
Rich love knows nought of 'thine that is not mine;'

Both have the strength and both the length thereof,
Both of us, of the love which makes us one.

5

*'Amor che a nulla amato amar perdona.'**
DANTE

*'Amor m'addusse in sì gioiosa spene.'**
PETRARCA

O my heart's heart, and you who are to me
More than myself myself, God be with you,
Keep you in strong obedience leal* and true
To Him whose noble service setteth free,
Give you all good we see or can foresee,
Make your joys many and your sorrows few,
Bless you in what you hear and what you do,
Yea, perfect you as He would have you be,
So much for you; but what for me, dear friend?
To love you without stint and all I can
Today, tomorrow, world without an end;
To love you much and yet to love you more,
As Jordan at his flood sweeps either shore;
Since woman is the helpmeet made for man.

6

'Or puoi la quantitate
*Comprender de l'amor che a te mi scalda.'**
DANTE

*'Non vo'che da tal nodo amor mi sciolglia.'**
PETRARCA

Trust me, I have not earned your dear rebuke,
I love, as you would have me, God the most;
Would lose not Him, but you, must one be lost,
Nor with Lot's wife* cast back a faithless look
Unready to forego what I forsook;
This say I, having counted up the cost,
This, tho' I be the feeblest of God's host,
The sorriest sheep Christ shepherds with His crook.

Yet while I love my God the most, I deem
  That I can never love you overmuch;
    I love Him more, so let me love you too;
  Yea, as I apprehend it, love is such
I cannot love you if I love not Him,
    I cannot love Him if I love not you.

7

*'Qui primavera sempre ed ogni frutto.'**

DANTE

*'Ragionando con meco ed io con lui.'**

PETRARCA

'Love me, for I love you' – and answer me,
  'Love me, for I love you' – so shall we stand
  As happy equals in the flowering land
Of love, that knows not a dividing sea.
Love builds the house on rock and not on sand,
  Love laughs what while the winds rave desperately;
And who hath found love's citadel unmanned?
  And who hath held in bonds love's liberty?
My heart's a coward tho' my words are brave—
  We meet so seldom, yet we surely part
  So often; there's a problem for your art!
    Still I find comfort in his Book, who saith,
Tho' jealousy be cruel as the grave,
    And death be strong, yet love is strong as death.

8

*'Come dicesse a Dio: D'altro non calme.'**

DANTE

*'Spero trovar pietà non che perdono.'**

PETRARCA

'I, if I perish, perish' – Esther spake:
  And bride of life or death she made her fair
  In all the lustre of her perfumed hair
And smiles that kindle longing but to slake.
She put on pomp of loveliness, to take
  Her husband thro' his eyes at unaware;

She spread abroad her beauty for a snare,
Harmless as doves and subtle as a snake.
She trapped him with one mesh of silken hair,
She vanquished him by wisdom of her wit,
And built her people's house that it should stand:—
If I might take my life so in my hand,
And for my love to Love put up my prayer,
And for love's sake by Love be granted it!

9

'*O dignitosa coscienza e netta!*'*

DANTE

'*Spirto più acceso di virtuti ardenti.*'*

PETRARCA

Thinking of you, and all that was, and all
That might have been and now can never be,
I feel your honoured excellence, and see
Myself unworthy of the happier call:
For woe is me who walk so apt to fall,
So apt to shrink afraid, so apt to flee,
Apt to lie down and die (ah, woe is me!)
Faithless and hopeless turning to the wall.
And yet not hopeless quite nor faithless quite,
Because not loveless; love may toil all night,
But take at morning; wrestle till the break
Of day, but then wield power with God and man: —
So take I heart of grace as best I can,
Ready to spend and be spent for your sake.

10

'*Con miglior corso e con migliore stella.*'*

DANTE

'*La vita fugge e non s'arresta un' ora.*'*

PETRARCA

Time flies, hope flags, life plies a wearied wing;
Death following hard on life gains ground apace;
Faith runs with each and rears an eager face,
Outruns the rest, makes light of everything,

Spurns earth, and still finds breath to pray and sing;
While love ahead of all uplifts his praise,
Still asks for grace and still gives thanks for grace,
Content with all day brings and night will bring.
Life wanes; and when love folds his wings above
Tired hope, and less we feel his conscious pulse,
Let us go fall asleep, dear friend, in peace:
A little while, and age and sorrow cease;
A little while, and life reborn annuls
Loss and decay and death, and all is love.

11

'*Vien dietro a me e lascia dir le genti.*'*
DANTE

'*Contando i casi della vita nostra.*'*
PETRARCA

Many in aftertimes will say of you
'He loved her' – while of me what will they say?
Not that I loved you more than just in play,
For fashion's sake as idle women do.
Even let them prate; who know not what we knew
Of love and parting in exceeding pain,
Of parting hopeless here to meet again,
Hopeless on earth, and heaven is out of view.
But by my heart of love laid bare to you,
My love that you can make not void nor vain,
Love that foregoes you but to claim anew
Beyond this passage of the gate of death,
I charge you at the Judgment make it plain
My love of you was life and not a breath.

12

'*Amor, che ne la mente mi ragiona.*'*
DANTE

'*Amor vien nel bel viso di costei.*'*
PETRARCA

If there be any one can take my place
And make you happy whom I grieve to grieve,
Think not that I can grudge it, but believe

I do commend you to that nobler grace,
That readier wit than mine, that sweeter face;
Yea, since your riches made me rich, conceive
I too am crowned, while bridal crowns I weave,
And thread the bridal dance with jocund pace.
For if I did not love you, it might be
That I should grudge you some one dear delight;
But since the heart is yours that was mine own,
Your pleasure is my pleasure, right my right,
Your honourable freedom makes me free,
And you companioned I am not alone.

13

*'E drizzeremo glí occhi al Primo Amore.'**

DANTE

*'Ma trovo peso non de la mie braccia.'**

PETRARCA

If I could trust mine own self with your fate,
Shall I not rather trust it in God's hand?
Without Whose Will one lily doth not stand,
Nor sparrow fall at his appointed date;
Who numbereth the innumerable sand,
Who weighs the wind and water with a weight,
To Whom the world is neither small nor great,
Whose knowledge foreknew every plan we planned.
Searching my heart for all that touches you,
I find there only love and love's goodwill
Helpless to help and impotent to do,
Of understanding dull, of sight most dim;
And therefore I commend you back to Him
Whose love your love's capacity can fill.

14

*'E la Sua Volontade è nostra pace.'**

DANTE

*'Sol con questi pensier, con altre chiome.'**

PETRARCA

Youth gone, and beauty gone if ever there
Dwelt beauty in so poor a face as this;

Youth gone and beauty, what remains of bliss?
I will not bind fresh roses in my hair,
To shame a cheek at best but little fair,—
Leave youth his roses, who can bear a thorn,—
I will not seek for blossoms anywhere,
Except such common flowers as blow with corn.
Youth gone and beauty gone, what doth remain?
The longing of a heart pent up forlorn,
A silent heart whose silence loves and longs;
The silence of a heart which sang its songs
While youth and beauty made a summer morn,
Silence of love that cannot sing again.

1880

*Later Life: A Double Sonnet of Sonnets**

1

Before the mountains were brought forth, before
Earth and the world were made, then God was God:
And God will still be God, when flames shall roar
Round earth and heaven dissolving at His nod:
And this God is our God, even while His rod
Of righteous wrath falls on us smiting sore:
And this God is our God for evermore
Thro' life, thro' death, while clod returns to clod.
For tho' He slay us we will trust in Him;
We will flock home to Him by divers ways:
Yea, tho' He slay us we will vaunt His praise,
Serving and loving with the Cherubim,
Watching and loving with the Seraphim,
Our very selves His praise thro' endless days.

2

Rend hearts and rend not garments for our sins;
Gird sackcloth not on body but on soul;
Grovel in dust with faces toward the goal
Nor won, nor neared; he only laughs who wins.
Not neared the goal, the race too late begins;
All left undone, we have yet to do the whole;

The sun is hurrying west and toward the pole
Where darkness waits for earth with all her kins.
Let us today while it is called today
Set out, if utmost speed may yet avail—
The shadows lengthen and the light grows pale:
For who thro' darkness and the shadow of death,
Darkness that may be felt, shall find a way,
Blind-eyed, deaf-eared, and choked with failing breath?

3

Thou Who didst make and knowest whereof we are made,
Oh bear in mind our dust and nothingness,
Our wordless tearless dumbness of distress;
Bear Thou in mind the burden Thou hast laid
Upon us, and our feebleness unstayed
Except Thou stay us: for the long long race
Which stretches far and far before our face
Thou knowest, – remember Thou whereof we are made.
If making makes us Thine then Thine we are,
And if redemption we are twice Thine own:
If once Thou didst come down from heaven afar
To seek us and to find us, how not save?
Comfort us, save us, leave us not alone,
Thou Who didst die our death and fill our grave.

4

So tired am I, so weary of today,
So unrefreshed from foregone weariness,
So overburdened by foreseen distress,
So lagging and so stumbling on my way,
I scarce can rouse myself to watch or pray,
To hope, or aim, or toil for more or less,—
Ah, always less and less, even while I press
Forward and toil and aim as best I may.
Half-starved of soul and heartsick utterly,
Yet lift I up my heart and soul and eyes
(Which fail in looking upward) toward the prize:
Me, Lord, Thou seest tho' I see not Thee;
Me now, as once the Thief in Paradise,*
Even me, O Lord my Lord, remember me.

5

Lord, Thou Thyself art Love and only Thou;
  Yet I who am not love would fain love Thee;
  But Thou alone being Love canst furnish me
With that same love my heart is craving now.
Allow my plea! for if Thou disallow,
  No second fountain can I find but Thee;
  No second hope or help is left to me,
No second anything, but only Thou.
O Love accept, according my request;
  O Love exhaust, fulfilling my desire;
  Uphold me with the strength that cannot tire,
Nerve me to labour till Thou bid me rest,
  Kindle my fire from Thine unkindled fire,
And charm the willing heart from out my breast.

6

We lack, yet cannot fix upon the lack:
  Not this, nor that; yet somewhat, certainly.
  We see the thing we do not yearn to see
Around us: and what see we glancing back?
Lost hopes that leave our hearts upon the rack,
  Hopes that were never ours yet seemed to be,
  For which we steered on life's salt stormy sea
Braving the sunstroke and the frozen pack.
If thus to look behind is all in vain,
  And all in vain to look to left or right,
Why face we not our future once again,
Launching with hardier hearts across the main,
  Straining dim eyes to catch the invisible sight,
And strong to bear ourselves in patient pain?

7

To love and to remember; that is good:
  To love and to forget; that is not well:
  To lapse from love to hatred; that is hell
And death and torment, rightly understood.
Soul dazed by love and sorrow, cheer thy mood;
  More blest art thou than mortal tongue can tell:
  Ring not thy funeral but thy marriage bell,

And salt with hope thy life's insipid food.
Love is the goal, love is the way we wend,
  Love is our parallel unending line
    Whose only perfect Parallel is Christ,
Beginning not begun, End without end:
    For He Who hath the Heart of God sufficed,
  Can satisfy all hearts, – yea, thine and mine.

8

We feel and see with different hearts and eyes:—
  Ah Christ, if all our hearts could meet in Thee
  How well it were for them and well for me,
Our hearts Thy dear accepted sacrifice.
Thou, only Life of hearts and Light of eyes,
  Our life, our light, if once we turn to Thee,
  So be it, O Lord, to them and so to me;
Be all alike Thine own dear sacrifice.
Thou Who by death hast ransomed us from death,
  Thyself God's sole well-pleasing Sacrifice,
    Thine only sacred Self I plead with Thee:
    Make Thou it well for them and well for me
That Thou hast given us souls and wills and breath,
  And hearts to love Thee, and to see Thee eyes.

9

Star Sirius and the Pole Star dwell afar
  Beyond the drawings each of other's strength:
  One blazes thro' the brief bright summer's length
Lavishing life-heat from a flaming car;
  While one unchangeable upon a throne
  Broods o'er the frozen heart of earth alone,
Content to reign the bright particular star
  Of some who wander or of some who groan.
They own no drawings each of other's strength,
  Nor vibrate in a visible sympathy,
    Nor veer along their courses each toward each:
  Yet are their orbits pitched in harmony
Of one dear heaven, across whose depth and length
    Mayhap they talk together without speech.

10

Tread softly! all the earth is holy ground.
  It may be, could we look with seeing eyes,
  This spot we stand on is a Paradise
Where dead have come to life and lost been found,
Where Faith has triumphed, Martyrdom been crowned,
  Where fools have foiled the wisdom of the wise;
  From this same spot the dust of saints may rise,
And the King's prisoners come to light unbound.
O earth, earth, earth, hear thou thy Maker's Word:
  'Thy dead thou shalt give up, nor hide thy slain'—
  Some who went weeping forth shall come again
  Rejoicing from the east or from the west,
As doves fly to their windows, love's own bird
  Contented and desirous to the nest.[1]

11

Lifelong our stumbles, lifelong our regret,
  Lifelong our efforts failing and renewed,
  While lifelong is our witness, 'God is good:'
Who bore with us till now, bears with us yet,
Who still remembers and will not forget,
  Who gives us light and warmth and daily food;
  And gracious promises half understood,
And glories half unveiled, whereupon to set
Our heart of hearts and eyes of our desire;
  Uplifting us to longing and to love,
Luring us upward from this world of mire,
  Urging us to press on and mount above
  Ourselves and all we have had experience of,
Mounting to Him in love's perpetual fire.

12

A dream there is wherein we are fain to scream,
  While struggling with ourselves we cannot speak:

[1] 'Quali colombe dal disio chiamate
Con l'ali aperte e ferme al dolce nido
Volan per l'aer dal voler portate.'
DANTE

And much of all our waking life, as weak
And misconceived, eludes us like the dream.
For half life's seemings are not what they seem,
And vain the laughs we laugh, the shrieks we shriek;
Yea, all is vain that mars the settled meek
Contented quiet of our daily theme.
When I was young I deemed that sweets are sweet:
But now I deem some searching bitters are
Sweeter than sweets, and more refreshing far,
And to be relished more, and more desired,
And more to be pursued on eager feet,
On feet untired, and still on feet tho' tired.

13

Shame is a shadow cast by sin: yet shame
Itself may be a glory and a grace,
Refashioning the sin-disfashioned face;
A nobler bruit* than hollow-sounded fame,
A new-lit lustre on a tarnished name,
One virtue pent within an evil place,
Strength for the fight, and swiftness for the race,
A stinging salve, a life-requickening flame.
A salve so searching we may scarcely live,
A flame so fierce it seems that we must die,
An actual cautery* thrust into the heart:
Nevertheless, men die not of such smart;
And shame gives back what nothing else can give,
Man to himself, – then sets him up on high.

14

When Adam and when Eve left Paradise
Did they love on and cling together still,
Forgiving one another all that ill
The twain had wrought on such a different wise?
She propped upon his strength, and he in guise
Of lover tho' of lord, girt to fulfil
Their term of life and die when God should will;
Lie down and sleep, and having slept arise.
Boast not against us, O our enemy!
Today we fall, but we shall rise again;

We grope today, tomorrow we shall see:
What is today that we should fear today?
A morrow cometh which shall sweep away
Thee and thy realm of change and death and pain.

15

Let woman fear to teach and bear to learn,
Remembering the first woman's first mistake.
Eve had for pupil the inquiring snake,
Whose doubts she answered on a great concern;
But he the tables so contrived to turn,
It next was his to give and her's to take;
Till man deemed poison sweet for her sweet sake,
And fired a train by which the world must burn.
Did Adam love his Eve from first to last?
I think so; as we love who works us ill,
And wounds us to the quick, yet loves us still.
Love pardons the unpardonable past:
Love in a dominant embrace holds fast
His frailer self, and saves without her will.

16

Our teachers teach that one and one make two:
Later, Love rules that one and one make one:
Abstruse the problems! neither need we shun,
But skilfully to each should yield its due.
The narrower total seems to suit the few,
The wider total suits the common run;
Each obvious in its sphere like moon or sun;
Both provable by me, and both by you.
Befogged and witless, in a wordy maze
A groping stroll perhaps may do us good;
If cloyed we are with much we have understood,
If tired of half our dusty world and ways,
If sick of fasting, and if sick of food;—
And how about these long still-lengthening days?

17

Something this foggy day, a something which
  Is neither of this fog nor of today,
  Has set me dreaming of the winds that play
Past certain cliffs, along one certain beach,
  And turn the topmost edge of waves to spray:
  Ah pleasant pebbly strand so far away,
So out of reach while quite within my reach,
  As out of reach as India or Cathay!
I am sick of where I am and where I am not,
  I am sick of foresight and of memory,
  I am sick of all I have and all I see,
    I am sick of self, and there is nothing new;
Oh weary impatient patience of my lot!—
    Thus with myself: how fares it, Friends, with you?

18

So late in Autumn half the world's asleep,
  And half the wakeful world looks pinched and pale;
  For dampness now, not freshness, rides the gale;
And cold and colourless comes ashore the deep
With tides that bluster or with tides that creep;
  Now veiled uncouthness wears an uncouth veil
  Of fog, not sultry haze; the blight and bale
Have done their worst, and leaves rot on the heap.
So late in Autumn one forgets the Spring,
  Forgets the Summer with its opulence,
The callow birds that long have found a wing,
  The swallows that more lately gat them hence:
Will anything like Spring, will anything
  Like Summer, rouse one day the slumbering sense?

19

Here now is Winter, Winter, after all,
  Is not so drear as was my boding dream
  While Autumn gleamed its latest watery gleam
On sapless leafage too inert to fall.
Still leaves and berries clothe my garden wall
  Where ivy thrives on scantiest sunny beam;
  Still here a bud and there a blossom seem

Hopeful, and robin still is musical.
Leaves, flowers and fruit and one delightful song
  Remain; these days are short, but now the nights
  Intense and long, hang out their utmost lights;
Such starry nights are long, yet not too long;
Frost nips the weak, while strengthening still the strong
  Against that day when Spring sets all to rights.

20

A hundred thousand birds salute the day:—
  One solitary bird* salutes the night:
Its mellow grieving wiles our grief away,
  And tunes our weary watches to delight;
It seems to sing the thoughts we cannot say,
  To know and sing them, and to set them right;
Until we feel once more that May is May,
  And hope some buds may bloom without a blight.
This solitary bird outweighs, outvies,
  The hundred thousand merry-making birds
Whose innocent warblings yet might make us wise
Would we but follow when they bid us rise,
  Would we but set their notes of praise to words
And launch our hearts up with them to the skies.

21*

A host of things I take on trust: I take
  The nightingales on trust, for few and far
  Between those actual summer moments are
When I have heard what melody they make.
So chanced it once at Como on the Lake:
  But all things, then, waxed musical; each star
  Sang on its course, each breeze sang on its car,
All harmonies sang to senses wide awake.
All things in tune, myself not out of tune,
  Those nightingales were nightingales indeed:
  Yet truly an owl had satisfied my need,
And wrought a rapture underneath that moon,
  Or simple sparrow chirping from a reed;
For June that night glowed like a doubled June.

22*

The mountains in their overwhelming might
   Moved me to sadness when I saw them first,
And afterwards they moved me to delight;
   Struck harmonies from silent chords which burst
   Out into song, a song by memory nursed;
For ever unrenewed by touch or sight
Sleeps the keen magic of each day or night,
   In pleasure and in wonder then immersed.
All Switzerland behind us on the ascent,
All Italy before us we plunged down
   St Gothard, garden of forget-me-not:
   Yet why should such a flower choose such a spot?
Could we forget that way which once we went
   Tho' not one flower had bloomed to weave its crown?

23

Beyond the seas we know, stretch seas unknown
   Blue and bright-coloured for our dim and green;
   Beyond the lands we see, stretch lands unseen
With many-tinted tangle overgrown;
And icebound seas there are like seas of stone,
   Serenely stormless as death lies serene;
   And lifeless tracts of sand, which intervene
Betwixt the lands where living flowers are blown.
This dead and living world befits our case
   Who live and die: we live in wearied hope,
We die in hope not dead; we run a race
Today, and find no present halting-place;
   All things we see lie far within our scope,
And still we peer beyond with craving face.

24

The wise do send their hearts before them to
   Dear blessed Heaven, despite the veil between;
   The foolish nurse their hearts within the screen
Of this familiar world, where all we do
Or have is old, for there is nothing new:
   Yet elder far that world we have not seen;
   God's Presence antedates what else hath been:

Many the foolish seem, the wise seem few.
Oh foolish fond folly of a heart
  Divided, neither here nor there at rest!
    That hankers after Heaven, but clings to earth;
    That neither here nor there knows thorough mirth,
Half-choosing, wholly missing, the good part:—
  Oh fool among the foolish, in thy quest.

25

When we consider what this life we lead
  Is not, and is: how full of toil and pain,
  How blank of rest and of substantial gain,
Beset by hunger earth can never feed,
And propping half our hearts upon a reed;
  We cease to mourn lost treasures, mourned in vain,
  Lost treasures we are fain and yet not fain
To fetch back for a solace of our need.
For who that feel this burden and this strain,
  This wide vacuity of hope and heart,
Would bring their cherished well-beloved again:
  To bleed with them and wince beneath the smart,
To have with stinted bliss such lavish bane,
  To hold in lieu of all so poor a part?

26

This Life is full of numbness and of balk,
  Of haltingness and baffled short-coming,
  Of promise unfulfilled, of everything
That is puffed vanity and empty talk:
Its very bud hangs cankered on the stalk,
  Its very song-bird trails a broken wing,
  Its very Spring is not indeed like Spring,
But sighs like Autumn round an aimless walk.
This Life we live is dead for all its breath;
  Death's self it is, set off on pilgrimage,
  Travelling with tottering steps the first short stage:
    The second stage is one mere desert dust
    Where Death sits veiled amid creation's rust:—
Unveil thy face, O Death who art not Death.

27

I have dreamed of Death: – what will it be to die
  Not in a dream, but in the literal truth
  With all Death's adjuncts ghastly and uncouth,
The pang that is the last and the last sigh?
Too dulled, it may be, for a last good-bye,
  Too comfortless for any one to soothe,
  A helpless charmless spectacle of ruth
Thro' long last hours, so long while yet they fly.
So long to those who hopeless in their fear
  Watch the slow breath and look for what they dread:
While I supine with ears that cease to hear,
    With eyes that glaze, with heart pulse running down
  (Alas! no saint rejoicing on her bed),
    May miss the goal at last, may miss a crown.

28

In life our absent friend is far away:
  But death may bring our friend exceeding near,
  Show him familiar faces long so dear
And lead him back in reach of words we say.
He only cannot utter yea or nay
  In any voice accustomed to our ear;
  He only cannot make his face appear
And turn the sun back on our shadowed day.
The dead may be around us, dear and dead;
  The unforgotten dearest dead may be
    Watching us with unslumbering eyes and heart;
Brimful of words which cannot yet be said,
    Brimful of knowledge they may not impart,
  Brimful of love for you and love for me.

1880

SELECTED FICTION

SELECTED FICTION

Christina Rossetti wrote short fiction at intervals from the late 1840s to the early 1880s, and sought to publish it. Apart from *Maude* none of her stories has ever been reprinted, and this selection includes all except those with a specifically doctrinal purpose, which she herself originally proposed omitting from her single collection, *Commonplace and Other Short Stories*, issued in 1870.

Sadly, *Folio Q, Case* 2, which William Rossetti described as the best tale she ever wrote, is also missing, because it is unavailable. Having submitted it unsuccessfully to *Blackwood's* and the *Cornhill* (where it sounds as if it would have been excellent company for Elizabeth Gaskell's tales of the unexpected) in 1860, Christina burnt it, having been told – probably by a critic and possibly by *Blackwood's* – that it touched on a 'dangerous moral question', of unidentified nature. All we know is that *Folio Q, Case* 2 concerned a man whose doom it was to have no reflection. Clearly a supernatural, Gothick tale, it joins the lost masterpieces of literature.

The extant stories range in style from satire to piety by way of fairy-tale and allegory. They were written for adults, children and teenagers, and vary in length from 2,000 to 20,000 words. Hans Christian Andersen, Maria Edgeworth, Lewis Carroll and Jane Austen are among the influences. Each story is here prefaced by a brief introduction, and particular words or phrases are elucidated in the Notes.

Maude: A Story for Girls

This is Christina Rossetti's earliest story, composed in 1849–50 and drawing on her own experience as a shy and awkward but also ambitious adolescent. Like her heroine, the author had seen her verses 'handed about and admired' with the printing of Verses *in 1847, prompting enquiries as to what made the poems 'so broken-hearted, as was mostly the case'. Like Maude, too, Christina Rossetti had been caught up in a wave of youthful religious fervour such as that which sweeps 'Sister Magdalen' into becoming a nun. Later, Christina confessed to having 'like many young people' felt a vague impulse towards 'the convent threshold', but it was in truth her sister Maria who was most inspired by the religious life.*

Maude *is thus a* künstlerroman *or portrait of the artist as a young woman. It also indirectly reflects Christina Rossetti's adolescent breakdown, when she felt obscurely unworthy of receiving communion. As her brother remarked when editing this three-part tale for publication, the worst thing Maude appears to have done 'is that, when she had written a good poem, she felt it to be good' – thereby transgressing the bounds of proper feminine modesty, perhaps, but hardly sufficient to cause such a spiritual crisis. But youthful anguish is not so simply explained or assuaged, and Maude's painful, illogical, foolish feelings are authentically rendered here – and indeed simultaneously mocked for their affectation. We may note that she does not remove the 'surreptitious sprig of bay' Cousin Agnes introduces into her garland, and though there is no satisfactory ending to her story except an improbable traffic accident, it must be conceded that the best romantic heroines characteristically expire in melodramatic manner. At a deeper level, the conflict Maude experiences between her desire to be a good Christian (like Magdalen), a good wife (like cousin Mary) and a good poet (like Maude) is one that can only be resolved by death.*

The bouts-rimés *game that Maude makes the others play was a favourite pursuit of Christina and her brothers during 1848–9; some examples are included in the selection of* Poems. *The productions in* Maude *poke fun at the element of pretentiousness in this, for though Maude's spiteful sonnet about hideous old ladies fit to drown is judged the winner, Sister Magdalen's poem is clearly the best. Self-reflexive satire and irony are densely layered in this curious tale.*

As befitted such a youthful effort, Christina made only a half-hearted attempt to publish Maude, especially after it was criticised by the Marchioness of Bath, Aunt Charlotte's employer, who objected to the 'commonplaces' of its conversation. But she did not destroy the manuscript, and with a brief introduction William issued the story in 1887, after his sister's death.

PART FIRST

I

'A penny for your thoughts,' said Mrs Foster one bright July morning as she entered the sitting-room with a bunch of roses in her hand, and an open letter: 'A penny for your thoughts,' said she, addressing her daughter, who, surrounded by a chaos of stationery, was slipping out of sight some scrawled paper. This observation remaining unanswered, the mother, only too much accustomed to inattention, continued: 'Here is a note from your Aunt Letty; she wants us to go and pass a few days with them. You know Tuesday is Mary's birthday, so they mean to have some young people and cannot dispense with your company.'

'Do you think of going?' said Maude at last, having locked her writing-book.

'Yes, dear: even a short stay in the country may do you good, you have looked so pale lately. Don't you feel quite well? Tell me.'

'Oh yes; there is not much the matter, only I am tired and have a headache. Indeed, there is nothing at all the matter; besides, the country may work wonders.'

Half-satisfied, half-uneasy, Mrs Foster asked a few more questions, to have them all answered in the same style; vain questions, put to one who, without telling lies, was determined not to tell the truth.

When once more alone, Maude resumed the occupations which her mother's entrance had interrupted. Her writing-book was neither commonplace-book, album,* scrap-book, nor diary; it was a compound of all these, and contained original compositions not intended for the public eye, pet extracts, extraordinary little sketches, and occasional tracts of journal. This choice collection she now proceeded to enrich with the following sonnet:—

Yes, I too could face death and never shrink:
But it is harder to bear hated life;
To strive with hands and knees weary of strife;
To drag the heavy chains whose every link
Galls to the bone; to stand upon the brink
Of the deep grave, nor drowse, though it be rife
With sleep; to hold with steady hand the knife
Nor strike home: this is courage as I think.
Surely to suffer is more than to do:
To do is quickly done; to suffer is
Longer and fuller of heart-sicknesses:

Each day's experience testifies of this:
Good deeds are many, but good lives are few;
Thousands taste the full cup; who drains the lees?

having done which she yawned, leaned back in her chair, and wondered how she should fill up the time till dinner.

Maude Foster was just fifteen. Small though not positively short, she might easily be overlooked but would not easily be forgotten. Her figure was slight and well-made, but appeared almost high-shouldered through a habitual shrugging stoop. Her features were regular and pleasing; as a child she had been very pretty; and might have continued so but for a fixed paleness, and an expression, not exactly of pain, but languid and preoccupied to a painful degree. Yet even now, if at any time she became thoroughly aroused and interested, her sleepy eyes would light up with wonderful brilliancy, her cheeks glow with warm colour, her manner become animated, and drawing herself up to her full height she would look more beautiful than ever she did as a child. So Mrs Foster said, and so unhappily Maude knew. She also knew that people thought her clever, and that her little copies of verses were handed about and admired. Touching these same verses, it was the amazement of everyone what could make her poetry so broken-hearted as was mostly the case. Some pronounced that she wrote very foolishly about things she could not possibly understand; some wondered if she really had any secret source of uneasiness; while some simply set her down as affected. Perhaps there was a degree of truth in all these opinions. But I have said enough; the following pages will enable my readers to form their own estimate of Maude's character.

Meanwhile let me transport them to another sitting-room; but this time it will be in the country with a delightful garden look-out.

Mary Clifton was arranging her mother's special nosegay when that lady entered.

'Here, my dear, I will finish doing the flowers. It is time for you to go to meet your aunt and cousin; indeed, if you do not make haste, you will be too late.'

'Thank you, mamma; the flowers are nearly done;' and Mary ran out of the room.

Before long she and her sister were hurrying beneath a burning sun towards the railway station. Through having delayed their start to the very last moment, neither had found time to lay hands on a parasol; but this was little heeded by two healthy girls, full of life and spirits, and longing, moreover, to spy out their friends. Mary wanted one day of fifteen; Agnes was almost a year older: both were well-grown and well-made, with fair hair, blue eyes, and fresh complexions. So far they were alike: what differences existed in other respects remain to be seen.

'How do you do, aunt? How do you do, Maude?' cried Mary, making a sudden dart forward as she discovered our friends, who, having left the station, had already made some progress along the dusty road. Then relinquishing her aunt to Agnes, she seized upon her cousin, and was soon deep in the description of all the pleasures planned for the auspicious morrow.

'We are to do what we like in the morning: I mean, nothing particular is arranged; so I shall initiate you into all the mysteries of the place; all the cats, dogs, rabbits, pigeons, etc.; above all, I must introduce you to a pig, a special *protégé* of mine: that is, if you are inclined, for you look wretchedly pale, aren't you well, dear?'

'Oh yes, quite well, and you must show me everything. But what are we to do afterwards?'

'Oh! afterwards we are to be intensely grand. All our young friends are coming, and we are to play at round games (you were always clever at round games), and I expect to have great fun. Besides, I have stipulated for unlimited strawberries and cream; also sundry tarts are in course of preparation. By the way, I count on your introducing some new game among us benighted rustics; you who come from dissipated London.'

'I fear I know nothing new, but will do my best. At any rate, I can preside at your toilet, and assist in making you irresistible.'

Mary coloured and laughed; then thought no more of the pretty speech, which sounded as if carefully prepared by her polite cousin. The two made a strong contrast: one was occupied by a thousand shifting thoughts of herself, her friends, her plans, what she must do, and what she would do; the other, whatever might employ her tongue, and to a certain extent her mind, had always an undercurrent of thought intent upon herself.

Arrived at the house, greetings were duly and cordially performed; also an introduction to a new and very fat baby, who received Maude's advances with a howl of intense dismay. The first day of a visit is often no very lively affair: so perhaps all parties heard the clock announce bed-time without much regret.

II

The young people were assembled in Mary's room, deep in the mysteries of the toilet.

'Here is your wreath, Maude; you must wear it for my sake, and forgive a surreptitious sprig of bay* which I have introduced,' said Agnes, adjusting the last white rose, and looking affectionately at her sister and cousin.

Maude was arranging Mary's long fair hair with good-natured anxiety to display it to the utmost advantage.

'One more spray of fuchsia; I was always sure fuchsia would make a beautiful head-dress. There, now you are perfection; only look; look, Agnes. Oh, I beg your pardon; thank you; my wreath is very nice, only I have not earned the bay.' She still did not remove it; and when placed on her dark hair it well became the really intellectual character of her face. Her dress was entirely white; simple, fresh, and elegant. Neither she nor Agnes would wear ornaments, but left them to Mary, in whose honour the entertainment was given, and who in all other respects was arrayed like her sister.

In the drawing-room Mary proceeded to set in order the presents received that morning – a handsomely bound Bible from her father, and a small prayer-book with cross and clasp from her mother; a bracelet of Maude's hair from her aunt; a cornelian heart from Agnes; and a pocket *bonbonnière** from her cousin, besides pretty trifles from her little brothers. In the midst of arrangements and re-arrangements the servant entered with a large bunch of lilies from the village school-children and the announcement that Mr and Mrs Savage were just arrived with their six daughters.

Gradually the guests assembled; young and old, pretty and plain; all alike seemingly bent on enjoying themselves; some with gifts, and all with cordial greetings for Mary, for she was a general favourite. There was slim Rosanna Hunt, her scarf arranged with artful negligence to hide a slight protrusion of one shoulder; and sweet Magdalen Ellis, habited as usual in quiet colours. Then came Jane and Alice Deverell, twins so much alike that few besides their parents knew them apart with any certainty; and their fair brother Alexis, who, had he been a girl, would have increased the confusion. There was little Ellen Potter, with a round rosy face like an apple, looking as natural and good-humoured as if, instead of a grand French governess, she had had her own parents with her like most of the other children; and then came three rather haughty-looking Miss Stantons, and pale Hannah Lindley the orphan; and Harriet Eyre, a thought too showy in her dress.

Mary, all life and spirits, hastened to introduce the new-comers to Maude; who, perfectly unembarrassed, bowed and uttered little speeches with the manner of a practical woman of the world; while the genuine, unobtrusive courtesy of Agnes did more towards making their guests comfortable than the eager good nature of her sister, or the correct breeding of her cousin.

At length the preliminaries were all accomplished, every one having found a seat, or being otherwise satisfactorily disposed of. The elders of the party were grouped here and there, talking and looking on; the very small children were accommodated in the adjoining apartment with a gigantic Noah's Ark: and the rest of the young people being at liberty to amuse themselves as fancy might prompt, a general appeal was made to Miss Foster for some game, novel, entertaining, and ingenious; or, some of the more diffident hinted, easy.

'I really know nothing new,' said Maude; 'you must have played at "Proverbs", "What's my thought like", "How do you like it", and "Magic music": – or stay, there is one thing we can try – "*Bouts-rimés*".'

'What?' asked Mary.

'"*Bouts-rimés*": it is very easy. Some one gives rhymes – mamma can do that – and then all of us fill them up as we think fit. A sonnet is the best form to select; but, if you wish, we could try eight, or even four lines.'

'But I am certain I could not make a couplet,' said Mary, laughing. 'Of course you would get on capitally, and Agnes might manage very well, and Magdalen can do anything; but it is quite beyond me: do pray think of something more suitable to my capacity.'

'Indeed I have nothing else to propose. This is very much better than mere common games; but if you will not try it, that ends the matter;' and Maude leaned back in her chair.

'I hope—' began Mary; but Agnes interposed:

'Suppose some of us attempt "*Bouts-rimés*"; and you meanwhile can settle what we shall do afterwards. Who is ready to test her poetic powers? – What, no one? Oh, Magdalen, pray join Maude and me.'

This proposal met with universal approbation, and the three girls retreated to a side-table, Mary, who supplied the rhymes, exacting a promise that only one sonnet should be composed. Before the next game was fixed upon, the three following productions were submitted for judgment to the discerning public. The first was by Agnes:

Would that I were a turnip white,
Or raven black,
Or miserable hack
Dragging a cab from left to right;
Or would I were the showman of a sight,
Or weary donkey with a laden back,
Or racer in a sack,
Or freezing traveller on an Alpine height;
Or would I were straw-catching as I drown,
(A wretched landsman I who cannot swim),
Or watching a lone vessel sink,
Rather than writing; I would change my pink
Gauze for a hideous yellow satin gown,
With deep-cut scolloped edges and a rim.

'Indeed, I had no idea of the sacrifice you were making,' observed Maude. 'You did it with such heroic equanimity. Might I, however, venture to hint that my sympathy with your sorrows would have been greater had they been expressed in metre.'

'There's gratitude for you,' cried Agnes gaily; 'what have you to expect, Magdalen?' and she went on to read her friend's sonnet:

I fancy the good fairies dressed in white,
Glancing like moon-beams through the shadows black;
Without much work to do for king or hack.
Training perhaps some twisted branch aright;
Or sweeping faded Autumn leaves from sight
To foster embryo life; or binding back
Stray tendrils; or in ample bean-pod sack
Bringing wild honey from the rocky height;
Or fishing for a fly lest it should drown;
Or teaching water-lily heads to swim,
Fearful that sudden rain might make them sink;
Or dyeing the pale rose a warmer pink;
Or wrapping lilies in their leafy gown,
Yet letting the white peep beyond the rim.

'Well, Maude?'

'Well, Agnes; Miss Ellis is too kind to feel gratified at hearing that her verses make me tremble for my own: but such as they are, listen:

Some ladies dress in muslin full and white,
Some gentlemen in cloth succinct and black;
Some patronise a dog-cart, some a hack,
Some think a painted clarence only right.
Youth is not always such a pleasing sight:
Witness a man with tassels on his back;
Or woman in a great-coat like a sack
Towering above her sex with horrid height.
If all the world were water fit to drown
There are some whom you would not teach to swim;
Rather enjoying if you saw them sink;
Certain old ladies dressed in girlish pink,
With roses and geraniums on their gown:
Go to the Bason, poke them o'er the rim.'

'What a very odd sonnet,' said Mary after a slight pause; 'but surely men don't wear tassels.'

Her cousin smiled. 'You must allow for poetical licence; and I have literally seen a man in Regent Street wearing a sort of hooded cloak with one tassel. Of course everyone will understand the Bason to mean the one in St James' Park.'*

'With these explanations your sonnet is comprehensible,' said Mary; and Magdalen added with unaffected pleasure: 'And without them it was by far the best of the three.'

Maude now exerted herself to amuse the party; and soon proved that ability was not lacking. Game after game was proposed and played at; and her fun seemed inexhaustible, for nothing was thought too nonsensical or too noisy for the occasion. Her good humour and animation were infectious: Miss Stanton incurred forfeits with the blandest smile; Hannah Lindley blushed and dimpled as she had not done for many months, Rosanna never perceived the derangement of her scarf; little Ellen exulted in freedom from school-room trammels; the twins guessed each other's thoughts with marvellous facility; Magdalen laughed aloud; and even Harriet Eyre's dress looked scarcely too gay for such an entertainment. Well was it for Mrs Clifton that the strawberries, cream, and tarts had been supplied with no niggard hand: and very meagre was the remnant left when the party broke up at a late hour.

III

Agnes and Mary were discussing the pleasures of the preceding evening as they sat over the unusually late breakfast, when Maude joined them. Salutations being exchanged and refreshments supplied to the last comer, the conversation was renewed.

'Who did you think was the prettiest girl in the room last night? our charming selves, of course, excepted,' asked Mary; 'Agnes and I cannot agree on this point.'

'Yes,' said her sister; 'we quite agree as to mere prettiness; only I maintain that Magdalen is infinitely more attractive than half the handsome people one sees. There is so much sense in her face and such sweetness. Besides, her eyes are really beautiful.'

'Miss Ellis has a characteristic countenance; but she appeared to me very far from the belle of the evening. Rosanna Hunt has much more regular features.'

'Surely you don't think Rosanna prettier than Jane and Alice,' interrupted Mary; 'I suppose I never look at those two without fresh pleasure.'

'They have good fair complexions, eyes, and hair, certainly,' and Maude glanced rather pointedly at her unconscious cousin; 'but to me they have a wax-dollish air which is quite unpleasant. I think one of the handsomest faces in the room was Miss Stanton's.'

'But she has such a disagreeable expression,' rejoined Mary hastily: then colouring, she half-turned towards her sister, who looked grave, but did not speak.

A pause ensued; and then Agnes said, 'I remember how prejudiced I felt against Miss Stanton when first she came to live here, for her appearance and manners are certainly unattractive: and how ashamed of myself I was when we heard that last year, through all the bitterly cold weather, she rose at six, though she never has a fire in her room, that she might have time before breakfast to make clothes for some of the poorest people in the village. And in spring, when the scarlet fever was about, her mother would not let her go near the sick children for fear of contagion; so she saved up all her pocket money to buy wine and soup* and such things for them as they recovered.'

'I dare say she is very good,' said Maude; 'but that does not make her pleasing. Besides, the whole family have that disagreeable expression, and I suppose they are not all paragons. But you have both finished breakfast, and make me ashamed by your diligence. What is that beautiful piece of work?'

The sisters looked delighted: 'I am so glad you like it, dear Maude. Mary and I are embroidering a cover for the lectern in our church; but we feared you might think the ground dull.'

'Not at all; I prefer those quiet shades. Why, how well you do it: is it not very difficult? Let me see if I understand the devices. There is the Cross and the Crown of Thorns;* and those must be the keys of St Peter, with, of course, the sword of St Paul. Do the flowers mean anything?'

'I am the Rose of Sharon and the Lily of the Valley,' answered Agnes, pointing. 'That is the Balm of Gilead – at least, it is what we will call so; there are myrrh and hyssop, and that is a palm-branch. The border is to be vine-leaves and grapes; with fig-leaves at the corners, thanks to Mary's suggestions. Would you like to help us? There is plenty of room at the frame.'

'No; I should not do it well enough, and have no time to learn, as we go home to-morrow. How I envy you,' she continued in a low voice, as if speaking rather to herself than to her hearers: 'you who live in the country, and are exactly what you appear, and never wish for what you do not possess. I am sick of display, and poetry, and acting.'

'You do not act,' replied Agnes, warmly. 'I never knew a more sincere person. One difference between us is that you are less healthy and far more clever than I am. And this reminds me: Miss Savage begged me to ask you for some verses to put in her album. Would you be so very obliging? Any that you have by you would do.'

'She can have the sonnet I wrote last night.'

Agnes hesitated: 'I could not well offer her that, because—'

'Why? she does not "tower". Oh! I suppose she has some reprehensible old lady in her family, and so might feel hurt at my lynch-law.'

PART SECOND

I

Rather more than a year had elapsed since Maude parted from her cousins; and now she was expecting their arrival in London every minute: for Mrs Clifton, unable to leave her young family, had gratefully availed herself of Mrs Foster's offer to receive Agnes and Mary during the early winter months, that they might take music and dancing lessons with their cousin.

At length the rumbling of an approaching cab was heard; then a loud knock and ring. Maude started up: but instead of running out to meet her guests, began poking vigorously at the fire, which soon sent a warm, cheerful light through the apartment, enabling her, when they entered, to discern that Agnes had a more womanly air than at their last meeting, that Mary had out-grown her sister, and that both were remarkably good-looking.

'First let me show you your room; and then we can settle comfortably to tea; we are not to wait for mamma. She thought you would not mind sleeping together,* as our house is so small; and I have done my best to arrange things for your taste, for I know of old how you have only one taste between you. Look, my room is next yours, so we can help each other very cosily: only pray don't think of unpacking now; there will be plenty of time this evening, and you must be famished: come.'

But Agnes lingered still, eager to thank her cousin for the good-natured forethought which had robbed her own apartment of flower-vases and inkstand for the accommodation of her guests. The calls of Mary's appetite were however imperious; and very soon the sisters were snugly settled on a sofa by the fire, while Maude, in a neighbouring arm-chair, made tea.

'How long it seems since my birthday party,' said Mary, as soon as the eatables had in some measure restored her social powers. 'Why, Maude, you are grown quite a woman; but you look more delicate than ever, and very thin: do you still write verses?' Then without waiting for a reply: 'Those which you gave Miss Savage for her album were very much admired; and Magdalen Ellis wished at the time for an autograph copy, only she had not courage to trouble you. But perhaps you are not aware that poor Magdalen has done with albums and such like, at least for the present: she has entered on her noviciate in the Sisterhood of Mercy established near our house.'

'Why poor?' said Maude. 'I think she is very happy.'

'Surely you would not like such a life,' rejoined her cousin. 'They have not proper clothes on their beds,* and never go out without a thick veil, which must half-blind them. All day long they are at prayers, or teaching children, or attending the sick, or making things for the poor, or something. Is that to your taste?'

Maude half-sighed; and then answered: 'You cannot imagine

me either fit or inclined for such a life; still I can perceive that those who are so are very happy. When I was preparing for confirmation, Mr Paulson offered me a district;* but I did not like the trouble, and mamma thought me too unwell to be regular. I have regretted it since, though: yet I don't fancy I ever could have talked to the poor people or have done the slightest good. Yes, I continue to write now and then as the humour seizes me; and if Miss Ellis—'

'Sister Magdalen,' whispered Agnes.

'If Sister Magdalen will accept it, I will try and find her something admissible even within convent walls. But let us change the subject. On Thursday we are engaged to tea at Mrs Strawdy's. There will be no sort of party, so we need not dress* or take any trouble.'

'Will my Aunt go with us?' asked Agnes.

'No. Poor mamma has been ailing for some time, and is by no means strong; so, as Mrs Strawdy is an old schoolfellow of hers, and a most estimable person, she thinks herself justified in consigning you to my guardianship. On Saturday we must go shopping, as Aunt Letty says you are to get your winter things in London; and I can get mine at the same time. On Sunday – or does either of you dislike Cathedral services?'

Agnes declared they were her delight; and Mary, who had never attended any, expressed great pleasure at the prospect of hearing what her sister preferred to all secular music.

'Very well,' continued Maude: 'we will go to St Andrew's* then, and you shall be introduced to a perfect service; or, at any rate, to perhaps the nearest English approach to vocal perfection. But you know you are to be quite at home here; so we have not arranged any particular plans of amusement, but mean to treat you like ourselves. And now it is high time for you to retire.'

When Thursday arrived Agnes and Mary were indisposed with colds; so Mrs Foster insisted that her daughter should make their excuses to Mrs Strawdy. In a dismal frame of mind, Maude, assisted by her sympathising cousins, performed her slight preliminary toilet.

'You have no notion of the utter dreariness of this kind of invitation. I counted on your helping me through the evening, and now you fail me. Thank you, Mary; I shall not waste *eau de Cologne* on my handkerchief. Good-night both: mind you go to bed early, and get up quite well tomorrow. Good-night.'

The weather was foggy and raw as Maude stepped into the street; and proved anything but soothing to a temper already fretted; so by the time she had arrived at her destination, removed her walking things, saluted her hostess, and apologised for her cousins, her countenance had assumed an expression neither pleased nor pleasing.

'Let me present my nieces to you, my dear,' said Mrs Strawdy, taking her young friend by the hand and leading her towards the fire: 'This is Miss Mowbray, or, as you must call her, Annie; that is Caroline, and that Sophy. They have heard so much of you, that any further introduction is needless'; here Maude bowed rather stiffly: 'but as you are early people, you will excuse our commencing with tea, after which we shall have leisure for amusement.'

There was nothing so genuinely kind and simple as Mrs Strawdy's manner, that even Maude felt mollified, and resolved on doing her best not only towards suppressing all appearance of yawns, but also towards bearing her part in the conversation.

'My cousins will regret their indisposition more than ever, when they learn of how much pleasure it has deprived them,' said she, civilly addressing Miss Mowbray.

A polite bend, smile, and murmur formed the sole response, and once more a subject had to be started.*

'Have you been very gay lately? I begin to acquire the reputation of an invalid; and so my privacy is respected.'

Annie coloured and looked excessively embarrassed; at last she answered in a low hesitating voice: 'We go out extremely little, partly because we never dance.'

'Nor I either; it really is too fatiguing: yet a ball-room is no bad place for a mere spectator. Perhaps, though, you prefer the Theatre?'

'We never go to the play,'* rejoined Miss Mowbray, looking more and more uncomfortable.

Maude ran on: 'Oh, I beg your pardon, you do not approve of such entertainments. I never go, but only for want of someone to take me.' Then addressing Mrs Strawdy: 'I think you know my aunt, Mrs Clifton?'

'I visited her years ago with your mamma,' was the answer: 'when you were quite a little child. I hope she continues in good health. Pray remember me to her and to Mr Clifton when you write.'

'With pleasure. She has a large family now, eight children.'

'That is indeed a large family,' rejoined Mrs Strawdy, intent meanwhile on dissecting a cake with mathematical precision: 'you must try a piece, it is Sophy's own manufacture.'

Despairing of success in this quarter, Maude now directed her attention to Caroline, whose voice she had not heard once in the course of the evening.

'I hope you will favour us with some music after tea; in fact, I can take no denial. You look too blooming to plead a cold, and I feel certain you will not refuse to indulge my love for sweet sounds: of your ability to do so I have heard elsewhere.'

'I shall be most happy; only you must favour us in return.'

'I will do my best,' answered Maude, somewhat encouraged; 'but my own performances are very poor. Are you fond of German songs? they form my chief resource.'

'Yes, I like them much.'

Baffled in this quarter also, Miss Foster wanted courage to attack Sophy, whose countenance promised more cake than conversation. The meal seemed endless: she fidgeted under the table with her fingers; pushed about a stool on the noiselessly-soft carpet until it came in contact with someone's foot; and at last fairly deprived Caroline of her third cup of coffee, by opening the piano and claiming the fulfilment of her promise.

The young lady complied with obliging readiness. She sang some simple airs, mostly religious, not indeed with much expression, but in a voice clear and warbling as a bird's. Maude felt consoled for all the contrarieties of the day; and was bargaining for one more song before taking Caroline's place at the instrument, when the door opened to admit Mrs and Miss Savage; who having only just reached town, and hearing from Mrs Foster that her daughter was at the house of a mutual friend, resolved on begging the hospitality of Mrs Strawdy, and renewing their acquaintance.

Poor Maude's misfortunes now came thick and fast. Seated between Miss Savage and Sophia Mowbray, she was attacked on either hand with questions concerning her verses. In the first place, did she continue to write? Yes. A flood of ecstatic compliments followed this admission: she was so young, so much admired, and, poor thing, looked so delicate. It was quite affecting to think of her lying awake at night meditating those sweet verses – ('I sleep like a top,' Maude put in, drily) – which so delighted her friends, and would so charm the public if only Miss Foster could be induced to publish. At last the bystanders were called upon to intercede for a recitation.

Maude coloured with displeasure; a hasty answer was rising to her lips, when the absurdity of her position flashed across her mind so forcibly that, almost unable to check a laugh in the midst of her annoyance, she put her handkerchief to her mouth. Miss Savage, impressed with a notion that her request was about to be complied with, raised her hand, imploring silence; and settled herself in a listening attitude.

'You will excuse me,' Maude at last said very coldly; 'I could not think of monopolising every one's attention. Indeed you are extremely good, but you must excuse me.' And here Mrs Savage interposed, desiring her daughter not to tease Miss Foster; and Mrs Strawdy seconded her friend's arguments by a hint that supper would make its appearance in a few minutes.

Finally the maid announced that Miss Foster was 'fetched'; and Maude, shortening her adieus and turning a deaf ear to Annie's suggestions that their acquaintance should not terminate with the first meeting, returned home dissatisfied with her circumstances, her friends, and herself.

III

It was Christmas Eve. All day long Maude and her cousins were hard at work putting up holly and mistletoe in wreaths, festoons, or bunches, wherever the arrangement of the rooms admitted of such embellishment. The picture-frames were hidden behind foliage and bright berries; the bird-cages were stuck as full of green as though it had been Summer. A fine sprig of holly was set apart as a centre-bit for the pudding of next day: scratched hands and injured gowns were disregarded: hour after hour the noisy bustle raged: until Mrs Foster, hunted from place to place by her young relatives, heard, with inward satisfaction, that the decorations were completed.

After tea Mary set the backgammon board in array and challenged her aunt to their customary evening game: Maude, complaining of a headache, and promising either to wrap herself in a warm shawl or to go to bed, went to her room, and Agnes, listening to the rattle of the dice, at last came to the conclusion that her presence was not needed downstairs, and resolved to visit the upper regions. Thinking that her cousin was lying down tired and might have fallen asleep, she forbore knocking; but opened the door softly and peeped in.

Maude was seated at a table surrounded by the old chaos of stationery; before her lay the locking manuscript-book, into which she had just copied something. That day she had appeared more than usually animated: and now supporting her forehead upon her hand, her eyes cast down till the long lashes nearly rested upon her cheeks, she looked pale, languid, almost in pain. She did not move, but let her visitor come close to her without speaking. Agnes thought she was crying.

'Dear Maude, you have overtired yourself. Indeed, for all our sakes, you should be more careful:' here Agnes passed her arm affectionately round her friend's neck: 'I hoped to find you fast asleep, and instead of this you have been writing in the cold.'

'You will stay to Communion tomorrow?' asked Maude after a short silence, and without replying to her cousin's remarks; even these few words seemed to cost her an effort.

'Of course I shall; why, it is Christmas Day: at least I trust to do so. Mary and I have been thinking how nice it will be for us all to receive together: so I want you to promise that you will pray for us at the Altar, as I shall for you. Will you?'

'I shall not receive tomorrow,'* answered Maude; then hurrying on as if to prevent the other from remonstrating: 'No: at least I will not profane Holy Things; I will not add this to all the rest. I have gone over and over again, thinking I should come right in time, and I do not come right. I will go no more.'

Agnes turned quite pale: 'Stop,' she said, interrupting her cousin: 'stop; you cannot mean – you do not know what you are saying. You will go no more? Only think if the struggle is so hard now, what it will be when you reject all help.'

'I do not struggle.'

'You are ill tonight,' rejoined Agnes very gently; 'you are tired and over-excited. Take my advice, dear; say your prayers and get to bed. But do not be very long; if there is anything you miss and will tell me of, I will say it in your stead. Don't think me unfeeling: I was once on the very point of acting as you propose. I was perfectly wretched: harassed and discouraged on all sides. But then it struck me – you won't be angry? – that it was so ungrateful to follow my own fancies, instead of at least endeavouring to do God's Will: and so foolish too; for if our safety is not in obedience, where is it?'

Maude shook her head: 'Your case is different. Whatever your faults may be (not that I perceive any), you are trying to correct them; your own conscience tells you that. But I am not trying. No one will say that I cannot avoid putting myself forward and displaying my verses. Agnes, you must admit so much.'

Deep-rooted indeed was that vanity which made Maude take pleasure, on such an occasion, in proving the force of arguments directed against herself. Still Agnes would not yield; but resolutely did battle for the truth.

'If hitherto it has been so, let it be so no more. It is not too late; besides, think for one moment what will be the end of this. We must all die: what if you keep to your resolution, and do as you have said, and receive the Blessed Sacrament no more?' – Her eyes filled with tears.

Maude's answer came in a subdued tone: 'I do not mean never to communicate again. You remember Mr Paulson told us last Sunday that sickness and suffering are sent for our correction. I suffer very much. Perhaps a time will come when these will have done their work on me also; when I shall be purified indeed and weaned from the world. Who knows? the lost have been found, the dead quickened.' She paused as if in thought; then continued: 'You partake of the Blessed Sacrament in peace, Agnes, for you are good; and Mary, for she is harmless: but your conduct cannot serve to direct mine, because I am neither the one nor the other. Some day I may be fit again to approach the Holy Altar, but till then I will at least refrain from dishonouring it.'

Agnes felt almost indignant. 'Maude, how can you talk so? this is not reverence. You cannot mean that for the present you will indulge vanity and display; that you will court admiration and applause; that you will take your fill of pleasure until sickness, or it may be death, strips you of temptation and sin together. Forgive me; I am sure you never meant this: yet what else does a deliberate resolution to put off doing right come to? – and if you are determined at once to do your best, why deprive yourself of the appointed means of grace? Dear Maude, think better of it;' and Agnes knelt beside her cousin, and laid her head against her bosom.

But still Maude, with a sort of desperate wilfulness, kept saying: 'It is of no use; I cannot go tomorrow; it is of no use.' She hid her face, leaning upon the table and weeping bitterly; while Agnes, almost discouraged, quitted the room.

Maude, once more alone, sat for some time just as her cousin left her. Gradually the thick, low sobs became more rare; she was beginning to feel sleepy. At last she roused herself with an effort, and commenced undressing; then it struck her that her prayers had still to be said. The idea of beginning them frightened her, yet she could not settle to sleep without saying something. Strange prayers they must have been, offered with a divided heart and a reproachful conscience. Still they were said at length; and Maude lay down harassed, wretched, remorseful, everything but penitent. She was nearly asleep, nearly unconscious of her troubles, when the first stroke of midnight sounded.

PART THIRD

I

Agnes Clifton to Maude Foster

12th June 18—

My dear Maude,

Mamma has written to my aunt that Mary's marriage is fixed for the 4th of next month: but as I fear we cannot expect you both so many days before the time, I also write, hoping that you at least will come without delay. At any rate, I shall be at the station tomorrow afternoon with a chaise for your luggage, so pray take pity on my desolate condition, and avail yourself of the three o'clock train. As we are both bridesmaids elect, I thought it would be very nice for us to be dressed alike, so have procured double quantity of everything; thus you will perceive no pretence remains for your lingering in smoky London.

You will be amused when you see Mary: I have already lost my companion. Mr Herbert calls at least once a day, but sometimes oftener; so all day long Mary is on the alert. She takes much more interest in the roses over the porch than was formerly the case; the creepers outside the windows require continual training, not to say hourly care: I tell her the constitution of the garden must have become seriously weakened lately. One morning I caught her before the glass, trying the effect of syringa (the English orange-blossom, you know) in her hair. She looked such a darling. I hinted how flattered Mr Herbert would feel when I told him; which provoked her to offer a few remarks on old maids. Was it not a shame?

Last Thursday Magdalen Ellis was finally received into the Sisterhood of Mercy. I wished much to be present, but could not, as the whole affair was conducted quite privately; only her parents were admitted. However, I made interest for a lock of her beautiful hair,* which I prize highly. It makes me sad to look at it; yet I know she has chosen well; and will, if she perseveres, receive hereafter an abundant recompense for all she has forgone here. Sometimes I think whether such a life can be suited to me; but then I could not leave mamma: indeed, that is just what Magdalen felt so much. I met her yesterday walking with some poor children. Her veil was down, nearly hiding her face; still I fancy she looked thoughtful, but very calm and happy. She says she always prays for me, and asked my prayers; so I begged her to remember you and Mary. Then she enquired how you are; desiring her kindest love to you, and assuring me she makes no doubt your name will be known at some future period: but checking herself almost immediately, she added that she could fancy you very different, as pale Sister Maude. This surprised me, I can fancy nothing of the sort. Then, having nearly reached my home, we parted.

What a document I have composed; I who have not one minute to spare from Mary's trousseau. Will you give my love to my aunt; and request her from me to permit your immediately coming to your affectionate cousin,

Agnes M. Clifton

P.S. – Mary would doubtless send a message were she in the room; I conjecture her to be lurking about somewhere on the watch. Good-bye: or rather, Come.

Maude handed the letter to her mother. 'Can you spare me, mamma? I should like to go, but not if it is to inconvenience you.'

'Certainly you shall go, my dear. It is a real pleasure to hear you express interest on some point, and you cannot be with anyone I approve of more than Agnes. But you must make haste with the packing now. I will come and help you in a few minutes.'

Still Maude lingered. 'Did you see about Magdalen? I wonder what made her think of me as a Sister. It is very nice of her; but then she is so good she never can conceive what I am like. Mamma, should you mind my being a nun?'

'Yes, my dear; it would make me miserable. But for the present take my advice and hurry a little, or the train will leave without you.'

Thus urged, Maude proceeded to bundle various miscellaneous goods into a trunk; the only article on the safety of which she bestowed much thought being the present destined for Mary: a sofa-pillow worked in glowing shades of wool and silk. This she wrapped carefully in cloth, and laid at the bottom: then over it all else was heaped without much ceremony. Many were the delays occasioned by things mislaid, which must be looked for, ill-secured, which must be re-arranged; or remembered too late, which yet could not be dispensed with, and so must be crammed in somewhere. At length, however, the tardy preparations were completed; and Maude, enveloped in two shawls, though it was the height of summer, stepped into a cab; promising strict conformity to her mother's injunction that both the windows should be kept closed.

Half-an-hour had not elapsed when another cab drove up to the door; and out of it Maude was lifted perfectly insensible. She had been overturned; and, though no limb was broken, had neither stirred nor spoken since the accident.

II

Maude Foster to Agnes Clifton

2nd July 18—

My dear Agnes,
You have heard of my mishap? it keeps me not bed-ridden, but sofa-ridden. My side is dreadfully hurt; I looked at it this morning for the first time, but hope never again to see so shocking a sight. The pain now and then is extreme; though not always so; sometimes, in fact, I am unconscious of any injury.

Will you convey my best love and wishes to Mary, and tell her how much I regret being away from her at such a time, especially as mamma will not hear of leaving me.

The surgeon comes twice a day to dress my wounds; still, all the burden of nursing falls on poor mamma. How I wish you were here to help us both; we should find plenty to say.

But, perhaps, ere many months are past I shall be up and about, when we may go together on a visit to Mary; a most delightful possibility. By the way, how I should love a baby of hers, and what a pretty little creature it ought to be. Do you think Mr Herbert handsome? hitherto I have only had a partial opinion.

Ugh, my side! it gives an awful twinge now and then. You need not read my letter; but I must write it, for I am unable to do anything else. Did the pillow reach safely? It gave me so much pleasure to work it for Mary, who, I hope, likes it. At all events. if not to her taste, she may console herself with the reflection that is unique; for the pattern was my own designing.

Here comes dinner; good-bye. When will anything so welcome as your kind face gladden the eyes of your affectionate

Maude Foster?

P.S. – I have turned tippler lately on port wine three times a day. 'To keep you up,' says my doctor: while I obstinately refuse to be kept up, but insist on becoming weaker and weaker. Mind you write me a full history of your grand doings on a certain occasion: not omitting a detailed account of the lovely bride, her appearance, deportment, and toilet. Good-bye once more: when shall I see you all again?

III

Three weeks had passed away. A burning sun seemed baking the very dust in the streets, and sucking the last remnant of moisture from the straw spread in front of Mrs Foster's house, when the sound of a low muffled ring was heard in the sick-room and Maude, now entirely confined to her bed, raising herself on one arm, looked eagerly towards the door; which opened to admit a servant with the welcome announcement that Agnes had arrived.

After tea Mrs Foster, almost worn out with fatigue, went to bed, leaving her daughter under the care of their guest. The first greetings between the cousins had passed sadly enough. Agnes perceived at a glance that Maude was, as her last letter hinted, in a most alarming state; while the sick girl, well aware of her condition, received her friend with an emotion which showed she felt it might be for the last time. But soon her spirits rallied.

'I shall enjoy our evening together so much, Agnes,' said she, speaking now quite cheerfully. 'You must tell me all the news. Have you heard from Mary since your last despatch to me?'

'Mamma received a letter this morning before I set off; and she sent it, hoping to amuse you. Shall I read it aloud?'

'No; let me have it myself.' Her eye travelled rapidly down the well-filled pages, comprehending at a glance all the tale of happiness. Mr and Mrs Herbert were at Scarborough; they would thence proceed to the Lakes; and thence, most probably, homewards, though a prolonged tour was mentioned as just possible. But both plans seemed alike pleasing to Mary; for she was full of her husband, and both were equally connected with him.

Maude smiled as paragraph after paragraph enlarged on the same topic. At last she said: 'Agnes, if you could not be yourself, but must become one of us three: I don't mean as to goodness, of course, but merely as regards circumstances, would you change with Sister Magdalen, with Mary, or with me?'

'Not with Mary, certainly. Neither should I have courage to change with you; I never should bear pain so well: nor yet with Sister Magdalen; for I want her fervour of devotion. So at present I fear you must even put up with me as I am. Will that do?'

There was a pause. A fresh wind had sprung up, and the sun was setting.

At length Maude resumed: 'Do you recollect last Christmas Eve when I was so wretched, what shocking things I said? How I rejoice that my next Communion was not indeed delayed till sickness had stripped me of temptation and sin together.'

'Did I say that? It was very harsh.'

'Not harsh: it was just and right as far as it went; only something more was required. But I never told you what altered me. The truth is, for a time I avoided as much as possible frequenting our parish church, for fear of remarks. Mamma, knowing how I love St Andrew's, let me go there very often by myself because the walk is too long for her. I wanted resolution to do right; yet, believe me, I was very miserable; how I could say my prayers at that period is a mystery. So matters went on; till one day as I was returning from a shop, I met Mr Paulson. He enquired immediately whether I had been staying in the country. Of course I answered, No. Had I been ill? again, No. Then gradually the whole story came out. I never shall forget the shame of my admissions; each word seemed forced from me, yet at last, all was told. I will not repeat all we said then, and on a subsequent occasion when he saw me at church: the end was, that I partook of the Holy Communion on Easter Day. That was indeed a Feast.'

Then changing the conversation abruptly, Maude said: 'Agnes, it would only pain mamma to look over everything if I die; will you examine my verses and destroy what I evidently never intended to be seen. They might all be thrown away together, only mamma is so fond of them. What will she do?' – and the poor girl hid her face in the pillows.

'But is there no hope, then?'

'Not the slightest, if you mean of recovery; and she does not know it. Don't go away when all's over, but do what you can to comfort her. I have been her misery from my birth till now; there is no time to do better, but you must leave me, please; for I feel completely exhausted. Or, stay one moment. I saw Mr Paulson again this morning, and he promised to come tomorrow to administer the Blessed Sacrament to me; so I count on you and mamma receiving with me, for the last time perhaps: will you?'

'Yes, dear Maude. But you are so young, don't give up hope. And now would you like me to remain here during the night? I can establish myself quite comfortably on your sofa.'

'Thank you, but it could only make me restless. Good-night, my own dear Agnes.'

'Good-night, dear Maude. I trust to rise early tomorrow, that I may be with you all the sooner.' So they parted.

That morrow never dawned for Maude Foster.

Agnes proceeded to perform the task imposed upon her, with scrupulous anxiety to carry out her friend's wishes. The locked book she never opened; but had it placed in Maude's coffin, with all its words of folly, sin, vanity; and, she humbly trusted, of true penitence also. She next collected the scraps of paper found in her cousin's desk and portfolio, or lying loose upon the table; and proceeded to examine them. Many of these were mere fragments, many half-effaced pencil scrawls, some written on torn backs of letters, and some full of incomprehensible abbreviations. Agnes was astonished at the variety of Maude's compositions. Piece after piece she committed to the flames, fearful lest any should be preserved not intended for general perusal: but it cost her a pang to do so; and to see how small a number remained for Mrs Foster. Of two only she took copies for herself.

The first was evidently composed subsequently to Maude's accident:

Fade, tender lily,*
  Fade, O crimson rose,
Fade every flower,
  Sweetest flower that blows.

Go, chilly Autumn,
  Come, O Winter cold;
Let the green stalks die away
  Into common mould.

Birth follows hard on death,
  Life on withering.
Hasten, we shall come the sooner
  Back to pleasant Spring.

The other was a sonnet, dated the morning before her death:

  What is it Jesus saith unto the soul?
  'Take up the Cross, and come, and follow me.'
This word He saith to all; no man may be
  Without the Cross, wishing to win the goal.
  Then take it bravely up, setting thy whole
Body to bear; it will not weigh on thee
Beyond thy utmost strength: take it; for He
  Knoweth when thou art weak, and will control
The powers of darkness that thou need'st not fear.
  He will be with thee, helping, strengthening,
Until it is enough: for lo, the day
Cometh when He shall call thee: thou shalt hear
  His voice that says: 'Winter is past, and Spring
Is come; arise, My Love, and come away.'

Agnes cut one long tress from Maude's head; and on her return home laid it in the same paper with the lock of Magdalen's hair. These she treasured greatly, and, gazing on them, would long and pray for the hastening of that eternal morning which shall reunite in God those who in Him, or for His sake, have parted here.

Amen for us all.

Family Correspondence

Under the title Corrispondenza Famigliare, *the text of this unfinished epistolary novel in Italian forms a sort of sequel to* Maude, *as the three young correspondents move from schoolroom to salon and party games to matrimony. It appeared in a privately printed young ladies' magazine entitled* The Bouquet culled from Marylebone Gardens *by Bluebell, Kingcup and Mignonette in 1852. Edited by Lady Hester Browne, daughter of the Marquess of Sligo, and Miss Hume Middlemass,* The Bouquet *offered a decorous display of talent, contributors each choosing a floral* nom de plume. *Christina appeared as 'Calta' (Marigold) and all her contributions were in Italian, probably owing to grandfatherly encouragement. Her first contributions, two neo-classical verses, applauded in the magazine as 'very elegant and pointed', were followed in April 1852 by the first instalment of the* Correspondence, *containing the first two letters between Angela-Maria, daughter of an Italian political refugee, and her English cousin Emma, entirely given over to fashion and frivolous pursuits.* The Bouquet*'s internal critic complimented Calta on her 'very lively and satirical Italian letters'; perhaps her identity was guessed at, for both her father and grandfather were relatively well-known figures.*

Subsequent instalments, introducing the pious Clorinda Knight, affianced to a curate, appeared in June, July and August, but the story then ended without explanation just as it was getting into its stride, over the words 'to be continued'.

In part a satire on aristocratic snobbery and social display (Christina Rossetti certainly never had a ballgown like that she bestowed on Emma), the storyline also incorporates elements of her own experience. Clorinda's visit to her mother-in-law is based on the month Christina spent during her engagement with James Collinson's family in Nottinghamshire – incidentally close to Hardwick Old Hall, which is very likely the inspiration for the ruined castle and oratory of Angela-Maria's picnic. The lake and deer, however, are probably lifted from Longleat, the Baths' seat in Somerset where Christina visited her Aunt Charlotte.

The two main characters reflect the author's bi-national inheritance, and Angela's fear for her father is based on the danger Gabriele Rossetti had been in when fleeing from Naples with a price on his head, and the ever-present anxiety in exile that his enemies were still active. Whether the authorical intention was for the young Neapolitan diplomat in the tale to fall in love with Angela (when her authorship of the album lines was revealed) and then effect the rescue or restoration of her father to his homeland, can only be guessed at. Emma, however, is surely riding hard for a social fall.

A private joke informs the footnote appended to Secretary Lancetti's poetic effusion, for the courtly lines were not Christina's, as she scrupulously avowed. They had been written three years before and attached to a bouquet from her grandfather, on the appearance of the Verses *which he had printed. Who chose the pseudonym 'Parsley' for Grandpapa is not recorded.*

Like Maude, Family Correspondence *is a juvenile effort which promised more, in terms of plot and literary accomplishment, than its author could deliver. Lively and observant, however, it offers a glimpse of Rossetti's youth nowhere else recorded, and looks forward to the social fiction of her maturity in* Commonplace.

NO. I

Angela-Maria de'Ruggieri to Emma Ward

My dearest Cousin,

Now that I am at school I will write often to give you my news. How I envy you! You are at home, happy, while I am here, miserable. I hate the schoolmistress; she's called Mrs Sharp. The assistants are Miss Compton for English and Mlle Dubois for French. The Miss is tall and the Mademoiselle is short; neither has any character. My companions range from the odious to the passable; I haven't found one who is truly amiable. The girl said to be the most talented is Amelia Etherage; fair, slim, lively, fifteen years old. The school beauty is a little nine-year-old named Gertrude Orme* (or Om, I don't know how it's spelt); she's truly charming, with big blue eyes, golden hair all curls, pretty mouth and the voice of a nightingale. But there's one detestable girl, Anna Green, only pronounced Grin; she's sixteen, just a month older than me, and tall, serious, boring. The other day I said to her at supper: In Italy we not eat beer; – she looked at me very disapprovingly and replied with one word: Drink. All the others started to laugh, except Elena Granby, who flushed and bit her lip.

Write soon and tell me your news. I do nothing but make mistakes if I try to speak in English and they all tease me. How different it was in Italy – there everyone courted and admired me. Oh, if only Papa were not involved in politics – but there's no use lamenting.

Give my respectful love to your dear mother, and greetings to your kind Sister, and believe me always your most affectionate Cousin,

Angela-Maria de'Ruggieri

NO. 2

Emma Ward to Angela-Maria de'Ruggieri

How I pity you, my poor dear Angela; you are badly off, but all the same you need not envy me. I languish a prisoner on the sofa; the other evening I went to a ball and injured my foot; as a result I'm immobile, and my ankle has swollen up huge.

But putting my woes aside, let me tell you of my glories. You remember the invitation I received to the Duchess of Bridport's* garden party? I went on Tuesday. Great thought attended my toilette: three dressmakers and two ladysmaids were engaged to accomplish it. It was, I may say without vanity, worthy of the occasion. A gown of white muslin sprinkled with silver flowers; a rose-pink silk mantle, edged with lace; a bonnet of rice-straw* garlanded with jessamine – my dear, doesn't that sound elegant? The main problem was the parasol: Mamma (who, between ourselves, has no taste) suggested one similar to the mantle; while my maid rhapsodised over green and gold; one said one thing, the other another; in the end I refused to listen any more; I shut myself in my room, and then the happiest idea came to me. What do you think of white silk, embroidered with alternate roses and jessamine?* And trimmed all around with a lace border two inches deep.

My labour was rewarded. The Caunter Ladies blanched with envy; and looked really wretched in blue and gold. The Misses Fairfax were ghastly in green; and Clorinda Knight made a pitiful sight all dressed in purple. In the evening the Duchess gave a ball for over five hundred people. I was clad entirely in white, with necklace, earrings, bracelets of pearl. On my entrance into the ballroom, all eyes turned. A royal prince asked me to dance; the Neapolitan ambassador brought me an ice; when I dropped my posy three lords raced to retrieve it. It was a veritable triumph. Clorinda sat alone on a bench all evening, with a poor curate talking to her. Oh how happy I was! At last Mamma said it was time to leave; the prince helped into my wraps, escorted me down the stair and was about to hand me into the carriage when, I don't know how, my foot stumbled and I all but fell. Since that night I have not and still cannot leave the house, and I've missed two parties.

Write as soon as you can, I'm dying of boredom. That hateful parrot died all of sudden, and Mamma has acquired an even more detestable monkey. Keep me in your thoughts and believe me your most affectionate

Emma Ward

P.S. I hear that Clorinda is to marry her curate. Much good may that do her.

To be continued

NO. 3

Angela-Maria de'Ruggieri to Emma Ward

My dearest Emma,

Be kind enough to forward the enclosed letter to Clorinda, whose address I've mislaid. I don't at all see the absurdity of her engagement, and would like to send my warm wishes for her happiness. When I met her at your house she seemed a very nice young woman; and I hope her curate will indeed be good for her. What's his name? I'd like to make a little gift for the bride-to-be, but I can't decide what to offer. What do you think of a sofa cushion? I made one not long ago and it was very pretty; but perhaps it would be better to send a purse; I am very good at netting.*

On Tuesday it was Mrs Sharp's birthday, and we had a holiday. We took breakfast at nine-thirty instead of the usual eight o'clock. I'm beginning to like Mrs Sharp; she is very good and never laughs at my mistakes, but corrects them, politely.

We had put our little present on the table, and she expressed her gratification. Breakfast was excellent: coffee, tea, ham, marmalade, porridge, cream cheese and rolls. Elena Granby sat beside me and acted as interpreter. Her Italian is good but her accent is horrible.

It was a beautiful day; and Mrs Sharp proposed we should visit a ruined castle some two miles from here. This fine idea was greeted with applause from us all, and around eleven thirty we set off. A boy and donkey went ahead earlier in the morning with provisions; and in the evening we were due to return by boat.

I can't describe the beauty of the weather. The sun shone with Italian splendour; a gentle breeze cooled the air and wafted the fragrance of a hundred flowers; trees offered welcome shade and birds sang in the branches; butterflies fluttered, and at every step we saw daisies and wild roses. Mademoiselle knows all about botany and made various observations on the subject, useful of course, but not interesting.

The ruins are those of a baronial castle; they rise on a hillock in the middle of a great park. At first sight I was disappointed, but when I mounted the mossy stair and passed down long corridors; when I saw daylight streaming through the stained glass of the oratory,* the only chamber where windows survive; when I called to mind those who were once as young and as full of life and hope as I am now, and had perhaps seen the same refulgence of red and gold and purple – then I felt all the majesty of the scene. A gentle melancholy bathed my soul; I was alone, my companions having gone ahead; when all unexpectedly I heard the sweet voice of Gertrude singing a well-known air. A thousand echoes made up the chorus, and when the song was over, these sustained the notes.

I regained my friends in the large room they call the Giants' Hall; why I don't know, unless it's on account of the huge height of the walls. Mrs Sharp had just discovered my absence; she begged me not to leave the other girls again.

Around two thirty we sat down to table, if so I may describe the floor. Somehow, the most ordinary dishes become exquisite on such occasions. So it was with us. Bread, cold meats, salad and fruit have never tasted so delicious. We sat on the ground; Mrs Sharp settled herself with dignity in a window alcove, I've never seen anything so beautiful as that window, the panes remained in the shape of a cross, and all was ivy-covered.

At five exactly we started towards the river where a boat was waiting. Besides the lake which adorns the park was a fine herd of deer; not far off hinds and fawns nibbled the sward. We arrived home a little after suppertime, so tired that without anything more to eat or drink we went striaght to bed and slept soundly.

Now goodbye my dear; keep me in your thoughts, and believe me your most affectionate

Angela-Maria de'Ruggieri

Thursday

NO. 4

Angela-Maria de'Ruggieri to Clorinda Knight

My Dear Miss Knight,

It would give me great pleasure if you would accept my most cordial wishes for your future happiness. My cousin Emma has given me your news which fills my heart with sincere delight; in expressing my own satisfaction I am thinking of another's, who shall remain unnamed.

This boarding school, I have discovered, also houses a most amiable relative of yours named Elena Granby, who overwhelms me with kindness; indeed, the affection she shows me I return with all my heart.

I should be honoured to receive a letter* from you; but I dare not request one, now that a more tender friendship occupies your thoughts. With renewed good wishes, I have the honour to sign myself, my dear Miss Knight, your devoted servant and friend,

Angela-Maria de'Ruggieri

(to be continued)

NO. 5

Clorinda Knight to Angela-Maria de'Ruggieri

My dear Miss Ruggieri,

Your letter was most gratifying; I can't say how sweet it is to think that one so worthy as yourself should honour me with your friendship.

I ought to have answered your letter sooner; but I did not see it until late last night when I returned from a short stay with my future mother-in-law. This lady, Mrs Foster, showered me with kindnesses; and since business obliged her son to be away for several weeks she invited me to visit, wishing to know me better. I fear she will have been disappointed; but as for me, I declare she is amiable in the highest degree. Although no longer young she has preserved a dignified beauty that inspires respect and love; her conversation is full of wit and wisdom. She greatly resembles her son, of whom she speaks with the tenderest affection.

I very much hope Mr Foster* will obtain the living of Clarendon. The rectory is charming, all covered with roses. The present rector, an old friend of the family, is being preferred to a Prebendary at the Cathedral of G—. Clarendon church is beautiful too, built in cruciform shape, with an ancient tower on the north side; the bells are reputed to be amongst the best in England. There are also excellent parish schools, and I shall consider myself lucky if I can teach there.

I am very pleased to hear you have made acquaintance with my cousin Elena. The better you know her, the more you'll like her,

I'm sure. She has lost both parents and I hope that when her education is completed she will make her home with us.

You must pardon me the liberty of having taken up so much of your time with such a long account of my own affairs. But truly, I've done so without realising my excessive chatter; so it is to speak of what one loves. Be kind enough to give my most affectionate greetings to Elena, and believe me, my dear Miss Ruggieri, always your most humble servant and friend,

Clorinda Knight

NO. 6

Emma Ward to Angela-Maria de'Ruggieri

I'm in despair. And why? I'll tell you with all my heart, because you and only you can give me any help in my present lamentable position.

The other evening, we went, Mamma and I, to a conversazione.* It was a disastrous evening. To begin with, the dressmaker only sent round my dress at the very last moment; so I was obliged to wear something that didn't suit me and was trimmed in pink of too dark a hue. Aren't you sorry for me, my dear? But don't be too sorry yet, for I haven't told you the half of my troubles.

We arrived rather late and could hardly find anywhere to sit. An ugly old man, younger son of a Duke, stationed himself before me and talked almost the whole evening. I did nothing but yawn, visibly, but it was no use.

He talked about literature, philosophy, fiction, painting, opera; and finally he told me that the Countess of Crawley* would give anything for a couple of verses for her album,* to accompany an air of her own composition. You should know that this Countess attracts the attention of all Society in this regard. She was a nobody, originally, but having married the richest peer in Ireland, who was as old as her grandfather, she can now do as she pleases, with stupendous dinner parties, magnificent dances and the best receptions of the Season.* So, flattering myself that I could be of service, I told my old man that I'd be happy to meet the Countess's requirements. Then came the introduction. Lady Crawley was enchanted by my offer, and promised to send round the album in the morning; in which happy moment even my old man seemed agreeable. I came home very very contented. I had always heard that anyone can write verses in Italian, the rhymes come of their own accord, and even improvisation isn't difficult in this beautiful tongue. Alas! I've been three hours at work and have produced just four and a half lines, with only a single rhyme. So I beg you to rescue me from my plight. Have pity on me and pen me a few stanzas, dearest Angela; I flatter myself you won't refuse.

I was most interested in your account of the excursion to the castle. Try to find out if the gracious Gertrude belongs to the family of Lord Towers, they share the same name. If so, this would be a favourable acquaintance for you.

I've no time to write more; but once again repeat my plea to you. Mamma sends greetings; and I am forever your most affectionate cousin,

Emma Ward

NO. 7

Angela-Maria de'Ruggieri to Emma Ward

My dearest Emma,
I'm truly pleased to be of some small service to you. I hope the following lyric will satisfy her ladyship the Countess; and in return for my endeavour I ask only to remain anonymous.

The blushing rose,
Sweet in scent and hue
Is fair to see
But will never be,
My love-in-a-mist,
Rival to you.

My misty lady,
Flower on stem's side
Each one is claimed
For Love's high aim;
But flowers will fade
While you abide.

For days it's done nothing but rain; it's very tiresome. Your letter gave me the greatest pleasure. To speak truly, this dull evening seems quite delightful compared with a week of rain in the country. Morning after morning I get up full of hope; but gaze out of the front door and you see the plane trees dancing, gaze out of the back window and you'll see ducks and geese enjoying themselves. Since we can't go out and it's wet and cold, Mrs Sharp encourages us to take excercise in dances which involve most jumping. You should see us leaping like lunatics. There's no one to play, so everyone has to sing the tune themselves. Gertrude sings much the best, and dances well too; as for the rest, some do better, some worse. You remember Anna Green? It's a real joy to see her jumping like a giraffe, all out of time, with an owlish expression. Oh, if Elena saw this squib, how she'd scold! She's tried in vain to make us friends.

Now I must tell you something that gives me great anxiety. Papa was in the habit of writing every other day, sending me all his news and asking for mine. More than a week has passed and I haven't had a single line. In his last letter he said he was in good health, had much business, and was thinking of going out of town for a few days. I replied the next day and have since sent two more letters, but there's been no response. A thousand fearful thoughts are whirling through my brain and I don't know which to trust. If Papa had been ill it would have been simple to ask someone to write to me; if he had had an accident, he could have done the same. I can't believe that a quiet stay in the country would make him forgetful of his loving daughter. I'm very afraid that some political affair has induced him to leave England; and who knows whether some impulsive plan has not taken him to Italy? However, so far I've consoled myself that this is not so, and that very soon I shall get a letter which will make me blush at the foolishness of my fears.

I think Mrs Sharp is very pleased with the progress I am making in English. From time to time, when we've nothing else to do, Elena makes me read a chapter of Miss Edgeworth,* and then I listen to her repeat some poetry for the pronunciation. The other day Amelia Etherage asked me to help her with her French exercise. That was a great compliment, because at first she used to look me up and down pityingly, as if I was a complete imbecile. She is really very talented; no half-year goes by without her receiving at least one prize.

Clorinda has written me the gayest letter. She seems truly happy. The curate is a Mr Foster and I hope will very soon become rector of Clarendon.

Write to me as soon as you can, and let me know if my verses are satisfactory. I hope to have a letter first thing tomorrow; if I don't get one, I shall send another to Papa, though who knows if it will reach him. My head aches with such thinking; goodbye, my dear

Emma, have pity on me and believe me always your most affectionate cousin

Angela-Maria de'Ruggieri

NO. 8

Emma Ward to Angela-Maria de'Ruggieri

Dearest Angela,

I can't thank you enough for the little song you sent. It's exactly what I wanted; I copied it, without any signature, into the Countess's album, and went to return the volume in person. When she read your verses she embraced me effusively, thanking me a thousand times and showing how immensely pleased she was. She has invited me to a party next week; and says that she wants to sing it before the guests. While we were talking, I taking great care not to betray your secret, in came the Neapolitan ambassador, accompanied by a new secretary just arrived in England. Lady Crawley at once showed them the verses. They read them and congratulated me on my knowledge of the beautiful language, and on my poetic gift. With utmost truth, as you know, I replied that I did not deserve such praise, but the more I protested, the more they heaped me with compliments; and a little while later I returned home. But the worst is yet to tell; early this morning, even before I was dressed, the maid brought up a wonderful bouquet of red and white roses. On the paper in which it was wrapped were written the following verses:

These roses which I give to you
Are symbolic
By their colours set apart
Of your spirit and your heart.

And the brightest red red rose
Like a queen
Whose high forehead rises proud
Of all flowers o'ertops the cloud

And through pure and noble singing
You excel,
Shining brighter than all other maidens
Like the Moon amidst the heavens.

While the brightest whitest rose
Symbolises

That pure truth in you discerned
And the heart whose faith ne'er turned.**

The signature was that of Lancetti, my Mr Secretary.

Don't scold me for my unwilling deceit, my dear. It's now too late to correct the mistake. Nobody would believe me unless I were to reveal the name of the true author, and I know you don't want me to do that. I hope that very soon the verses will be forgotten, and then the wrong of a moment will matter no longer. I shall continue to declare myself unworthy of such praise, and it won't be my fault if I'm not believed.

Do not torment yourself by anticipating troubles that may never come. If I did this at every request, every evening, it would be a cause of grief. Moreover, even if your father has left the country, it is not certain that he has gone to Italy; and even if it should prove to be, we read of so many miraculous escapes that we may always hope for the best.

I am confident you won't betray me; if the error were revealed, I should be mortified. I'll give you a full account without fail of the Countess's evening party. Between ourselves, no-one ever speaks of the Earl, who's a cipher in his own house; but Lady Crawley treats him very well, and always appears when they give a party. I haven't time to write any more, but am and will always be your most affectionate cousin

Emma Ward

(to be continued)

** These delightful verses are not mine; I am obliged for them to my honoured friend PARSLEY

– MARIGOLD

[Original footnote in August 1852 issue of *The Bouquet from Marylebone Gardens*. No more instalments of *Family Correspondence* appeared.]

Nick

Written in the early 1850s, Nick* *derives its folk-tale form from the stories Christina Rossetti read to the young pupils attending her mother's day- school, but it is not really a tale for children. It was first published in the* National Magazine *in 1857. It is full of violence, envy and spite, emotions seldom endorsed in her poetry, although given expression in some of the more Gothick pieces, such as* 'Will These Hands Ne'er be Clean' *and* 'Sister Maude', *and which belie her reputation for what Sara Coleridge called 'goodyism' – a form of ostentatious piety much practised by Puseyites.*

In 1853, when Nick *was first submitted to a publisher named Addey, the author wove a facetious fantasy on the subject which hints at the seriousness of her literary hopes. 'I have conceived a first-rate scheme for rebuilding the shattered fortunes of our house,' she told her brother, suggesting humorously that the text be forwarded to Addey's business manager together with her portrait. Then, she continued:*

> *Man of business (a susceptible individual of great discernment) risks the loss of his situation by immediately forwarding me a cheque for £20, and sets his subs to work on an elegant edition of 'Nick.' Addey returns; is at first furious; but, seeing the portrait, and with a first-rate business head perceiving at a glance its capabilities, has it engraved, prefixed to 'N', and advertized all over the civilized world. The book spreads like wild-fire. Addey at the end of 2 months, struck by a late remorse, and having an eye to future contingencies, sends me a second cheque for £200; on which we subsist for a while. At the publication of the 20th edition Mrs A (a mild person of few words) expires; charging her husband to do me justice. He promises with one suppressed sob. Next day a third cheque for £2000 reaches me. This I divide; assigning half to Maria for her dowry, and handing the rest to Mamma. I then collapse. Exeunt Omnes.*

There dwelt in a small village, not a thousand miles from Fairyland, a poor man, who had no family to labour for or friend to assist. When I call him poor, you must not suppose he was a homeless wanderer, trusting to charity for a night's lodging; on the contrary, his stone house, with its green verandah and flower-garden, was the prettiest and snuggest in all the place, the doctor's only excepted. Neither was his store of provisions running low: his farm supplied him with milk, eggs, mutton, butter, poultry, and cheese in abundance; his fields with hops and barley for beer, and wheat for bread; his orchard with fruit and cider; and his kitchen-garden with vegetables and wholesome herbs. He had, moreover, health, an appetite to enjoy all these good things, and strength to walk about his possessions. No, I call him poor because, with all these, he was discontented and envious. It was in vain that his apples were the largest for miles around, if his neighbour's vines were the most productive by a single bunch; it was in vain that his lambs were fat and thriving, if some one else's sheep bore twins: so, instead of enjoying his own prosperity, and being glad when his neighbours prospered too, he would sit grumbling and bemoaning himself as if every other man's riches were his poverty. And thus it was that one day our friend Nick leaned over Giles Hodge's* gate, counting his cherries.

'Yes,' he muttered, 'I wish I were sparrows to eat them up, or a blight to kill your fine trees altogether.'

The words were scarcely uttered when he felt a tap on his shoulder, and looking round, perceived a little rosy woman, no bigger than a butterfly, who held her tiny fist clenched in a menacing attitude. She looked scornfully at him, and said: 'Now listen, you churl, you! henceforward you shall straightway become everything you wish; only mind, you must remain under one form for at least an hour.' Then she gave him a slap in the face, which made his cheek tingle as if a bee had stung him, and disappeared with just so much sound as a dewdrop makes in falling.

Nick rubbed his cheek in a pet, pulling wry faces and showing his teeth. He was boiling over with vexation, but dared not vent it in words lest some unlucky wish should escape him. Just then the sun seemed to shine brighter than ever, the wind blew spicy from the south; all Giles's roses looked redder and larger than before, while his cherries seemed to multiply, swell, ripen. He could refrain no longer, but, heedless of the fairy-gift he had just received, exclaimed, 'I wish I were sparrows eating—' No sooner said than done: in a moment he found himself a whole flight of hungry birds, pecking, devouring, and bidding fair to devastate the envied cherry-trees. But honest Giles was on the watch hard by; for that very morning it had struck him he must make nets for the protection of his fine fruit. Forthwith he ran home, and speedily returned with a revolver furnished with quite a marvellous array of barrels.* Pop, bang – pop, bang! he made short work of the sparrows, and soon reduced the enemy to one crestfallen biped with broken leg and wing, who limped to hide himself under a holly-bush. But though the fun was over, the hour was not; so Nick must needs sit out his allotted time. Next a pelting shower came down, which soaked him through his torn, ruffled feathers; and then, exactly as the last drops fell and the sun came out with a beautiful rainbow, a tabby cat pounced upon him. Giving himself up for lost, he chirped in desperation, 'O, I wish I were a dog to worry you!' Instantly – for the hour was just passed – in the grip of his horrified adversary, he turned at bay, a savage bull-dog. A shake, a deep bite, and poor puss was out of her pain. Nick, with immense satisfaction, tore her fur to bits, wishing he could in like manner exterminate all her progeny. At last, glutted with vengence, he lay down beside his victim, relaxed his ears and tail, and fell asleep.

Now that tabby-cat was the property and special pet of no less a personage than the doctor's lady; so when dinner-time came, and not the cat, a general consternation pervaded the household. The kitchens were searched, the cellars, the attics; every apartment was ransacked; even the watch-dog's kennel was visited. Next the stable was rummaged, then the hay-loft; lastly, the bereaved lady wandered disconsolately through her own private garden into the shrubbery, calling 'Puss, puss,' and looking so intently up the trees as not to perceive what lay close before her feet. Thus it was that, unawares, she stumbled over Nick, and trod upon his tail.

Up jumped our hero, snarling, biting, and rushing at her with such blind fury as to miss his aim. She ran, he ran. Gathering up his strength, he took a flying-leap after his victim; her foot caught in the spreading root of an oaktree, she fell, and he went over her head, clear over, into a bed of stinging-nettles. Then she found breath to raise that fatal cry,* 'Mad dog!' Nick's blood curdled in his veins; he would have slunk away if he could; but already a stout labouring-man, to whom he had done many an ill turn in the time of his humanity, had spied him, and, bludgeon in hand, was preparing to give chase. However, Nick had the start of him, and used it too; while the lady, far behind, went on vociferating, 'Mad dog, mad dog!' inciting doctor, servants, and vagabonds to the pursuit. Finally, the whole village came pouring out to swell the hue and cry.

The dog kept ahead gallantly, distancing more and more the asthmatic doctor, fat Giles, and, in fact, all his pursuers except the bludgeon-bearing labourer, who was just near enough to persecute his tail. Nick knew the magic hour must be almost over, and so kept forming wish after wish as he ran, – that he were a viper only to get trodden on, a thorn to run into some one's foot, a man-trap in the path, even the detested bludgeon to miss its aim and break. This wish crossed his mind at the propitious moment; the bull-dog vanished, and the labourer, overreaching himself, fell flat on his face, while his weapon struck deep into the earth, and snapped.

A strict search was instituted after the missing dog, but without success. During two whole days the village children were exhorted to keep indoors and beware of dogs; on the third an inoffensive bull pup was hanged, and the panic subsided.

Meanwhile the labourer, with his shattered stick, walked home in silent wonder, pondering on the mysterious disappearance. But the puzzle was beyond his solution; so he only made up his mind not to tell his wife the whole story till after tea. He found her preparing for that meal, the bread and cheese set out, and the kettle singing softly on the fire. 'Here's something to make the kettle boil, mother,' said he, thrusting our hero between the bars and seating himself; 'for I'm mortal tired and thirsty.'

Nick crackled and blazed away cheerfully, throwing out bright sparks, and lighting up every corner of the little room. He toasted the cheese to a nicety, made the kettle boil without spilling a drop, set the cat purring with comfort, and illuminated the pots and pans into splendour. It was provocation enough to be burned; but to contribute by his misfortune to the well-being of his tormentors was still more aggravating. He heard, too, all their remarks and wonderment about the supposed mad-dog, and saw the doctor's lady's own maid bring the labourer five shillings as a reward for his exertions. Then followed a discussion as to what should be purchased with the gift, till at last it was resolved to have their best window glazed with real glass. The prospect of their grandeur put the finishing-stroke to Nick's indignation. Sending up a sudden flare, he wished with all his might that he were fire to burn the cottage.

Forthwith the flame leaped higher than ever flame leaped before. It played for a moment about a ham,* and smoked it to a nicety; then, fastening on the woodwork above the chimney-corner, flashed full into a blaze. The labourer ran for help, while his wife, a timid woman, with three small children, overturned two pails of water on the floor, and set the beer-tap running. This done, she hurried, wringing her hands, to the door, and threw it wide open. The sudden draught of air did more mischief than all

Nick's malice, and fanned him into quite a conflagration. He danced upon the rafters, melted a pewter-pot and a pat of butter, licked up the beer, and was just making his way towards the bedroom, when through the thatch and down the chimney came a rush of water. This arrested his progress for the moment; and before he could recover himself, a second and a third discharge from the enemy completed his discomfiture. Reduced ere long to one blue flame, and entirely surrounded by a wall of wet ashes, Nick sat and smouldered; while the good-natured neighbours did their best to remedy the mishap, – saved a small remnant of beer, assured the labourer that his landlord was certain to do the repairs, and observed that the ham would eat 'beautiful'.

Our hero now had leisure for reflection. His situation precluded all hope of doing further mischief; and the disagreeable conviction kept forcing itself upon his mind that, after all, he had caused more injury to himself than to any of his neighbours. Remembering, too, how contemptuously the fairy woman had looked and spoken, he began to wonder how he could ever have expected to enjoy her gift. Then it occurred to him, that if he merely studied his own advantage without trying to annoy other people, perhaps his persecutor might be propitiated; so he fell to thinking over all his acquaintances, their fortunes and misfortunes; and, having weighed well their several claims on his preference, ended by wishing himself the rich old man who lived in a handsome house just beyond the turnpike.* In this wish he burned out.

The last glimmer had scarcely died away, when Nick found himself in a bed hung round with faded curtains, and occupying the centre of a large room. A night-lamp, burning on the chimney-piece, just enabled him to discern a few shabby old articles of furniture, a scanty carpet, and some writing materials on a table. These objects looked somewhat dreary; but for his comfort he felt an inward consciousness of a goodly money-chest stowed away under his bed, and of sundry precious documents hidden in a secret cupboard in the wall.

So he lay very cosily, and listened to the clock ticking, the mice squeaking, and the house-dog barking down below. This was, however, but a drowsy occupation; and he soon bore witness to its somniferous influence by sinking into a fantastic dream about his money-chest. First, it was broken open, then shipwrecked, then burned; lastly, some men in masks, whom he knew instinctively to be his own servants, began dragging it away. Nick started up, clutched hold of something in the dark, found his last dream true, and the next moment was stretched on the floor – lifeless, yet not insensible – by a heavy blow from a crowbar.

The men now proceeded to secure their booty, leaving our hero where he fell. They carried off the chest, broke open and ransacked the secret closet, overturned the furniture, to make sure that no hiding-place of treasure escaped them, and at length, whispering together, left the room. Nick felt quite discouraged by his ill success, and now entertained only one wish – that he was himself again. Yet even this wish gave him some anxiety; for he feared that if the servants returned and found him in his original shape they might take him for a spy, and murder him in downright earnest. While he lay thus cogitating two of the men reappeared, bearing a shutter and some tools. They lifted him up, laid him on the shutter, and carried him out of the room, down the backstairs, through a long vaulted passage, into the open air. No word was spoken; but Nick knew they were going to bury him.*

An utter horror seized him, while, at the same time, he felt a strange consciousness that his hair would not stand on end because he was dead. The men set him down, and began in silence to dig his grave. It was soon ready to receive him; they threw the body roughly in, and cast upon it the first shovelful of earth.

But the moment of deliverance had arrived. His wish suddenly found vent in a prolonged unearthly yell. Damp with night dew, pale as death, and shivering from head to foot, he sat bolt upright, with starting, staring eyes and chattering teeth. The murderers, in mortal fear, cast down their tools, plunged deep into a wood hard by, and were never heard of more.

Under cover of night Nick made the best of his way home, silent and pondering. Next morning he gave Giles Hodge a rare tulip-root, with full directions for rearing it; he sent the doctor's wife a Persian cat twice the size of her lost pet; the labourer's cottage was repaired, his window glazed, and his beer-barrel replaced by unknown agency; and when a vague rumour reached the village that the miser was dead, that his ghost had been heard bemoaning itself, and that all his treasures had been carried off, our hero was one of the few persons who did not say, 'And served him right, too.'

Finally, Nick was never again heard to utter a wish.

Hero

Probably written in the mid-1850s, after reading Hans Andersen – whose work was introduced to the British public by Mary Howitt, friend and mentor to Christina Rossetti – Hero *was first published in 1865, in* The Argosy. *A metamorphosis tale, it dramatises the fantasy of desire for beauty, riches and surpassing fame within the framework of a traditional warning against the selfish pursuit of eminence, thus playing out the eternal female conflict between eager ambition and modest contentment. Hero, too, as her odd name suggests, aspires to the heroic status a Victorian girl could only contemplate in fiction, not dream of attaining in life, where self-realisation was held to be egocentric and unseemly. But behind – or literally, within – Hero stand her alter egos Princess Lily and diva Melice Rapta, alluring figures respectively of the young Queen Victoria (recipient of the renowned Koh-i-noor diamond) and the 'unrivalled songstress' Jenny Lind. The account of Madame Rapta's final performances, incidentally, appears to be drawn from the Italian opera in London, which Christina Rossetti enjoyed in her youth, before religious scruples compelled her to relinquish theatre-going. And though in the end Hero gives up glory in favour of marriage and motherhood, her splendid adventures are full of verve and spirit in the style of the most satisfying Cinderella story. Thematically, it forms a link between* 'The Lowest Room' *and* 'Goblin Market', *heralding the latter's blend of fairy fantasy and moral narrative.*

'Oh, wad some power the giftie gie us!'*

BURNS

If you consult the authentic map of Fairyland (recently published by Messrs Moon, Shine, and Co.) you will notice that the emerald-green line which indicates its territorial limit, is washed towards the south by a bold expanse of sea, undotted by either rocks or islands. To the north-west it touches the work-a-day world, yet is effectually barricaded against intruders by an impassable chain of mountains; which, enriched throughout with mines of gems and metals, presents on Man-side a leaden sameness of hue, but on Elf-side glitters with diamonds and opals as with ten thousand fire-flies. The greater portion of the west frontier is, however, bounded, not by these mountains, but by an arm of the sea, which forms a natural barrier between the two countries; its eastern shore peopled by good folks and canny neighbours, gay sprites, graceful fairies, and sportive elves; its western by a bold tribe of semi-barbarous fishermen.

Nor was it without reason that the first settlers selected this fishing-field, and continued to occupy it, though generation after generation they lived and died almost isolated. Their swift, white-sailed boats ever bore the most delicate freights of fish to the markets of Outerworld – and not of fish only; many a waif and stray from Fairyland washed ashore amongst them. Now a fiery carbuncle* blazed upon the sand; now a curiously-wrought ball of gold or ivory was found imbedded amongst the pebbles. Sometimes a sunny wave threw up a rose-coloured winged shell or jewelled starfish; sometimes a branch of unfading seaweed, exquisitely perfumed. But though these treasures, when once secured, could be offered for sale and purchased by all alike, they were never, in the first instance, discovered except by children or innocent young maidens; indeed, this fact was of such invariable occurrence, and children were so fortunate in treasure-finding, that a bluff mariner would often, on returning home empty-handed from his day's toil, despatch his little son or daughter to a certain sheltered stretch of shingle, which went by the name of 'the children's harvest-field;' hoping by such means to repair his failure.

Amongst this race of fishermen was none more courageous, hospitable, and free-spoken than Peter Grump the widower; amongst their daughters was none more graceful and pure than his only child Hero,* beautiful, lively, tender-hearted, and fifteen; the pet of her father, the pride of her neighbours, and the true love of Forss,* as sturdy a young fellow as ever cast a net in deep water, or rowed against wind and tide for dear life.

One afternoon Hero, rosy through the splashing spray and sea-wind, ran home full-handed from the harvest-field.

'See here, father!' she cried, eagerly depositing a string of sparkling beads upon the table: 'see, are they not beautiful?'

Peter Grump examined them carefully, holding each bead up to the light, and weighing them in his hand.

'Beautiful indeed!' echoed Forss, who unnoticed, at least by the elder, had followed Hero into the cottage. 'Ah, if I had a sister to find me fairy treasures, I would take the three months' long journey to the best market of Outerworld, and make my fortune there.'

'Then you would rather go the three months' journey into Outerworld than come every evening to my father's cottage?' said Hero, shyly.

'Truly I would go to Outerworld first, and come to you

afterwards,' her lover answered, with a smile; for he thought how speedily on his return he would have a tight house of his own, and a fair young wife, too.

'Father,' said Hero presently, 'if, instead of gifts coming now and then to us, I could go to Giftland and grow rich there, would you fret after me?'

'Truly,' answered honest Peter, 'if you can go and be Queen of Fairyland, I will not keep you back from such eminence;' for he thought, 'my darling jests; no one ever traversed those mountains or that inland sea, and how should her little feet cross over?'

But Hero, who could not read their hearts, said within herself, 'They do not love me as I love them. Father should not leave me to be fifty kings; and I would not leave Forss to go to Fairyland, much less Outerworld.'

Yet from that day forward Hero was changed; their love no longer seemed sufficient for her; she sought after other love and other admiration. Once a lily was ample head-dress, now she would heighten her complexion with a wreath of gorgeous blossoms; once it was enough that Peter and Forss should be pleased with her, now she grudged any man's notice to her fellow-maidens. Stung by supposed indifference, she suffered disappointment to make her selfish. Her face, always beautiful, lost its expression of gay sweetness; her temper became capricious, and instead of cheerful airs she would sing snatches of plaintive or bitter songs. Her father looked anxious, her lover sad; both endeavoured, by the most patient tenderness, to win her back to her former self; but a weight lay on their hearts when they noticed that she no longer brought home fairy treasures, and remembered that such could be found only by the innocent.

One evening Hero, sick alike of herself and of others, slipped unnoticed from the cottage, and wandered seawards. Though the moon had not yet risen, she could see her way distinctly, for all Fairycoast flashed one blaze of splendour. A soft wind bore to Hero the hum of distant instruments and songs, mingled with ringing laughter; and she thought, full of curiosity, that some festival must be going on amongst the little people; perhaps a wedding.

Suddenly the music ceased, the lights danced up and down, ran to and fro, clambered here and there, skurried round and round with irregular precipitate haste, while the laughter was succeeded by fitful sounds of lamentation and fear. Hero fancied some precious thing must have been lost, and that a minute search was going on. For hours the commotion continued, then gradually, spark by spark, the blaze died out, and all seemed once more quiet; yet still the low wail of sorrow was audible.

Weary at length of watching, Hero arose; and was just about to turn homewards, when a noisy, vigorous wave leaped ashore, and deposited something shining at her feet.

She stooped. What could it be?

It was a broad, luminous shell, fitted up with pillows and an awning. On the pillows and under the scented canopy lay fast asleep a little creature, butterfly-winged and coloured like a rose-leaf. The fish who should have piloted her had apparently perished at his post, some portion of his pulp still cleaving to the shell's fluted lip; while unconscious of her faithful adherent's fate, rocked by wind and wave, the Princess Royal of Fairyland had floated fast asleep to Man-side. Her disappearance it was which had occasioned such painful commotion amongst her family and affectionate lieges;* but all their lamentations failed to rouse her; and not till the motion of the water ceased did she awake to find herself, vessel and all, cradled in the hands of Hero.

During some moments the two stared at each other in silent amazement; then a suspicion of the truth flashing across her mind, Princess Fay sat upright on her couch and spoke,—

'What gift shall I give you that so I may return to my home in peace?'

For an instant Hero would have answered, 'Give me the love of Forss;' but pride checked the words, and she said, 'Grant me, wherever I am, to become the supreme object of admiration.'

Princess Fay smiled. 'As you will,' said she; 'but to effect this you must come with me to my country.'

Then, whilst Hero looked round for some road which mortal feet might traverse, Fay uttered a low, bird-like call. A slight frothing ensued, at the water's edge, close to the shingle, whilst one by one mild, scaly faces peered above the surface, and vigorous tails propelled their owners. Next, three strong fishes combining themselves into a raft, Hero seated herself on the centre back, and holding fast her little captive, launched out upon the water.

Soon they passed beyond where mortal sailor had ever navigated, and explored the unknown sea. Strange forms of seals and porpoises, marine snails and unicorns contemplated them with surprise, followed reverentially in their wake, and watched them safe ashore.

But on Hero their curious ways were lost, so absorbed was she by ambitious longings. Even after landing, to her it seemed nothing that her feet trod on sapphires, and that both birds and fairies made their nests in the adjacent trees. Blinded, deafened, stultified by self, she passed unmoved through crystal streets, between fountains of rainbow, along corridors carpeted with butterflies' wings, up a staircase formed from a single tusk, into the opal presence-chamber, even to the foot of the carnelian dormouse on which sat enthroned Queen Fairy.

Till the Queen said, 'What gift shall I give you, that so my child may be free from you and we at peace?'

Then again Hero answered, 'Grant me, wherever I am, to become the supreme object of admiration.'

Thereat a hum and buzz of conflicting voices ran through the apartment. The immutable statutes of Fairycourt enacted that no captured fairy could be set free except at the price named by the captor; from this necessity not even the blood-royal was exempt, so that the case was very urgent; on the other hand, the beauty of Hero, her extreme youth, and a certain indignant sorrow which spoke in her every look and tone, had enlisted such sympathy on her side as made the pigmy nation loth to endow her with the perilous pre-eminence she demanded.

'Clear the court,' shrilled the usher of the golden rod, an alert elf, green like a grasshopper. Amid the crowd of non-voters Hero, bearing her august prisoner, retired from the throne-room.

When recalled to the assembly an imposing silence reigned, which was almost instantly broken by the Queen. 'Maiden,' she said, 'it cannot be but that the dear ransom of my daughter's liberty must be paid. I grant you, wherever you may appear, to become the supreme object of admiration. In you every man shall find his taste satisfied. In you one shall recognise his ideal of loveliness, another shall bow before the impersonation of dignity. One shall be thrilled by your voice, another fascinated by your wit and inimitable grace. He who prefers colour shall dwell upon your complexion, hair, eyes; he who worships intellect shall find in you his superior; he who is ambitious shall feel you to be a prize more august than an empire. I cannot ennoble the taste of those who look upon you: I can but cause that in you all desire shall be gratified. If sometimes you chafe under a trivial homage, if sometimes you are admired rather for what you have than for what you are, accuse your votaries, – accuse, if you will, yourself, but accuse not me. In consideration, however, of your utter inexperience, I and my trusty counsellors have agreed for one year to retain your body here, whilst in spirit you at will become one with the reigning object of admiration. If at the end of the year you return to claim this pre-eminence as your own proper attribute, it shall then be unconditionally granted: if, on the contrary, you then or even sooner desire to be released from a gift whose sweetness is alloyed by you know not how much of bitter shortcoming and disappointment, return, and you shall at once be relieved of a burden you cannot yet estimate.'

So Hero quitted the presence, led by spirits to a pleasance screened off into a perpetual twilight. Here, on a rippling lake, blossomed lilies. She lay down among their broad leaves and cups, cradled by their interlaced stems; rocked by warm winds on the rocking water; she lay till the splash of fountains, and the chirp of nestlings, and the whisper of spiced breezes, and the chanted monotone of an innumerable choir, lulled to sleep her soul, lulled to rest her tumultous heart, charmed her conscious spirit into a heavy blazing diamond, – a glory by day, a lamp by night, and a world's wonder* at all times.

Let us leave the fair body at rest, and crowned with lilies, to follow the restless spirit, shrined in a jewel, and cast ashore on Man-side.

No sooner was this incomparable diamond picked up and carried home than Hero's darling wish was gratified. She outshone every beauty, she eclipsed the most brilliant eyes of the colony. For a moment the choicest friend was superseded, the dearest mistress overlooked. For a moment – and this outstripped her desire – Peter Grump forgot his lost daughter and Forss his lost love. Soon greedy admiration developed into greedy strife: her spark kindled a conflagration. This gem, in itself an unprecedented fortune; should this gem remain the property of a defenceless orphan to whom mere chance had assigned it? From her it was torn in a moment: then the stronger wrested it from the strong, blows revenged blows, until, as the last contender bit the dust in convulsive death, the victor, feared throughout the settlement for his brute strength and brutal habits, bore off the prize toward the best market of Outerworld.

It irked Hero to nestle in that polluted bosom and count the beatings of that sordid heart; but when at the end of the three months' long journey, she found herself in a guarded booth, enthroned on a cushion of black velvet, by day blazing even in the full sunshine, by night needing no lamp save her own lustre; when she heard the sums running up from thousands into millions which whole guilds of jewellers, whole caravans of merchant princes, whole royal families clubbed their resources to offer for her purchase, it outweighed all she had undergone of disgust and tedium. Finally, two empires, between which a marriage was about to be contracted and a peace ratified, outbid all rivals and secured the prize.

Princess Lily, the august bride-elect, was celebrated far and near for courteous manners and delicate beauty. Her refusal was more gracious, her reserve more winning, than the acquiescence or frankness of another. She might have been more admired, or even envied, had she been less loved. If she sang, her hearers loved her; thus love forestalled admiration, and happy in the one she never missed the other.

Only on her wedding-day, for the first time, she excited envy; for in her coronet appeared the inestimable jewel, encircling her sweet face with a halo of splendour. Hero eclipsed the bride, dazzled the bridegroom, distracted the queen-mother, and thrilled the whole assembly. Through all the public solemnities of the day Hero reigned supreme: and when, the state parade being at length over, Lily unclasped her gems and laid aside her cumbrous coronet, Hero was handled with more reverential tenderness than her mistress.

The bride leaned over her casket of treasure and gazed at the inestimable diamond. 'Is it not magnficient?' whispered she.

'What?' said the bridegroom: 'I was looking at you.'

So Lily flushed up with delight, and Hero experienced a shock. Next the diamond shot up one ray of dazzling momentary lustre; then lost its supernatural brilliancy, as Hero quitted the gem for the heart of Lily.

Etiquette required that the young couple should for some days remain in strict retirement. Hero now found herself in a secluded palace, screened by the growth of many centuries. She was waited on by twenty bridesmaids only less noble than their princess; she was worshipped by her bridegroom and reflected by a hundred mirrors. In Lily's pure heart she almost found rest: and when the young prince, at dawn, or lazy noon, or mysterious twilight – for indeed the process went on every day and all day – praised his love's eyes, or hair, or voice, or movements, Hero thought with proud eagerness of the moment when, in her own proper person, she might claim undisputed pre-eminence.

The prescribed seclusion, however, drew to a close, and the royal pair must make their entrance on public life. Their entrance coincided with another's exit.

Melice Rapta had for three successive seasons thrilled the world by her voice, and subdued it by her loveliness. She possessed the demeanour of an empress, and the winning simplicity of a child, genius and modesty, tenderness and indomitable will. Her early years had passed in obscurity, subject to neglect, if not unkindness; it was only when approaching womanhood developed and matured her gifts that she met with wealthy protectors and assumed their name: for Melice was a foundling.

No sooner however did her world-wide fame place large resources at her command, than she anxiously sought to trace her unknown parentage; and, at length, discovered that her high-born father and plebeian mother – herself sole fruit of their concealed marriage – were dead. Once made known to her kindred, she was eagerly acknowledged by them; but rejecting more brilliant offers, she chose to withdraw into a private sphere, and fix her residence with a maternal uncle, who, long past the meridian of life, devoted his energies to botanical research and culture.

So, on the same evening, Lily and her husband entered on their public duties, and Melice took leave for ever of a nation of admirers.

When the prince and princess appeared in the theatre, the whole house stood up, answering their smiles and blushes by acclamations of welcome. They took their places on chairs of state under an emblazoned canopy, and the performance commenced.

A moonless night: three transparent ghosts flit across the scene, bearing in their bosoms unborn souls. They leave behind tracks of light from which are generated arums. Day breaks – Melice enters; she washes her hands in a fountain, singing to the splash of the water; she plucks arums, and begins weaving them into a garland, still singing.

Lily bent forward to whisper something to her husband; but he raised his hand, enforcing 'Hush!' as through eyes and ears his soul drank deep of beauty. The young wife leaned back with good-humoured acquiescence; but Hero?

In another moment Hero was singing in the unrivalled songstress, charming and subduing every heart. The play proceeded; its incidents, its characters developed. Melice outshone, outsang herself; warbling like a bird, thrilling with entreaty, pouring forth her soul in passion. Her voice commanded an enthusiastic silence, her silence drew down thunders of enthusiastic applause. She acknowledged the honour with majestic courtesy; then, for the first time, trembled, changed colour: would have swept from the presence like a queen, but merely wept like a woman.

It was her hour of supreme triumph.

Next day she set out for her uncle's residence, her own selected home.

Many a long day's journey separated her from her mother's village, and her transit thither assumed the aspect of a ceremonial progress. At every town on her route orations and emblems awaited her; whilst from the capital she was quitting, came, pursuing her, messages of farewell, congratulation, entreaty. Often an unknown cavalier rode beside her carriage some stage of the journey; often a high-born lady met her on the road, and, taking a last view of her countenance, obtained a few more last words from the most musical mouth in the world.

At length the goal was reached. The small cottage, surrounded by its disproportionately extensive garden, was there; the complex forcing-houses, pits, refrigerators, were there; Uncle Treeh was there, standing at the open door to receive his newly-found relative.

Uncle Treeh was rather old, rather short, not handsome; with an acute eye, a sensitive mouth, and spectacles. With his complexion of sere brown, and his scattered threads of white hair, he strikingly resembled certain plants of the cactus tribe, which, in their turn, resemble withered old men.

All his kind face brightened with welcome as he kissed his fair niece, and led her into his sitting-room. On the table were spread for her refreshment the choicest products of his gardens: ponderous pine-apples, hundred-berried vine clusters, currants large as grapes and sweet as honey. For a moment his eyes dwelt on a human countenance with more admiration than on a vegetable; for a moment, on comparing Melice's complexion with an oleander, he awarded the palm to the former.

But a week afterwards, when Melice, leaning over his shoulder, threatened to read what he was writing, Treeh looked good-naturedly conscious, and, abandoning the letter to her mercy, made his escape into a neighbouring conservatory.

She reads as follows:—

MY FRIEND,—

You will doubtless have learned how my solitude has been invaded by my sister's long-lost daughter, a peach-coloured damsel, with commeline* eyes, and hair darker than chestnuts. For one whole evening I suspended my beloved toils and devoted myself to her: alas! next day, on revisiting Lime Alley, house B, pot 37, I found that during my absence a surreptitious slug had devoured three shoots of a tea-rose. Thus nipped in the bud, my cherished nursling seemed to upbraid me with neglect, and so great was my vexation, that, on returning to company, I could scarcely conceal it. From that hour I resolved that no mistaken notions of hospitality should ever again seduce me from the true aim of my existence. Nerved by this resolution, I once more take courage; and now write to inform you that I am in hourly expectation of beholding pierce the soil (loam, drenched with liquid manure) the first sprout from that unnamed alien seed,* which was brought to our market, three months ago, by a seafaring man of semi-barbarous aspect. I break off to visit my hoped-for seedling.

At this moment the door, hastily flung open, startled Melice, who, looking up, beheld Treeh, radiant and rejoicing, a flowerpot in his hand. He hurried up to her, and, setting his load on the table, sank upon his knees. 'Look!' he cried.

'Why, uncle,' rejoined Melice, when curious examination revealed to her eyes a minute living point of green, 'this marvel quite eclipses me!'

A pang of humiliation shot through Hero, an instantaneous sharp pang; the next moment she was burrowing beneath the soil in the thirsty sucking roots of a plant not one-eighth of an inch high.

Day by day she grew, watched by an eye unwearied as that of a lover. The green sheath expanded fold after fold, till from it emerged a crumpled leaf, downy and notched. How was this first-born of an unknown race tended; how did fumigations rout its infinitesimal foes, whilst circles of quicklime barricaded it against the invasion of snails! It throve vigorously, adding leaf to leaf and shoot to shoot: at length, a minute furry-bud appeared.

Uncle Treeh, the most devoted of foster-fathers, revelled in ecstasy; yet it seemed to Hero that his step was becoming feebler, and his hand more tremulous. One morning he waited on her as usual, but appeared out of breath and unsteady: gradually he bent more and more forward, till, without removing his eyes from the cherished plant, he sank huddled on the conservatory floor.

Three hours afterwards hurried steps and anxious faces sought the old man. There, on the accustomed spot, he lay, shrunk together, cold, dead; his glazed eyes still riveted on his favourite nursling.

They carried away the corpse – could Treeh have spoken he would have begged to lie where a delicate vine might suck nourishment from his remains – and buried it a mile away from the familiar garden; but no one had the heart to crush him beneath a stone. The earth lay lightly upon him; and though his bed was unvisited by one who would have tended it – for Melice, now a wife, had crossed the sea to a distant home – generations of unbidden flowers, planted by winds and birds, blossomed there.

During one whole week Hero and her peers dwelt in solitude, uncared for save by a mournful gardener, who loved and cherished the vegetable family for their old master's sake. But on the eighth day came a change: all things were furbished up, and assumed their most festive aspect; for the new owners were hourly expected.

The door opened. A magnificently attired lady, followed by two children and a secondary husband, sailed into the narrow passage, casting down with her robe several flower-pots. She glanced around with a superior air, and was about to quit the scene without a word, when the gardener ventured to remark, 'Several very rare plants, madam.'

'Yes, yes,' she cried, 'we knew his eccentric tastes, poor dear old man!' and stepped doorwards.

One more effort: 'This, madam,' indicating Hero, 'is a specimen quite unique.'

'Really,' said she; and observed to her husband as she left the house, 'These useless buildings must be cleared away. This will be the exact spot for a ruin: I adore a ruin!'

A ruin? – Hero's spirit died in the slighted plant. Was it to such taste as this she must condescend? such admiration as this she must court? Merely to receive it would be humiliation. A passionate longing for the old lost life, the old beloved love, seized her; she grew tremulous, numbed: 'Ah,' she thought, 'this is death!'

A hum, a buzz, voices singing and speaking, the splash of fountains, airy laughter, rustling wings, the noise of a thousand leaves and flowercups in commotion. Sparks dancing in the twilight, dancing feet, joy and triumph; unseen hands loosing succous,* interlacing stalks from their roots beneath the water; towing a lily-raft across the lake, down a tortuous inland creek, through Fairy-harbour, out into the open sea.

On the lily-raft lay Hero, crowned with lilies, at rest. A swift tide was running from Fairycoast to Man-side: every wave heaving her to its silver crest bore her homewards; every wind whistling from the shore urged her homewards. Seals and unicorns dived on either hand, unnoticed. All the tumbling porpoises in the ocean could not have caught her eye.

At length, the moon-track crossed, she entered the navigable sea. There all was cold, tedious, dark; not a vessel in sight, not a living sound audible. She floated farther: something black loomed through the obscurity; could it be a boat? yes, it was certainly a distant boat; then she perceived a net lowered into the water; then saw two fishermen kindle a fire, and prepare themselves to wait, it might be for hours. Their forms thrown out against the glare struck Hero as familiar: that old man, stooping more than his former wont; that other strong and active figure, not so broad as in days of yore; – Hero's heart beat painfully: did they remember yet? did they love yet? was it yet time?

Nearer and nearer she floated, nearer and nearer. The men were wakeful, restless; they stirred the embers into a blaze, and sat waiting. Then softly and sadly arose the sound of a boat-song:—

PETER GRUMP

If underneath the water
   You comb your golden hair
With a golden comb, my daughter,
   Oh, would that I were there.
If underneath the wave
You fill a slimy grave,
Would that I, who could not save,
         Might share.

FORSS

If my love Hero queens it
  In summer Fairyland,
  What would I be
  But the ring on her hand?
Her cheek when she leans it
  Would lean on me:—
Or sweet, bitter-sweet,
  The flower that she wore
When we parted, to meet
  On the hither shore
  Anymore? nevermore.

Something caught Forss's eye; he tried the nets, and finding them heavily burdened began to haul them in, saying, 'It is a shoal of white fish; no, a drift of white seaweed'; – but suddenly he cried out: 'Help, old father! It is a corpse, as white as snow!'

Peter ran to the nets, and with the younger man's aid rapidly drew them in. Hero lay quite still, while very gently they lifted the body over the boat-side, whispering one to another: 'It is a woman – she is dead!' They laid her down where the fire-light shone full upon her face – her familiar face.

Not a corpse, O Peter Grump: not a corpse, O true Forss, staggering as from a death-blow. The eyes opened, the face dimpled into a happy smile; with tears, and clinging arms, and clinging kisses, Hero begged forgiveness of her father and her lover.

I will not tell you of the questions asked and answered, the return home, the wonder and joy which spread like wildfire through the colony. Nor how in the moonlight Forss wooed and won his fair love; nor even how at the wedding danced a band of strangers, gay and agile, recognised by none save the bride. I will merely tell you how in after years, sitting by her husband's fireside, or watching on the shingle for his return, Hero would speak to her children of her own early days. And when their eyes kindled while she told of the marvellous splendour of Fairyland, she would assure them, with a convincing smile, that only home is happy: and when, with flushed cheeks and quickened breath, they followed the story of her brief pre-eminence, she would add, that though admiration seems sweet at first, only love is sweet first, and last, and always.

The Lost Titian

The best of Christina Rossetti's surviving stories, a sparkling tale of artistic rivalry and Renaissance Italy, The Lost Titian *was written towards the end of 1855 and first published in 1856 in the American magazine* The Crayon *– appropriately so, since the magazine was devoted to the fine arts.*

As the author stressed when the story was re-issued, noting with amusement that one or two 'kindest friends' had taken it to be based on a genuine tradition of a lost masterpiece by the great artist of the title, the work is entirely fictional. Nevertheless, it draws both on Rossetti's Italian inheritance – the linguistic flourishes are among its most beguiling aspects – and on the implicit rivalry between the three leading figures of the PRB: John Everett Millais (who was currently being hailed as the Titian of his time), William Holman Hunt and the author's brother Dante Gabriel Rossetti who, when this piece was written, had like Giannuccione in the story 'promised everything and fulfilled nothing'.

The Lost Titian *is not a* conte-à-clef, *however. There is no resemblance between the character of Gianni and that of Holman Hunt, for example, and the tale is rather a lively historical fiction on the theme of wordly ambition and envy, brilliantly executed in glowing colours to match the imaginary art it so deftly describes. It is also a disguised allegory of the allure of the senses – thus encompassing the World, the Flesh, and even the Devil, who makes an appearance as a flaming painted dragon.*

'A lie with a circumstance.'
WALTER SCOTT

The last touch was laid on. The great painter stood opposite the masterpiece of the period; the masterpiece of his life.

Nothing remained to be added. The orange drapery was perfect in its fruit-like intensity of hue; each vine-leaf was curved, each tendril twisted, as if fanned by the soft south wind; the sunshine brooded drowsily upon every dell and swelling upland: but a tenfold drowsiness slept in the cedar shadows. Look a moment, and those cymbals must clash, that panther* bound forward; draw nearer, and the songs of those ripe, winy lips must become audible.

The achievement of his life glowed upon the easel, and Titian was satisfied.

Beside him, witnesses of his triumph, stood his two friends – Gianni the successful, and Giannuccione the universal disappointment.

Gianni ranked second in Venice; second in most things, but in nothing first. His *colorito** paled only before that of his illustrious rival, whose supremacy, however, he ostentatiously asserted. So in other matters. Only the renowned Messer Cecchino was a more sonorous singer; only fire-eating Prince Barbuto a better swordsman; only Arrigo il Biondo a finer dancer or more sculpturesque beauty; even Caterina Suprema, in that contest of gallantry which has been celebrated by so many pens and pencils, though she awarded the rose of honour to Matteo Grande, the wit, yet plucked off a leaf for the all but victor Gianni.

A step behind him lounged Giannuccione, who had promised everything and fulfilled nothing. At the appearance of his first picture – 'Venus whipping Cupid with feathers plucked from his own wing' – Venice rang with his praises, and Titian foreboded a rival: but when, year after year, his works appeared still lazily imperfect, though always all but perfect, Venice subsided into apathetic silence, and Titian felt that no successor to his throne had as yet achieved the purple.

So these two stood with the great master in the hour of his triumph: Gianni loud, and Giannuccione hearty, in his applauses.

Only these two stood with him: as yet Venice at large knew not what her favourite had produced. It was, indeed, rumoured, that Titian had long been at work on a painting which he himself accounted his masterpiece, but its subject was a secret; and while some spoke of it as an undoubted *Vintage of red grapes,* others maintained it to be a *Dance of wood-nymphs*; while one old gossip whispered that, whatever else the painting might contain, she knew whose sunset-coloured tresses* and white brow would figure in the foreground. But the general ignorance mattered little; for, though words might have named the theme, no words could have described a picture which combined the softness of a dove's breast with the intensity of an October sunset: a picture of which the light almost warmed, and the fruit actually bloomed and tempted.*

Titian gazed upon his work, and was satisfied: Giannuccione gazed upon his friend's work, and was satisfied: only Gianni gazed upon his friend and upon his work, and was enviously dissatisfied.

'Tomorrow,' said Titian, – 'tomorrow Venice shall behold what she has long honoured by her curiosity. Tomorrow, with music and festivity, the unknown shall be unveiled; and you, my friends, shall withdraw the curtain.'

The two friends assented.

'Tomorrow,' he continued, half amused, half thoughtful, 'I know whose white brows will be knit, and whose red lips will pout. Well, they shall have their turn: but blue eyes are not always in season; hazel eyes, like hazel nuts, have their season also.'

'True,' chimed the chorus.

'But tonight,' he pursued, 'let us devote the hours to sacred friendship. Let us with songs and bumpers* rehearse tomorrow's festivities, and let your congratulations forestall its triumphs.'

'Yes, *evviva!*'* returned the chorus, briskly; and again '*evviva!*'

So, with smiles and embraces, they parted. So they met again at the welcome coming of Argus-eyed night.*

The studio was elegant with clusters of flowers, sumptuous with crimson, gold-bordered hangings, and luxurious with cushions and perfumes. From the walls peeped pictured fruit and fruit-like faces, between the curtains and in the corners gleamed moonlight-tinted statues; whilst on the easel reposed the beauty of the evening, overhung by budding boughs, and illuminated by an alabaster lamp burning scented oil. Strewn about the apartment lay musical instruments and packs of cards. On the table were silver dishes, filled with leaves and choice fruits; wonderful vessels of Venetian glass, containing rare wines and iced waters; and footless goblets, which allowed the guest no choice but to drain his bumper.

That night the bumpers brimmed. Toast after toast was quaffed to the success of tomorrow, the exaltation of the unveiled beauty, the triumph of its author.

At last Giannuccione, flushed and sparkling, rose: 'Let us drink,' he cried, 'to our host's success tomorrow: may it be greater than the past, and less than the future!'

'Not so,' answered Titian, suddenly; 'not so: I feel my star culminate.'

He said it gravely, pushing back his seat, and rising from table. His spirits seemed in a moment to flag, and he looked pale in the moonlight. It was as though the blight of the evil eye* had fallen upon him.

Gianni saw his disquiet, and laboured to remove it. He took a lute from the floor, and tuning it, exerted his skill in music. He wrung from the strings cries of passion, desolate sobs, a wail as of one abandoned, plaintive, most tender tones as of the *solitario passero*.* The charm worked: vague uneasiness was melting into delicious melancholy. He redoubled his efforts; he drew out tinkling notes joyful as the feet of dancers; he struck notes like fire, and, uniting his voice to the instrument, sang the glories of Venice and of Titian. His voice, full, mellow, exultant, vibrated through the room; and, when it ceased, the bravos of his friends rang out an enthusiastic chorus.

Then, more stirring than the snap of castanets on dexterous fingers; more fascinating, more ominous, than a snake's rattle, sounded the music of the dice-box.

The stakes were high, waxing higher, and higher; the tide of fortune set steadily towards Titian. Giannuccione laughed and played, played and laughed with reckless good nature, doubling and redoubling his bets apparently quite at random. At length, however, he paused, yawned, laid down the dice, observing that it would cost him a good six months' toil to pay off his losses – a remark which elicited a peculiar smile of intelligence from his companions – and, lounging back upon the cushions, fell fast asleep.

Gianni also had been a loser: Gianni the imperturbable, who won and lost alike with steady hand and unvarying colour. Rumour stated that one evening he lost, won back, lost once more, and finally regained his whole property unmoved: at last only relinquishing the game, which fascinated, but could not excite him, for lack of an adversary.

In like manner he now threw his possessions, as coolly as if they been another's, piecemeal into the gulph. First his money went, then his collection of choice sketches; his gondola followed, his plate, his jewelry. These gone, for the first time he laughed.

'Come,' he said, '*amico mio*,* let us throw the crowning cast. I stake thereon myself; if you win, you may sell me to the Moor tomorrow, with the remnant of my patrimony; to wit, one house, containing various articles of furniture and apparel; yea, if aught else remains to me, that also do I stake: against these set you your newborn beauty, and let us throw for the last time; lest it be said cogged dice* are used in Venice, and I be taunted with the true proverb, – "*Save me from my friends, and I will take care of my enemies.*" '

'So be it,' mused Titian, 'even so. If I gain, my friend shall not suffer; if I lose, I can but buy back my treasure with this night's winnings. His whole fortune will stand Gianni in more stead than my picture; moreover, luck favours me. Besides, it can only be that my friend jests, and would try my confidence.'

So argued Titian, heated by success, by wine and play. But for these, he would freely have restored his adversary's fortune, though it had been multiplied tenfold, and again tenfold, rather than have risked his life's labour on the hazard of the dice.

They threw.

Luck had turned, and Gianni was successful.

Titian, nothing doubting, laughed as he looked up from the table into his companion's face; but no shadow of jesting lingered there. Their eyes met, and read each other's heart at a glance.

One, discerned the gnawing envy of a life satiated: a thousand mortifications, a thousand inferiorities, compensated in a moment.

The other, read an indignation that even yet scarcely realised the treachery which kindled it; a noble indignation, that more upbraided the false friend than the destroyer of a life's hope.

It was a nine-days' wonder in Venice what had become of Titian's masterpiece; who had spirited it away, – why, when, and where. Some explained the mystery by hinting that Clementina Beneplacida, having gained secret access to the great master's studio, had there, by dint of scissors, avenged her slighted beauty, and in effigy defaced her nut-brown rival. Others said that Giannuccione, paying tipsy homage to his friend's performance, had marred its yet moist surface.* Others again averred, that in a moment of impatience, Titian's own sponge flung against the canvas, had irremediably blurred the principal figure. None knew, none guessed the truth. Wonder fulfilled its little day, and then, subsiding, was forgotten: having, it may be, after all, as truly amused Venice the volatile as any work of art could have done, though it had robbed sunset of its glow, its glory, and its fire.

But why was the infamy of that night kept secret?

By Titian, because in blazoning abroad his companion's treachery, he would subject himself to the pity of those from whom he scarcely accepted homage; and, in branding Gianni as a traitor, he would expose himself as a dupe.

By Gianni, because had the truth got wind, his iniquitous prize might have been wrested from him, and his malice frustrated in the moment of triumph; not to mention that vengeance had a subtler relish when it kept back a successful rival from the pinnacle of fame, than when it merely exposed a friend to humiliation. As artists, they might possibly have been accounted rivals; as astute men of the world, never.

Giannuccione had not witnessed all the transactions of that night. Thanks to his drunken sleep, he knew little; and what he guessed, Titian's urgency induced him to suppress. It was, indeed, noticed how, from that time forward, two of the three inseparables appeared in a measure, estranged from the third; yet all outward observances of courtesy were continued, and, if embraces had ceased, bows and doffings never failed.

For weeks, even for months, Gianni restrained his love for play, and, painting diligently, laboured to rebuild his shattered fortune. All prospered in his hands. His sketches sold with unprecedented readiness, his epigrams charmed the noblest dinner-givers, his verses and piquant little airs won him admission into the most exclusive circles. Withal, he seemed to be steadying. His name no more pointed stories of drunken frolics in the purlieus of the city, of mad wagers in the meanest company, of reckless duels with nameless adversaries. If now he committed follies, they were committed in the best society; if he sinned, it was, at any rate, in a patrician *casa;** and, though his morals might not yet be flawless, his taste was unimpeachable.* His boon companions grumbled, yet could not afford to dispense with him; his warmest friends revived hopes which long ago had died away into despair. It was the heyday of his life: fortune and Venice alike courted him; he had but to sun himself in their smiles, and accept their favours.

So, nothing loth, he did, and for a while prospered. But, as the extraordinary stimulus flagged, the extraordinary energy flagged with it. Leisure returned, and with leisure the allurements of old pursuits. In proportion as his expenditure increased, his gains lessened; and, just when all his property, in fact, belonged to his creditors, he put the finishing stroke to his obvious ruin, by staking and losing at the gambling-table what was no longer his own.

That night beheld Gianni grave, dignified, imperturbable, and a beggar. Next day, his creditors, princely and plebeian, would be upon him: everything must go; not a scrap, not a fragment, could be held back. Even Titian's masterpiece would be claimed; that prize for which he had played away his soul, by which, it may be, he had hoped to acquire a world-wide fame, when its mighty author should be silenced for ever in the dust.

Yet tomorrow, not tonight, would be the day of reckoning; tonight, therefore, was his own. With a cool head he conceived, with a steady hand he executed, his purpose. Taking coarse pigments, such as, when he pleased, might easily be removed, he daubed over those figures which seemed to live, and that wonderful background, which not Titian himself could reproduce; then on the blank surface, he painted a dragon, flaming, clawed, preposterous. One day he would recover his dragon, recover his Titian under the dragon, and the world should see.

Next morning the crisis came.

After all, Gianni's effects were worth more than had been supposed. They included Giannuccione's *Venus whipping Cupid* – how obtained, who knows? – a curiously wrought cup, by a Florentine goldsmith,* just then rising into notice; within the hollow of the foot was engraved *Benvenuto Cellini*, surmounted by an outstretched hand, symbolic of welcome, and quaintly allusive* to the name; a dab by Giorgione, a scribble of the brush by Titian, and two feet square of genuine Tintoret.* The creditors brightened; there was not enough for honesty, but there was ample for the production of a most decorous bankrupt.

His wardrobe was a study of colour; his trinkets, few but choice, were of priceless good taste. Moreover, his demeanour was unimpeachable and his delinquencies came to light with the best grace imaginable. Some called him a defaulter, but all admitted he was a thorough gentleman.

Foremost in the hostile ranks stood Titian; Titian, who now, for the first time since that fatal evening, crossed his rival's threshold. His eye searched eagerly among the heap of nameless canvasses for one forgotten beauty, who had occasioned him such sore heartache; but he sought in vain; only in the forefront sprawled a dragon, flaming, clawed, preposterous; grinned, twinkled, erected his tail, and flouted him.

'Yes,' said Gianni, answering his looks, not words, yet seeming to address the whole circle, '*Signori miei,** these compose all my gallery. An immortal sketch, by Messer Tiziano' – here a complimentary bow – 'a veritable Giorgione; your own work, Messer Robusti, which needs no comment of mine to fix its value. A few productions by feebler hands, yet not devoid of merit. These are all. The most precious part of my collection was destroyed (I need not state, accidentally), three days ago by fire. That dragon, yet moist, was designed for mine host, Bevilacqua Mangiaruva;* but this morning, I hear, with deep concern, of his sudden demise.'

Here Lupo Vorace* of the *Orco decapitato** stepped forward.

He, as he explained at length, was a man of few words (this, doubtless, in theory); but to make a long story short, so charmed was he by the scaly monster that he would change his sign, accept the ownerless dragon, and thereby wipe out a voluminous score which stood against his debtor. Gianni, with courteous thanks, explained that the dragon, still moist, was unfit for immediate transport; that it should remain in the studio for a short time longer; and that, as soon as its safety permitted, he would himself convey it to the inn of his liberal creditor. But on this point Lupo was inflexible. In diffuse but unvarying terms he claimed instant possession of Gianni's masterstroke. He seized it, reared it face upwards on to his head, and by his exit broke up the conclave of creditors.

What remains can be briefly told.

Titian, his last hope in this direction wrecked, returned to achieve, indeed, fresh greatness: but not the less returned to the tedium of straining after an ideal once achieved, but now lost for ever. Giannuccione, half amused, half mortified, at the slighting mention made of his performances, revenged himself in an epigram, of which the following is a free translation: –

Gianni my friend and I both strove to excel,
But, missing better, settled down in well.
Both fail, indeed; but not alike we fail –
My forte being Venus' face, and his a dragon's tail.

Gianni, in his ruin, took refuge with a former friend; and there, treated almost on the footing of a friend, employed his superabundant leisure on concocting a dragon superior in all points to its predecessor; but, when this was almost completed, this which was to ransom his unsuspected treasure from the clutches of Lupo, the more relentless clutches of death fastened upon himself.

His secret died with him.

An oral tradition of a somewhere extant lost Titian having survived all historical accuracy, and so descended to another age, misled the learned Dr Landau* into purchasing a spurious work for the Gallery of Lunenberg; and even more recently induced Dr Dreieck to expend a large sum on a nominal Titian, which he afterwards bequeathed to the National Museum of Saxe Eulenstein. The subject of this latter painting is a *Vintage of red grapes*, full of life and vigour, exhibiting marked talent, but clearly assignable to the commencement of a later century.

There remains, however, a hope that some happy accident may yet restore to the world the masterpiece of one of her most brilliant sons.

Reader, should you chance to discern over wayside inn or metropolitan hotel a dragon pendent, or should you find such an effigy amid the lumber of a broker's shop, whether it be red, green, or piebald, demand it importunately, pay for it liberally, and in the privacy of home scrub it. It *may* be that from behind the dragon will emerge a fair one, fairer than Andromeda,* and that to you will appertain the honour of yet further exalting Titian's greatness in the eyes of a world.*

Vanna's Twins

Vanna's Twins, *a story full of sentiment, appears to have been written in 1869/70 on the same wave of nursery memories that produced* SingSong, *and is infused with affectionate homage towards Christina Rossetti's own happy infancy in a largely Italian family. Vanna's children, it may be noted, are named Felice Maria and Maria Gioconda.*

They live in H—, a seaside town not a million miles from Hastings, where their author spent many recuperative holidays, often arriving with her luggage in search of lodgings like the narrator. Their parents, Cola and Vanna, are surely denizens of Little Italy, the community of émigrés, and are also Neapolitans, like Christina Rossetti's own father. Like him, too, they dream of returning home, to Vascitammò. Gabriele Rossetti's birthplace was Vasto, in the Abruzzi.

The catastrophe that overwhelms the twins is that of the Babes in the Wood, without a happy ending. Around this time, Rossetti contemplated re-telling a series of traditional fairy-tales, to match and complement her nursery rhymes, and it may be that Vanna's Twins *is the only survivor of the project, with a more tragic ending to suit the age. At the same time, the ending is also happy, for by dying in the snowstorm Vanna's babes are forever infants, everlastingly spared the pain and decay of growing old.*

Vanna's Twins *was first published with* Commonplace *in 1870.*

There I stood on the platform at H—, girt by my three boxes, one carpet-bag, strapful of shawls and bundle of umbrellas; there I stood, with a courteous station-master and two civil porters assuring me that not one lodging was vacant throughout H— . At another time such an announcement might not have greatly signified, for London, whence I came, was less than three hours off; but on this particular occasion it did matter because I was weakened by recent illness, the journey down had shaken me, I was hungry and thirsty for my tea, and, through fear of catching cold, I had wrapped up overmuch; so that when those polite officials stated that they could not point out a lodging for me I felt more inclined to cry than I hope anybody suspected. One of the porters, noticing how pale and weak I looked, good-naturedly volunteered to go to the three best hotels, and see whether in one of them, I could be housed for the moment; and though the expensiveness of such a plan secretly dismayed me, I saw nothing better than to accept his offer. Meanwhile, I retreated into the waiting-room wishing him success; but wondering should he not succeed, what would become of me for the night.

Happily for me, my troubles were not aggravated by imaginary difficulties. I was turned forty-five,* and looked not a day younger; an age at which there is nothing alarming in finding oneself alone in a strange place, or compelled to take a night journey by rail. So I sat on the waiting-room sofa, shut my eyes to ease, if possible, a racking headache, and made up my mind that, at the worst, I could always take the mail-train back to London.

After all, I had not long to wait. Within ten minutes of leaving me my porter returned with the news that, if I did not mind a very unfashionable, but quite respectable, quarter of H—, he had just heard of a first floor vacated half-an-hour before my arrival, and ready, if I pleased, to receive me. I merely asked, was it clean? and being assured that there was not a tidier young woman in all H— than 'Fanny', that her husband was a decent optician and stone-cutter, and that for cleanliness any of their floors might be eaten off, I felt only too thankful to step into a fly,* and accompany my boxes to an abiding place. Before starting, I happened to ask the name of my landlord, and was answered, somewhat vaguely, by my porter, 'We call them Cole.'

The report of a coming lodger had travelled before me, and I found Mr Cole and his Fanny awaiting me at their shop-door. But what a Mr Cole and what a Fanny. He was a tall, stout foreigner, about thirty years of age, ready with tucked-up shirt sleeves and athletic arms to bear my boxes aloft; she was the comeliest of young matrons, her whole face one smile, her ears adorned by weighty gold pendents, and with an obvious twin baby borne in each arm. Husband and wife alike addressed me as 'Meess', and displayed teeth of an enviable regularity and whiteness as they smiled or spoke. Thus much I saw at a first glance.

Too tired for curiosity, I toiled up the narrow staircase after my boxes, washed my dusty face and hot hands, and stepped into my little sitting-room, intending to lie down on the sofa, and wait as patiently as might be whilst tea, which I had already ordered, was got ready. A pleasant surprise met me. I suppose the good-natured porter may have forewarned Mr Cole of my weakness and wants; be this as it may, there stood the tea ready brewed, and flanked by pats of butter, small rolls, a rasher, and three eggs* wrapped up in a clean napkin. After this, my crowning pleasure for the day was to step into a bed soft as down could make it, and drop to sleep between sheets fragrant of lavender.

A few days' convalescence at H— did more for me than as many weeks' convalescence in London had effected. Soon I strolled about the beach without numbering the breakwaters, or along the country roads, taking no count of the milestones; and went home to meals as hungry as a school-girl, and slept at nights like a baby. One of my earliest street-discoveries was that my landlord's name, as inscribed over his window, was not Cole, but Cola (Nicola) Piccirillo; and a very brief sojourn under his roof instructed me that the Fanny of my friend the porter was called Vanna (Giovanna) by her husband. They were both Neapolitans of the ex-kingdom,* though not of the city, of Naples; whenever I asked either of them after the name of their native place, they invariably answered me in a tone of endearment, by what sounded more like 'Vascitammò' than aught else I know how to spell; but when my English tongue uttered 'Vascitammò' after them, they would shake their heads and repeat the uncatchable word; at last it grew to be a standing joke between us that when I became a millionnaire my courier Cola and my maid Vanna should take the twins and me to see Vascitammò.

I never thought of changing my lodgings, though, as time went on, it would have been easy to do so, and certainly the quarter we inhabited was not fashionable. A laborious not an idle, community environed our doors and furnished customers to the shop: it was some time before I discovered that *l'amico* Piccirillo held a store for polished stones and marine curiosities* in the bazaar of H—. He liked to be styled an optician; but whilst he sold and repaired spectacles, driving a prosperous trade amongst the fishing population who surrounded us, and supplying them with cheap telescopes, compasses, and an occasional magic-lantern,* he was not too proud to eke out his gains by picking up and preparing marine oddities, pebbles, or weeds. After we became intimate I more than once rose at three or four in the morning, as the turn of the tide dictated, and accompanied him on a ramble of exploration. He scrambled about slippery, jagged rocks as sure-footed as a wild goat; and if ever my climbing powers failed at some critical pass, thought nothing of lifting me over the difficulty, with that courteous familiarity which, in an Italian, does not cease to be respectful. I was rather lucky in spying eligible stones, which I contributed to his basket; and then, when we got home, he would point out to his wife what '*la Signora*'* had found '*per noi due e per li piccini.*'* I understood a little Italian and they a little English, so we generally, in spite of the Neapolitan blurring accent, made out each other's meaning.

Vanna was one of the prettiest women I ever saw, if indeed I ought to term merely pretty a face which, with good features, contained eyes softer and more lustrous than any others I remember; their colour I never made out, but when she lowered the large eyelids, their long black lashes seemed to throw half her face into shadow. I don't know that she was clever except as a housewife, but in this capacity she excelled, and was a dainty cook over her shining pots and pans: her husband's '*due maccheroni*'* often set me hankering, as I spied them done to a turn and smoking hot; though I confess that when Cola brought home a cuttle-fish and I saw it dished up as a '*calamarello*'* my English prejudice asserted itself.

'Mr and Mrs Cole' were unique in my small experience of people, but surely the twins must have remained unique in anybody's experience. What other babies were ever so fat or so merry? To see their creased arms was enough till one saw their creased legs, and then their arms grew commonplace. I never once heard them cry: a clothes-basket formed their primitive bassinette, and there they would sprawl, tickling each other and chuckling. They chuckled at their father, mother, myself, or any stranger who would toss them, or poke a finger into their cushions of fat. They crowed over their own teething, and before they could speak seemed to bandy intuitive jokes, and chuckled in concert. Well were they named Felice* Maria and Maria Gioconda.* At first sight, they were utterly indistinguishable apart; but experiment proved that Felice was a trifle heavier than his sister, and that fingers could go a hair's-breadth farther round her fat waist than round his. When I made their acquaintance their heads were thickly plaistered with that scurf* which apparently an Italian custom leaves undisturbed; but as this wore off, curly black down took its place, and balanced the large, dark eyes and silky eyebrows and lashes, which both inherited from their mother. What we, in our insularity, term the English love of soap and water was shared by Vanna, and it was one of my amusements to see the twins in their tub. Often, if hastily summoned to serve behind the counter, Vanna would leave them in the tub to splash about, and throw each other down and pick each other up, for a quarter of an hour together; and if I hinted that this might not be perfectly safe for them, she invariably assured me that in her '*paese*'* all the babies toddled about the shore, and into the sea and out again so soon as ever they could toddle. '*E che male vi* *potrebb' essere? non vi son coccodrilli:'** an argument no less apposite to the tub than to the sea.

As I possessed a small competence* and no near home-ties, I felt under no constraint to leave H— sooner than suited my humour; so, though I had originally intended to remain there no longer than seven or eight weeks, month after month slipped away till a whole year had elapsed, and found me there still. In a year one becomes thoroughly acquainted with daily associates, and from being prepossessed by their engaging aspect, I had come to love and respect Piccirillo and his wife. Both were good Catholics, and evinced their orthodoxy as well by regularity at mass and confession as by strict uprightness towards customers and kindliness towards neighbours. Once when a fishing-boat was lost at sea, and its owner, Ned Gough, left well-nigh penniless, Cola, who was ingenious in preparing marine oddities,* arranged a group of young skate in their quaint hoods and mantles, and mounted them on a green board amongst seaweed bushes as a party of gipsies; this would have been raffled for, and the proceeds given to the ruined boatman, had I not taken a fancy to the group, and purchased it. And the first time the twins walked out alone was when they crossed over the road hand in hand, each holding an orange as a present to a little sick girl opposite. Both parents watched them safe over, and I heard one remark to the other, that '*Nossignore*'* would bless them.

It was mid-May when I arrived at H—, and about mid-May of the year following I returned to London. A legal question had meanwhile arisen touching my small property; and this took so long to settle, that during many and many months I remained in doubt whether I should continue adequately provided for, or be reduced to work in some department or other for my living. The point was ultimately decided in my favour, but not before much vexation and expense had been incurred on both sides. At the end of three years from quitting H— I made up my mind to return and settle there for good: no special ties bound me to London, and I knew of no people under whose roof I would so gladly make my solitary home as with Piccirillo and his wife; besides, the twins were an attraction. As to the optician's shop being in an out-of-the-way quarter, that I cared nothing for, having neither the tastes nor the income for fashionable society: so, after a preliminary letter or two had passed between us, I found myself one glowing afternoon in June standing once again on the H—

platform, not in the forlorn position I so vividly remembered, but met by Cola, broader than ever in figure, and smiling his broadest, who whipped up my trunks with his own hands on to the fly, and took his place by the driver.

Vanna came running out to meet me at the carriage door, seizing and kissing both my hands; and before I even alighted two sturdy urchins had been made to kiss *'la Signora's* hand. Ten minutes more and I was seated at tea, chatting to Vanna, and renewing acquaintance with my old friends Felice and Gioconda. This was effected by the presentation to them of a lump of sugar apiece, for which each again kissed my hand, fortunately before their mouths had become sticky by suction.

They were the funniest little creatures imaginable, and two of the prettiest. Felice was still just ahead of Gioconda in bulk, but so much like her that (as I found afterwards) if for fun they exchanged hats I got into a complete mental muddle as to which was which, confused by the discrepant hats and frocks. There was no paid Roman Catholic school in H—, but the good nuns of St L— taught the little boys and girls of their congregation; and morning after morning I used to see the twins start for school hand in hand, with dinner as well as books in their bags; for St L—* was too far from their home to admit of going and returning twice in one day. All the neighbours were fond of them; and often before their destination was reached a hunch of cake from some good-natured rough hand had found its way into one or other bag, to be shared in due course.

At their books they were *'proprio maravigliosi'*,* as Vanna phrased it; whilst Cola, swelling with paternal pride under a veil of humility, would observe, '*Non c'è male, nè lui nè lei*'.* I believe they really were clever children and fond of their books: at any rate, one Holy Innocents' Day* they brought home a prize, a little story in two volumes, one volume apiece; for, as the kind nuns had remarked, they were like one work in two volumes themselves, and should have one book between them. That night they went to bed and fell asleep hand in hand as usual, but each holding in the other hand a scarlet-bound volume, so proud were they. They were but seven years old, and had never yet slept apart: never yet, and, as it turned out, never at all.

The Christmas when this happened was one of the brightest and pleasantest I recollect; night after night slight frost visited us, but day after day it melted away, whilst sea and sky spread clear and blue in the sunshine. In other countries much snow had fallen and was still falling, but snow had not yet reached our shores.

Christmas, as usual, brought a few bills to me, and likewise to my friends. Of theirs the heaviest was the doctor's bill, for the twins had caught scarlatina in the summer, and had got well on a variety of pills and draughts. Then Cola bethought himself of certain money due to him at a coast-guard station not many miles from H—, and which would just suffice to pay the doctor; and one Saturday, a day or two after Twelfth Day,* he took the first afternoon train to E—,* this being the nearest point on the line to his destination, and went to look after his debtor, telling Vanna that he might not be back before the latest train came into H—.

So Vanna took her seat behind the counter, and looked up the road towards St L—, watching for her little ones to come racing home from school, for school broke up early on Saturdays. As she sat, she knitted something warm and useful, for she was never idle, and hummed in her low, sweet voice the first words of a Christmas carol. I only know those first words, so pathetic in their devout simplicity:—

Tu scendi dalle stelle, O Re del Cielo,*
E vieni in una grotta al freddo al gelo:
O Bambino mio divino
Io Ti voglio sempre amar!
O Dio beato
E quanto Ti costò l' avermi amato.

She was thus occupied as I crossed the shop on my way upstairs, and whilst I paused to say a word in passing, a young woman, her face swollen with crying, came up, who, almost without stopping, called out: 'O Fanny, Fanny, my three are down with the fever, and I'm running for the doctor!' and in speaking she was gone.

Sympathetic tears had gathered in Vanna's kind eyes when I looked at her. '*Non hanno padre,*'* she said, half apologetically; and I then recollected who the young woman was, and that her children were worse than fatherless. Poor Maggie Crowe! deserted by a good-for-nothing husband she worked hard to keep her little ones out of the workhouse; did charing,* took in needlework, went out nursing when she could get a job, and now her three children were 'down with the fever', and she had had to leave them alone in her wretched hovel on the east cliff to run a mile and more into H— to fetch the parish doctor. We soon saw her tearing back as she had come, not stopping now to speak.

I went to my room, and looking into my charity-purse* found that I could afford five shillings out of it for this poor family, and settled mentally that I would take them round next day after church. At the moment I was feeling tired and disinclined to stir, and I concluded the parish doctor, who bore a character for kindness, would certainly for that night supply his patients with necessaries.

Just after the clock struck three I heard a bustle below; the twins had come home and were talking eagerly to their mother in their loud, childish voices. I heard Vanna answer them once or twice; then she spoke continuously, seeming to tell them something, and I heard both reply, '*Mamma sì*'.* A few minutes later I was surprised to see them from my window trotting along the street, but not in the direction from which they had just come, and bearing between them a market-basket, each of them holding it by one handle.

A suspicion of their errand crossed my mind, and I hurried downstairs to warn Vanna that a few snowflakes had already fallen and more hung floating in the still air. She had noticed this of herself, but replied that they knew their way quite well, and it was not far to go; indeed, she could not feel easy without sending up a few oranges left from Twelfth Day for the sick children. Her own had had the fever, they had promised her to go straight and return straight without loitering, and though she looked somewhat anxious, she concluded bravely: '*Nossignore avrà cura di loro.*'*

I went back to my room thoroughly mortified at the rebuke which her alacrity administered to my laziness. How much less would it not have cost me to set off at once with my five shillings than it cost poor Vanna to send her little ones, tired as perhaps they were, to what, for such short legs, was a considerable distance. From my window, moreover, I soon could not help perceiving that not only the snow, rare at first, had begun to fall rapidly and in large flakes, but that the sky lowered dense and ominous over the east cliff. I felt sure that there, and thither it was that the twins were bound, it must already be snowing heavily.

Four o'clock struck, but Felice and Gioconda had not come back. I heard Vanna closing the shop. In another five minutes she came up to me dressed in bonnet and shawl, with a pale face that told its own story of alarm. Still she would not acknowledge herself frightened, but tried to laugh, as she apologized for leaving me alone in the house, assured me that no one could possibly be calling at that hour, and protested that she would not be out long. If the twins arrived in her absence she was sure I would kindly let them sit by my fire till her return; then, fairly breaking down and crying, she left me, repeating, '*Non son che piccini, poveri piccini, poveri piccini miei.*'*

A couple of men with lighted lanterns stood waiting for her in the street; one of them made her take his arm, and I knew by the voice that it was Ned Gough. Hour after hour struck, and they did not return.

About seven o'clock I heard a loud knocking; and running down to open the door, for being left alone in the house I had locked up and made all safe, I found Piccirillo, who on account of the snow had hastened home by an earlier train than he had mentioned, and was now much amazed at finding the house closed and no light burning below. When he understood what had happened he seemed beside himself with agitation and terror. Flinging up his arms he rushed from the house, calling out, '*Vanna, Vanna mia! dove sei? rispondimi: figli miei, rispondetemi.*'* Neighbours came about him, offering what comfort they could think of: but what comfort could there be? He, too, must set off in the snow to seek his poor lost babies and their mother; and soon he started, lantern and stick in hand, ejaculating, and making vows as he went. '*Dio mio, Dio mio, abbi pietà di noi.*'*

All through the long night it snowed and snowed: at daybreak it was snowing still. Soon after daybreak the seekers returned, cold, silent, haggard; Piccirillo carrying his wife, who lay insensible in his arms. After hours of wandering they had met somewhere out towards the east cliff, and Vanna, at sight of her husband, had dropped down utterly spent. She had gone straight to Maggie Crowe's cottage, and found that the twins had safely left the cottages there and started homewards; Felice tired but manful, poor little Gioconda trudging wearily along, and clinging to her brother. Maggie had tried to keep them at the cottage as it was already snowing heavily, and the little girl had cried and wanted to stay and warm herself; but her brother said 'No', they had promised not to loiter, his siter would be good and not cry, he would take care of her; so whilst Maggie was busy with her own sick children, the twins had started. Beyond this, not one of the searching party could trace them; the small footmarks must have been effaced almost as soon as imprinted on the snow; and any one of the surface inequalities of that snow-waste, which now stretched right and left for miles, might be the mound to cover two such feeble wayfarers.

For three days the frost held and our suspense lasted; then the wind veered from north round to west, a rapid thaw set in, and a few hours ended hope and fear alike. The twins were found huddled together in a chalky hollow close to the edge of the cliff, and almost within sight of Maggie's hovel: Gioconda with her head thrust into the market-basket, Felice with one arm holding the basket over his sister, and with the other clasping her close to him. Her fat hands met round his waist, and clasped between them was a small silver cross I had given her at Christmas, and which she had worn round her neck.

Lovely and pleasant in their lives, in their death they were not divided; but as they had always shared one bed, they now shared one coffin and one grave.

After a while Piccirillo and his wife recovered from their passionate grief; but Vanna drooped more and more as spring came on, and clothed the small grave with greenness. They had no other child, and the house was silent indeed and desolate. Once I heard them talking to each other of 'Vascitammò': Vanna said something I did not catch, and then Cola anwered her, *'Sì, Vanna mia, ritorneremo; tolga Iddio che io perda te ancora.'**

So I knew that we should soon have to part. They came upstairs together to me one evening, and with real kindliness explained that all their plans were altered on account of Vanna's failing health, and that they must go home to their own country lest she should die. Vanna cried and I cried, and poor Cola fairly cried too. I promised them that the little grave shall never fall into neglect whilst I live, and in thanking me they managed to say through their tears, – *'Nossignore è buono, e certo li avrà benedetti.'**

The business was easily disposed of, for though small, it was a thriving concern, and capable of extension. Other affairs did not take long to settle; and one morning I saw my kind friends off by an early train, on their road through London to 'Vascitammò', which now neither the twins nor I shall ever see.

Speaking Likenesses

'I have tried to write a little prose story, such as might do for a child's Xmas volume,' Christina Rossetti wrote to Macmillan in 1874, with 'an eye to the market'. She added that 'properly speaking, it consists of three short stories in a common framework – but the whole is not long'. It was inspired, as she acknowledged, by the phenomenal success of Lewis Carroll's *Alice in Wonderland*, whose author the Rossettis had met in 1863.

The three stories – about eight-year-old Flora, Edith and Maggie – followed on from Rossetti's book of nursery rhymes for younger children. They are told to a group of inquisitive girls by an irascible aunt, whose questions and replies both frame and link the separate tales. They are distinctly harsher in tone than *SingSong*, dealing not inappropriately with some painful childhood experiences – a quarrelsome birthday party, a failed endeavour to light a fire, and an arduous and frightening errand – in a mode somewhat reminiscent of the Brothers Grimm, whose tales Christina knew as a child. Though Wonderland is also a cruel world in many respects, Rossetti's 'Nowhere' (her original title) is far darker in mood, and her audience hardly have time to enjoy the pleasures of naughtiness before they are brought up against the lesson.

This sombre cast has prejudiced critics against the stories, but there is a good deal to be said against sentimentality in writing for children. Recently, too, feminist scholars have found much to discuss in relation to the representations of gender and sexuality in the text. Moreover, it is important to read the three stories as episodes in a single narrative. The three young heroines are story-sisters – or at least friends: Flora's sugarplums and Edith's doll come from the very shop kept by Maggie's grandmother – and the 'common framework' pointed out by the author offers a clue to the conclusion, for the quarrels, failures and trials the heroines endure are countered and resolved in the final tale, when Maggie retraces her steps, withstands the temptations of spite, sloth and greed, and is rewarded with three baby animals and a happy ending.

The supporting figures of *Speaking Likenesses* – with its shape-shifting furniture, hall of mirrors, fierce queen and talking animals – offer both homage and a concealed critique of *Alice in Wonderland* and *Through the Looking-Glass*. The greedy Mouth Boy is surely stepbrother to Tweedledum and Tweedledee, and when the aunt reintroduces Sticky, Quills and Co into Maggie's episode – 'Oh, Aunt, are these those monstrous children over again? Yes, Ella, you really can't expect me not to utilize such a brilliant idea twice' – she is glancing at Carroll's reinvention of the March Hare and Mad Hatter as Heigha and Hatta. The story-telling aunt also complements the avuncular narrator of the Alice tales.

As to the revised title, 'very likely you did not so deeply ponder upon *my text as to remark that my small heroines perpetually encounter "speaking (literally speaking) likenesses" or embodiments or caricatures of themselves of their faults', wrote author to publisher. 'This premised, I think the title boasts of some point and neatness.' Though more minatory than is now favoured for children's fiction, the curious wit and humour of* Speaking Likenesses *and its inimitably obnoxious aunt should commend the text to adult readers.*

FLORA*

Come sit round me, my dear little girls, and I will tell you a story. Each of you bring her sewing, and let Ella take pencils and colour-box, and try to finish some one drawing of the many she has begun. What, Maude! pouting over that nice clean white stocking because it wants a darn? Put away your pout and pull out your needle, my dear; for pouts make a sad beginning to my story. And yet not an inappropriate beginning, as some of you may notice as I go on. Silence! Attention! All eyes on occupations, not on me lest I should feel shy! Now I start my knitting and my story together.

Whoever saw Flora on her birthday morning, at half-past seven o'clock on that morning, saw a very pretty sight. Eight years old to a minute, and not awake yet. Her cheeks were plump and pink, her light hair was all tumbled, her little red lips were held together as if to kiss some one; her eyes also, if you could have seen them, were blue and merry, but for the moment they had gone fast asleep and out of sight under fat little eyelids. Wagga the dog was up and about, Muff the cat was up and about, chirping birds were up and about; or if they were mere nestlings and so could not go about (supposing, that is, that there were still a few nestlings so far on in summer), at least they sat together wide awake in the nest, with wide open eyes and most of them with wide open beaks, which was all they could do: only sleepy Flora slept on, and dreamed on, and never stirred.

Her mother stooping over the child's soft bed woke her with a kiss. 'Good morning, my darling, I wish you many happy returns of the day,' said the kind, dear mother: and Flora woke up to a sense of sunshine, and of pleasure full of hope. To be eight years old when last night one was merely seven, this is pleasure: to hope for birthday presents without any doubt of receiving some, this also is pleasure. And doubtless you now think so, my children, and it is quite right that so you should think: yet I tell you, from the sad knowledge of my older experience, that to every one of you a day will most likely come when sunshine, hope, presents and pleasure will be worth nothing to you in comparison with the unattainable gift of your mother's kiss.

On the breakfast table lay presents for Flora: a story-book full of pictures from her father, a writing-case from her mother, a gilt pincushion like a hedgehog from nurse, a box of sugar-plums and a doll from Alfred her brother and Susan her sister; the most tempting of sugar-plums, the most beautiful of curly-pated dolls, they appeared in her eyes.

A further treat was in store. 'Flora,' said her mother, when admiration was at last silent and breakfast over: 'Flora, I have asked Richard, George, Anne and Emily to spend the day with you and with Susan and Alfred. You are to be queen of the feast, because it is your birthday; and I trust you will all be very good and happy together.'

Flora loved her brother and sister, her friend Emily, and her cousins Richard, George and Anne: indeed I think that with all their faults these children did really love each other. They had often played together before; and now if ever, surely on this so special occasion they would play pleasantly together. Well, we shall see.

Anne with her brothers arrived first: and Emily having sent to ask permission, made her appearance soon after accompanied by a young friend, who was spending the holidays with her, and whom she introduced as Serena.

[What an odd name, Aunt! – Yes, Clara, it is not a common name, but I knew a Serena once; though she was not at all like this Serena, I am happy to say.]

Emily brought Flora a sweet-smelling nosegay; and Serena protested that Flora was the most charming girl she had ever met, except of course dearest Emily.

'Love me,' said Serena, throwing her arms round her small hostess and giving her a clinging kiss: 'I will love you so much if you will only let me love you.'

The house was a most elegant house, the lawn was a perfect park, the elder brother and sister frightened her by their cleverness: so exclaimed Serena: and for the moment silly little

Flora felt quite tall and superior, and allowed herself to be loved very graciously.

After the arrivals and the settling down, there remained half-an-hour before dinner, during which to cultivate acquaintance and exhibit presents. Flora displayed her doll and handed round her sugar-plum box. 'You took more than I did and it isn't fair,' grumbled George at Richard: but Richard retorted, 'Why, I saw you picking out the big ones.' 'Oh,' whined Anne, 'I'm sure there were no big ones left when they came to me.' And Emily put in with a smile of superiority: 'Stuff, Anne: you got the box before Serena and I did, and *we* don't complain.' 'But there wasn't one,' persisted Anne. 'But there were dozens and dozens,' mimicked George, 'only you're such a greedy little baby.' 'Not one,' whimpered Anne. Then Serena remarked soothingly: 'The sugar-plums were most delicious, and now let us admire the lovely doll. Why, Flora, she must have cost pounds and pounds.'

Flora, who had begun to look rueful, brightened up: 'I don't know what she cost, but her name is Flora, and she has red boots with soles. Look at me opening and shutting her eyes, and I can make her say Mamma. Is she not a beauty?' 'I never saw half such a beauty,' replied smooth Serena. Then the party sat down to dinner.

Was it fact? Was it fancy? Each dish in turn was only fit to be found fault with. Meat underdone, potatoes overdone, beans splashy, jam tart not sweet enough, fruit all stone; covers clattering, glasses reeling, a fork or two dropping on the floor. Were these things really so? or would even finest strawberries and richest cream have been found fault with, thanks to the children's mood that day?

[Were the dishes all wrong, Aunt? – I fancy not, Ella; at least, not more so than things often are in this world without upsetting every one's patience. But hear what followed.]

Sad to say, what followed was a wrangle. An hour after dinner blindman's buff in the garden began well and promised well: why could it not go on well? Ah, why indeed? for surely before now in that game toes have been trodden on, hair pulled, and small children overthrown. Flora fell down and accused Alfred of tripping her up, Richard bawled out that George broke away when fairly caught, Anne when held tight muttered that Susan could see in spite of bandaged eyes. Susan let go, Alfred picked up his little sister, George volunteered to play blindman in Susan's stead: but still pouting and grumbling showed their ugly faces, and tossed the apple of discord to and fro as if it had been a pretty plaything.

[What apple, Aunt? – The Apple of Discord,* Clara, which is a famous apple your brothers would know all about, and you may ask them some day. Now I go on.]

Would you like, any of you, a game of hide-and-seek in a garden, where there are plenty of capital hiding-places and all sorts of gay flowers to glance at while one goes seeking? I should have liked such a game, I assure you, forty years ago. But these children on this particular day could not find it in their hearts to like it. Oh dear no. Serena affected to be afraid of searching along the dusky yew alley unless Alfred went with her; and at the very same moment Flora was bent on having him lift her up to look down into a hollow tree in which it was quite obvious Susan could not possibly have hidden. 'It's my birthday,' cried Flora; 'it's my birthday.' George and Richard pushed each other roughly about till one slipped on the gravel walk and grazed his hands, when both turned cross and left off playing. At last in sheer despair Susan stepped out of her hiding-place behind the summer-house: but even then she did her best to please everybody, for she brought in her hand a basket full of ripe mulberries which she had picked up off the grass as she stood in hiding.

Then they all set to running races across the smooth sloping lawn: till Anne tumbled down and cried, though she was not a bit hurt; and Flora, who was winning the race against Anne, thought herself ill-used and so sat and sulked. Then Emily smiled, but not good-naturedly, George and Richard thrust each a finger into one eye and made faces at the two cross girls, Serena fanned herself, and Alfred looked at Susan, and Susan at Alfred, fairly at their wits' end.

An hour yet before tea-time: would another hour ever be over? Two little girls looking sullen, two boys looking provoking: the sight was not at all an encouraging one. At last Susan took pouting Flora and tearful Anne by the hand, and set off with them for a walk perforce about the grounds; whilst Alfred fairly dragged Richard and George after the girls, and Emily arm-in-arm with Serena strolled beside them.

The afternoon was sunny, shady, breezy, warm, all at once. Bees were humming and harvesting as any bee of sense must have done amongst so many blossoms: leafy boughs danced with their dancing shadows; bell flowers rang without clappers:—

[Could they, Aunt? – Well, not exactly, Maude: but you're coming to much more wonderful matters!]

Now and then a pigeon cooed its soft water-bottle note; and a long way off sheep stood bleating.

Susan let go the little hot hands she held, and began as she walked telling a story to which all her companions soon paid attention – all except Flora.

Poor little Flora: was this the end of her birthday? was she eight years old at last only for this? Her sugar-plums almost all gone and not cared for, her chosen tart not a nice one, herself so cross and miserable: is it really worth while to be eight years old and have a birthday, if this is what comes of it?

'—So the frog did not know how to boil the kettle;* but he only replied: I can't bear hot water,' went on Susan telling her story. But Flora had no heart to listen, or to care about the frog. She lagged and dropped behind not noticed by any one, but creeping along slowly and sadly by herself.

Down the yew alley she turned, and it looked dark and very gloomy as she passed out of the sunshine into the shadow. There were twenty yew trees on each side of the path, as she had counted over and over again a great many years ago when she was learning to count; but now at her right hand there stood twenty-one: and if the last tree was really a yew tree at all, it was at least a very odd one, for a lamp grew on its topmost branch. Never before either had the yew walk led to a door: but now at its further end stood a door with bell and knocker, and 'Ring also' printed in black letters on a brass plate; all as plain as possible in the lamplight.

Flora stretched up her hand, and knocked and rang also.

She was surprised to feel the knocker shake hands with her, and to see the bell handle twist round and open the door. 'Dear me,' thought she, 'why could not the door open itself instead of troubling the bell?' But she only said, 'Thank you,' and walked in.

The door opened into a large and lofty apartment, very handsomely furnished. All the chairs were stuffed arm-chairs, and moved their arms and shifted their shoulders to accommodate sitters. All the sofas arranged and rearranged their pillows as convenience dictated. Footstools glided about,* and rose or sank to meet every length of leg. Tables were no less obliging, but ran on noiseless castors here or there when wanted. Tea-trays ready set out, saucers of strawberries, jugs of cream, and plates of cake, floated in, settled down, and floated out again empty, with considerable tact and good taste: they came and went through a square hole high up in one wall, beyond which I presume lay the kitchen. Two harmoniums, an accordion, a pair of kettledrums and a peal of bells played concerted pieces behind a screen, but kept silence during conversation. Photographs and pictures made the tour of the apartment, standing still when glanced at and going on when done with. In case of need the furniture flattened itself against the wall, and cleared the floor for a game, or I dare say a dance. Of these remarkable details some struck Flora in the first few minutes after her arrival, some came to light as time went on. The only uncomfortable point in the room, that is, as to furniture, was that both ceiling and walls were lined throughout with looking-glasses: but at first this did not strike Flora as any disadvantage; indeed she thought it quite delightful, and took a long look at her little self full length.

[Jane and Laura, don't *quite* forget the pocket-handkerchiefs you sat down to hem. See how hard Ella works at her fern leaves, and what pains she is taking to paint them nicely. Yes, Maude, that darn will do: now your task is ended, but if I were you I would help Clara with hers.]

The room was full of boys and girls, older and younger, big and little. They all sat drinking tea at a great number of different tables; here half a dozen children sitting together, here more or fewer; here one child would preside all alone at a table just the size for one comfortably. I should tell you that the tables were like telescope tables; only they expanded and contracted of themselves without extra pieces, and seemed to study everybody's convenience.

Every single boy and every single girl stared hard at Flora and went on staring: but not one of them offered her a chair, or a cup of tea, or anything else whatever. She grew very red and uncomfortable under so many staring pairs of eyes: when a chair did what it could to relieve her embarrassment by pressing gently against her till she sat down. It then bulged out its own back comfortably into hers, and drew in its arms to suit her small size. A footstool grew somewhat taller beneath her feet. A table ran up with tea for one; a cream-jug toppled over upon a saucerful of strawberries, and then righted itself again; the due quantity of sifted sugar sprinkled itself over the whole.

[How could it sprinkle itself? – Well, Jane, let us suppose it sprang up in its china basin like a fountain; and overflowed on one side only, but that of course the right side, whether it was right or left.]

Flora could not help thinking everyone very rude and ill-natured to go on staring without speaking, and she felt shy at having to eat with so many eyes upon her: still she was hot and thirsty, and the feast looked most tempting. She took up in a spoon one large, very large strawberry with plenty of cream; and was just putting it into her mouth when a voice called out crossly: 'You shan't, they're mine.' The spoon dropped from her startled hand, but without any clatter: and Flora looked round to see the speaker.

[Who was it? Was it a boy or a girl? – Listen, and you shall hear, Laura.]

The speaker was a girl enthroned in an extra high armchair; with a stool as high as an ottoman under her feet, and a table as high as a chest of drawers in front of her. I suppose as she had it so she liked it so, for I am sure all the furniture laid itself out to be obliging. Perched upon her hair she wore a coronet made of tinsel; her face was a red face with a scowl: sometimes perhaps she looked nice and pretty, this time she looked ugly. 'You shan't, they're mine,' she repeated in a cross grumbling voice: 'it's my birthday, and everything is mine.'

Flora was too honest a little girl to eat strawberries that were not given her: nor could she, after this, take a cup of tea without leave. Not to tantalize her, I suppose, the table glided away with its delicious untasted load; whilst the armchair gave her a very gentle hug as if to console her.

If she could only have discovered the door Flora would have fled through it back into the gloomy yew-tree walk, and there have moped in solitude, rather than remain where she was not made welcome: but either the door was gone, or else it was shut to and lost amongst the multitude of mirrors. The birthday Queen, reflected over and over again in five hundred mirrors, looked frightful, I do assure you: and for one minute I am sorry to say that Flora's fifty million-fold face appeared flushed and angry too; but she soon tried to smile good-humouredly and succeeded, though she could not manage to feel very merry.

[But, Aunt, how came she to have fifty million faces? I don't understand. – Because in such a number of mirrors there were not merely simple reflections, but reflections of reflections, and reflections of reflections and reflections, and so on and on and on, over and over again, Maude: don't you see?]

The meal was ended at last: most of the children had eaten and stuffed quite greedily; poor Flora alone had not tasted a morsel. Then with a word and I think a kick from the Queen, her high footstool scudded away into a corner: and all the furniture taking the hint arranged itself as flat as possible round the room, close up against the walls.

[And across the door? – Why, yes, I suppose it may have done so, Jane: such active and willing furniture could never be in the way anywhere. – And was there a chimney corner? – No, I think not: that afternoon was warm we know, and there may have been a different apartment for winter. At any rate, as this is all make-believe, I say No. Attention!]

All the children now clustered together in the middle of the empty floor; elbowing and jostling each other, and disputing about what game should first be played at. Flora, elbowed and jostled in their midst, noticed points of appearance that quite surprised her. Was it themselves, or was it their clothes? (only who indeed would wear such clothes, so long as there was another suit in the world to put on?) One boy bristled with prickly quills like a porcupine, and raised or depressed them at pleasure; but he usually kept them pointed outwards. Another instead of being rounded like most people was facetted at very sharp angles. A third caught in everything he came near, for he was hung round with hooks like fishhooks. One girl exuded a sticky fluid and came off on the fingers; another, rather smaller, was slimy and slipped through the hands. Such exceptional features could not but prove inconvenient, yet patience and forbearance might still have done something towards keeping matters smooth: but these unhappy children seemed not to know what forbearance was; and as to patience, they might have answered me nearly in the words of a celebrated man – 'Madam, I never saw patience.'

[Who was the celebrated man, Aunt? – Oh, Clara, you an English girl and not know Lord Nelson!* But I go on.]

'Tell us some new game,' growled Hooks threateningly, catching in Flora's hair and tugging to get loose.

Flora did not at all like being spoken to in such a tone, and the hook hurt her very much. Still, though she could not think of anything new, she tried to do her best, and in a timid voice suggested 'Les Grâces'.*

'That's a girl's game,' said Hooks contemptuously.

'It's as good any day as a boy's game,' retorted Sticky.

'I wouldn't give *that* for your girl's games,' snarled Hooks, endeavouring to snap his fingers, but entangling two hooks and stamping.

'Poor dear fellow!' drawled Slime, affecting sympathy.

'It's quite as good,' harped on Sticky: 'It's as good or better.'

Angles caught and would have shaken Slime, but she slipped through his fingers demurely.

'Think of something else, and let it be new,' yawned Quills, with quills laid for a wonder.

'I really don't know anything new,' answered Flora half crying: and she was going to add, 'But I will play with you at any game you like, if you will teach me'; when they all burst forth into a yell of 'Cry, baby, cry! – Cry, baby, cry!' – They shouted it, screamed it, sang it: they pointed fingers, made grimaces, nodded heads at her. The wonder was she did not cry outright.

At length the Queen interfered: 'Let her alone; – who's she? It's *my* birthday, and we'll play at Hunt the Pincushion.'*

So Hunt the Pincushion it was. This game is simple and demands only a moderate amount of skill. Select the smallest and weakest player (if possible let her be fat: a hump is best of all), chase her round and round the room, overtaking her at short intervals, and sticking pins into her here or there as it happens: repeat, till you choose to catch and swing her; which concludes the game. Short cuts, yells, and sudden leaps give spirit to the hunt.

[Oh, Aunt, what a horrid game! surely there cannot be such a game? – Certainly not, Ella: yet I have seen before now very rough cruel play, if it can be termed play. – And did they get a poor little girl with a hump? – No, Laura, not this time: for]

The Pincushion was poor little Flora. How she strained and ducked and swerved to this side or that, in the vain effort to escape her tormentors! Quills with every quill erect tilted against her, and needed not a pin: but Angles whose corners almost cut her, Hooks who caught and slit her frock, Slime who slid against and passed her, Sticky who rubbed off on her neck and plump bare arms, the scowling Queen, and the whole laughing scolding pushing troop, all wielded longest sharpest pins, and all by turns overtook her.

Finally the Queen caught her, swung her violently round, let go suddenly, – and Flora losing her balance dropped upon the floor. But at least that game was over.

Do you fancy the fall jarred her? Not at all: for the carpet grew to such a depth of velvet pile below her, that she fell quite lightly.

Indeed I am inclined to believe that even in that dreadful sport of Hunt the Pincushion, Flora was still better off than her stickers: who in the thick of the throng exasperated each other and fairly maddened themselves by a free use of cutting corners, pricking quills, catching hooks, glue, slime, and I know not what else. Slime, perhaps, would seem not so much amiss for its owner: but then if a slimy person cannot be held, neither can she hold fast. As to Hooks and Sticky they often in wrenching themselves loose got worse damage than they inflicted: Angles many times cut his own fingers with his edges: and I don't envy the individual whose sharp quills are flexible enough to be bent point inwards in a crush or a scuffle. The Queen must perhaps be reckoned exempt from particular personal pangs: but then, you see, it was her birthday! And she must still have suffered a good deal from the eccentricities of her subjects.

The next game called for was Self Help.* In this no adventitious aids were tolerated, but each boy depended exclusively on his own resources. Thus pins were forbidden: but every natural advantage, as a quill or fishhook, might be utilized to the utmost.

[Don't look shocked, dear Ella, at my choice of words; but remember that my birthday party is being held in the Land of Nowhere. Yet who knows whether something not altogether unlike it has not ere now taken place in the Land of Somewhere? Look at home, children.]

The boys were players, the girls were played (if I may be allowed such a phrase): all except the Queen who, being Queen, looked on, and merely administered a slap or box on the ear now and then to some one coming handy. Hooks, as a Heavy Porter, shone in this sport; and dragged about with him a load of attached captives, all vainly struggling to unhook themselves. Angles, as an Ironer, goffered or fluted several children by sustained pressure. Quills, an Engraver, could do little more than prick and scratch with some permanence of result. Flora falling to the share of Angles had her torn frock pressed and plaited after quite a novel fashion: but this was at any rate preferable to her experience as Pincushion, and she bore it like a philosopher.

Yet not to speak of the girls, even the boys did not as a body extract unmixed pleasure from Self Help; but much wrangling and some blows allayed their exuberant enjoyment. The Queen as befitted her lofty lot did, perhaps, taste of mirth unalloyed; but if so, she stood alone in satisfaction as in dignity. In any case, pleasure palls in the long run.

The Queen yawned a very wide loud yawn: and as everyone yawned in sympathy the game died out.

A supper table now advanced from the wall to the middle of the floor, and armchairs enough gathered round it to seat the whole party. Through the square hole, – not, alas! through the door of poor Flora's recollection, – floated in the requisite number of plates, glasses, knives, forks, and spoons; and so many dishes and decanters filled with nice things as I certainly never saw in all my lifetime, and I don't imagine any of you ever did.

[How many children were there at supper? – Well, I have not the least idea, Laura, but they made quite a large party: suppose we say a hundred thousand.]

This time Flora would not take so much as a fork without leave: wherefore as the Queen paid not the slightest attention to her, she was reduced to look hungrily on while the rest of the company feasted, and while successive dainties placed themselves before her and retired untasted. Cold turkey, lobster salad, stewed mushrooms, raspberry tart, cream cheese, a bumper of champagne, a méringue, a strawberry ice, sugared pine apple, some greengages: it may have been quite as well for her that she did not feel at liberty to eat such a mixture: yet it was none the less tantalizing to watch so many good things come and go without taking even one taste, and to see all her companions stuffing without limit. Several of the boys seemed to think nothing of a whole turkey at a time: and the Queen consumed with her own mouth and of sweets alone one quart of strawberry ice, three pine apples, two melons, a score of méringues, and about four dozen sticks of angelica, as Flora counted.

After supper there was no need for the furniture to withdraw: for the whole birthday party trooped out through a door (but still not through Flora's door) into a spacious playground. What they may usually have played at I cannot tell you; but on this occasion a great number of bricks happened to be lying about on all sides mixed up with many neat piles of stones, so the children began building houses: only instead of building from without as most bricklayers do, they built from within, taking care to have at hand plenty of bricks as well as good heaps of stones, and inclosing both themselves and the heaps as they built; one child with one heap of stones inside each house.

[Had they window panes at hand as well? – No, Jane, and you will soon see why none were wanted.]

I called the building material bricks: but strictly speaking there were no bricks at all in the playground, only brick-shaped pieces of glass instead. Each of these had the sides brilliantly polished; whilst the edges, which were meant to touch and join, were ground, and thus appeared to acquire a certain tenacity. There were bricks (so to call them) of all colours and many different shapes and sizes. Some were fancy bricks wrought in open work, some were engraved in running patterns, others were cut into facets or blown into bubbles. A single house might have its blocks all uniform, or of twenty different fashions.

Yet, despite this amount of variety, every house built bore a marked resemblance to its neighbour: colours varied, architecture agreed. Four walls, no roof, no upper floor; such was each house: and it needed neither window nor staircase.

All this building occupied a long long time, and by little and little a very gay effect indeed was produced. Not merely were the glass blocks of beautiful tints; so that whilst some houses glowed like masses of ruby, and others shone like enormous chrysolites or sapphires, others again showed the milkiness and fiery spark of a hundred opals, or glimmered like moonstone: but the playground was lighted up, high, low, and on all sides, with coloured lamps. Picture to yourselves golden twinkling lamps like stars high overhead, bluish twinkling lamps like glowworms down almost on the ground; lamps like illuminated peaches, apples, apricots, plums, hung about with the profusion of a most fruitful orchard. Should we not all have liked to be there with Flora, even if supper was the forfeit?

Ah no, not with Flora: for to her utter dismay she found that she was being built in with the Queen. She was not called upon to build: but gradually the walls rose and rose around her, till they towered clear above her head; and being all slippery with smoothness, left no hope of her ever being able to clamber over them back into the road home, if indeed there was any longer such a road anywhere outside. Her heart sank within her, and she could scarcely hold up her head. To crown all, a glass house which contained no vestige even of a cupboard did clearly not contain a larder: and Flora began to feel sick with hunger and thirst, and to look forward in despair to no breakfast to-morrow.

Acoustics must have been most accurately studied,—

[But, Aunt, what are acoustics? – The science of sounds, Maude: pray now exercise your acoustical faculty.]

As I say, they must have been most accurately studied, and to practical purpose, in the laying out of this particular playground; if, that is, to hear distinctly everywhere whatever might be uttered anywhere within its limits, was the object aimed at. At any rate, such was the result.

Their residences at length erected, and their toils over, the youthful architects found leisure to gaze around them and bandy compliments.

First: 'Look,' cried Angles, pointing exultantly: 'just look at Quills, as red as fire. Red doesn't become Quills. Quills' house would look a deal better without Quills.'

'Talk of becomingness,' laughed Quills, angrily, 'you're just the colour of a sour gooseberry, Angles, and a greater fright than we've seen you yet. Look at him, Sticky, look whilst you have the chance:' for Angles was turning his green back on the speaker.

But Sticky – no wonder, the blocks *she* had fingered stuck together! – Sticky was far too busy to glance around; she was engrossed in making faces at Slime, whilst Slime returned grimace for grimace. Sticky's house was blue, and turned her livid: Slime's house – a very shaky one, ready to fall to pieces at any moment, and without one moment's warning: – Slime's house, I say, was amber-hued, and gave her the jaundice. These advantages were not lost on the belligerents, who stood working each other up into a state of frenzy, and having got long past variety, now did nothing but screech over and over again: Slime: 'You're a sweet beauty,' – and Sticky (incautious Sticky!): 'You're another!'

Quarrels raged throughout the playground. The only silent tongue was Flora's.

Suddenly, Hooks, who had built an engraved house opposite the Queen's bubbled palace (both edifices were pale amethyst coloured, and trying to the complexion), caught sight of his fair neighbour, and, clapping his hands, burst out into an insulting laugh.

'You're another!' shrieked the Queen (the girls all alike seemed well-nigh destitute of invention). Her words were weak, but as she spoke she stooped: and clutched – shook — hurled – the first stone.

'Oh don't, don't, don't,' sobbed Flora, clinging in a paroxysm of terror, and with all her weight, to the royal arm.

That first stone was, as it were, the first hail-stone of the storm: and soon stones flew in every direction and at every elevation. The very atmosphere seemed petrified. Stones clattered, glass shivered, moans and groans resounded on every side. It was as a battle of giants: who would excel each emulous peer, and be champion among giants?

The Queen. All that had hitherto whistled through mid-air were mere pebbles and chips compared with one massive slab which she now heaved up – poised – prepared to launch—

'Oh don't, don't, don't,' cried out Flora again, almost choking with sobs. But it was useless. The ponderous stone spun on, widening an outlet through the palace wall on its way to crush Hooks. Half mad with fear, Flora flung herself after it through the breach—

And in one moment the scene was changed. Silence from human voices and a pleasant coolness of approaching twilight surrounded her. High overhead a fleet of rosy grey clouds went sailing away from the west, and outstripping these, rooks on flapping black wings flew home to their nests in the lofty elm trees, and cawed as they flew. A few heat-drops pattered down on a laurel hedge hard by, and a sudden gust of wind ran rustling through the laurel leaves. Such dear familiar sights and sounds told Flora that she was sitting safe within the home precincts: yes, in the very yew-tree alley, with its forty trees in all, not one more, and with no mysterious door leading out of it into a hall of misery.

She hastened indoors. Her parents, with Alfred, Susan, and the five visitors, were just sitting down round the tea-table, and nurse was leaving the drawing-room in some apparent perturbation.

Wagga wagged his tail, Muff came forward purring, and a laugh greeted Flora. 'Do you know,' cried George, 'that you have been fast asleep ever so long in the yew walk, for I found you there? And now nurse was on her way to fetch you in, if you hadn't turned up.'

Flora said not a word in answer, but sat down just as she was, with tumbled frock and hair, and a conscious look in her little face that made it very sweet and winning. Before tea was over, she had nestled close up to Anne, and whispered how sorry she was to have been so cross.

And I think if she lives to be nine years old and give another birthday party, she is likely on that occasion to be even less like the birthday Queen of her troubled dream than was the Flora of eight years old: who, with dear friends and playmates and pretty presents, yet scarcely knew how to bear a few trifling disappointments, or how to be obliging and good-humoured under slight annoyances.

EDITH

'Aunt, Aunt!'

'What, girls?'

'Aunt, do tell us the story of the frog who couldn't boil the kettle.'

'But I was not there to hear Susan tell the story.'

'Oh, but you know it, Aunt.'

'No, indeed I do not. I can imagine reasons why a frog would not and should not boil a kettle, but I never heard any such stated.'

'Oh, but try. You know, Aunt, you are always telling *us* to try.'

'Fairly put, Jane, and I will try, on condition that you all help me with my sewing.'

'But we got through our work yesterday.'

'Very well, Maude, as you like: only no help no story. I have too many poor friends* ever to get through *my* work. However, as I see thimbles coming out, I conclude you choose story and labour. Look, these breadths must be run together, three and three. Ella, if you like to go to your music, don't stay listening out of ceremony: still, if you do stay, here are plenty of buttonholes to overcast. Now are we all seated and settled? Then listen. The frog and his peers will have to talk, of course; but that seems a marvel scarcely worth mentioning after Flora's experience.'

Edith and a teakettle were spending one warm afternoon together in a wood. Before proceeding with my story, let me introduce each personage to you more particularly.

The wood should perhaps be called a grove rather than a wood, but in Edith's eyes it looked no less than a forest. About a hundred fine old beech-trees stood together, with here and there an elegant silver birch drooping in their midst. Besides these there was one vine which, by some freak, had been planted near the centre of the group, and which, year after year, trailing its long graceful branches over at least a dozen neighbours, dangled bunches of pale purple grapes among its leaves and twisted tendrils. The kettle was of brilliant copper, fitted up with a yellow glass handle: it was also on occasion a pleasing singer. Edith was a little girl who thought herself by no means such a very little girl, and at any rate as wise as her elder brother, sister, and nurse. I should be afraid to assert that she did not reckon herself as wise as her parents: but we must hope not, for her own sake.

The loving mother had planned a treat for her family that afternoon. A party of friends and relations were to assemble in the beech-wood, and partake of a gipsy tea : some catch-singing might be managed, cold supper should be laid indoors, and if the evening proved very delightful, the open-air entertainment might be prolonged till full-moonrise.

Preparations were intrusted to nurse's care, others of the household working under her, and she promising to go down to the beeches at least half an hour before the time fixed for the party, to see that all was ready. An early dinner throughout the house and no lessons in the schoolroom set the afternoon free for the gipsy feast.

After dinner Edith dressed her doll in its best clothes, tied on its broad-brimmed hat and veil, and hooked a miniature parasol into its waistband. Her sister was busy arranging flowers for the supper-table, her brother was out taking a walk, nurse was deep in jams, sandwiches, and delicacies in general; for nurse, though going by her old name, and still doing all sorts of things for her old baby, was now in fact housekeeper.

None of these could bestow much attention on Edith, who, doll in arm, strolled along into the kitchen, and there paused to watch cook rolling puff paste at her utmost speed. Six dozen patty-pans stood in waiting, and yawned as they waited.

Edith set down her doll on the window-seat and began to talk, whilst cook, with a good-natured red face, made her an occasional random answer, right or wrong as it happened.

'What are we to have besides sandwiches and tarts?'

'Cold fowls, and a syllabub, and champagne, and tea and coffee, and potato-rolls, and lunns,* and tongue, and I can't say what besides.'

'Where are the fowls, cook?'

'In the larder, where they ought to be, Miss Edith, not lying about in a hot kitchen.'

'Do you like making tarts?'

'I like tarts, but not often.'

'Cook, you're not attending to what I say.'

'No, the attendance is just what I should not have liked.'

Edith looked about till a bright copper kettle on a shelf caught her eye. 'Is that the kettle for tea?'

'Yes, miss.'

The doll gazing out of window was forgotten, while, mounting on a stool, Edith reached down the kettle.

'I will carry the kettle out ready.'

'The fire will have to be lighted first,' answered cook, as she hurried her tarts into the oven, and ran out to fetch curled parsley from the kitchen-garden.

'I can light the fire,' called out Edith after her, though not very anxious to make herself heard: and thus it happened that cook heard nothing beyond the child's voice saying something or other of no consequence.

So Edith found a box of lucifers,* and sallied forth kettle in hand. Striking on the burnished copper, the sun's rays transformed that also into a resplendent portable sun of dazzling aspect. The beautiful sunshine bathed garden, orchard, field, lane and wood; bathed flower, bush and tree; bathed bird, beast and butterfly. Frisk, the Newfoundland dog, and Cosy, the Persian cat, meeting their young mistress, turned round, to give her their company. Crest, the cockatoo, taking a constitutional on the lawn, fluttered up to her shoulder and perched there. The four went on together, Frisk carrying the kettle in his mouth, and Crest pecking at the match-box. Several lucifers dropped out, and not more than six reached their destination.

Edith knew that the gipsy party was to be held just where the vine grew, and thither she directed her steps. A pool, the only pool in the wood, gleamed close at hand, and mirrored in its still depths the lights, shadows, and many greens of beech-tree, birch-tree, and vine. How she longed for a cluster of those purple grapes* which, hanging high above her head, swung to and fro with every breath of wind; now straining a tendril, now displacing a leaf, now dipping towards her but never within reach. Still, as Edith was such a very wise girl, we must not suppose she would stand long agape after unattainable grapes: nor did she. Her business just then was to boil a kettle, and to this she bent her mind.

Three sticks and a hook dependent therefrom suggested a tripod erected for the kettle: and so it was.

[Why a tripod, Aunt? – I have been wondering at the no remarks, but here comes one at last. Three sticks, Maude, are the fewest that can stand up firmly by themselves; two would tumble down, and four are not wanted. The reel? here it is: and then pass it to Clara.]

Within the legs of the tripod lay a fagot,* supported on some loose bricks. The fagot had been untied, but otherwise very little disturbed.

By standing on the fagot, Edith made herself more than tall enough to hang the kettle on its hook: then jumping down she struck her first match. A flash followed; and in one instant the match went out, as might have been expected in the open air and with no shelter for the flame. She struck a second lucifer, with the like result: a third, a fourth, with no better success. After this it was high time to ponder well before sacrificing a fifth match; for two only remained in the broken box.

Edith sat down to reflect, and stayed quiet so long, with her cheek leaning on her hand and her eyes fixed on a lucifer, that the aborigines of the wood grew bold and gathered round her.

[Who were the aborigines, Aunt? – The natives of the wood, Laura; the creatures born and bred there generation after generation.]

A squirrel scampered down three boughs lower on the loftiest beech-tree, and cracked his beechmast audibly. A pair of wood pigeons advanced making polite bows. A mole popped a fleshy nose and a little human hand out of his burrow – popped them in, and popped them out again. A toad gazed deliberately round him with his eye like a jewel. Two hedgehogs came along and seated themselves near the toad. A frog—

[*The* frog, Aunt? – Yes, Laura,]

– *the* frog hopped at a leisurely pace up the pond bank, and squatted among the long grasses at its edge.

The wonder is that Frisk, Cosy, and Crest, let this small fry come and go at pleasure and unmolested; but, whatever their motive may have been, they did so. They sat with great gravity right and left of their mistress, and kept themselves to themselves.

Edith's situation had now become, as it seems to me, neither pleasant nor dignified. She had volunteered to boil a kettle, and could not succeed even in lighting a fire. Her relations, friends, and other natural enemies would be arriving, and would triumph over her: for if her fire would not light, her kettle would certainly never boil. She took up the fifth lucifer and prepared to strike – paused – laid it back in the box: for it was her last but one. She sat on thinking what to do, yet could think of nothing to the purpose: of nothing better, that is, than of striking the match and running the risk. What should she do?

She had not even so much as half an eye to spare for the creatures around her, whilst they on their side concentrated their utmost attention on her. The pigeons left off bowing: the squirrel did not fetch a second beechmast.

'Oh dear!' exclaimed Edith at last; 'what shall I do?'

Two voices, like two gurgling bottles, answered, 'Couldn't you fly away, dear?' and the two pigeons bowed like one pigeon.

Edith was so thoroughly preoccupied by her troubles as to have very little room left in her mind for surprise: still, she did just glance at the pigeons before answering, 'I wish you'd advise something sensible, instead of telling me to fly without wings.'

'If you can only get so much as one twig to light,' called out the squirrel hopefully, 'I'll fan the flame with my tail.'

'Ah,' retorted Edith, 'but that's just it: how am I to light the first twig with lucifers that do nothing but go out?'

A pause. 'What should you say,' suggested the mole, rubbing his hands together, 'to my rearranging the sticks?'

'Very well,' answered Edith, 'do what you please.' But she looked as if she did not expect much good to result from the mole's co-operation.

However, the mole clambered up one of the bricks, and then by pushing and pulling with his handy little hands, really did arrange the sticks in a loose heap full of hollows and tunnels for admitting currents of air; and so far matters looked promising.

The two hedgehogs sat silent and staring; why they came and why they stayed never appeared from first to last; but the frog hopped past them, and enquired, with a sudden appearance of interest, 'Does not the kettle want filling?' No one noticed what he said, so he added under his breath, 'Perhaps it is full already.'

[Was it full, Aunt? – No, Maude, there was not a drop in it: so after all it was fortunate that it hung above black sticks instead of over a blazing fire, or it would soon have been spoilt. Remember, girls, never put an empty kettle on the fire, or you and it will rue the consequence.]

The toad peered with his bright eye in among the sticks. 'I should vote,' said he mildly, 'that the next lucifer be held and struck inside the heap, to protect the spark from draughts.'

[How came the toad to be so much cleverer than his neighbours, Aunt? – Well, Jane, I suppose such a bright thought may have occurred to him rather than to the rest, because toads so often live inside stones: at least, so people have said. And suppose his father, grandfather and great-grandfather all inhabited stones, the idea of doing everything inside something may well have come naturally to him.]

The toad's suggestion roused Edith from despondency to action. She knelt down by the tripod, although just there the ground was sprinkled with brickdust and sawdust; thrust both hands in amongst the wood, struck a match, saw it flash, – and die out. 'Try again,' whispered the toad; and as she could devise no better plan she tried again.

This sixth and last venture was crowned with success. One twig caught fire, as a slight crackling followed by a puff of smoke attested. The squirrel took his seat on a brick and whisked his tail to and fro. The hedgehogs turning their backs on the smoke, sniffed in the opposite direction; waiting as I suppose for the event, though they showed not the least vestige of interest in it.

'Now,' cried the frog hopping up and down in his excitement and curiosity, 'now to boil the kettle.'

But the first spark of success was followed by a dim, smoky, fitful smouldering which gave merely the vaguest promise of a coming blaze. A pair of bellows would have answered far better than the squirrel's tail: and though, with a wish to oblige, the two wood-pigeons fluttered round and round the tripod, they did not the slightest good.

Just then a fox bustled up, and glanced askance at Frisk: but receiving a reassuring and friendly nod, joined the party under the shady vine-branches. This fox was a tidy person, and like most foxes always carried about a brush* with him: so without more ado he went straight up to Edith, and gave her dusty frock a thorough brushing all round. Next he wrapped his fore paws about the vine, and shook it with all his force; but as no grapes fell, though several bunches bobbed up and down and seemed ready to drop into his mouth, he gave one leap upwards off all four feet at once towards the lowest cluster he could spy; this also failing he shook his head, turned up his nose, shrugged his shoulders, muttered, 'They must be sour,' (and this once I suspect the fox was right) trotted away, and was soon lost to view among the beech-trees.

'Now,' cried the frog once more, 'now for the kettle.'

'Boil it yourself,' retorted Edith.

So the frog did not know how to boil the kettle, but he only replied, 'I can't bear hot water.' This you may remark was a startling change of tone in the frog: but I suppose he was anxious to save his credit. Now if he had only taken time to look at what was under his very eyes, he might have saved his credit without belying his principles: for

The fire had gone out!

And here my story finishes: except that I will just add how

As Edith in despair sat down to cry,

As the pigeons withdrew bowing and silent,

As the squirrel scudded up his beech-tree again,

As the mole vanished underground,

As the toad hid himself behind a toadstool,

As the two hedgehogs yawned and went away yawning,

As the frog dived,

As Frisk wagged, Cosy purred, and Crest murmured, 'Pretty Cockatoo,' to console their weeping mistress,

Nurse arrived on the ground with a box of lucifers in one hand, two fire-wheels* in the other, and a half-a-dozen newspapers under her arm, and exclaimed, 'Oh my dear child, run indoors as fast as you can: for your mother, father, brother and sister are hunting up and down all over the house looking for you; and cook is half out of her wits because she cannot find the kettle.'

MAGGIE

'My dear children, what is all this mysterious whispering about?'

'It's Jane, Aunt.'

'Oh, Maude, I'm sure it's you quite as much.'

'Well then, Jane and Maude, what is it?'

'We were only saying that both your stories are summer stories, and we want you to tell us a winter story some day. That's all, Aunty dear.'

'Very well, Maudy dear; but don't say "only", as if I were finding fault with you. If Jane and you wish for a winter story, my next shall freeze hard. What! now? You really do allow me very little time for invention!'

'And please, Aunt, be wonderful.'

'Well, Laura, I will try to be wonderful; but I cannot promise first-rate wonders on such extremely short notice. Ella, you sitting down too? Here is my work for you all, the same as yesterday, and here comes my story.'

Old Dame Margaret kept the village fancy shop. Her window was always filled with novelties and attractions, but about Christmastide, it put forth extra splendours, and as it were blossomed gorgeously. Flora's doll, her sugar-plum box and hedgehog pincushion, came I should say from this very window; and though her hoops and sticks for *les grâces* can scarcely have looked smart enough for a place of honour, they emerged probably from somewhere behind the counter.

[Did Edith's doll come out of the window too? – Yes, Clara, if Flora's did I have no doubt Edith's did; for as they say in the Arabian Nights,* 'each was more beautiful than the other'.]

In spite of her gay shop, Dame Margaret was no fine lady, but a nice simple old woman who wore plain clothes, and made them last a long time: and thus it was that over and over again she found money to give or lend among her needy neighbours. If a widow's cow died, or a labourer's cottage was burnt down, or if half-a-dozen poor children were left orphans, Dame Margaret's purse would be the first to open, and the last to shut; though she was very cautious as to helping idlers who refused to help themselves, or drunkards who would only do more harm with more money.

I dare say her plain clothes and her plain table (for she kept a plain table too) were what enabled her, amongst other good deeds, to take home little Maggie, her orphan granddaughter, when the child was left almost without kith or kin to care for her. These two were quite alone in the world: each was the other's only living relation, and they loved each other very dearly.

Hour after hour on Christmas Eve, business raged in Dame Margaret's shop. I shrink from picturing to myself the run on burnt almonds, chocolate, and 'sweeties' of every flavour, all done up in elegant fancy boxes; the run on wax dolls, wooden dolls, speaking dolls, squeaking dolls; the run on woolly lambs and canaries with removable heads; the run on everything in general. Dame Margaret and Maggie at her elbow had a busy time behind their counter, I do assure you.

[Did Maggie serve too? – Yes, Jane; and it was her delight to run up steps and reach down goods from high shelves.]

About three o'clock, the shop happened for a moment to be empty of customers, and Dame Margaret was glancing complacently round upon her diminished stock, when her eye lighted on some parcels which had been laid on a chair and forgotten. 'Oh dear, Maggie,' exclaimed she, 'the doctor's young ladies have left behind them all the tapers* for their Christmas tree, and I don't know what besides.' Now that doctor resided with his family in a large house some distance out of the village, and the road to it lay through the outskirts of an oak forest.

'Let me take them, Granny,' cried Maggie eagerly: 'and perhaps I may get a glimpse of the Christmas tree.'

'But it will soon be dark.'

'Oh, Granny, I will make haste: do, please, let me go.'

So kind Dame Margaret answered, 'Yes; only be sure to make great haste:' and then she packed up the forgotten parcels very carefully in a basket. Not merely the red tapers, but a pound of vanilla chocolate, a beautiful bouncing ball, and two dozen crackers, had all been left behind.

Basket on arm, Maggie started for the doctor's house: and as she stepped out into the cold open air it nipped her fingers and ears, and little pug-nose. Cold? indeed it was cold, for the thermometer marked *half-a-dozen* degrees of frost; every pond and puddle far and near was coated with thick sheet ice, or turned to block ice from top to bottom; every branch of every bare oak shivered in a keen east wind. How the poor little birds kept warm, or whether in fact any did keep warm on the leafless boughs, I cannot tell: I only know that many a thrush and sparrow died of cold that winter, whilst robin redbreast begged crumbs at cottage windows. His snug scarlet waistcoat could scarcely keep hungry robin's heart warm; and I am afraid to think about his poor little pretty head with its bright eye.

Maggie set off on her journey with a jump and a run, and very soon got a fall: for without any suspicion of what awaited her she set her foot on a loose lump of ice, and down she went, giving the back of her head a sounding thump. She was up again directly, and ran on as if nothing had happened; but whether her brain got damaged by the blow, or how else it may have been, I know not; I only know that the thwack seemed in one moment to fill the atmosphere around her with sparks, flames and flashes of lightning; and that from this identical point of time commenced her marvellous adventures.

Were the clouds at play? they went racing across the sky so rapidly! Were the oaks at play? they tossed their boughs up and down in such rattling confusion! Maggie on her travels began to think that she too should dearly like a game of play, when an opening in the forest disclosed to her a green glade, in which a party of children were sporting together in the very freest and easiest manner possible.

Such a game! Such children! If they had not been children they must inevitably have been grasshoppers. They leaped over oaks, wrestled in mid-air, bounded past a dozen trees at once; two and two they spun round like whirlwinds; they darted straight up like balloons; they tossed each other about like balls. A score of dogs barking and gambolling in their midst were evidently quite unable to keep up with them.

[Didn't they all get very hot, Aunt? – Very hot indeed, Maude, I should think.]

The children's cheeks were flushed, their hair streamed right out like comets' tails; you might have heard and seen their hearts beat, and yet no one appeared in the least out of breath. Positively they had plenty of breath amongst them to time their game by singing.

'One, two, three,' they sang,—

'One, two, three,' they sang,—

'One, two, three,' they sang, 'and away,' – as they all came clustering like a swarm of wasps round astonished Maggie.

How she longed for a game with them! She had never in her life seen anything half so funny, or so sociable, or so warming on a cold day. And we must bear in mind that Maggie had no play-fellows at home, and that cold winter was just then at its very coldest. 'Yes,' she answered eagerly; 'yes, yes; what shall we play at?'

A glutinous-looking girl in pink cotton velvet proposed: 'Hunt the pincushion.'

'No, Self Help,' bawled a boy clothed in something like porcupine skin.

[Oh, Aunt, are these those monstrous children over again? – Yes, Ella, you really can't expect me not to utilize such a brilliant idea twice.]

'No, running races,' cried a second girl, wriggling forward through the press like an eel.

'No, this' – 'No, that,' – 'No, the other,' shouted every one in general, bounding here, spinning there, jumping up, clapping hands, kicking heels, in a tempest of excitement.

'Anything you please,' panted Maggie, twirling and leaping in emulation, and ready to challenge the whole field to a race; when suddenly her promise to make haste crossed her mind – her fatal promise, as it seemed to her; though you and I, who have as it were peeped behind the scenes, may well believe that it kept her out of no very delightful treat.

She ceased jumping, she steadied her swinging basket on her arm, and spoke resolutely though sadly: 'Thank you all, but I mustn't stop to play* with you, because I promised Granny to make haste. Good-bye;' – and off she started, not venturing to risk her decision by pausing or looking back; but feeling the bouncing ball bouncing in her basket as if it too longed for a game, and hearing with tingling ears a shout of mocking laughter which followed her retreat.

The longest peal of laughter came to an end. Very likely, as soon as Maggie vanished from view among the oak-trees the boisterous troop ceased laughing at her discomfiture; at any rate, they did not pursue her; and she soon got beyond the sound of their mirth, whilst one by one the last echoes left off laughing and hooting at her. Half glad that she had persisted in keeping her word, yet half sorry to have missed so rare a chance, Maggie trudged on solitary and sober. A pair of wood pigeons alighting almost at her feet pecked about in the frozen path, but could not find even one mouthful for their little empty beaks: then, hopeless and silent, they fluttered up and perched on a twig above her head. The sight of these hungry creatures made Maggie hungry from sympathy; yet it was rather for their sakes than for her own that she lifted the cover of her basket and peered underneath it, to see whether by any chance kind Granny had popped in a hunch or so of cake, – alas! not a crumb. Only there lay the chocolate, sweet and tempting, looking most delicious through a hole in its gilt paper.

Would birds eat chocolate, wondered Maggie,—

[Would they, Aunt? – Really, I hardly know myself, Laura: but I should suppose some might, if it came in their way.]

—and she was almost ready to break off the least little corner and try, when a sound of rapid footsteps coming along startled her; and hastily shutting her basket, she turned to see who was approaching.

A boy: and close at his heels marched a fat tabby cat, carrying in her mouth a tabby kitten. Or was it a real boy? He had indeed arms, legs, a head, like ordinary people: but his face exhibited only one feature, and that was a wide mouth. He had no eyes; so how he came to know that Maggie and a basket were standing in his way I cannot say: but he did seem somehow aware of the fact; for the mouth, which could doubtless eat as well as speak, grinned, whined, and accosted her: 'Give a morsel to a poor starving beggar.'

'I am very sorry,' replied Maggie, civilly; and she tried not to stare, because she knew it would be rude to do so, though none the less amazed was she at his aspect; 'I am very sorry, but I have nothing I can give you.'

'*Nothing*, with all that chocolate!'

'The chocolate is not mine, and I cannot give it you,' answered Maggie bravely; yet she felt frightened; for the two stood all alone together in the forest, and the wide mouth was full of teeth and tusks, and began to grind them.

'Give it me, I say. I tell you I'm starving:' and he snatched at the basket.

'I don't believe you are starving,' cried Maggie, indignantly, for he looked a great deal stouter and sleeker than she herself did; and she started aside, hugging her basket close as the beggar darted out a lumpish-looking hand to seize it. 'I'm hungry enough myself, but I wouldn't be a thief!' she shouted back to her tormentor, whilst at full speed she fled away from him, wondering secretly why he did not give chase, for he looked big enough and strong enough to run her down in a minute: but after all, when she spoke so resolutely and seemed altogether so determined, it was he that hung his head, shut his mouth, and turned to go away again faster and faster, till he fairly scudded out of sight among the lengthening shadows.

Had this forest road always been so long? Never before certainly had it appeared so extremely long to Maggie. Hungry and tired, she lost all spirit, and plodded laggingly forward, longing for her journey's end, but without energy enough to walk fast. The sky had turned leaden, the wind blew bleaker than ever, the bare boughs creaked and rattled drearily. Poor desolate

Maggie! drowsiness was creeping over her, and she began to wish above all things that she might just sit down where she stood and go fast asleep: never mind food, or fire, or bed; only let her sleep.

[Do you know, children, what would most likely have happened to Maggie if she had yielded to drowsiness and slept out there in the cold? – What, Aunt? – Most likely she would never have woke again. And then there would have been an abrupt end to my story.]

Yet she recollected her promise to make haste, and went toiling on and on and on, step after tired step. At length she had so nearly passed through the forest that five minutes more would bring her into the by-road which led straight to the doctor's door, when she came suddenly upon a party of some dozen persons sitting toasting themselves around a glowing gipsy fire, and all yawning in nightcaps or dropping asleep.

They opened their eyes half-way looked at her and shut them again. They all nodded. They all snored. Whoever woke up yawned; whoever slept snored. Merely to see them and hear them was enough to send one to sleep.

A score or so of birds grew bold, hopped towards the kindly fire, and perched on neighbouring shoulder, hand, or nose. No one was disturbed, no one took any notice.

If Maggie felt drowsy before, she felt ready to drop now: but remembering her promise, and rousing herself by one last desperate effort, she shot past the tempting group. Not a finger stirred to detain her, not a voice proffered a word, not a foot moved, not an eye winked.

At length the cold long walk was ended, and Maggie stood ringing the doctor's door-bell, wide awake and on tiptoe with enchanting expectation: for surely now there was a good prospect of her being asked indoors, warmed by a fire, regaled with something nice, and indulged with a glimpse of the Christmas tree bending under its crop of wonderful fruit.

Alas, no! The door opened, the parcel was taken in with a brief 'Thank you,' and Maggie remained shut out on the sanded doorstep.

Chilled to the bone, famished, cross, and almost fit to cry with disappointment, Maggie set off to retrace her weary steps. Evening had closed in, the wind had lulled, a few snowflakes floated about in the still air and seemed too light to settle down. If it looked dim on the open road, it looked dimmer still in the forest: dim, and solitary, and comfortless.

Were all the sleepers gone clean away since Maggie passed scarcely a quarter of an hour before? Surely, yes: and moreover not a trace of their glowing fire remained, not one spark, not one ember. Only something whitish lay on the ground where they had been sitting: could it be a nightcap? Maggie stooped to look, and picked up, not a nightcap, but a wood-pigeon with ruffled feathers and closed eyes, which lay motionless and half frozen in her hand. She snuggled it tenderly to her, and kissed its poor little beak and drooping head before she laid it to get warm within the bosom of her frock. Lying there, it seemed to draw anger and discontent out of her heart: and soon she left off grumbling to herself, and stepped forward with renewed energy, because the sooner the pigeon could be taken safe indoors out of the cold, the better.

Mew, mew, mew: such a feeble pitiful squeak of a mew! Just about where the Mouth had met her a mew struck upon Maggie's ears, and wide she opened both ears and eyes to spy after the mewer. Huddled close up against the gnarled root of an oak, crouched a small tabby kitten all alone, which mewed and mewed and seemed to beg for aid. Maggie caught up the helpless creature, popped it into her empty basket, and hurried forward.

But not far, before she paused afresh: for suddenly, just in that green glade where the grasshopper children in general and one glutinous girl in particular had stood hooting her that very afternoon, her foot struck against some soft lump, which lay right in her path and made no effort to move out of harm's way. What could it be? She stooped, felt it, turned it over, and it was a short-haired smooth puppy, which put one paw confidingly into her hand, and took the tip of her little finger between its teeth with the utmost friendliness. Who could leave such a puppy all abroad on such a night? Not Maggie, for one. She added the puppy to her basketful, – and a basketful it was then! – and ran along singing quite merrily under her burden.

And when, the forest shades left behind her, she went tripping along through the pale clear moonlight, in one moment the sky before her flashed with glittering gold,* and flushed from horizon to zenith with a rosy glow; for the northern lights came out, and lit up each cloud as if it held lightning, and each hill as if it smouldered ready to burst into a volcano. Every oak-tree seemed to turned to coral, and the road itself to a pavement of dusky carnelian.

Then at last she once more mounted a door-step and rang a door-bell, but this time they were the familiar step and bell of home. So now when the door opened she was received, not with mere 'Thank you,' but with a loving welcoming hug; and not only what she carried, but she herself also found plenty of light and warmth awaiting all arrivals, in a curtained parlour set out for tea. And whilst Maggie thawed, and drank tea, and ate buttered toast in Granny's company, the pigeon thawed too, and cooed and pecked up crumbs until it perched on the rail of a chair, turned its head contentedly under its wing, and dropped fast asleep; and the kitten thawed too, and lapped away at a saucerful of milk, till it fell asleep on the rug; and the puppy – well, I cannot say the puppy thawed too, because he was warm and cordial when Maggie met him; but he wagged his stumpy tail, stood bolt upright and begged, munched tit-bits, barked, rolled over, and at last settled down under the table to sleep: after all which, Dame Margaret and Maggie followed the good example set them, and went to bed and to sleep.

Commonplace

Commonplace is the longest and sharpest of Christina Rossetti's fictional works, a long short story or novella in several chapters. Written in 1868/9 and published as the title-piece in her only collection, it traces the lives of the three Charlmont sisters and satirises mid-Victorian mercenary marriage, contrasting Jane's soulless espousal of wealth in the shape of businessman Mr Durham with Catherine's decision to remain single and Lucy's late, unexpected love-match with good Arthur Tresham.

It was very much 'in the Miss Austen-ish vein' as Christina's brother Gabriel remarked, and indeed boasts a disastrous picnic and a garrulous chaperone in Miss Drum to rival Emma*'s Miss Bates, while the maiden ladies of Mrs Gaskell's* Cranford *(1853) also come to mind. Manners, money and morals are the theme, and there are also Austenish amateur dramatics and a number of misunderstandings, all related by a cool, witty narrator who judges nicely but seldom condemns; even pert little Jane is destined only to suffer from meanness of spirit. The comedy of the drawing-room charades is subtly drawn (where, one wonders, did Christina Rossetti witness any such entertainment?) and satire is laced with sympathy throughout. The characters' interrelations are well worked out, so that even while Mr Durham is being mocked by Jane for vulgarity, his daughter Stella reveals his essential goodheartedness. The supporting cast is deftly drawn, and the title leaves us guessing as to whether or not it is ironic.*

Christina Rossetti wrote no more stories of social comment, but had she pursued this vein she might have developed a true talent for witty moral tales; both her eye and her pen were acute.

CHAPTER I

Brompton-on-Sea – any name not in 'Bradshaw'* will do – Brompton-on-Sea in April.

The air keen and sunny; the sea blue and rippling, not rolling; everything green, in sight and out of sight, coming on merrily. Birds active over straws and fluff; a hardy butterfly abroad for a change; a second hardy butterfly dancing through mid-air, in and out, and round about the first. A row of houses all alike stands facing the sea – all alike so far as stucco fronts and symmetrical doors and windows could make them so: but one house in the monotonous row was worth looking at, for the sake of more numerous hyacinths and early roses in its slip of front garden, and on several of its window-sills. Judging by appearances, and for once judging rightly, this must be a private residence on an esplanade full of lodging-houses.

A pretty house inside too, snug in winter, fresh in summer; now in mid-spring sunny enough for an open window, and cool enough for a bright fire in the breakfast-room.

Three ladies sat at the breakfast-table, three maiden ladies, obviously sisters by strong family likeness, yet with individual differences strong also. The eldest, Catherine, Miss Charlmont, having entered her thirty-third year, had taken on all occasions to appearing in some sort of cap.* She began the custom at thirty, when also she gave up dancing, and adopted lace over her neck and arms in evening dress. Her manner was formal and kindly, savouring of the provinces rather than of the capital; but of the provinces in their towns, not in their old country seats. Yet she was a well-bred gentlewoman in all essentials, tall and fair, a handsome member of a handsome family. She presided over the tea and coffee, and, despite modern usage, retained a tea-tray.

Opposite her sat Lucy, less striking in featuress and complexion, but with an expression of quicker sensibility. Rather pretty and very sweet-looking, not turned thirty as yet, and on some points treated by Catherine as still a young thing. She had charge of the loaf and ham, and, like her elder sister, never indulged in opening letters till every one at table had been served.

The third, Jane, free of meat-and-drink responsibilities, opened letters or turned over the newspaper as she pleased. She was youngest by many years, and came near to being very beautiful. Her profile was almost Grecian, her eyes were large, and her fair hair grew in wavy abundance. At first sight she threw Catherine and Lucy completely into the shade; afterwards, in spite of their additional years, they sometimes were preferred, for her face only of the three could be thought insipid. Pleasure and displeasure readily showed themselves in it, but the pleasure would be frivolous and the displeasure often unreasonable. A man might fall in love with Jane, but no one could make a friend of her; Catherine and Lucy were sure to have friends, however they might lack lovers.

On the morning when our story commences the elders were busied with their respective charges, whilst Jane already sipped her tea and glanced up and down the Births, Marriages, and Deaths, in the 'Times' Supplement.* There she sat, with one elbow on the table and her long lashes showing to advantage over downcast eyes. Dress was with her a matter for deep study, and her pink-and-white breakfast suit looked as fresh and blooming as April's self. Her hair fell long and loose over her shoulders, in becoming freedom; and Catherine gazing at her felt a motherly pride in the pretty creature to whom, for years, she had performed a mother's duty; and Lucy felt how young and fresh Jane was, and remembered that she herself was turned twenty-nine: but if the thought implied regret it was untinctured by envy.

Jane read aloud: " 'Halbert to Jane;" I wish I were Jane. And here, positively, are two more Janes, and not me. 'Catherine' – that's a death. Lucy, I don't see you anywhere. Catherine was eighty-nine, and much respected. "Mrs Anstruther of a son and heir." I wonder if those are the Anstruthers I met in Scotland: she was very ugly, and short. "Everilda Stella," – how can anybody be Everilda?' Then, with a sudden accession of interest, 'Why, Lucy, Everilda Stella has actually married your Mr Hartley!'

Lucy started, but no one noticed her. Catherine said, 'Don't say "your" Mr Hartley, Jane: that is not a proper way of speaking about a married gentleman to an unmarried lady. Say "the Mr Hartley you know," or, "the Mr Hartley you have met in London." Besides, I am acquainted with him also; and very likely it is a different person. Hartley is not an uncommon name.'

'Oh, but it is that Mr Hartley, sister,' retorted Jane, and she read:

' "On Monday the 13th, at the parish-church, Fenton, by the Rev. James Durham, uncle of the bride, Alan Hartley, Esq. of the Woodlands, Gloucestershire, to Everilda Stella, only child and presumptive heiress of George Durham, Esq. of Orpingham Place, in the same county." '

CHAPTER II

Forty years before the commencement of this story, William Charlmont, an Indian army-surgeon,* penniless, except for his pay, had come unexpectedly into some hundreds a-year, left him by a maiden great-aunt, who had seen him but once, and that when he was five years old, on which occasion she boxed his ears for misspelling 'elephant'. His stoicism under punishment, for he neither roared nor whined, may have won her heart; at any rate, from whatever motive, she, years afterwards, disappointed three nephews and a female first cousin by leaving every penny she was worth to him. This moderate accession of fortune justified him in consulting both health and inclination by exchanging regimental practice in India for general practice* in England and a combination of apparently trifling circumstances led him, soon after his return home, to settle at the then infant watering-place of Brompton-on-Sea, of which the reputation had just been made by a royal duke's* visit; and the tide of fashion was setting to its shore.

The house in which our story opens then stood alone, and belonged to a clergyman's widow. As she possessed, besides, an only daughter, and but a small life annuity – nothing more – she sought for a lodger, and was glad to find one in the new medical practitioner. The widow, Mrs Turner, was, and felt herself to be, no less a gentlewoman when she let lodgings than when with her husband and child she had occupied the same house alone; no less so when after breakfast she donned a holland apron and helped Martha, the maid, to make Mr Charlmont's bed, than when in old days she had devoted her mornings to visiting and relieving her poorer neighbours.

Her daughter, Kate, felt their altered fortunes more painfully; and showed, sometimes by uncomfortable bashfulness, sometimes by anxious self-assertion, how much importance she attached to the verdict of Mrs Grundy. Her mother's holland apron was to her a daily humiliation, and single-handed Martha an irritating shortcoming. She chilled old friends by declining invitations, because her wardrobe lacked variety, and shunned new acquaintances lest they should call at some moment when herself or her mother might have to answer the door. A continual aim at false appearances made her constrained and affected; and persons who would never have dwelt upon the fact that Mrs Turner let lodgings, were certain to have it recalled to mind by Miss Turner's uneasiness.

But Kate owned a pretty face, adorned by a pink-and-white complexion, most refreshing to eyes that had ached under an Indian sun. At first Mr Charlmont set her down as merely affected and silly; then he began to dwell on the fact that, however silly and affected, she was indisputably pretty; next he reflected that reverses of fortune deserve pity and demand every gentleman's most courteous consideration. In himself such consideration at once took the form of books lent from his library; of flowers for the drawing-room, and fruit for dessert. Kate, to do her justice, was no flirt, and saw without seeing his attentions; but her more experienced mother seeing, pondered, and seized, or made, an opportunity for checking her lodger's intimacy. Mr Charlmont, however, was not to be rebuffed; opposition made him earnest, whilst the necessity of expressing his feelings gave them definiteness: and not many months later Kate, with the house for her dowry, became Mrs William Charlmont, the obnoxious lodger developed into an attached and dear husband, and Mrs Turner retired on the life annuity to finish her days in independence.

A few years passed in hopes and disappointments. When hope had dwindled to despondency a little girl came – Catherine; after another few years a second girl, named Lucy in memory of her grandmother Turner, who had not lived to see her namesake. Then more years passed without a baby; and in due course the sisters were sent to Miss Drum's school as day-boarders, their mother having become ailing and indolent.

Time went on, and the girls grew wiser and prettier – Catherine very pretty. When she was nearly twelve years old, Mr Charlmont said one evening to his wife, 'I have made my will, Kate, and left everything to you in the first instance, and between the children after you.' And she answered, blushing – she was still comely, and a blush became her: – 'O William, but suppose another baby should come?' 'Well, I should make my will over again,' he replied: but he did not guess why his wife blushed and spoke eagerly; he had quite given up such hopes.

Mr Charlmont was fond of boating, and one day, when the girls were at home for the Easter holidays, he offered to take them both for a row; but Catherine had a bad cold, and as Lucy was not a good sailor, he did not care to take charge of her without her sister. His wife never had liked boating. Thus it was that he went alone. The morning was dull and chilly; but there was no wind, and the sea was almost smooth. He took dinner and fishing tackle in the boat with him, and gave notice that he should not be at home till the evening.

No wind, no sun; the day grew duller and duller, dimmer and dimmer. A smoke-like fog, beginning on land, spread from the cliffs to the beach, from the beach over the water's edge; further and further it spread, beyond sight; it might be for miles over the sea. No wind blew to shift the dense fog which hid seamarks and landmarks alike. As day waned towards evening, and darkness deepened, all the fisher-folk gathered on the beach in pain and fear for those at sea. They lit a bonfire, they shouted, they fired off an old gun or two, such as they could get together, and still they watched, and feared, and hoped. Now one boat came in, now another; some guided by the glare, some by the sound of the firing: at last, by midnight, every boat had come in safe, except Mr Charlmont's.

As concerned him, that night was only like all nights and all days afterwards; for neither man, nor boat, nor waif, nor stray from either, ever drifted ashore.

Mrs Charlmont took the news of her husband's disappearance very quietly indeed. She did not cry or fret, or propose any measures for finding him; but she bade Catherine be sure to have tea ready when he came in. This she repeated every day, and often in the day; and would herself sit by a window looking out towards the sea, smiling and cheerful. If any one spoke to her she would answer at random, but quite cheerfully. She rose or went to bed when her old nurse called her, she ate and drank when food was set before her; but she originated nothing, and seemed indifferent to everything except the one anxiety, that tea should be ready for her husband on his return.

The holidays over, Lucy went back to Miss Drum's, trudging to and fro daily; but Catherine stayed at home to keep house and sit with her poor dazed mother.

A few months and the end came. One night nurse insisted with unusual determination on the girls going to bed early; but before daybreak Catherine was roused out of her sleep to see a new little sister and her dying mother.

Life was almost gone, and with the approach of death a sort of of consciousness had returned. Mrs Charlmont looked hard at Catherine, who was crying bitterly, and taking her hand said distinctly: 'Catherine, promise to stay here ready for your father when he comes on shore – promise some of you to stay here: don't let him come on shore and find me gone and no one – don't let the body come on shore and find us all gone and no one – promise me, Catherine!'

And Catherine promised.

Mr Charlmont died a wealthy man. He had enjoyed a large lucrative practice, and had invested his savings profitably: by his will, and on their mother's death, an ample provision remained for his daughters. Strictly speaking, it remained for Catherine and Lucy: the baby, Jane, was unavoidably left dependent on her sisters; but on sisters who, in after-life, never felt that their own right to their father's property was more obvious or more valid than hers.

Mr Charlmont had appointed but one trustee for his daughters – Mr Drum, only brother of their schoolmistress, a thoroughly honest lawyer, practising and thriving in Brompton-on-Sea; a man somewhat younger than himself, who had speculated adroitly both with him and for him. On Mrs Charlmont's death, Mr Drum proposed sending the two elder girls to a fashionable boarding-school near London, and letting nurse, with a wet-nurse under her, keep house in the old home with baby: but Catherine set her face against this plan, urging her promise to her dying mother as a reason for not going away; and so held to her point that Mr Drum yielded, and agreed that the girls, who could not bear to be parted, should continue on the same terms as before at his sister's school. Miss Drum, an intimate friend of their mother's, engaged to take them into such suitable society as might offer until Catherine should come of age; and as she resided within two minutes' walk of their house, this presented no difficulty. At twenty-one, under their peculiar circumstances, Catherine was to be considered old enough to chaperone her sisters. Nurse, a respectable elderly woman, was to remain as housekeeper and personal attendant on the children; and a wet-nurse, to be succeeded by a nursery-girl, with two other maids, completed the household.

Catherine, though only in her thirteenth year, already looked grave, staid, and tall enough for a girl of sixteen, when these arrangements were entered into. The sense of responsibility waxed strong within her, and with the motherly position came something of the motherly instinct of self-postponement to her children.

CHAPTER III

The last chapter was parenthetical, this takes up the broken thread of the story.

Breakfast over, and her sisters gone their several ways, Lucy Charlmont seized the 'Times' Supplement and read the Hartley-Durham paragraph over to herself: – 'On Monday the 13th, at the parish church, Fenton, by the Rev. James Durham, uncle of the bride, Alan Hartley, Esq., of the Woodlands, Gloucestershire, to Everilda Stella, only child and presumptive heiress of George Durham, Esq., of Orpingham Place, in the same county.'

There remained no lurking-place for doubt. Mr Hartley, – 'her' Mr Hartley, as Jane dubbed him – had married Everilda Stella, a presumptive heiress. Thus concluded Lucy's one romance.

Poor Lucy! the romance had been no fault of hers, perhaps not even a folly: it had arisen thus. When Miss Charlmont was twenty-one Lucy was eighteen, and had formally come out* under her sister's wing; thenceforward going with her to balls and parties from time to time, and staying with her at friends' houses in town or country. This paying visits had entailed the necessity of Jane's having a governess. Miss Drum had by that time 'relinquished tuition', as she herself phrased it, and retired on a comfortable competence earned by her own exertions; therefore, to Miss Drum's school Jane could not go. Lucy, when the subject was started, declared, with affectionate impulsiveness, that she would not pay visits at all, or else that she and Catherine might pay them separately; but Catherine, who considered herself in the place of mother to both her sisters, and whose standard of justice to both alike was inflexible, answered, 'My dear' – when Miss Charlmont said 'my dear' it ended a discussion – 'My dear, Jane must have a governess. She shall always be with us in the holidays, and shall leave the schoolroom for good when she is eighteen, and old enough to enter society, but at present I must think of you and your prospects.'* So Jane had a fashionable governess, fresh from a titled family, and versed in accomplishments and the art of dress, whilst Catherine commenced her duties as chaperone. Lucy thought that her sister, handsomer than herself and not much older, might have prospects too, and tried hard to discover chances for her; but Catherine nursed no such fancies on her own account. Her promise to her dying mother, that some one of them should always be on the spot at Brompton-on-Sea, literally meant at the moment, she resolved as literally to fulfil, even whilst she felt that only by one not fully in her right mind could such a promise have been exacted. Grave and formal in manner, dignified in person, and in disposition reserved, though amiable, she never seemed to notice, or to return, attentions paid her by any man of her acquaintance; and if one of these ever committed himself so far as to hazard an offer, she kept his secret and her own.

Lucy, meanwhile, indulged on her own account the usual hopes and fears of a young woman. At first all parties and visits were delightful, one not much less so than another; then a difference made itself felt between them; some parties turned out dull, and some visits tedious. The last year of Lucy's going everywhere with Catherine, before, that is, she began dividing engagements with Jane, – for until Lucy should be turned thirty, self-chaperoning* was an inadmissible enormity in Miss Charlmont's eyes, in spite of what she had herself done; as she said, her own had been an exceptional case, – in that last year the two sisters had together spent a month with Dr Tyke, whose wife had been before marriage another Lucy Charlmont, and a favourite cousin of their father's: concerning her, tradition even hinted that, in bygone years, she had refused the penniless army surgeon.

Be this as it may, at Mrs Tyke's house in London, the sisters spent one certain June, and then and there Lucy 'met her fate', as with a touch of sentiment, bordering on sentimentality, she recorded in her diary one momentous first meeting. Alan Hartley was a nephew of Dr Tyke's – handsome, and clever on the surface, if not deep within. He had just succeeded his father* at the Woodlands, had plenty of money, no profession, and no hindrance to idling away any amount of time with any pretty woman who was pleasant company. Such a woman was Lucy Charlmont. He harboured no present thoughts of marriage, but she did; he really did pay just as much attention to a dozen girls elsewhere, but she judged by his manner to herself, and drew from it a false conclusion. That delightful June came to an end, and he had not spoken; but two years later occurred a second visit, as pleasant and as full of misunderstanding as the first. Meanwhile, she had refused more than one offer. Poor Lucy Charlmont: her folly, even if it was folly, had not been very blameable.

The disenchantment came no less painfully than unexpectedly: and Lucy, ready to cry, but ashamed of crying for such a cause, thrust the Supplement out of sight, and sitting down, forced herself to face the inevitable future. One thing was certain, she could not meet Alan – in her thoughts he had long been Alan, and now it cost her an effort of recollection to stiffen him back into Mr Hartley – she must not meet Mr Hartley till she could reckon on seeing him and his wife with friendly composure. Oh! why – why – why had she all along misunderstood him, and he never understood her? Not to meet him, it would be necessary to decline the invitation from Mrs Tyke, which she had looked forward to and longed for during weeks past, and which, in the impartial judgment of Miss Charlmont, it was her turn, not Jane's, to accept; which, moreover, might arrive by any post. Jane she knew would be ready enough to pay a visit out of turn, but Catherine would want a reason; and what reason could she give? On one point, however, she was determined, that, with or without her reasons being accepted as reasonable, go she would not. Then came the recollection of a cracker she had pulled with him, and kept in her pocket-book ever since; and of a card he had left for her and her sister, or, as she had fondly fancied, mainly for herself, before the last return from Mrs Tyke's to Brompton-on-Sea. Treasures no longer to be treasured, despoiled treasures, – she denied herself the luxury of a sigh, as she thrust them between the bars of the grate and watched them burn.

CHAPTER IV

'Lucy, Jane,' said Miss Charlmont, some days afterwards, addressing her sisters, and holding up an open letter, – 'Mrs Tyke has sent a very kind invitation, asking me, with one of you, to stay a month at her house, and to fix the day. It is your turn, Lucy; so, if you have no objection, I shall write, naming next Thursday for our journey to London. Jane, I shall ask Miss Drum to stay with you during our absence; I think she will be all the better for a change, and there is no person more fit to have the charge of you. So don't be dull, dear, till we come back.'

But Jane pouted, and said in a cross tone, 'Really, sister, you need not settle everything now for me, as if I were a baby. I don't want Miss Drum, who is as old as the hills and as solemn. Can't you write to Mrs Tyke and say, that I cannot be left alone here? What difference could it make in her large house?'

For once Catherine answered her favourite sister with severity, 'Jane, you know why it is impossible for us all to leave home together. This is the last year you will be called upon to remain behind, for after Lucy's next birthday it is agreed between us that she will take turns with me in chaperoning you. Do not make what may be our last excursion together unpleasant by your unkindness.'

Still Jane was not silenced. 'At any rate, it need not be Miss Drum. I will stay here alone, or I will have somebody more amusing than Miss Drum.'

Before Catherine could reply, Lucy with an effort struck into the dispute. 'Jane, don't speak like that to our sister; I should be ashamed to speak to her so. Still, Catherine,' she continued, without noticing a muttered retort from the other, 'after all, I am going to side with Jane on the main point, and ask you to take her to Notting Hill,* and leave me at home to keep house with dear old Miss Drum. This really was my own wish before Jane spoke, so pray let us not say another word on the subject.'

But Catherine saw how pale and languid she looked, and stood firm. 'No, Lucy, that would be unreasonable; Jane ought not to have made any difficulty. You have lost your colour lately and your appetite, and need a change more than either of us. I shall write to Mrs Tyke, promising her and the doctor your company next Thursday; Jane will make up her mind like a good girl, and I am sure you, my dear, will oblige me by not withholding your assent.'

For the first time 'my dear' did not close the debate. 'Catherine,' said Lucy, earnestly, whilst, do what she would, tears gathered in her eyes, 'I am certain you will not press me further, when I assure you that I do not feel equal to paying this visit. I have felt weak lately,' she went on hurriedly, 'and I cannot tell you how much I long for the quiet of a month at home rather than in that perpetual bustle. Merely for my own sake, Jane must go.'

Catherine said no more just then; but later, alone with Lucy, resumed the subject so far as to ask whether she continued in the same mind, and answered her flurried 'yes' by no word of remonstrance, but by an affectionate kiss. This was all which passed between them; neither then nor afterwards did the younger sister feel certain whether Catherine had or had not guessed her secret.

Miss Drum was invited to stay with Lucy in her solitude, and gladly accepted the invitation. Lucy was her favourite, and when they were together, they petted each other* very tenderly.

Jane, having gained her point, recovered her good humour, and lost no time in exposing the deficiencies of her wardrobe. 'Sister,' she said, smiling her prettiest and most coaxing smile, 'you can't think how poor I am, and how few clothes I've got.'

Catherine, trying to appear serenely unconscious of the drift of this speech, replied, 'Let us look over your wardrobe, dear, and we will bring it into order. Lucy will help, I know, and we can have Miss Smith to work here too, if necessary.'

'Oh dear no!' cried Jane; 'there is no looking over what does not exist. If it comes to furbishing up old tags and rags, here I stay.

Why, you're as rich as Jews, you and Lucy, and could give me five pounds a-piece without ever missing it; and not so much of a gift either, for I'm sure poor papa would never have left me such a beggar if he had known about me.'

This argument had been used more than once before. Catherine looked hurt. Lucy said, 'You should remember that you have exactly the same allowance for dress and pocket-money that we have ourselves, and we both make it do.'

'Of course,' retorted Jane, with latent spitefulness; 'and when I'm as old and wise as you two, I may manage as well; but at present it is different. Besides, if I spend most on dress, you spend most on books and music, and dress is a great deal more amusing. And if I dressed like an old fright, I should like to know who'd look at me. You don't want me to be another old maid, I suppose.'

Lucy flushed up, and tried to keep her temper in silence: her sore point had been touched. Catherine, accustomed in such cases to protest first and yield afterwards, but half ashamed that Lucy's eye should mark the process from beginning to end, drew Jane out of the room, and with scarcely a word more wrote her a cheque for ten pounds, and dropped the subject of looking over her wardrobe.

An hour after the sisters had started for London, Miss Drum arrived to take their place.

Miss Drum was tall in figure, rather slim and well preserved, with pale complexion, hair, and eyes, and an unvarying tone of voice. She was mainly describable by negatives. She was neither unladylike, nor clever, nor deficient in education. She was old, but not very infirm; and neither an altogether obsolete nor a youthful dresser, though with some tendency towards the former style. Propriety was the most salient of her attributes, and was just too salient to be perfect. She was not at all amusing; in fact, rather tiresome, with an unflagging intention of being agreeable. From her Catherine acquired a somewhat old-fashioned formality; from her, also, high principles, and the instinct of self-denial. And because unselfishness, itself a negative, was Miss Drum's characteristic virtue, and because her sympathy, however prosy in expression, was sterling in quality, therefore Lucy, sore with unavowed heart-sorrow, could bear her companionship, and run down to welcome her at the door with affectionate cordiality.

CHAPTER V

London-Bridge Station, with its whirl of traffic, seems no bad emblem of London itself: vast, confused, busy, orderly, more or less dirty; implying enormous wealth in some quarter or other; providing luxuries for the rich, necessaries for the poor; thronged by rich and poor alike, idle and industrious, young and old, men and women.

London-Bridge Station at its cleanest is soiled by thousands of feet passing to and fro: on a drizzling day each foot deposits mud in its passage, takes and gives mud, leaves its impress in mud; on such a day the Station is not attractive to persons fresh from the unfailing cleanliness of sea coast and inland country; and on such a day, when, by the late afternoon, the drizzle had done, and the platform had suffered each its worst, – on such a day Miss Charlmont and her pretty sister, fresh and fastidious from sea salt and country sweetness, arrived at the Station.

Dr Tyke's carriage was there to meet the train. Dr Tyke's coachman, footman, and horses were fat, as befitted a fat master, whose circumstances and whose temperament might be defined as fat also; for ease, good-nature, and fat have an obvious affinity.

'Should the hood* be up or down?' The rain had ceased, and Miss Charlmont, who always described London as stifling, answered, 'Up.' Jane, leaning back with an elegant ease, which nature had given and art perfected, felt secretly ashamed of Catherine, who sat bolt upright, according to her wont, and would no more have lolled in an open carriage than on the high-backed, scant-seated chair of her school-days.

The City looked at once dingy and glaring; dingy with unconsumed smoke, and glaring here and there with early-lighted gas. When Waterloo Bridge had been crossed matters brightened somewhat, and Oxford Street showed not amiss. Along the Edgware Road dirt and dinginess re-asserted their sway; but when the carriage finally turned into Notting Hill, and drove amongst the Crescents, Roads, and Gardens of that cleanly suburb, a winding-up shower, brisk and brief, not drizzly, cleared the way for the sun, and finished off the afternoon with a rainbow.

Dr Tyke's abode was named Appletrees House, though the orchard whence the name was derived had disappeared before the memory of the oldest inhabitant. The carriage drew up, the door swung open: down the staircase came flying a little, slim woman, with outstretched hands and words of welcome; auburn-haired, though she had outlived the last of the fifties, and cheerful, though the want of children had not ceased to be felt as a hopeless disappointment: a pale-complexioned, high-voiced, little woman, all that remained of that fair cousin Lucy of bygone years and William Charlmont.

Behind her, and more deliberately, descended her husband, elastic of step, rotund of figure, bright-eyed, rosy, white-headed, not altogether unlike a robin redbreast that had been caught in the snow. Mrs Tyke had a habit of running on with long-winded, perfectly harmless commonplaces; but notwithstanding her garrulity, she never uttered an ill-natured word or a false one. Dr Tyke, burdened with an insatiable love of fun, and a ready, if not a witty, wit, was addicted to venting jokes, repartees, and so-called anecdotes; the last not always unimpeachably authentic.

Such were the hosts. The house was large and light, with a laboratory for the Doctor, who dabbled in chemistry, and an aviary for his wife, who doted on pets. The walls of the sitting-rooms were hung with engravings, not with family portraits, real or sham: in fact, no sham was admitted within doors, unless imaginary ancedotes and quotations must be stigmatized as shams; and as to these, when taxed with invention, the Doctor would only reply by his favourite Italian phrase: '*Se non è vero è ben trovato.*'*

'Jane,' said Mrs Tyke, as three ladies sat over a late breakfast, the Doctor having already retreated to the laboratory and his newspaper: – 'Jane, I think you have made a conquest.'

Jane looked down in silence, with a conscious simper. Catherine spoke rather anxiously: 'Indeed, Cousin Lucy, I have noticed what you allude to, and I have spoken to Jane about not encouraging Mr Durham. He is not at all a man she can really like, and she ought to be most careful not to let herself be misunderstood. Jane, you ought indeed.'

But Jane struck merrily in: 'Mr Durham is old enough and – ahem! – handsome enough to take care of himself, sister. And, besides,' with a touch of mimicry, which recalled his pompous manner, 'Orpingham Place, my dear madam, Orpingham Place is a very fine place, a very fine place indeed. Our pineapples can really hardly be got rid of, and our prize pigs can't see out of their eyes; they can't indeed, my dear young lady, though it's not pretty talk for a pretty young lady to listen to. – Very well, if the pines* and the pigs are smitten, why shouldn't I marry the pigs and the pines?'

'Why not?' cried Mrs Tyke with a laugh; but Miss Charlmont, looking disturbed, rejoined: 'Why not, certainly, if you like Mr Durham; but do you like Mr Durham? And, whether or not, you ought not to laugh at him.'

Jane pouted: 'Really one would think I was a child still! As to Mr Durham, when he knows his own mind and speaks, you may be quite sure I shall know my own mind and give him his answer. – Orpingham Place, my dear Miss Catherine, the finest place in the county; the finest place in three counties, whatever my friend the Duke may say. A charming neighbourhood, Miss Catherine; her Grace the Duchess, the most affable woman you can imagine, and my lady the Marchioness, a fine woman – a very fine woman. But they can't raise such pines as my pines; they can't do it, you know; they haven't the means, you know. – Come now, sister, don't look cross; when I'm Mrs Durham you shall have your slice off the pigs and the pines.'

CHAPTER VI

Everilda Stella, poor Lucy's unconscious rival, had married out of the schoolroom. Pretty she was not, but with much piquancy of face and manner, and a talent for private theatricals. These advantages, gilded, perhaps, by her reputation as presumptive heiress, attracted to her a suitor, to whose twenty years' seniority she felt no objection. Mr Hartley wooed and won her in the brief space of an Easter holiday; and bore her, nothing loth, to London, to enjoy the gaieties of the season. Somewhat to the bridegroom's annoyance, Mr Durham accompanied the newly-married couple to town, and shared their pretty house at Kensington.

Alan Hartley, a favourite nephew of Dr Tyke, had, as we know, been very intimate at his house in old days. Now he was proud to present his little wife of sixteen to his uncle and aunt, though somewhat mortified at having also to introduce his father-in-law, whose pompous manners, and habit of dragging titled personages into his discourse, put him to the blush. Alan had dropped Everilda, and called his wife simply Stella; her father dubbed her Pug; Everilda she was named, in accordance with the taste of her peerage-studious mother. This lady was accustomed to describe herself as a north-country family – a Leigh of the Leazes; which conveyed an old-manorial notion to persons unacquainted with Newcastle-on-Tyne.* But this by the way: Mrs Durham had died before the opening of our tale.

At their first visit they were shown into the drawing-room by a smiling maid-servant, and requested to wait, as Dr and Mrs Tyke were expected home every moment. Stella looked very winning in her smart hat and feather and jaunty jacket, and Alan would have abandoned himself to all the genial glow of a bridegroom, but for Mr Durham's behaviour. That gentleman began by placing his hat on the floor between his feet, and flicking his boots with a crimson silk pocket-handkerchief. This done, he commenced a survey of the apartment, accompanied by an apt running comment, – 'Hem, no pictures – cheap engravings; a four-and-sixpenny Brussels carpet; a smallish mirror, wants regilding. Pug, my pet, that's a neat antimacassar: see if you can't carry off the stitch in your eye. A piano – a harp; fiddlestick!'

When Dr and Mrs Tyke entered, they found the Hartleys looking uncomfortable, and Mr Durham red and pompous after his wont; also, in opening the door, they caught the sound of 'fiddlestick!' All these symptoms, with the tact of kindness, they ignored. The bride was kissed, the father-in-law taken for granted, and Alan welcomed as if no one in the room had looked guilty.

'Come to lunch and take a hunch,' said the Doctor, offering his arm to Stella. 'Mother Bunch is rhyme, but not reason; you shall munch and I will scrunch – that's both. "Ah! you may well look surprised," as the foreign ambassador admitted when the ancient Britons noticed that he had no tail. But you won't mind when you know us better; I'm no worse than a barrel-organ.'

Yet with all Dr Tyke's endeavour to be funny, and this time it cost him an effort, and with all his wife's facile commonplaces, two of the guests seemed ill at ease. Alan felt, as it were with every nerve, the impression his father-in-law must produce, while Stella, less sensitive for herself, was out of countenance for her husband's sake. Mr Durham, indeed, was pompous and unabashed as ever; but whilst he answered commonplace remarks by remarks no less commonplace, he appeared to be, as in fact he was, occupied in scrutinizing, and mentally valuing, the plate and china.

'Charming weather,' said Mrs Tyke, with an air of intelligent originality.

'Yes, ma'am; fine weather, indeed; billing and cooing weather; ha! ha!' with a glance across the table. 'Now I dare say your young ladies know what to do in this weather.'

'We have no children,' and Mrs Tyke whispered, lest her husband should hear. Then, after a pause, 'I dare say Orpingham Place was just coming into beauty when you left.'

Mr Durham thrust his thumbs into his waistcoat-pockets, and leaned back for conversation. 'Well, I don't know what to say to that, – I don't indeed; I don't know which the season is when Orpingham Place is *not* in beauty. Its conservatories were quite a local lion last winter – quite a local lion, as my friend the Duke remarked to me; and he said he must bring the Duchess over to see them, and he did bring her Grace* over; and I gave them a luncheon in the largest conservatory, such as I don't suppose they sit down to every day. For the nobility have blood, if you please, and the literary beggars are welcome to all the brains they've got' (the Doctor smiled, Alan winced visibly); 'but you'll find it's us city men who've got backbone, and backbone's the best to wear, as I observed to the Duke that very day when I gave him such a glass of port as he hasn't got in his cellar. I said it to him, just as I say it to you, ma'am, and he didn't contradict me; in fact, you know, he couldn't.'

After this it might have been difficult to start conversation afresh, when, happily, Jane entered, late for luncheon, and with an apology for her sister, who was detained elsewhere. She went through the necessary introductions, and took her seat between Dr Tyke and Mr Durham, thus commanding an advantageous view of the bride, whom she mentally set down as nothing particular in any way.

Alan had never met Jane before. He asked her after Miss Charlmont and Lucy, after Lucy especially, who was 'a very charming old friend' of his, as he explained to Stella. For some minutes Mr Durham sat silent, much impressed by Jane's beauty and grace; this gave people breathing-time for the recovery of ease and good humour; and it was not till Dr Tyke had uttered three successive jokes, and every one, except Mr Durham, had laughed at them, that the master of Orpingham Place could think of any remark worthy of his attractive neighbour; and then, with much originality, he too observed, – 'Charming weather, Miss Jane.'

And Jane answered with a smile; for was not this the widower of Orpingham Place?

That Mr Durham's conversation on subsequent occasions gained in range of subject, is clear from Jane's quotations in the last chapter. And that Mr Durham was alive to Jane's fascinations appeared pretty evident, as he not only called frequently at Appletrees House, but made up parties, to which Dr and Mrs Tyke, and the Miss Charlmonts, were invariably asked.

CHAPTER VII

Gaiety in London, sadness by the sea.

Lucy did her very best to entertain Miss Drum with the cheerfulness of former visits; in none of which had she shown herself more considerate of the old lady's tastes than now. She made breakfast half-an-hour earlier than usual; she culled for her interesting scraps from the newspaper; she gave her an arm up and down the Esplanade on sunny days; she reclaimed the most unpromising strayed stitches in her knitting; she sang her old-fashioned favourite ballads for an hour or so before teatime, and after tea till bed-time played energetically at backgammon: yet Miss Drum was sensible of a change. All Lucy's efforts could not make her cheeks rosy and plump, and her laugh spontaneous; could not make her step elastic or her eyes bright.

It is easy to ridicule a woman nearly thirty years old for fancying herself beloved without a word said, and suffering deeply under disappointment: yet Lucy Charlmont was no contemptible person. However at one time deluded, she had never let a hint of her false hopes reach Mr Hartley's observation; and however now disappointed, she fought bravely against a betrayal of her plight. Alone in her own room she might suffer visibly and keenly, but with any eye upon her she would not give way. Sometimes it felt as if the next moment the strain on her nerves might wax unedurable; but such a next moment never came, and she endured still. Only, who is there strong enough, day after day, to strain strength to the utmost, and yet give no sign?

'My dear,' said Miss Drum, contemplating Lucy over her spectacles and across the backgammon-board one evening when the eyes looked more sunken than ever, and the whole face more haggard, 'I am sure you do not take exercise enough. You really must do more than give me an arm on the Esplanade; all your bloom is gone, and you are much too thin. Promise me that you will take at least one long walk in the day whenever the weather is not unfavourable.'

Lucy stroked her old friend's hand fondly: 'I will take walks when my sisters are at home again; but I have not you here always.'

Miss Drum insisted: 'Do not say so, my dear, or I shall feel bound to go home again; and that I should not like at all, as we both know. Pray oblige me by promising.'

Thus urged, Lucy promised, and in secret rejoiced that for at least an hour or two of the day she should thenceforward be alone, relieved from the scrutiny of those dim, affectionate eyes. And truly she needed some relief. By day she could forbid her thoughts to shape themselves, even mentally, into words, although no effort could banish the vague, dull sorrow which was all that might now remain to her of remembrance. But by night, when sleep paralysed self-restraint, then her dreams were haunted by distorted spectres of the past; never alluring or endearing – for this she was thankful – but sometimes monstrous, and always impossible to escape from. Night after night she would awake from such dreams, struggling and sobbing, with less and less conscious strength to resume daily warfare.

Soon she allowed no weather to keep her indoors at the hour for walking, and Miss Drum, who was a hardy disciple of the old school, encouraged her activity. She always sought the sea, not the smooth, civilised esplanade, but the rough, irreclaimable shingle; – to stray to and fro till the last moment of her freedom; to and fro, to and fro, at once listless and unresting, with wide, absent eyes fixed on the monotonous waves, which they did not see. Gradually a morbid fancy grew upon her that one day she should behold her father's body washed ashore, and that she should know the face: from a waking fancy, this began to haunt her dreams with images unutterably loathsome. Then she walked no more on the shingle, but took to wandering along green lanes and country roads.

But no one struggling persistently against weakness fails to overcome: also, however prosaic the statement may sound, air and exercise *will* take effect on persons of sound constitution. Something of Lucy's lost colour showed itself, by fits and starts at first, next steadily; her appetite came back, however vexed she might feel at its return; at last fatigue brought sounder sleep, and the hollow eyes grew less sunken. This refreshing sleep was the turning-point in her case; it supplied strength for the day, whilst each day in its turn brought with it fewer and fewer demands upon her strength. Seven weeks after Miss Drum exacted the promise, Lucy, though graver of aspect, and at heart sadder than before Alan Hartley's wedding, had recovered in a measure her look of health and her interest in the details of daily life. She no longer greatly dreaded meeting her sisters when at length their much-prolonged absence should terminate; and in spite of some nervousness in the anticipation, felt confident that even a sight of Mr and Mrs Hartley would not upset the outward composure of her decorum.

Miss Drum triumphed in the success of her prescription, and brought forward parallel instances within her own experience. 'That is right,' she would say, 'my dear; take another slice of the mutton where it is not overdone. There is nothing like exercise for giving an appetite, only the mutton should not be overdone. You cannot remember Sarah Smith, who was with me before your dear mother entrusted you to my care; but I assure you three doctors had given her over as a confirmed invalid when I prescribed for her;' and the old lady laughed gently at her own wit. 'I made her take a walk every day, let the weather be what it might; and gave her nice, juicy mutton to eat, with a change to beef, or a chicken, now and then for variety; and very soon you would not have known her for the same girl; and Dr Grey remarked, in his funny way, that I ought to be an M.D.* myself.' Or, again: 'Lucy, my dear, you recollect my French assistant,* Mademoiselle Leclerc, what a fine, strong young woman she was when you knew her. Now when she first came to me she was pale and peaking, afraid of wet feet or an open window; afraid of this, that, and the other, always tired, and with no appetite except for sweets. Mutton and exercise made her what you remember; and before she went home to France to marry an old admirer, she thanked me with tears in her eyes for having made her love mutton. She said "love" when she should have said "like"; but I was too proud and pleased to correct her English then. I only answered, "Ah, dear Mademoiselle, always love your husband and love your mutton."'

Lucy had a sweet, plaintive voice, to which her own secret sorrow now added a certain simple pathos; and when in the twilight she sang 'Alice Grey', or 'She wore a wreath of roses', or some other old favourite, good Miss Drum would sit and listen till the tears gathered behind her spectacles. Were tears in the singer's eyes also? She thought now with more tenderness than ever before of the suitors she had rejected in her hopeful, happy youth, especially of a certain Mr Tresham, who had wished her all happiness as he turned to leave her in his dignified regret. She had always had a great liking for Mr Tresham, and now she could feel for him.

CHAPTER VIII

On the 28th of June, four letters came to Lucy by the first delivery: –

I

My dear Lucy,

Pray do not think me thoughtless if I once more ask whether you will sanction an extension of our holiday. Mrs Tyke presses us to remain with her through July, and Dr Tyke is no less urgent. When I hinted that their hospitality had already been trespassed upon, the doctor quoted Hone* (as he said: I doubt if it is there): –

'In July
No good-bye;
In August
Part we must.'

I then suggested that you may be feeling moped at home, and in want of change; but, of course, the Doctor had still an answer ready: – Tell Lucy from me, that if she takes you away I shall take it very ill, as the homœopath said when his learned brother substituted cocoa-nibs for champagne.' And all the time Cousin Lucy was begging us to stay, and Jane was looking at me so earnestly: in short, dear Lucy, if 'No' must be said, pray will you say it; for I have been well-nigh talked over.

And, indeed, we must make allowances for Jane, if she seems a little selfish; for, to let you into a secret, I believe she means to accept Mr Durham if he makes her the offer we all are expecting from him. At first I was much displeased at her giving him any encouragement, for it appeared to me impossible that she could view his attentions with serious approbation: but I have since become convinced that she knows her own mind, and is not trifling with him. How it is possible for her to contemplate union with one so unrefined and ostentatious I cannot conceive, but I have no power to restrain her; and when I endeavoured to exert my influence against him, she told me in the plainest terms that she preferred luxury with Mr Durham to dependence without him. Oh, Lucy, Lucy! have we ever given her cause to resent her position so bitterly? Were she my own child, I do not think I could love her more or care for her more anxiously: but she has never understood me, never done me justice. I speak of myself only, not of you also, because I shall never marry, and all I have has been held simply in trust for her: with you it is, and ought to be, different.

But you must not suffer for Jane's wilfulness. If you are weary of our absence I really must leave her under Cousin Lucy's care – for she positively declines to accompany me home at present – and return to every-day duties. I am sick enough of pleasuring, I do assure you, as it is; though, were Mr Durham a different man, I should only rejoice, as you may suppose.

Well, as to news, there is not much worth transmitting. Jane has been to the Opera three times, and to the English play once. Mr Durham sends the boxes, and Dr and Mrs Tyke never tire of the theatre. The last time they went to the Opera they brought home with them to supper Mr Tresham, whom you may recollect our meeting here more than once, and who has lately returned to England from the East. Through some misunderstanding he expected to see you instead of me, and looked out of countenance for a moment: then he asked after you, and begged me to remember him to you when I wrote. He appeared much interested in hearing our home news, and concerned when I mentioned that you have seemed less strong lately. Pray send compliments for him when next you write, in case we should see him again.

Mr Hartley I always liked, and now I like his wife also: she is an engaging little thing, and gets us all to call her Stella. You, I am sure, will be fond of her when you know her. How I wish her father resembled her! She is as simple and as merry as a bird, and witnesses Mr Durham's attentions to Jane with perfect equanimity. As to Mr Hartley, he seems as much amused as if the bulk of his wife's enormous fortune were not at stake; yet any one must see the other man is in earnest. Stella is reckoned a clever actress, and private theatricals of some sort are impending. I say 'of some sort', because Jane, who is indisputably the beauty of our circle, would prefer *tableaux vivants;** and I know not which will carry her point.

My love to Miss Drum. Don't think me selfish for proposing to remain longer away from you; but, indeed, I am being drawn in two opposite directions by two dear sisters, of whom I only wish that one had as much good sense and good taste as the other.

Your affectionate sister,
Catherine Charlmont

II

My dear Lucy,

I know Catherine is writing, and will make the worst of everything, just as if I was cut out to be an old maid.

Surely at my age one may know one's own mind; and, though I'm not going to say before I am asked whether I like Mr Durham, we are all very well aware, my dear Lucy, that I like money and comforts. It's one thing for Catherine and you, who have enough and to spare, to split hairs as to likes and dislikes; but it's quite another for me who have not a penny of my own, thanks to poor dear papa's blindness. Now do be a dear, and tell sister she is welcome to stay this one month more; for, to confess the truth, if I remain here alone I may find myself at my wit's end for a pound or two one of these days. Dress is so dear, and I had rather never go out again than be seen a dowdy; and if we are to have *tableaux* I shall want all sorts of things. I don't hold at all with charades* and such nonsense, in which people are supposed to be witty; give me a piece in which one's arms are of some use; but of course, Stella, who has no more arm than a pump-handle, votes for theatricals.

The Hartleys are coming to-day, and, of course, Mr Durham, to take us after luncheon to the Crystal Palace.* There is a grand concert coming off, and a flower-show, which would all be yawny enough but for the toilettes.* I dare say I shall see something to set me raving; just as last time I was at the Botanic Gardens, I pointed out the loveliest suit of Brussels lace over white silk; but I might as well ask Catherine for wings to fly with.

Good-bye, my dear Lucy. Don't be cross this once, and when I have a house of my own, I'll do you a good turn.

Your affectionate sister,
Jane

P.S. I enclose Mr Durham's photograph, which he fished and fished to make me ask for, so at last I begged it to gratify the poor man. Don't you see all Orpingham Place in his speaking countenance?

III

My dearest Lucy,

You owe me a kindness to balance my disappointment at missing your visit. So please let Catherine know that she and Jane may give us a month more. Dr Tyke wishes it no less than I do, and Mr Durham perhaps more than either of us; but a word to the wise.

Your affectionate cousin,
Lucy C. Tyke

P.S. The Doctor won't send regards, because he means to write to you himself.

IV

Dear Lucy,

If you agree with the snail, you find your house just the size for one; and lest bestial example should possess less force than human, I further remind you of what Realmah the Great affirms, – 'I met two blockheads, but the one sage kept himself to himself.' All which sets forth to you the charms of solitude, which, as you are such a proper young lady, is, of course, the only anybody you can be in love with, and of whose society I am bent on affording you prolonged enjoyment.

This can be effected, if your sisters stay here another month, and indeed you must not say us nay; for on your 'yes' hangs a tale which your 'no' may for ever forbid to wag. Miss Catherine looks glummish, but Jenny* is all sparkle and roses, like this same month of June; and never is she more sparkling or rosier than when the master of Orpingham Place hails her with that ever fresh remark, 'Fine day, Miss Jane.' Don't nip the summer crops of Orpingham Place in the bud, or, rather, don't retard them by unseasonable frost; for I can't fancy my friend will be put off with anything less than a distinct 'no'; and when it comes to that, I think Miss Jane, in her trepidation, will say 'yes.' And if you are a good girl, and let the little one play out her play, when she has come into the sugar and spice and all that's nice, you shall come to Notting Hill this very next May, and while the sun shines make your hay.

Your venerable cousin's husband
(by which I merely mean),
Your cousin's venerable husband,
Francis Tyke, M.D.

N.B. I append M.D. to remind you of my professional status, and so quell you by the weight of my advice.

Lucy examined the photograph of Mr Durham with a double curiosity, for he was Mr Hartley's father-in-law as well as Jane's presumptive suitor. She looked, and saw a face not badly featured, but vulgar in expression; a figure not amiss, but ill at ease in its studied attitude and superfine clothes. Assuredly it was not George Durham, but the master of Orpingham Place who possessed attractions for Jane; and Lucy felt, for a sister who could be thus attracted, the sting of a humiliation such as her own baseless hopes had never cost her.

Each of her correspondents was answered with judicious variation in the turn of the sentences. To Jane she wrote dryly, returning Mr Durham's portrait wrapped in a ten-pound note; an arrangement which, in her eyes, showed a symbolic appropriateness, lost for the moment on her sister. Catherine she answered far more affectionately, begging her on no account to curtail a visit which might be of importance to Jane's prospects; and on the flap of the envelope, she added compliments to Mr Tresham.

CHAPTER IX

Mr Tresham had loved Lucy Charlmont sincerely, and until she refused him had entertained a good hope of success. Even at the moment of refusal she avowed the liking for him which all through their acquaintance had been obvious; and then, and not till then, it dawned upon him that her indifference towards himself had its root in preference for another. But he was far too honourable a man either to betray or to aim at verifying his suspicion; and though he continued to visit at Dr Tyke's, where Alan Hartley was so often to be seen idling away time under the comfortable conviction that he was doing no harm to himself or to any one else, it was neither at once, nor of set purpose, that Arthur Tresham penetrated Lucy's secret. Alan and himself had been College friends; he understood him thoroughly; his ready good-nature, which seemed to make every one a principal person in his regard; his open hand that liked spending; his want of deep or definite purpose; his unconcern as to possible consequences. Then Lucy, – in whom Mr Tresham had been on one point wofully mistaken, – she was so composed and so cordial to all her friends; there was about her such womanly sweetness, such unpretentious, dignified reserve towards all: her face would light up so brightly when he, or any other, spoke what interested her, not seldom, certainly, when *he* spoke: – even after a sort of clue had come into his hands, it was some time before he felt sure of any difference between her manner to Alan and to others. When the conviction forced itself upon him, he grieved more for her than for himself; he knew his friend too intimately to mistake his pleasure in being amused for any anxiety to make himself beloved; he knew about Alan much that Lucy did not and could not guess, and from the beginning inferred the end.

In the middle of that London season Catherine and Lucy returned to Brompton-on-Sea; and before August had started the main stream of tourists from England to the continent, Mr Tresham packed up his knapsack, and staff in hand, set off on a solitary expedition, of undetermined length, to the East.* He was neither a rich nor a poor man; had been called to the bar,* but without pursuing his profession, and was not tied to any given spot; he went away to recruit his spirits, and, having recovered them, stayed on out of sheer enjoyment. Yet, when one morning his eye lighted on the Hartley-Durham marriage in the 'Times' Supplement, home feeling stirred within him; and he who, twenty-four hours earlier, knew not whether he might not end his days beside the blue Bosphorus, on the evening of that same day had started westward.

He felt curious, he would not own to himself that he felt specially interested, to know how Lucy fared; and he felt curious, in a minor degree, to inspect her successful rival. With himself Lucy had not yet had a rival; not yet, perhaps she might one day, he repeated to himself, only it had not happened yet. And then the sweet, dignified face rose before him kind and cheerful; cheerful still in his memory, though he guessed that now it must look saddened. He had never yet seen it with a settled expression of sadness, and he knew not how to picture it so.

Mr Drum – or Mr Gawkins Drum, as he scrupulously called himself, on account of a certain Mr Drum, who lived somewhere and went nowhere, and was held by all outsiders to be in his dotage – Miss Drum's brother, Mr Gawkins Drum, had for several years stood as a gay young bachelor of sixty. Not that, strictly speaking, any man (or, alas! any woman) can settle down at sixty and there remain; but at the last of a long series of avowed birthday parties, Mr Drum had drunk his own health as being sixty that very day; this was now some years ago, and still, in neighbourly parlance, Mr Drum was no more than sixty. At sixty-something-indefinite Gawkins brought home a bride, who confessed to sixty; and all Brompton-on-Sea indulged in a laugh at their expense, till it oozed out that the kindly old couple had gone through all the hopes and disappointments of a many years' engagement, begun at a reasonable age for such matters, and now terminated only because the bedridden brother, to whom the bride had devoted herself during an ordinary lifetime, had at last ended his days in peace. Mr and Mrs Gawkins Drum forestalled their neighbours' laugh by their own, and soon the laugh against them died out, and every one accepted their house as amongst the pleasantest resorts in Brompton-on-Sea.

Miss Drum, however, felt less leniently towards her brother and sister-in-law, and deliberately regarded them from a shocked point of view. The wedding took place at Richmond, where the bride resided; and the honeymoon came to an end whilst Lucy entertained her old friend, during that long visit at Notting Hill, which promised to colour all Jane's future.

'My dear,' said Miss Drum to her deferential listener; 'My dear, Sarah,' – and Lucy felt that that offending Sarah could only be the bride, – 'Sarah shall not suffer for Gawkins' folly and her own. I will not fail to visit her in her new home, and to notice her on all proper occasions, but I cannot save her from being ridiculous. I did not wait till I was sixty to make up my mind against wedlock, though perhaps' – and the old lady bridled – 'I also may have endured the preference of some infatuated man. Lucy, my dear, take an old woman's advice: marry, if you mean to marry, before you are sixty, or else remain like myself; otherwise, you make yourself simply ridiculous.'

And Lucy, smiling, assured her that she would either marry before sixty or not at all; and added, with some earnestness, that she did not think she should ever marry. To which Miss Drum answered with stateliness: 'Very well; do one thing or do the other, only do not become ridiculous.'

Yet the old lady softened that evening, when she found herself, as it were, within the radius of the contemned bride. Despite her sixty years, and in truth she looked less than her age, Mrs Gawkins Drum was a personable little woman, with plump red cheeks, gentle eyes, and hair of which the soft brown was threaded, but not overpowered, by grey. There was no affectation of youthfulness in her gown, which was of slate-coloured silk; nor in her cap, which came well on her head; nor in her manner to her guests, which was cordial; nor in her manner to her husband, which was affectionate, with the undemonstrative affectionateness that might now have been appropriate had they married forty years earlier.

Her kiss of welcome was returned frostily by Miss Drum, warmly by Lucy. Mr Drum at first looked a little sheepish under his sister's severe salutation. Soon all were seated at tea.

'Do you take cream and sugar?' asked the bride, looking at her new sister.

'No sugar, I thank you,' was the formal reply. 'And it will be better, Sarah, that you should call me Elizabeth. Though I am an old woman your years do not render it unsuitable, and I wish to be sisterly.'

'Thank you, dear Elizabeth,' answered Mrs Gawkins, cheerily; 'I hope, indeed, we shall be sisterly. It would be sad times with me if I found I had brought coldness into my new home.'

But Miss Drum would not thaw yet. 'Yes, I have always maintained, and I maintain still, that there must be faults on both sides if a marriage, if any marriage whatever, introduces dissension into a family circle. And I will do my part, Sarah.'

'Yes, indeed;' but Sarah knew not what more to say.

Mr Drum struck in, – 'Lucy, my dear' – she had been a little girl perched on his knee when her father asked him years before to be trustee, – 'Lucy, my dear, you're not in full bloom. Look at my old lady, and guess: what's a recipe for roses?'

'For shame, Gawkins!' cried both old ladies; one with a smile, the other with a frown.

Still, as the evening wore on, Miss Drum slowly thawed. Having, as it were once for all, placed her hosts in the position of culprits at the moral bar, having sat in judgment on them, and convicted them in the ears of all men (represented by Lucy), she admitted them to mercy, and dismissed them with a qualified pardon. What most softened her towards the offending couple was their unequivocal profession of rheumatism. When she unbendingly declined to remain seated at the supper-table one minute beyond half-past ten, she alleged rheumatism as her impelling motive; and Gawkins and Sarah immediately proclaimed their own rheumatic experience and sympathies. As Miss

Drum observed to Lucy on their way home, 'Old people don't confess to rheumatism if they wish to appear young.'

Thus the feud subsided, though Miss Drum to the end of her life occasionally spoke of her sister-in-law as 'that poor silly thing', and of her brother as of one who should have known better.

Whilst, on her side, Mrs Gawkins Drum remarked to her husband, 'What a very old-looking woman that Miss Charlmont is, if she's not thirty, as you say. I never saw such an old, faded-looking woman of her age.'

CHAPTER X

Parties ran high at Kensington and Notting Hill. Stella stood up for charades, Jane for *tableaux*. Mr Hartley naturally sided with his wife, Miss Charlmont held back from volunteering any opinion, Mrs Tyke voted for the last speaker, Dr Tyke ridiculed each alternative; at last Mr Durham ingeniously threw his weight into both scales, and won for both parties a partial triumph. 'Why not,' asked he, – 'why not let Pug speak, and Miss Jane be silent?'

This pacific suggestion once adopted, Dr Tyke proposed that a charade word should be fixed upon, and performed by speech or spectacle, as might suit the rival stars; for instance, Love-apple.*

But who was to be Love?

Everybody agreed in rejecting little boys;* and Jane, when directly appealed to, refused to represent the Mother of love and laughter; 'for', as she truly observed, 'that would not be Love, after all.' Mr Durham, looking laboriously gallant, aimed at saying something neat and pointed; he failed, yet Jane beamed a smile upon his failure. Then Dr Tyke proposed a plaster Cupid; this, after some disputing, was adopted, with vague accessories of processional Greek girls, to be definitely worked out afterwards. For 'Apple' Alan suggested Paris* and the rival goddesses, volunteering himself as Paris: Jane should be Venus, and Catherine would make a capital Juno. Jane accepted her own part as a matter of course, but doubted about her sister. 'Yes,' put in Miss Charlmont, decisively, 'I will be Juno, or anything else which will help us forward a little.' So that was settled; but who should be Minerva? Stella declined to figure as the patroness of wisdom, and Jane drily observed, that they ought all to be tall, or all to be short, in her idea. At last a handsome, not too handsome, friend, Lady Everett, was thought of to take the part. The last scene Dr Tyke protested he should settle himself with Stella, and not be worried any more about it. So those two went into committee together, and Alan edged in ere long for consultation; finally, Miss Charlmont was appealed to, and the matter was arranged amongst them without being divulged to the rest.

But all was peace and plenty, smiles and wax-candles, at Kensington, when at last the evening came for the performance. Mrs Hartley's drawing-rooms being much more spacious than Mrs Tyke's, had been chosen for convenience, and about two hundred guests assembled to hear Stella declaim and see Jane attitudinise, as either faction expressed it. Good-natured Mrs Tyke played the hostess, whilst Mrs Hartley remained occult in the green-room. Dr Tyke was manager and prompter. Mr Durham, vice Paris-Hartley, welcomed people in a cordial, fussy manner, apologising for the smallness of London rooms, and regretfully alluding to the vast scale of Orpingham Place, 'where a man can be civil to his friends without treading on their toes or their tails – ha! ha!'

But there is a limit to all things, even fussiness has an end. At last every one worth waiting for had arrived, been received, been refreshed. Orpingham Place died out of the conversation. People exchanged commonplaces, and took their seats; having taken their seats they exchanged more commonplaces. 'What's the word?' – 'It's such a bore guessing: I never guess anything.' – 'People ought to tell the word beforehand.' – 'What a horrible man! Is that Mr Hartley?' – 'No, old Durham; backbone Durham.' – 'Why backbone?' – 'Don't know; hear him called so.' – 'Isn't there a Beauty somewhere?' – 'Don't know; there's the Beast,' – and the hackneyed joke received the tribute of a hackneyed laugh.

The manager's bell rang, the curtain drew up.

A plaster cast of Cupid, with fillet, bow, and quiver, on an upholstery pedestal, stood revealed. Music, commencing behind the scenes, approached; a file of English-Grecian maidens,* singing and carrying garlands, passed across the stage towards a pasteboard temple, presumably their desired goal, although they glanced at their audience, and seemed very independent of Cupid on his pedestal. There were only six young ladies; but they moved slowly, with a tolerable space interposed between each and each, thus producing a processional effect. They sang, in time and in tune, words by Dr Tyke; music (not in harmony, but in unison, to ensure correct execution) by Arthur Tresham: –

Love hath a name of Death:
He gives a breath
And takes away.
Lo we, beneath his sway,
Grow like a flower;
To bloom an hour,
To droop a day,
And fade away.

The first Anglo-Greek had been chosen for her straight nose, the last for her elegant foot; the intermediate four, possessing good voices, bore the burden of the singing. They all moved and sang with self-complacent ease, but without much dramatic sentiment, except the plainest of the six, who assumed an air of languishment.

Some one suggested 'cupid-ditty,' but without universal acceptance. Some one else, on no obvious grounds, hazarded 'Bore, Wild Boar': a remark which stung Dr Tyke, as playwright, into retorting, 'Boreas.'

The second scene was dumb show. Alan Hartley as Paris, looking very handsome in a tunic and sandals, and flanked by the largest-sized, woolly toy lambs, sat, apple in hand, awaiting the rival goddesses. A flourish of trumpets announced the entrance of Miss Charlmont, a stately crowned Juno, robed in amber-coloured cashmere, and leading in a leash a peacock, with train displayed, and ingeniously mounted on noiseless wheels. She swept grandly in, and held out one arm, with a studied gesture, for the apple; which, doubtless, would have been handed to her then and there, had not warning notes on a harp ushered in Lady Everett: a modest, sensible-looking Minerva, robed and stockinged in blue, with a funny Athenian owl* perched on her shoulder, and a becoming helmet on her head. Paris hesitated visibly, and seemed debating whether or not to split the apple and the difference together, when a hubbub, as of birds singing, chirping, calling, cleverly imitated by Dr Tyke and Stella on water-whistles, heralded the approach of Venus. In she came, beautiful Jane Charlmont, with a steady, gliding step, her eyes kindling with victory, both her small hands outstretched for the apple so indisputably hers, her lips parted in a triumphant smile. Her long, white robe flowed classically to the floor; two doves, seeming to nestle in her hair, billed and almost cooed; but her face eclipsed all beside it; and when Paris, on one knee, deposited the apple within her slim, white fingers, Juno forgot to look indignant and Minerva scornful.

After this the final scene fell dead and flat. In vain did Stella whisk about as the most coquettish of market-girls of an undefined epoch and country, balancing a fruit-basket on her head, and crying, 'Grapes, melons, peaches, love-apples', with the most natural inflections. In vain did Arthur Tresham beat down the price of peaches and Alan Hartley bid for love-apples: – Jane had attained one of her objects, and eclipsed her little friend for that evening.

The *corps dramatique** was to sit down to supper in costume; a point arranged ostensibly for convenience, secretly it may be for vanity's sake: only Stella laid her fruit-basket aside, and Miss Charlmont released her peacock. Lady Everett continued to wear the helmet, which did not conceal her magnificent black hair (she had been a Miss Moss before marriage, Clara Lyon Moss), and Jane retained her pair of doves.

But during the winding up of the charade, more of moment had occurred off the stage than upon it. Jane, her part over, left the other performers to their own devices, and quietly made her way into a conservatory which opened out of the room devoted for that evening to cloaks and hoods. If she expected to be followed she was not disappointed. A heavy step, and an embarrassed clearance of throat, announced Mr Durham. He bustled up to her, where she sat fanning herself and showing white and brilliant against a background of flowers and leaves, whilst he looked at once sheepish and pompous, awkward and self-satisfied; not a lady's man assuredly.

'Hem – haw – Miss Jane, you surpassed yourself. I shall always think of you now as Venus; I shall, indeed.' Jane smiled benignantly. 'Poor Pug's nose is quite out of joint; it is, indeed. But the chit has got a husband, and can snap her fingers at all of us.' Jane surveyed him with grave interrogation, then cast down her lustrous eyes, and slightly turned her shoulder in his direction. Abashed, he resumed: 'But really, Miss Jane, now wasn't Venus a married lady too? and couldn't we—?' Jane interrupted him: 'Pray give me your arm, Mr Durham;' she rose: 'let us go back to the company. I don't know what you are talking about, unless you mean to be rude and very unkind:' the voice broke, the large, clear eyes softened to tears; she drew back as he drew nearer. Then Mr Durham, ill-bred, but neither scheming nor cold-hearted, pompous and fussy, but a not ungenerous man for all that, – then Mr Durham spoke: 'Don't draw back from me, Miss Jane, but take my arm for once to lead you back to the company, and take my hand for good. For I love and admire you, Miss Jane; and if you will take an oldish man for your husband, you shall never want for money or for pleasure while my name is good in the City.'

Thus in one evening Jane Charlmont attained both her objects.

Supper was a very gay meal, as brilliant as lights, glass, and plate could make it. People were pleased with the night's entertainment, with themselves, and with each other. Mr Durham, with an obtrusive air of festivity, sat down beside Jane, and begged his neighbours not to inconvenience themselves, as they did not mind squeezing. Jane coloured, but judged it too early to frown. Mr Durham, being somewhat old-fashioned, proposed healths: the fair actresses were toasted, the Anglo-Greeks in a bevy, the distinguished stars one by one. Mr Tresham returned thanks for the processional six; Dr Tyke for Miss Charlmont, Sir James Everett and Mr Hartley for their respective wives.

Then Jane's health was drunk: who would rise to return thanks? Mr Durham rose: 'Hem – haw—' said he: 'haw – hem – ladies and gentlemen, allow me to return thanks for the Venus of the evening – I mean for the Venus altogether, whose health you have done me the honour to drink' – knowing smiles circled round the table. 'Done us, I should say: not that I unsay what I said; quite the contrary, and I'm not ashamed to have said it. I will only say one word more in thanking you for the honour you have done her and all of us: the champagne corks pop, and suggest popping; but after popping mum's the word. Ladies and gentlemen, my very good friends, I drink your very good health.'

And the master of Orpingham Place sat down.

CHAPTER XI

Lucy received the news of Jane's engagement with genuine vexation, and then grew vexed with herself for feeling vexed. Conscience took alarm, and pronounced that envy and pride had a share in her vexation. Self retorted: It is not envy to see that Jane is mercenary, nor pride to dislike vulgarity. Conscience insisted: It is envy to be annoyed by Jane's getting married before you, and it is pride to brand Mr Durham as vulgar, and then taboo him as beyond the pale. Self pleaded: No one likes growing old and being made to feel it; and who would not deprecate a connection who will put one out of countenance at every turn? But Conscience secured the last word: If you were younger than Jane, you would make more allowances for her; and if Mr Durham were engaged to any one except your sister, you would think it fair not to condemn him as destitute of every virtue because he is underbred.

Thus did Conscience get the better of Self. And Lucy gulped down dignity and disappointment together when, in reply to Miss Drum's, 'My dear, I hope your sisters are well, and enjoying their little gaieties,' she said, cheerfully: 'Now, really, you should give me something for such wonderful news: Jane is engaged to be married.'

There was nothing Miss Drum relished more than a wedding 'between persons suited to each other, and not ridiculous on the score of age and appearance', as she would herself pointedly have defined it. Now Jane was obviously young enough and pretty enough to become a bride; so Miss Drum was delighted, and full of interest and of inquiries, which Lucy found it rather difficult to answer satisfactorily.

'And who is the favoured gentleman, my dear?'

'Mr Durham, of Orpingham Place, in Gloucestershire. Very rich it seems, and a widower. His only daughter', Lucy hurried on with an imperceptible effort, 'married that Mr Hartley Catherine and I used to meet so often at Notting Hill. She was thought to be a great heiress; but I suppose this will make some difference.'

'Then he is rather old for Jane?'

'He is not yet fifty it seems, though of course that is full old. By what he says, Orpingham Place must be a very fine country-seat; and Jane appears cut out for wealth and pleasure, she has such a power of enjoying herself;' and Lucy paused.

Miss Drum, dropping the point of age, resumed: 'Now what Durham will this be, my dear? I used to know a Sir Marcus Durham – a gay, hunting Baronet. He was of a north-country family; but this may be a branch of the same stock. He married an Earl's daughter, Lady Mary; and she used to take precedence, let who would be in the room, which was not thought to be in very good taste when the dowager Lady Durham was present. Still an Earl's daughter ought to understand good breeding, and that was how she acted; I do not wish to express any opinion. Perhaps Mr Durham may have a chance of the Baronetcy, for Sir Marcus left no children, but was succeeded by a bachelor brother; and then Jane will be "my lady" some day.'

'No,' replied Lucy; 'I don't think that likely. Mr Durham is enormously wealthy, by what I hear; but not of a county family.* He made his fortune in the City.'

Miss Drum persisted: 'The cadets of even noble families have made money by commerce over and over again. It is no disgrace to make a fortune; and I see no reason why Mr Durham should not be a baronet some day. Many a City man has been as fine a gentleman as any idler at court. Very likely Mr Durham is an elegant man of talent, and well connected; if so, a fortune is no drawback, and the question of age may be left to the lady's decision.'

Lucy said no more: only she foresaw and shrank from the approaching day of undeceiving which should bring Mr Durham to Brompton-on-Sea.

Once set off on the subject of family, there was no stopping Miss Drum, who, having had no proveable great-grandfather, was sensitive on the score of pedigree.

'You might not suppose it now, Lucy, but it is well known that our family name of Drum, though less euphonious than that of Durham, is in fact the same. I made the observation once to Sir Marcus, and he laughed with pleasure, and often afterwards addressed me as cousin. Lady Mary did not like the suggestion; but no one's fancies can alter a fact:' and the old lady looked stately, and as if the Drum-Durham theory had been adopted and emblazoned by the College of Heralds; whereas, in truth, no one besides herself, not even the easy-tempered Gawkins, held it.

Meanwhile, all went merrily and smoothly at Notting Hill. As Jane had said, she was old enough to know her own mind, and apparently she knew it. When Mr Durham presented her with a set of fine diamonds, she dropped naturally into calling him George; and when he pressed her to name the day, she answered, with an assumption of girlishness, that he must talk over all those dreadful things with Catherine.

To Miss Charlmont he had already opened his mind on the subject of settlements: Jane should have everything handsome and ample, but Pug must not lose her fortune either. This Catherine, deeming it right and reasonable, undertook to explain to Jane. Jane sulked a little to her sister, but displayed only a smiling aspect to her lover, feeling in her secret heart that her own nest was being particularly well feathered: for not only were Mr Durham's new marriage settlements most liberal, in spite of Stella's prospective twenty thousand pounds on coming of age, and twenty thousand at her father's demise; but Catherine, of her own accord, provided that at her death all her share of their father's property should descend to Jane, for her own separate use, and at her own absolute disposal.* The younger sister, indeed, observed with safe generosity: 'Suppose you should marry, too, some day?' But Catherine, grateful for any gleam of unselfishness in her favourite sister, answered warmly and decisively: 'I never meant to marry, and I always meant what fortune I had to be yours at last: only, dear, do not again think hardly of our poor father's oversight.'

Mr Durham was urgent to have the wedding-day fixed, and Jane reluctant merely and barely for form's sake. A day in August was named, and the honeymoon pre-devoted to Paris and Switzerland. Then Miss Charlmont pronounced it time to return home; and was resolute that the wedding should take place at Brompton-on-Sea, not at Notting Hill as the hospitable Tykes proposed.

Jane was now nothing loth to quit town; Mr Durham unwilling to lose her, yet willing as recognising the step for an unavoidable preliminary. Nevertheless, he felt hurt at Jane's indifference to the short separation; whilst Jane, in her turn, felt worried at his expecting any show of sentiment from her, though, having once fathomed his feelings, she kept the worry to herself and produced the sentiment. He looked genuinely concerned when they parted at London-Bridge Station; but Jane never in her life had experienced a greater relief than now, when the starting train left him behind on the platform. A few more days, and it would be too late to leave him behind: but she consoled herself by reflecting that without him she might despair of ever seeing Paris; Switzerland was secondary in her eyes.

Miss Drum had often set as a copy,* 'Manners make the Man', and explained to her deferential pupils how in that particular phrase 'Man' includes 'Woman'. Catherine in later life reflected that 'Morals make the Man' (including Woman) conveys a not inferior truth. Jane might have modified the sentence a trifle further, in employing it as an M copy, and have written, 'Money makes the Man'.

CHAPTER XII

Lucy welcomed her sisters home, after an absence of unprecedented duration, with warm-hearted pleasure, but Jane went far to extinguish the feeling.

In the heyday of her blooming youth and satisfaction, she was not likely to acquire any tender tact lacking at other times; and an elder sister, mentally set down in her catalogue of old maids, was fair game.

'Why, Lucy,' she cried, as they sat together the first evening, herself the only idler of the three, 'you look as old as George, and about as lively: Miss Drum must be catching.'

'Do leave Miss Drum alone,' Lucy answered, speaking hastily from a double annoyance. 'And if,' – she forced a laugh, – 'surely if my looks recall George to your mind they ought to please you.'

But Jane was incorrigible. 'My dear, George is Orpingham Place, and Orpingham Place is George; but your looks suggest some distinction between the two. Only think, he expected me to grow dismal at leaving him behind, and I did positively see his red pockethandkerchief fluttering in the breeze as we screamed out of the station. And he actually flattered himself I should not go out much till the wedding is over; catch me staying at home if I can help it! By-the-bye, did you mean a joke by wrapping his photograph up in the ten-pound note? it struck me afterwards as really neat in its way.'

'Oh, Jane!' put in Catherine, and more she might have added in reproof; but at that instant the door opened, and Mr Ballantyne was announced.

Mr Ballantyne was a solicitor, related to Mrs Gawkins Drum, and taken into partnership by that lady's husband shortly before their marriage. Judging by looks, Mr Ballantyne might have been own nephew to Miss Drum rather than to her sister-in-law, so neutral was he in aspect and manner; if ever any one liked him at first sight, it was because there was nothing on the surface to stir a contrary feeling; and if any one volunteered a confidence to him, it was justified by his habitual taciturnity, which suggested a mechanical aptitude at keeping a secret; yet, however appearances were against him, he was a shrewd man of business, and not deficient in determination of character.

He arrived by appointment to show Miss Charlmont the draft of her settlement on her sister, and take, if need be, further instructions. She was one to see with her own eyes rather than merely to hear with her own ears, and, therefore, retired with the papers to the solitude of her own room, leaving her sisters to entertain the visitor.

Thus left, Mr Ballantyne took a respectful look at Jane, whose good luck in securing the master of Orpingham Place he considered rare indeed. Looking at her he arrived at the conclusion that Mr Durham also had been lucky. Jane just glanced at Mr Ballantyne, mentally appraising him as a nonentity; but in that glance she saw his admiration; admiration always propitiated her, and she deigned to be gracious.

Various maiden ladies in Brompton-on-Sea would have been gracious to Mr Ballantyne from a different motive. Though still a youngish man he was a widower, already in easy circumstances, and with a prospect of growing rich. His regard for his late wife's memory was most decorous, but not such as to keep him inconsolable; and his only child, Frank, being no more than five years old and healthy, need scarcely be viewed as a domestic drawback; indeed, certain spinsters treated the boy with a somewhat demonstrative affection, but these ladies were obviously not in their teens.

Mr Ballantyne meanwhile, though mildly courteous to all, had not singled out any one for avowed preference. Possibly he liked Miss Edith Sims, a doctor's daughter, a bold equestrian, a first-rate croquet player; she hoped so sincerely, for she had unbecoming carroty hair and freckles; possibly he liked Lucy Charlmont, but she had never given the chance a thought. Of Miss Charlmont, whom he had seen twice, and both times exclusively on business, he stood in perceptible awe.

Catherine, finding nothing to object to in the draft, returned it to Mr Ballantyne with her full assent. Then tea was brought in, and Mr Ballantyne was asked to stay. His aptitude for carrying cups and plates, recognised and admired in other circles, here remained in abeyance; Miss Charlmont adhering to the old fashion of people sitting round the tea-table at tea no less formally than round the dining-table at dinner.

A plan for a picnic having been set on foot by the Gawkins Drums, Lucy had been invited, and had accepted before Jane's engagement was announced. So now Mr Ballantyne mentioned the picnic, taking for granted that Lucy would join, and empowered by the projectors to ask her sisters also; Jane brightened at the proposal, being secretly charmed at a prospect of appearing amongst her familiar associates as mistress elect of Orpingham Place; but Catherine demurred,—

'Thank you, Mr Ballantyne; I will call myself and thank Mrs Drum, but Mr Durham might object,* and I will stay at home with my sister. No doubt we shall find future opportunities of all meeting.'

'Dear me!' cried Jane; 'Mr Durham isn't Bluebeard; or, if he is, I had better get a little fun first. My compliments, please, and I shall be too glad to come.'

'Oh, Jane!' remonstrated Miss Charlmont; but it was a hopeless remonstrance. Jane, once bent on amusement, was not to be deterred by doubtful questions of propriety; and the elder sister, mortified, but more anxious for the offender's credit than for her own dignity, changed her mind perforce, and, with a sigh, accepted the invitation. If Jane was determined to go, she had better go under a middle-aged sister's eye; but the party promised to be a large one, including various strange gentlemen, and Catherine honestly judged it objectionable.

Jane, however, was overflowing with glee, and questioned Mr Ballantyne energetically as to who were coming. When he was gone she held forth to her sisters,—

'That hideous Edith Sims, of course she will ride over on Brunette, to show her figure and her bridle hand. I shall wear pink, and sit next her to bring out her freckles. I've not forgotten her telling people I had no fortune. Don't you see she's trying to hook Mr Ballantyne? you heard him say she has been consulting him about something or other. Let's drive Mr Ballantyne over in our carriage, and the baby can perch on the box.'

Lucy said, 'Nonsense, Jane; Mr Ballantyne has his own dog-cart, and he is tiresome enough without keeping him all to ourselves.'

And Catherine added, this time peremptorily, 'My dear, that is not to be thought of; I could not justify it to Mr Durham. Either you will drive over with Lucy and me, and any other person I may select, or you must find a carriage for yourself, as I shall not go to the picnic.'

CHAPTER XIII

The environs of Brompton-on-Sea were rich in spots adapted to picnics, and the Gawkins Drums had chosen the very prettiest of these eligible spots. Rocky Drumble, a green glen of the floweriest, but with fragments of rock showing here and there, possessed an echo point and a dripping well: it was, moreover, accredited by popular tradition with a love-legend, and, on the same authority, with a ghost for moonlight nights. Rocky Drumble was threaded from end to end by a stream which nourished water-cresses; at one season its banks produced wild strawberries, at another nuts, sometimes mushrooms. All the year round the glen was frequented by song-birds; not seldom a squirrel would scamper up a tree, or a rabbit sit upright on the turf, winking his nose. Rocky Drumble on a sunny summer-day was a bower of cool shade, and of a silence heightened, not broken, by sounds of birds and of water, the stream at hand, the sea not far off; a bower of sun-chequered shade, breaths of wind every moment shifting the shadows, and the sun making its way in, now here, now there, with an endless, monotonous changeableness.

On such a day the Charlmonts drove to their rendezvous in Rocky Drumble. The carriage held four inside; Miss Drum and Catherine sitting forward, with Lucy and Jane opposite. On the box beside the driver perched little Frank Ballantyne, very chatty and merry at first; but to be taken inside and let fall asleep when, as was foreseen, he should grow tired. The child had set his heart on going to the picnic, and good Miss Drum had promised to take care of him – Miss Drum nominally, Lucy by secret understanding, for the relief of her old friend.

Miss Drum wore a drawn silk bonnet, which had much in common with the awning of a bathing-machine. Catherine surmounted her inevitable cap by a broad-brimmed brown straw hat. Lucy wore a similar hat without any cap under it, but looked, in fact, the elder of the two. Jane, who never sacrified complexion to fashion, also appeared in a shady hat, dove-coloured, trimmed with green leaves, under which she produced a sort of apple-blossom effect, in a cloud of pink muslin over white, and white *appliqué* again over the pink. Catherine had wished her to dress soberly, but Jane had no notion of obscuring her beauties. She had bargained with Mr Durham that he was not to come down to Brompton-on-Sea till the afternoon before the wedding; and when he looked hurt at her urgency, had assumed an air at once affectionate and reserved assuring him that this course seemed to her due to the delicacy of their mutual relations. Five days were still wanting to the wedding-day, George was not yet inalienably at her elbow, and no moment could appear more favourable for enjoyment. Surely if a skeleton promised to preside at the next banquet, this present feast was all the more to be relished: for though, according to Jane's definition, George was Orpingham Place, she would certainly have entered upon Orpingham Place with added zest had it not entailed George.

Miss Charlmont had delayed starting till the very last moment, not wishing to make more of the picnic than could be helped; and when she with her party reached the Drumble, they found their friends already on the spot. The last-comers were welcomed with a good deal of friendly bustle, and half-a-dozen gentlemen, in scarcely more than as many minutes, were presented to Jane by genial little Mrs Drum, who had never seen her before, and was charmed at first sight. Jane, happily for Catherine's peace of mind, assumed an air of dignity in unison with her distinguished prospects: she was gracious rather than coquettish – gracious to all, but flattering to none; a change from former days, when her manner used to savour of coaxing. Edith Sims had ridden over on Brunette, and Jane, keeping her word as to sitting next her, produced the desired effect.

The Charlmonts coming late, every one was ready for luncheon on their arrival, and no strolling was permitted before the meal. As to the luncheon, it included everything usual and nothing unusual, and most of the company consuming it displayed fine, healthy appetites. Great attention was paid to Jane, who was beyond all comparison the best-looking woman present; whilst two or three individuals made mistakes between Catherine and Lucy, as to which was Miss Charlmont.

Poor Lucy! she had seldom felt more heavy-hearted than now, as she sat talking and laughing. She felt herself getting more and more worn-looking as she talked and laughed on, getting visibly older and more faded. How she wished that Frank, who had fallen asleep on a plaid after stuffing unknown sweets into his system – how she wished that Frank would wake and become troublesome, to give her some occupation less intolerable than 'grinning and bearing!'

Luncheon over, the party broke up, splitting into twos and threes, and scattering themselves here and there through the Drumble. Miss Charlmont attaching herself doggedly to Jane, found herself clambering up and down banks and stony excrescences in company with a very young Viscount and his tutor: as she clambered exasperation waxed within her at the futility of the young men's conversation and the complacency of Jane's rejoinders; certainly, had any one been studying Catherine's face (which nobody was), he would have beheld an unwonted aspect at a picnic.

Miss Drum, ostentatiously aged because in company with her brother and his bride, had chosen before luncheon was well over to wrap herself up very warmly, and ensconce herself for an avowed nap inside one of the flys. 'You can call me for tea,' she observed to Lucy; 'and when Frank tires you, you can leave him in the carriage with me.' But Frank was Lucy's one resource: minding him served as an excuse for not joining Mr Drum, who joked, or Mr Ballantyne, who covertly stared at her, or Edith Sims, who lingering near Mr Ballantyne talked of horses, or any other person whose conversation was more tedious than silence.

When Frank woke, he recollected that nurse had told him strawberries grew in the Drumble; a fact grasped by him without the drawback of any particular season. Off he started in quest of strawberries, and Lucy zealously started in his wake, not deeming it necessary to undeceive him. The little fellow wandered and peered about diligently awhile after imaginary strawberries; failing these, he suddenly clamoured for a game at hide-and-seek: he would hide, and Lucy must not look.

They were now among the main fragments of rock found in the Drumble, out of sight of their companions. Lucy had scarcely shut her eyes as desired, when a shout of delight made her open them still more quickly, in time to see Frank scampering, as fast as his short legs would carry him, after a scampering rabbit. He was running – she recollected it in an instant – headlong towards the stream, and was already some yards from her. She called after him, but he did not turn, only cried out some unintelligible answer in his babyish treble. Fear lent her speed; she bounded after him, clearing huge stones and brushwood with instinctive accuracy. She caught at his frock – missed it – caught at it again – barely grasped it – and fell, throwing him also down in her fall on stones and brambles, bruising and scratching herself severely: but the child was safe, and she knew it, before she fainted away, whilst even in fainting her hand remained tightly clenched on his frock.

Frank's frightened cries soon brought friends to their assistance. Lucy, still insensible, was lifted on to smooth turf, and then sprinkled with water till she came to herself. In few words, for she felt giddy and hysterical but was resolute not to give way, she accounted for the accident, blaming herself for having carelessly let the child run into danger. It was impossible for any carriage to drive so far along the Drumble, so she had to take some one's arm to steady her in walking to meet the fly. Mr Ballantyne, as pale as a sheet, offered his arm; but she preferred Mr Drum's, and leaned heavily on it for support.

Lucy was soon safe in the fly by Miss Drum's side, whose nap was brought to a sudden end, and who, waking scared and fidgety, was disposed to lay blame on every one impartially, beginning with herself, and ending, in a tempered form, with Lucy. The sufferer thus disposed of, and packed for transmission home, the remaining picnickers, influenced by Mrs Drum's obvious bias, declined to linger for rustic tea or other pleasures, and elected then and there to return to their several destinations. The party mustered round the carriages ready to take their seats: but where were Catherine and Jane, Viscount and tutor? Shouting was tried, whistling was tried, 'Cooee'* was tried by amateur Australians for the nonce: all in vain. At last Dr Sims stepped into the fly with Lucy, promising to see her safe home; Miss Drum, smelling-bottle in hand, sat sternly beside her; Frank, after undergoing a paternal box on the ear, was degraded from the coachman's box to the back seat, opposite the old lady, who turned towards him the aspect as of an ogress: and thus the first carriage started, with Edith reining in Brunette beside it. The others followed without much delay, one carriage being left for the truants; and its driver charged to explain, if possible without alarming the sisters, what had happened to cut short the picnic.

CHAPTER XIV

The day before the wedding Lucy announced that she still felt too much bruised and shaken to make one of the party, either at church or at breakfast. Neither sister contradicted her: Catherine, because she thought the excuse valid; Jane, because Lucy, not having yet lost the traces of her accident, must have made but a sorry bridesmaid: and, as Jane truly observed, there were enough without her, for her defection still left a bevy of eight bridesmaids in capital working order.

Brompton-on-Sea possessed only one hotel of any pretensions, – 'The Duke's Head', so designated in memory of that solitary Royal Duke who had once made brief sojourn beneath its roof.

He found it a simple inn, bearing the name and sign of 'The Three Mermaids'; the mermaids appearing in paint as young persons, with yellow hair and combs, and faces of a type which failed to account for their uninterrupted self-ogling in hand-mirrors; tails were shadowily indicated beneath waves of deepest blue. After the august visit this signboard was superseded by one representing the Duke as a gentleman of inane aspect, pointing towards nothing discoverable; and this work of art, in its turn, gave place to a simple inscription, 'The Duke's Head Hotel'.

Call it by what name you would, it was as snug a house of entertainment as rational man or reasonable beast need desire, with odd little rooms opening out of larger rooms and off staircases; the only trace now visible of the Royal Duke's sojourn (beyond the bare inscription of his title) being Royal Sentries in coloured paste-board effigy, the size of life, posted on certain landings and at certain entrances. All the windowsills bore green boxes of flowering plants, whence a sweet smell, mostly of mignonette, made its way within doors. The best apartments looked into a square courtyard, turfed along three sides, and frequented by pigeons; and the pigeon-house, standing in a turfy corner, was topped by a bright silvered ball.

The landlord of the 'Duke's Head', a thin, tallowy-complexioned man, with a manner which might also be described as unpleasantly oily or tallowy, was in a bustle that same day, and all his household was bustling around him: for not merely had the 'Duke's Head' undertaken to furnish the Durham-Charlmont wedding-breakfast with richness and elegance, but the bride-groom elect, whom report endowed with a pocketful of plums, the great Mr Durham himself, with sundry fashionable friends, was coming down to Brompton-on-Sea by the 5.30 train, and would put up for one night at the 'Duke's Head'. The waiters donned their whitest neckcloths, the waitresses their pinkest caps; the landlady, in crimson gown and gold-chain, loomed like a local Major; the landlord shone, as it were, snuffed and trimmed: never, since the era of that actual Royal Duke, had the 'Duke's Head' smiled such a welcome.

Mr Durham, stepping out of the carriage on to the railway platform, and followed by Alan Hartley, Stella, and Arthur Tresham, indulged hopes that Jane might be there to meet him, and was disappointed. Not that the matter had undergone no discussion. Miss Charlmont, that unavoidable drive home from the picnic with a young Viscount and a tutor for *vis-à-vis** still rankling in her mind, had said, 'My dear, there would be no impropriety in our meeting George at the Station, and he would certainly be gratified.' But Jane had answered, 'Dear me, sister! George will keep, and I've not a moment to spare; only don't stay at home for me.'

So no one met Mr Durham. But when he presented himself at the private house on the Esplanade, Jane showed herself all smiling welcome, and made him quite happy by her pretty ways. True, she insisted on his not spending the evening with her; but she hinted so tenderly at such restrictions vanishing on the morrow, and so modestly at remarks people might make if he did stay, that he was compelled to yield the point and depart in great admiration of her reserve, though he could not help recollecting that his first wooing had progressed and prospered without any such amazing proprieties. But then the mother of Everilda Stella had seen the light in a second-floor back room at Gateshead,* and had married out of a circle where polite forms were not in the ascendant; whereas Jane Charlmont looked like a Duchess, or an Angel, or Queen Venus herself, and was altogether a different person. So Mr Durham, discomfited, but acquiescent, retreated to the 'Duke's Head', and there consoled himself with more turtle-soup and crusty old port than Dr Tyke would have sanctioned. Unfortunately Dr and Mrs Tyke were not coming down till the latest train that night from London, so Mr Durham gorged unrebuked. He had seen Lucy, and taken rather a fancy to her, in spite of her blemished face, and had pressed her to visit Orpingham Place as soon as ever he and Jane should have returned from the Continent. He preferred Lucy to Catherine, with whom he never felt quite at ease; she was so decided and self-possessed, and so much better bred than himself. Not that Backbone Durham admitted this last point of superiority; he did not acknowledge, but he winced under it. Lucy on her side had found him better than his photograph; and that was something.

After tea she was lying alone on the drawing-room sofa in the pleasant summer twilight; alone, because her sisters were busy over Jane's matters upstairs; alone with her own thoughts. She was thinking of very old days, and of days not so old and much more full of interest. She tried to think of Jane and her prospects; but against her will Alan Hartley's image intruded itself on her reverie, and she could not banish it. She knew from Mr Durham that he had come down for the wedding; she foresaw that they must meet, and shrank from the ordeal, even whilst she wondered how he would behave and how she herself should behave. Alone, and in the half darkness, she burned with shame-faced dread of her own possible weakness, and mortified self-love wrung tears from her eyes as she inwardly prayed for help.

The door opened, the maid announced Mr and Mrs Hartley.

Lucy, startled, would have risen to receive them, but Stella was too quick for her, and seizing both her hands, pressed her gently backwards on the sofa. 'Dear Miss Charlmont, you must not make a stranger of me, and my husband is an old friend. Mayn't I call you Lucy?'

So this was Alan's wife, this little, winning woman, still almost a child; this winning woman, who had won the only man Lucy ever cared for. It cost Lucy an effort to answer, and to make her welcome by her name of Stella.

Then Alan came forward and shook hands, looking cordial and handsome, with that kind tone of voice and tenderness of manner which had deceived poor Lucy once, but must never deceive her again. He began talking of their pleasant acquaintanceship in days of yore, of amusements they had shared, of things done together, and things spoken and not forgotten; it required the proof positive of Stella seated there smiling in her hat and scarlet feather, and with the wedding-ring on her small hand, to show even now that Alan only meant friendliness, when he might seem to mean so much more.

Lucy revolted under the fascination of his manner; feeling angry with herself that he still could wield power over her fancy, and angry a little with him for having made himself so much to her and no more. She insisted on leaving the sofa, rang the bell for a second edition of tea, and sent up the visitors' names to her sisters. When they came down she turned as much shoulder as good breeding tolerated towards Alan, and devoted all the attention she could command to Stella. Soon the two were laughing together over some feminine little bit of fun; then Lucy brought out an intricate piece of tatting,* which, when completed, was to find its way to Notting Hill – the antimacassar of Mr Durham's first visit there being, in fact, her handiwork; and, lastly, Lucy, once more for the moment with pretty pink cheeks and brightened eyes, conveyed her new friend upstairs to inspect Jane's bridal dress, white satin, under Honiton lace.

When the visit was over, and Lucy safe in the privacy of her own room, a sigh of relief escaped her, followed by a sentiment of deep thankfulness; she had met Alan again, and he had disappointed her. Yes, the spectre which had haunted her for weeks past had, at length, been brought face to face and had vanished. Perhaps surprise at his marriage had magnified her apparent disappointment, perhaps dread of continuing to love another woman's husband had imparted a morbid and unreal sensitiveness to her feelings; be this as it might, she had now seen Alan again, and had felt irritated by the very manner that used to charm. In the revulsion of her feelings she was almost ready to deem herself fortunate and Stella pitiable.

She felt excited, exalted, triumphant rather than happy; a little pained, and, withal, very glad. Life seemed to glow within her, her blood to course faster and fuller, her heart to throb, lightened of a load. Recollections which she had not dared face alone, Mr Hartley, by recalling, had stripped of their dangerous charm; had stripped of the tenderness she had dreaded, and the sting under which she had writhed; for he was the same, yet not the same. Now, for the first time, she suspected him not indeed of hollowness, but of shallowness.

She threw open her window to the glorious August moon and stars, and, leaning out, drank deep of the cool night air. She ceased to think of persons, of events, of feelings; her whole heart swelled, and became uplifted with a thankfulness altogether new to her, profound, transporting. When at length she slept, it was with moist eyes and smiling lips.

CHAPTER XV

The wedding was over. Jane might have looked still prettier but for an unmistakable expression of gratified vanity; Mr Durham might have borne himself still more pompously but for a deep-seated, wordless conviction, that his bride and her family looked down upon him. Months of scheming and weeks of fuss had ended in a marriage, to which the one party brought neither refinement nor tact, and the other neither respect nor affection.

Wedding guests, however, do not assemble to witness exhibitions of respect or affection, and may well dispense with tact and refinement when delicacies not in season are provided; therefore, the party on the Esplanade waxed gay as befitted the occasion, and expressed itself in toasts of highly improbable import.

The going off was, perhaps, the least successful point of the show. Catherine viewed flinging shoes* as superstitious, Jane as vulgar; therefore no shoes were to be flung. Mr Durham might have made head against 'superstitious', but dared not brave 'vulgar'; so he kept to himself the fact that he should hardly feel thoroughly married without a tributary shoe, and meanly echoed Jane's scorn. But Stella, who knew her father's genuine sentiment, chose to ignore 'superstition' and 'vulgarity' alike; so, at the last moment, she snatched off her own slipper, and dexterously hurled it over the carriage, to Jane's disgust (no love was lost between the two young ladies), and to Mr Durham's inward satisfaction.

Lucy had not joined the wedding party, not caring overmuch to see Jane marry the man who served her as a butt; but she peeped wistfully at the going off, with forebodings in her heart, which turned naturally into prayers, for the ill-matched couple. In the evening, however, when many of the party had returned to London, the few real friends and familiar acquaintances who reassembled as Miss Charlmont's guests found Lucy in the drawing-room, wrapped up in something gauzily becoming to indicate that she had been ill, and looking thin under her wraps.

In Miss Charlmont's idea a wedding-party should be at once mirthful and grave, neither dull nor frivolous. Dancing and cards were frivolous, conversation might prove dull; games were all frivolous except chess, which, being exclusive, favoured general dullness. These points she had impressed several times on Lucy, who was suspected of an inopportune hankering after bagatelle;* and who now sat in the snuggest corner of the sofa, feeling shy, and at a loss what topic to start that should appear neither dull nor frivolous.

Dr Tyke relieved her by turning her embarrassment into a fresh channel: what had she been doing to make herself 'look like a turnip-ghost* before its candle is lighted?'

'My dear Lucy!' cried Mrs Tyke, loud enough for everybody to hear her, 'you really do look dreadful, as if you were moped to death. You had much better come with the Doctor and me to the Lakes.* Now I beg you to say yes, and come.'

Alan heard with good-natured concern; Arthur Tresham heard as if he heard not. But the first greeting had been very cordial between him and Lucy, and he had not seemed to remark her faded face.

'Yes,' resumed Dr Tyke. 'Now that's settled. You pack up

tonight and start with us to-morrow, and you shall be doctored with the cream of drugs for nothing.'

But Lucy said the plan was preposterous, and she felt old and lazy.

Mrs Tyke caught her up: 'Old? my dear child! and I feeling young to this day!'

And the Doctor added: 'Why not be preposterous and happy? "*Quel che piace giova*,"* as our sunny neighbours say. Besides, your excuses are incredible: "Not at home," as the snail answered to the woodpecker's rap.'

Lucy laughed, but stood firm; Catherine protesting that she should please herself. At last a compromise was struck: Lucy, on her cousins' return from their tour, should go to Notting Hill, and winter there if the change did her good. 'If not,' said she, wearily, 'I shall come home again, to be nursed by Catherine.'

'If not,' said Dr Tyke, gravely for once, 'we may think about our all seeing Naples* together.'

Edith Sims, her hair and complexion toned down by candle-light, sat wishing Mr Ballantyne would come and talk to her; and Mr Ballantyne, unmindful of Edith at the other end of the room, sat making up his mind. Before the accident in the Drumble he had thought of Lucy with a certain distinction, since that accident he had felt uncomfortably in her debt, and now he sat reflecting that, once gone for the winter, she might be gone for good so far as himself was concerned. She was nice-looking and amiable; she was tender towards little motherless Frank; her fortune stood above rather than below what he had proposed to himself in a second wife: – if Edith could have read his thoughts, she would have smiled less complacently when at last he crossed over to talk to her of Brunette and investments, and when later still he handed her in to supper. As it was, candlelight and content became her, and she looked her best.

Mrs Gawkins Drum, beaming with good will, and harmonious in silver-grey moire under old point lace, contrasted favourably with her angular sister-in-law, whose strict truthfulness forbade her looking congratulatory: for now that she had seen the 'elegant man of talent' of her previsions, she could not but think that Jane had married his money-bags rather than himself: therefore Miss Drum looked severe, and when viewed in the light of a wedding guest, ominous.

Catherine, no less conscientious than her old friend, took an opposite line, and laboured her very utmost to hide mortification and misgivings, and to show forth that cheerful hospitality which befitted the occasion when contemplated from an ideal point of view; but ease was not amongst her natural gifts, and she failed to acquire it on the spur of an easy moment. 'Manners make the Man', 'Morals make the Man', kept running obstinately in her head, and she could not fit Mr Durham to either sentence. In all Brompton-on-Sea there was no heavier heart that night than Catherine Charlmont's.

CHAPTER XVI

November had come, the Tykes were settled at home again, and Lucy Charlmont sat in a railway-carriage on her way from Brompton-on-Sea to Notting Hill. Wrapped up in furs, and with a novel open on her lap, she looked very snug in her corner; she looked, moreover, plumper and brighter than at Jane's wedding-party. But her expression of unmistakable amusement was not derived from the novel lying unread in her lap: it had its source in recollections of Mr Ballantyne, who had made her an offer the day before, and who had obviously been taken aback when she rejected his suit. All her proneness to bring herself in in the wrong could not make her fear that she had even for one moment said or done, looked or thought, what ought to have misled him: therefore conscience felt at ease, and the comic side of his demeanour remained to amuse her, despite a decorous wish to feel for him. He had looked so particularly unimpulsive in the act of proposing, and then had appeared so much more disconcerted than grieved at her positive 'No', and had hinted so broadly that he hoped she would not talk about his offer, that she could not imagine the matter very serious to him: and if not to him assuredly to nobody else. 'I dare say it will be Edith Sims at last,' mused she, and wished them both well.

A year earlier his offer might have been a matter of mere indifference to her, but not now; for her birthday was just over, and it was gratifying to find herself not obsolete even at thirty. This birthday had loomed before her threateningly for months past, but now it was over; and it became a sensible relief to feel and look at thirty very much as she had felt and looked at twenty-nine. Her mirror bore witness to no glaring accession of age having come upon her in a single night. 'After all,' she mused, 'life isn't over at thirty.'* Her thoughts flew before her to

Notting Hill; if they dwelt on any one in especial, it was not on Alan Hartley.

Not on Alan Hartley, though she foresaw that they must meet frequently; for he and Stella were at Kensington again, planning to stay there over Christmas. Stella she rather liked than disliked; and as she no longer deemed her lot enviable, to see more of her would be no grievance. Mr Tresham also was in London, and likely to remain there; for since his return from the East he had taken himself to task for idleness, and had joined a band of good men in an effort to visit and relieve the East-end poor* in their squalid homes. His hobby happened to be emigration, but he did not ride his hobby rough-shod over his destitute neighbours. He was in London hard at work, and by no means faring sumptuously every day; but glad sometimes to get a mouthful of pure night air and of something more substantial at Notting Hill. He and Lucy had not merely renewed acquaintance at the wedding-party, but had met more than once afterwards during a week's holiday he gave himself at the seaside; had met on the beach, or in country lanes, or down in some of the many drumbles. They had botanised in company; and one day had captured a cuttle-fish together, which Lucy insisted on putting safe back into the sea before they turned homewards. They had talked of what grew at their feet or lay before their eyes; but neither of them had alluded to those old days when first they had known and liked each other, though they obviously liked each other still.

Lucy, her thoughts running on some one who was not Alan, would have made a very pretty picture. A sort of latent smile pervaded her features without deranging them, and her eyes, gazing out at the dreary autumn branches, looked absent and soft; soft, tender, and pleased, though with a wistful expression through all.

The short, winter-like day had darkened by the time London Bridge was reached. Lucy stepped on to the platform in hopes of being claimed by Dr Tyke's man; but no such functionary appeared, neither was the fat coachman discernible along the line of vehicles awaiting occupants. It was the first time Lucy had arrived in London without being either accompanied or met at the Station, and the novel position made her feel shy and a little nervous; so she was glad to stand unobtrusively against a wall, whilst more enterprising individuals found or missed their luggage. She preferred waiting, and she had to wait whilst passengers craned their necks, elbowed their neighbours, blundered, bawled, worried the Company's servants, and found everything correct after all. At last the huge mass of luggage dwindled to three boxes, one carpet-bag, and one hamper, which were Lucy's own; and which, with herself, a porter consigned to a cab. Thus ended her anxieties.

From London Bridge to Notting Hill the cabman of course knew his way, but in the mazes of Notting Hill he appealed to his fare for guidance. Lucy informed him that Appletrees House stood in its own large garden, and was sure to be well lighted up; and that it lay somewhere to the left, up a steepish hill. A few wrong turnings first made and next retrieved, a few lucky guesses, brought them to a garden-wall, which a passing postman told them belonged to Dr Tyke's premises. Lucy thrust her head out, and thought it all looked very like, except that the house itself stood enveloped in grim darkness; she had never noticed it look so dark before: could it be that she had been forgotten and every one had gone out?

They drove round the little sweep and knocked; waited, and knocked again. It was not till the grumbling cabman had knocked loud and long a third time that the door was opened by a crying maid-servant, who admitted Lucy into the unlighted hall with the explanation: 'O Miss, Miss, master has had a fit, and mistress is taking on so you can hear her all over the place.' At the same instant a peal of screaming, hysterical laughter rang through the house.

Without waiting for a candle, Lucy ran stumbling up the broad staircase, guided at once by her familiarity with the house and by her cousin's screams. On the second-floor landing one door stood open revealing light at last, and Lucy ran straight in amongst the lights and the people. For a moment she was dazzled, and distinguished nothing clearly: in another moment she saw and understood all. Arthur Tresham and a strange gentleman were standing pale and silent at the fireplace, an old servant, stooping over the pillows, was busied in some noiseless way, and Mrs Tyke had flung herself face downwards on the bed beside her husband.

Her husband? No, not her husband any longer, for she was a widow.

CHAPTER XVII

A week of darkened windows, of condolence-cards and hushed

inquiries, of voices and faces saddened, of footsteps treading softly on one landing. A week of many tears and quiet sorrow; of many words, for in some persons grief speaks; and of half-silent sympathy, for in some even sympathy is silent. A week wherein to weigh this world and find it wanting, wherein also to realise the far more exceeding weight of the other. A week begun with the hope whose blossom goes up as dust, and ending with the sure and certain hope of the resurrection.

In goods and chattels, Mrs Tyke remained none the poorer for her husband's death. He had left almost everything to her and absolutely at her disposal, well knowing that their old faithful servants were no less dear to her than to himself, and having on his side no poor relations to provide for. His nephew Alan Hartley, and Mr Tresham, were appointed his executors. Alan the good-natured, addicted to shirking trouble in general, consistently shirked this official trouble in particular. Arthur Tresham did what little work there was to do, and did it in such a way as veiled his friend's shortcomings. Mrs Tyke, with a life-long habit of leaning on some one, came, as a matter of course, to lean on him, and appealed to him as to all sorts of details, without once considering whether the time he devoted to her service was reclaimed out of his work, or leisure, or rest; he best knew, and the knowledge remained with him. Alan, though sincerely sorry for his uncle's death, cut private jokes with Stella about his co-executor's frequent visits to Appletrees House, and ignored the shortcomings which curtailed their necessity.

Mrs Tyke in her bereavement, clung to Lucy, and was thoroughly amiable and helpless. She would sit for hours over the fire, talking and crying her eyes and her nose red, whilst Lucy wrote her letters, or grappled with her bills. Then they would both grow sleepy, and doze off in opposite chimney-corners. So the maid might find them when she brought up tea, or so Arthur when he dropped in on business, or possibly on pleasure. Mrs Tyke would sometimes merely open sleepy eyes, shake hands, and doze off again; but Lucy would sit up wide awake in a moment, ready to listen to all his long stories about his poor people. Soon she took to making things for them, which he carried away in his pocket, or, when too bulky for his pocket, in a parcel under the arm. At last it happened, that they began talking of old days, before he went to the East, and then each found that the other remembered a great deal about those old days. So gradually it came to pass that, from looking back together, they took also to looking forward together.

Lucy's courtship was most prosaic. Old women's flannel and old men's rheumatism alternated with some more usual details of love-making, and the exchange of rings was avowedly an exchange of old rings. Arthur presented Lucy with his mother's wedding-guard; but Lucy gave him a fine diamond solitaire which had been her father's, and the romantic corner of her heart was gratified by the inequality of the gifts. She would have preferred a little more romance certainly on his side; if not less sense, at least more sentiment; something reasonable enough to be relied upon, yet unreasonable enough to be flattering. 'But one cannot have everything,' she reflected, meekly remembering her own thirty years; and she felt what a deep resting-place she had found in Arthur's trusty heart, and how shallow a grace had been the flattering charm of Alan's manner. Till, weighing her second love against her first, tears, at once proud and humble, filled her eyes, and 'one cannot have everything' was forgotten in 'I can never give him back half enough.'

After the exchange of rings, she announced her engagement to Catherine and Mrs Tyke; to Jane also and Mr Durham in few words; and as all business connected with Dr Tyke's will was already satisfactorily settled, and Appletrees House about to pass into fresh hands, she prepared to return home. Mrs Tyke, too purposeless to be abandoned to her own resources, begged an invitation to Brompton-on-Sea, and received a cordial welcome down from both sisters. Arthur was to remain at work in London till after Easter; and then to join his friends at the seaside, claim his bride, and take her away to spend their honeymoon beside that beautiful blue Bosphorus which had made him forget her.

If there was a romantic moment in their courtship, it was the moment of parting at the noisy, dirty, crowded railway-station, when Arthur terrified Lucy, to her great delight, by standing on the carriage-step, and holding her hand locked fast in his own, an instant after the train had started.

CHAPTER XVIII

A short chapter makes fitting close to a short story.

In mid May, on a morning which set forth the perfection either of sunny spring warmth or of breezy summer freshness, Arthur Tresham and Lucy Charlmont took each other for better for worse, till death should them part. Mr Gawkins Drum gave away the bride; Miss Drum appeared auspicious as a rainbow; Catherine glowed and expanded with unselfish happiness; Mrs Gawkins Drum pronounced the bride graceful, elegant, but old-looking; Mr Durham contributed a costly wedding present, accompanied by a speech both ostentatious and affectionate; Jane displayed herself a little disdainful, a little cross, and supremely handsome; Alan and Stella – there was a young Alan now, a comical little fright, more like mother than father – Alan and Stella seemed to enjoy their friend's wedding as light-heartedly as they had enjoyed their own. No tears were shed, no stereotyped hypocrisies uttered, no shoes flung; this time a true man and a true woman who loved and honoured each other, and whom no man should put asunder, were joined together; and thus the case did not lend itself to any tribute of lies, miscalled white.

Four months after their marriage Mr Tresham was hard at work again in London among his East-end poor; while Lucy, taking a day's holiday at Brompton-on-Sea, sat in the old familiar drawing-room, Catherine's exclusively now. She had returned from the East blooming, vigorous, full of gentle fun and kindly happiness: so happy, that she would not have exchanged her present lot for aught except her own future; so happy, that it saddened her to believe Catherine less happy than herself.

The two sisters sat at the open window, alike yet unlike: the elder handsome, resolute, composed; the younger with the old wistful expression in her tender beautiful eyes. They had talked of Jane, who, though not dissatisfied with her lot, too obviously despised her husband; once lately, she had written of him as the 'habitation-tax' paid for Orpingham Place: of Jane, who was too worldly either to keep right in the spirit, or go wrong in the letter. They had talked, and they had fallen silent; for Catherine, who loved no one on earth as she loved her frivolous sister, could best bear in silence the sting of shame and grief for her sake.

Full in view of the drawing-room windows spread the sea, beautiful, strong, resistless, murmuring; the sea which had cast a burden on Catherine's life, and from which she now never meant to absent herself; the sea from which Lucy had fled in the paroxysm of her nervous misery.

At last Lucy spoke again very earnestly, – 'Oh, Catherine, I cannot bear to be so happy when I think of you! If only you, too, had a future.'

Catherine leaned over her happy sister and gave her one kiss, a rare sign with her of affectionate emotion. Then she turned to face the open sky and sea. – 'My dear,' she answered, whilst her eyes gazed beyond clouds and waves, and rested on one narrow streak of sunlight which glowed at the horizon, – 'My dear, my future seems further off than yours; but I certainly have a future, and I can wait.'

EXTRACTS FROM PROSE AND CORRESPONDENCE

EXTRACTS FROM PROSE AND CORRESPONDENCE

'They lack almost entirely the peculiar qualities which attract us in the letters of distinguished people,' wrote Virginia Woolf of Christina Rossetti's correspondence; '– they are not remarkable for their wit, nor do they tell us any secrets.'[1] But while no more confessional than her poetry, the letters do contain illuminating passages – sometimes no more than a sentence or phrase – giving a glimpse of Rossetti's personal and intellectual views available nowhere else in her writing. A selection of such passages is presented here, together with short extracts from her prose works which offer a wider-than-devotional window onto her memories, opinions, desires. Readers wishing to learn more about her contemplative writing are advised to go directly to Rossetti's devotional books published between 1874 and 1892, as listed in the checklist of her writings on page 476.

The selection here is necessarily brief, and arranged chronologically.

To W. E. Aytoun, Blackwood's Magazine, *1 August 1854*

William Edmonstoune Aytoun (1813–1865) was Professor of Rhetoric at Edinburgh University and a contributing editor to *Blackwood's Magazine*. Author of ballad-romances on Scottish themes, Aytoun had also recently published a satire on the Spasmodic school, which made him rather unlikely to approve of any verses in the as yet unfashionable 'Pre-Raphaelite' mode – unless CGR, like others, had taken the Spasmodic satire as a genuine article.

Rossetti was somewhat disingenuous in describing herself as a 'nameless rhymester': she had already published two poems in the *Athenaeum* (1848), and others in the *Germ* (1850).

[1] 'Letters of Christina Rossetti', *Essays of Virginia Woolf*, ed. Andrew McNeillie, Hogarth Press, London 1986, vol. 1, pp. 225–7.

A 'non avenue' is a dead end or cul-de-sac. There is no evidence that Aytoun favoured CGR with a reply or any comments on her work.

Sir,

As an unknown and unpublished writer, I beg leave to bespeak your indulgence for laying before you the enclosed verses.

I am not unaware, sir, that the editor of a magazine looks with dread and contempt upon the offerings of a nameless rhymester, and that the feeling is in nineteen cases out of twenty a just and salutary one. It is certainly not for me to affirm that I am the one-twentieth in question, but speaking as I am to a poet, I hope that I shall not be misunderstood as guilty of egotism or foolish vanity when I say that my love for what is good in the work of others teaches me that there is something above the despicable in mine; that poetry is with me, not a mechanism but an impulse and a reality, and that I know my aims in writing to be pure and directed to that which is true and right. I do not blush to confess that, with these feelings and beliefs, it would afford me some gratification to place my productions before others and ascertain how far what I do is expressive of mere individualism and how far it is capable of approving itself to the general sense. It would be a personal favour to me if you would look into the enclosed with an eye not inevitably to the waste paper basket, and a further obligation if, whatever the result, you would vouchsafe me a few words as to the fate of the verses. I am quite conscious that volunteer contributors have no right to expect this of an editor; I ask it simply as a courtesy. It is mortifying to have done something sincerely, offer it in good faith, and be treated as a 'non avenue'.

I am, Sir,
Your obedient servant
Christina G. Rossetti

To David Masson, Macmillan's Magazine, *19 January 1861*

David Masson (1822–1907) was the first editor of *Macmillan's Magazine*. In 1865 he was appointed Professor of English Literature at Edinburgh University. His wife was Rosalind Orme, daughter of a family well known to the Rossettis and herself a friend of CGR in the early 1850s – hence CGR's diffidence in submitting her verses, and her concluding sentiments.

The poems submitted with this letter included 'Up-hill' and 'A Birthday', which Masson immediately accepted and published; in turn this led his proprietor, Alexander Macmillan, to publish CGR's first collection, *Goblin Market and Other Poems* in 1862.

(In *The Rossetti-Macmillan Letters*, ed. L. M. Packer, 1963, p. 60, this letter is mistakenly identified as relating to poems submitted by CGR on behalf of Isa Craig.)

My dear Mr Masson,

Bored as you are with contributions, many of them doubtless being poems good or bad by unknown authors, I feel ashamed to add the enclosed to the heap: the more so as personal acquaintanceship might make it more unpleasant for you to decline them. Will you therefore give me credit for sincerity when I beg you to accept all or any of the enclosed for *Macmillan's Magazine* in case you think them of any use, and to pass upon them a condign sentence of rejection in the (highly probable) opposite case.

With William's and my own kindest regards to all at home, believe me.

Truly yours
Christina G. Rossetti

To Alexander Macmillan, 1 December 1863

Alexander Macmillan (1818–1896) was head of the publishing firm bearing his family name and the founder of the eponymous magazine, one of the leading periodicals of the day. *Goblin Market and Other Poems* was published by him in spring 1862. The cheque referred to here related to the publication of 'One Day' in *Macmillan's Magazine* in December 1863; CGR's enclosed receipt was for three guineas.

Adelaide Proctor (1825–1864) was a fellow poet, and close friend of Bessie Rayner Parkes, whom CGR also knew; she had published *Legends and Lyrics* (1858) and is chiefly remembered today as author of 'The Lost Chord', a poem more parodied than read. Jean Ingelow (1820–1897) was also a fellow poet, a 'new star in the firmament', whose *Poems* (1863), issued by Longmans, proved immediately popular; it went into numerous editions, causing CGR to confess to a distinct sense of envy. She and Ingelow became friends in 1865, one result being CGR's successful approach to Roberts Bros, Ingelow's American publisher.

Somewhat to CGR's chagrin, though much praised the first edition of *Goblin Market* proved a slow seller. Macmillan nevertheless regarded her as one of his firm's finest authors. Her second collection was compiled in 1865 and published in 1866 as *The Prince's Progress and Other Poems*.

My dear Mr Macmillan,

I enclose my receipt and many thanks for the cheque – and many more thanks for the kind words of encouragement you give me. Miss Proctor I am not afraid of: but Miss Ingelow (judging by extracts; I have not yet seen the actual volume) – would be a formidable rival to most men, and to any woman. Indeed I have been bewailing that she did not publish with you.

Few things within the range of probability would give me greater pleasure than to see in print my second volume: but I am sadly convinced that I have not by me materials, equal both in quantity and quality, to what are already before the public. And, if one conviction can go beyond another, I am yet more firmly convinced that my system of not writing against the grain is the right one, at any rate as concerns myself. Had a second edition of *Goblin Market* been called for, one considerably augmented would have been at once feasible: but a second volume must I fear stand over to the indefinite future.

Yours very truly
Christina G. Rossetti

To Dante Gabriel Rossetti, 10 February 1865

Written from Hastings, where CGR was completing *The Prince's Progress* and compiling her second collection for publication; DGR had evidently suggested replacing the Alchemist episode in the poem with a tournament.

Charles Cayley was currently completing 'a classic epic in quantitative hexameters' in the form of a transition of the *Iliad* in this metre; eleven-syllable hendecasyllabics are the metre of parts of Tennyson's 'Maud', and other poems.

My dear Gabriel,

I am indulging in a holiday from all attempt at *Progress* whilst Mamma is with me: she gone (alas!) I hope to set-to with a will. Thanks for annotations, to be attended to. Do you know, I don't think it would have done to write the Alchemist without the metric jolt, however unfortunate the original selection of such rhythm may have been: but we will file and polish. How shall I express my sentiments about the terrible tournament? Not a phrase to be relied on, not a correct knowledge on the subject, not the faintest impulse of inspiration, incites me to the tilt: and looming before me in horrible bugbeardom stand TWO tournaments in Tennyson's *Idylls*. Moreover, the Alchemist, according to original convention, took the place of the lists: remember this in my favour, please. You see, were you next to propose my writing a classic epic in quantitative hexameters or in the hendecasyllables which might almost trip-up Tennyson, what could I do? Only what I feel inclined to do in the present instance – plead goodwill but inability. Also (but this you may scorn as the blind partiality of a parent) my actual *Prince* seems to me invested with a certain artistic congruity of construction not lightly to be despised . . .

To Dante Gabriel Rossetti, April 1870

Written in response to a letter (which has not survived) from DGR, who was currently staying in Sussex, together with W. J. Stillman, former editor of *The Crayon*, while his own first collection *Poems* was published. DGR had apparently passed on Stillman's regret that CGR did not tackle larger, 'public' themes in the manner of Elizabeth Barrett Browning. But CGR's response in disingenuous: she knew that 'turning to politics or philanthropy' in verse did not necessarily lead to poetry. In any case she was always reluctant to announce a new publication or project before it was completed. 'Give me the withered leaves' is a self-mocking reference to her own 'Song'; she had already published two books and finished both *SingSong* and *Commonplace*, as well as having more than a few 'groans' (the joking family term for her melancholy laments) ready for publication, posthumous or otherwise.

. . . It is impossible to go on singing out-loud to one's one-stringed lyre. It is not in me, and therefore it will never come out of me, to turn to politics or philanthropy with Mrs Browning: such manysidedness I leave to a greater than I, and, having said my say, may well sit silent. 'Give me the withered leaves I chose' may include the dog-eared leaves of one's first, last, and only book. If ever the fire rekindles availably, *tanto meglio per me*: at the worst, I suppose a few posthumous groans may be found amongst my remains. Here is a great discovery, 'Women are not Men', and you must not expect me to possess a tithe of your capacities, though I humbly – or proudly – lay claim to family likeness . . .

To Augusta Webster, c. 1878–9

Augusta Webster (1837–1894) was a fellow poet, whose work CGR admired, a newspaper columnist and advocate of women's suffrage, focused at this date on extending the franchise to all householders on the same basis as men – which excluded non-householders such as adult sons living at home, and would have excluded married women such as Mrs Webster. CGR's reference to 'shooting ahead of her instructresses' alludes to the fact that the suffrage campaign was generally restricted to voting rights, not to the right of women to stand for election as Members of Parliament. CGR's views on these matters were complex and contradictory, leading her in the end to refuse public support for the female franchise.

. . . You express yourself with such cordial openness that I feel encouraged to endeavour also after self-expression – no easy matter sometimes. I write as I am thinking and feeling, but I premise that I have not even to my own apprehension gone deep into the question; at least not in the sense in which many who *have* studied it would require depth of me. In one sense I feel as if I had gone deep, for my objection seems to myself a fundamental one underlying the whole structure of female claims.

Does it not appear as if the Bible was based upon an understood unalterable distinction between men and women, their position, duties, privileges? Not arrogating to myself but most earnestly desiring to attain to the character of a humble orthodox Xtian, so does it appear to me; not only under the Old but also under the New Dispensation. The fact of the Priesthood being exclusively man's, leaves me in no doubt that the highest functions are not in this world open to both sexes: and if not all, then a selection must be made and a line drawn somewhere. – On the other hand if female rights are sure to be overborne for lack of female voting influence, then I confess I feel disposed to shoot ahead of my instructresses, and to assert that female *M. P's* are only right and reasonable. Also I take exception to the exclusion of married women from the suffrage – for who so apt as Mothers – all previous arguments allowed for the moment – to protect the interests of themselves and of their offspring? I do think if anything ever does sweep away the barrier of sex, and make the female not a giantess or a heroine but at once and full grown into a hero and a giant, it is that mighty maternal love which makes little birds and little beasts as well as little women matches for very big adversaries . . .

To Dante Gabriel Rossetti, 2 December 1881

Written when DGR was 'deeply melancholy' and agitated by 'matters of very old as well as more recent date' and when he expressed to WMR a desire to consult a priest. He never did so, however, and died some few months later in much the same state of gloom and guilt. In this letter CGR expresses both her love for DGR and her gratitude for the (then controversial) practice of confession in the Anglican Church. The 'first time' alluded to would seem to relate to a spiritual crisis such as described in *Maude*.

Isaac Williams (1802–1865) was a Tractarian poet, author of *The Cathedral* (1838).

My dearest Gabriel,

I write because I cannot but write, for you are continually in my thoughts and always in my heart, much more in our Mother's who sends you her love and dear blessing.

I want to assure you that, however harassed by memory or by anxiety you may be, I have (more or less) heretofore gone through the same ordeal. I have borne myself till I became unbearable by myself, and then I have found help in confession and absolution and spiritual counsel, and relief inexpressible. Twice in my life I tried to suffice myself with measures short of this, but nothing would do; the first time was of course in my youth before my general confession, the second time was when circumstances had led me (rightly or wrongly) to break off the practice. But now for years past I have resumed the habit, and I hope not to continue it profitlessly.

'Tis like frail man to love to walk on high,
But to be lowly is to be like God',

is a couplet (Isaac Williams) I thoroughly assent to.

I ease my own heart by telling you all this, and I hope I do not weary yours. Don't think of me merely as the younger sister whose glaring faults are known to you, but as a devoted friend also.

From Letter and Spirit: Notes on the Commandments, *1883*

Eve made a mistake, 'being *deceived*' she was in the transgression: Adam made no mistake: his was an error of will, hers partly of judgment; nevertheless both proved fatal. Eve equally with Adam was created sinless: each had a specially vulnerable point, but this apparently not the same point. It is no degree at variance with the Sacred Record to picture to ourselves Eve, that first and typical woman, as indulging quite innocently sundry refined tastes and aspirations, a castle-building spirit (if so it may be called) a feminine boldness and directness of aim combined with a no less feminine guessiness as to means. Her very virtues may have opened the door to temptation. By birthright gracious and accessible, she lends an ear to all petitions from all petitioners. She desires to instruct ignorance, to rectify misapprehension: 'unto the pure all things are pure', and she never suspects even the serpent . . .

. . . it is no light offence to traduce the dead, to blacken recklessly their memory, to cultivate not tenderness for them, helpless and inoffensive as they now lie with all their sins of omission or commission on their heads. Party feeling, whether called religious zeal or national antagonism or political creed, becomes simple malice and is simply devilish when it leads us not only to condemn opponents (or it may even be those merely to whom we ourselves are opposed) but to wish that they may really be as unworthy as history or rumour makes them, to court and hug and blaze abroad every tittle of evidence which tells against them, and turn a dull ear and lukewarm heart to everything which tells in their favour. 'Charity rejoiceth not in iniquity, but rejoiceth in the truth'. It is a solemn thing to write history.

To Edmund Gosse, 26 March 1884

Edmund Gosse (1848–1928), later famous as the author of *Father and Son* (1907), was at this time attempting to make a career in literature and literary journalism. He first met CGR around 1870, and in the early 1880s commissioned an article from her on Dante for the *Century Magazine* (New York), which appeared in 1884. At the same time, he had the idea of printing an interview with CGR on the origins of her 'poetic schooling', to which this letter is the response. There is no evidence that Gosse carried out the interview.

CGR's reference to feeling somewhat pre-engaged until Easter refers to her High Anglican practice of treating Lent as a solemn season when spiritual commitments were uppermost.

Mary Robinson's article appeared in *Harper's Magazine* in 1883, some six months after DGR's death. The cottage 30 miles from London was the home of CGR's maternal grandparents at Holmer Green in Buckinghamshire, the inspiration for some of the poems in *SingSong*. The 'early booklet . . . printed but not published' was *Verses* (1847), produced by CGR's grandfather, and circulated to family and friends.

. . . I may be described as habitually at home in the afternoon, and on hand and with solitude within easy reach; tho' until Easter I feel (in a sense) somewhat pre-engaged. So far your enterprise is easy. The difficulty will encounter you – if, that is, you ever nerve yourself to encounter it – one stage further on, when even your skill as an interviewer may fail to discover my poetic schooling. When was it, and what was it? I think Mary Robinson's very lifelike sketch of our family circle (*see* Harper's article on our Gabriel) shows for me as well as for him that whilst our 'school' was everything, it was no one definite thing. I, as last and least in the group, may remind you that besides the clever and cultivated parents who headed us all, I in particular beheld far ahead of myself the clever sister and two clever brothers who were a little (tho' but a little) my seniors. And as to acquirements I lagged out of all proportion behind them, and have never overtaken them to this day.

If any one thing schooled me in the direction supposed, it was perhaps the delightful idle liberty to prowl all alone about my Grandfather's cottage grounds some 30 miles from London, entailing in my childhood a long stage coach journey! This privilege came to an end when I was eight years old, if not earlier. The grounds were quite small and on the simplest scale – but in those days *to me* they were vast, varied, worth exploring. After those charming holidays ended, I remained pent up in London till I was a great girl of 14, when delight reawakened at the sight of primroses in a railway cutting – a prelude to many lovely country sights.

So you see all sorts of things may have influenced me, while nothing in particular trained me . . . Do you think it would help you at all to glance at that early booklet of mine, which was printed but not published in (I think) 1847? Perhaps you know of its existence, as now and then it crops up in a catalogue, or what not. I have a spare copy, if you would care for it . . .

From Time Flies: A Reading Diary, *1885*

The cottage referred to was at Holmer Green, where the Rossetti children spent holidays up till 1838; the incident described therefore took place before CGR was nine years old.

My first vivid experience of death (if so I may term it) occurred in early childhood in the grounds of a cottage.

This little cottage was my familiar haunt: its grounds were my inexhaustible delight. They then seemed to me spacious, though I now know them to have been narrow and commonplace.

So in these grounds, perhaps in the orchard, I lighted upon a dead mouse. The dead mouse moved my sympathy: I took him up, buried him comfortably in a mossy bed, and bore the spot in mind.

It may have been a day or two afterwards that I returned, removed the moss coverlet, and looked . . . a black insect emerged. I fled in horror, and for long years ensuing I never mentioned this ghastly adventure to anyone.

Now looking back at the incident I see that neither impulse was unreasonable, although the sympathy and the horror were alike childish.

Only now contemplating death from a wider and wiser viewpoint, I would fain reverse the order of these feelings: dwelling less and less on the mere physical disgust, while more and more on the rest and safety; on the perfect peace of death, please God.

From Time Flies: A Reading Diary, *1885*

The incident described took place at Holmer Green; CGR's companion was her sister Maria.

CGR was an active supporter of animal rights and the vigorous Victorian anti-vivisection movement, which campaigned for many years; dissection of live animals was still widely practised for observation and demonstration as well as research.

To this hour I remember a certain wild strawberry growing on a hedgerow bank, watched day by day while it ripened by a little girl and by my yet younger self.

My elder instructed me not to pluck it prematurely, and I complied.

I do not know which of us was to have had it at last, or whether we were to have halved it. As it was we watched, and as it turned out we watched in vain: for a snail, or some such marauder, must have forestalled us at a happy moment. One fatal day we found it half-eaten, and good for nothing.

Thus then we had watched in vain: or was it altogether in vain? On a very lowly level we had obeyed a counsel of prudence, and had practised self-restraint.

And shall the baulked watches of after-life prove in vain? 'Let patience have her perfect work'.

. . .

'Half-eaten and good for nothing' said I of the strawberry. I need not have expressed myself with such sweeping contempt.

Some small children may have been glad to finish up that wreck. Some children might not have disdained the final bite.

Yet to confine myself to snails and their peers: why should they not have a share in strawberries?

Man is very apt to contemplate himself out of all proportion to his surroundings . . .

Fruits for man, green herbs for other living creatures, including creepers on the earth, is the decree in Genesis. Thus for the Garden of Eden: and why not thus, as regards the spirit of the decree, here and now?

But man, alas! finds it convenient here to snap off a right and there to chip away a due. Greed grudges their morsel to hedgerow birds, and idleness robs the provident hare of his winter haystack, and science pares away at the living creature bodily. 'And what will ye do in the end thereof?'

From Time Flies: A Reading Diary, *1885*

The incident here described took place in a guest room at the All Saints' sanatorium and convalescent home in Eastbourne, Sussex, where CGR stayed in the 1870s while visiting her sister, a member of the All Saints' Sisterhood.

If ever I deciphered a 'Parable of Nature', surely I did so one summer night . . .

The gas was alight in my little room with its paperless bare wall.

On that wall appeared a spider, himself dark and defined, his shadow no less dark and scarcely if at all less defined.

They jerked, zigzagged, advanced, retreated, he and his shadow posturing in ungainly, indissoluble harmony. He seemed exasperated, fascinated, desperately endeavouring and utterly helpless.

What could it all mean? One meaning and one only suggested itself. That spider saw without recognising his black double, and was mad to disengage himself from the horrible pursuing inalienable presence.

I stood watching him awhile. (Presumably when I turned off the gas he composed himself)

To me this self-haunted spider appears a figure of each obstinate impenitent sinner, who having outlived enjoyment remains isolated irretrievably with his own horrible loathesome self.

And if thus in time, how throughout eternity?

From Time Flies: A Reading Diary, *1885*

Interruptions are vexatious.

Granted. But what is an interruption?

An interruption is something, is anything, which breaks in upon our occupation of the moment. For instance: a frivolous remark when we are absorbed, a selfish call when we are busy, an idle noise out of time, an intrusive sight out of place.

Now our occupations spring? . . . from within: for they are the outcome of our own will.

And interruptions arrive? . . . from without. Obviously from without, otherwise we could and would ward them off.

Our occupation, then, is that which we select. Our interruption is that which is sent us.

But hence it would appear that the occupation may be wilful, while the interruption must be Providential.

A startling view of occupations and interruptions!

. . .

Ah but, that which is frivolous, selfish, idle, intrusive, is clearly not Providential.

As regards the doer, no: as regards the sufferer, yes.

I think we quite often misconceive the genuine appointed occupation of a given moment, perhaps even of our whole lives. We take for granted that we ought to enjoy a pleasure, or complete a task, or execute a work, or serve someone we love: while what we are really then and there called to is to forego a pleasure, or break off a task, or leave a cherished work incomplete, or serve someone we find it difficult to love.

Interruptions seem well nigh to form the occupation of some lives.

Not an occupation one would choose; yet none the less profitable on that account . . .

To Lucy Brown Rossetti, 11 January 1886

Lucy Rossetti (1843–1894), elder daughter of Ford Madox Brown, married William Rossetti in 1874; in her later years she suffered pneumonia and spent much time away from London. This letter was written when she was on the Isle of Wight and CGR was in London, where she kept house for and nursed her elderly aunts. Olive, Arthur, Helen and Mary were CGR's nieces and nephew. Lizzie was DGR's wife, who died in 1862.

Katherine Tynan (1861–1931) was an Irish poet, now best known as a friend of W. B. Yeats, who called on CGR and WMR, bearing copies of her first collection, *Louise de la Vallière* (1885); that to CGR was inscribed 'to the first of living women poets by the last and least'. As a consequence of her fame, CGR was the recipient of many such volumes, which her scrupulous honesty made it difficult to praise – hence her humorous warning to Lucy and the children. Happily, Lucy Rossetti was a painter rather than a poet, and unlikely to press sonnets upon her sister-in-law.

My dear Lucy,

I felt an impulse to write to you on Saturday, but 'Time flew' and it remained undone. Now I sit down to respond to your last delightful letter. We get good news of you from William, whom we last saw on Friday: I hope when he has joined you – as he was then planning to do one day this week – you will rejoice his heart by coming into fuller bloom before his eyes. I wonder whether Miss Tynan told him what she told me, that she preferred your portrait to Lizzie's – and I wonder whether you will think this worth telling you! (I should appreciate it, were it I.) Miss Tynan is an agreeable young woman enough, and deferential to puff one up like puff-paste. She has given me a volume of *Vagrant Verse* by her friend Miss Rosa Mulholland, but I rate higher K.T.'s own muse. Sad to say, another unknown has presented me with a volume of Sonnets of which (so far as I have waded) the less said the better *as poetry*; my note of thanks turned out jejune, though the spirit is admirable and I found one point to praise. Don't you ever publish a volume unless you are quite sure you can excell (say) Mr W. Shakespeare; or, if not, at least don't bestow it on poor disconcerted me! a warning to be early and with absolute impartiality brought home to Olive, Arthur, Helen, Mary, who exhibit alarming tendencies. . . .

From The Face of the Deep: A Devotional Commentary on the Apocalypse, *1892*

Towards the end of her life CGR visited Brighton with her niece Olive, who observed that her aunt seemed hypnotised by the sight of the octopus in the aquarium.

. . . in the serpent tribe we observe ghastly, loathly, emblematic likenesses of Satan . . . silent, insinuating, gliding, they are upon us before we know that they are near. Yet of all living creatures which my memory records no one in Satanic suggestion approaches, to my own thinking, the octopus.

One single small octopus in an aquarium is all I have seen. It had a fascination for me. Inert as it often appeared, it bred and tickled a perpetual suspense: will it do something? will it emerge from the background of its water den? I have seen it swallow its live prey in an eyewink, change from a stony colour to an appalling lividness, elongate unequal feelers and set them flickering like a flame, sit still with an air of immemorial old age amongst the lifeless refuse of its once living meals. I had to remind myself that this vivid figure of wickedness was not in truth itself wickedness.

NOTES

Abbreviations

CGR Christina Georgina Rossetti
CP *Complete Poems of Christina Rossetti*, ed. R. W. Crump, 3 vols, 1979–90
DGR Dante Gabriel Rossetti
EBB Elizabeth Barrett Browning
FLR Frances Lavinia Rossetti (CGR's mother)
MFR Maria Francesca Rossetti
PW *Poetical Works of Christina Rossetti*, ed. William Michael Rossetti, 1904
WMR William Michael Rossetti

POETRY

Lyrics, Ballads and Shorter Poems

p. 3 Heaven: the second of CGR's compositions to be copied into the MS notebook.

p. 4 Charity: printed in *Verses* (1847). The MS text has a note by MFR: 'The foregoing verses are imitated from that beautiful little poem "Virtue" by George Herbert.'

p. 4 Lines to my Grandfather: CGR's grandfather, Gaetano Polidori, encouraged her writing and printed her first collection in 1847. These lines date from the time of CGR's breakdown in 1845 and preceded six months' poetic silence.

p. 5 Hope in Grief: written just before CGR's fifteenth birthday. Some phrases echo Isaac Williams (1802–1865), a Tractarian writer much read by CGR and MFR.

p. 6 On the Death of a Cat: MS title 'On the Death of Aunt Eliza's Cat aged ten years & a half'.

p. 9 Sappho: at this date the Greek poet Sappho, whose work is known only in fragments, was figured both as the 'tenth Muse' and as the pre-eminent classical poet of unhappy love, said to have killed herself in despair. In December 1848 CGR wrote a longer but less intense lament entitled 'What Sappho would have said had her leap cured instead of killing her', in reference to the legend that Sappho flung herself from the cliff of Leukos.

p. 9 Will These Hands Ne'er be Clean?: MS title 'To a Murderer'. The revised title comes from *Macbeth*, which may have furnished CGR's inspiration.

p. 10 Spring Quiet: published text contains several emendations, e.g. 'covert' for MS 'greenwood' and 'whitethorn' for MS 'myrtle'.

p. 11 Immalee: at the opening of Maturin's *Melmoth* (1820) Immalee is a child of Nature living on a tropical island, innocent of the world's woes. Around this date CGR based several other poems on Maturin's heroines, including 'Eva' (18 March 1847), 'Eleanor' (30 July 1847) and 'Isidora' (9 August 1847).

p. 12 Death's Chill Between: the first of CGR's poems to be published commercially, in the *Athenaeum*, 14 October 1848; never republished by CGR. MS title 'Anne of Warwick', in reference to the widow of the Prince of Wales, killed at Tewkesbury in 1471, although the poem is a more generalised expression of loss.

p. 13 Heart's Chill Between: the second of CGR's poems to be published in the Athenaeum, 21 October 1848; not republished by CGR. MS title 'The Last Hope'. According to WMR, 'it ought to have been better than it is' (PW, p. 467).

l.27 fright: cf. *bouts-rimés* sonnet 'So I grew half delirious' (see note to 'Sonnets Written to *Bouts-rimés*', below).

p. 14 Lines given with a Penwiper: a penwiper, made from small strips of cloth, was used to wipe excess ink from the nib.

p. 15 Undine: Undine is a water-spirit, subject of a famous painting by Daniel Maclise (1844).

p. 16 Sonnets Written to *Bouts-rimés*: four of over twenty surviving pieces written to rhyme words supplied by WMR and DGR, a favourite pastime at this date. 'I seek among the living' was completed in eight minutes and 'Is this August weather' in six. The first three were done while CGR was on holiday at Brighton and the fourth while staying with the Collinson family in Nottinghamshire. Other *bouts-rimés* are included in *Maude*.

p. 18 Song

l.4 cypress: symbol of mourning.
l.15 haply: perhaps.

p. 18 Song: first published in the *Germ* (1850). MS title 'A Song in a

Song', with three preceding stanzas framing the published text as the utterance of a girl now dead.

p. 18 Symbols

ll.5–6 matin/evensong: the use of church services for times of day indicates the poem's devotional purpose.

p. 19 **To Lalla**: 'Lalla' was Henrietta Polydore, CGR's younger and only cousin.

p. 20 **An End**: published in the *Germ* (1850).

p. 21 **Dream-Land**: published in the *Germ* (1850).

p. 22 **Remember**: cf. Shakespeare, Sonnet 71, 'No longer mourn for me'.

p. 25 **The Three Enemies**: the three traditional enemies of the Christian soul, according to the Anglican litany, representing the lures of physical pleasure, material wealth, glory and power, are here characterised as speakers in a dialogue, tempting the soul with ease, riches and fame. In each case the soul responds by citing Christ's suffering and sacrifice.

p. 27 **'Behold I stand at the door and knock'**: published in the *English Woman's Journal* (1861). The dialogue between a well-to-do householder and three needy supplicants dramatises the religious duty of alms-giving in the context of nineteenth-century poverty. The title is from *Revelation* 3: 19–20: 'As many as I love, I rebuke and chasten: be zealous therefore and repent. Behold, I stand at the door and knock: if any man hear my voice, and open the door, I will come in to him.' The idea of 'opening the door of one's heart' to Christ was a favourite Victorian religious trope. At the time of CGR's poem, William Holman Hunt had begun his famous painting on the same text, *The Light of the World* (Keble College, Oxford), though CGR had not yet seen it. For another poem on the same text, see *The Face of the Deep* (1892), p. 143.

ll.33–40: the speaker here is Christ, rather uncharitably threatening the householder with appropriate punishment.

p. 30 **Books in the Running Brooks**: MS title 'After a Picture in the Portland Gallery', presumably based on Shakespeare's *As You Like It*, from which the revised title is taken (Act II, Scene i).

l.51: cf. 'The heart knoweth its own bitterness'.

p. 31 **'To what purpose is this waste?'**: title from the disciples' rebuke to the woman who anointed Christ with precious ointment in Matthew 26:3. An early example of CGR's view of the relation between the human, natural and divine worlds; also an early example of the free-running metrical and rhyme scheme developed in 'Goblin Market'.

l.72 Undefiled: the lily is the Virgin Mary's emblem, symbolising purity.

p. 35 The P.R.B.: written at Frome, expressing CGR's nostalgia for the early days of the Pre-Raphaelite Brotherhood (*c.* 1848–50). See Introduction for members of PRB; CGR was correct rather than coy in omitting the name of James Collinson, who formally resigned from the PRB in 1850.

1. l.4 Woolner in a distant land: Thomas Woolner was currently in Australia.
   ll.6–7 two good pictures: *The Girlhood of Mary Virgin* (1849) and *Ecce Ancilla* (1850), since when DGR had not exhibited.
   l.12 by the column: WMR was art critic of the *Spectator*.
2. l.3 land of Cheops: Egypt.
   l.4 vulgar optic: i.e. DGR's refusal to exhibit.
   l.6 His B.s: i.e. his 'Brothers' in the PRB.
   l.6: Coptic: seems chosen merely for the rhyme.
   l.11 A.R.A: Associate of the Royal Academy.

p. 36 The World: 'the world' is a term embracing everything secular and self-indulgent, in opposition to the spiritual and divine; cf. Bunyan's *Pilgrim's Progress from this World to that which is to come* (1678). 'Worldliness' was the trait CGR most deplored in herself and others.

p. 37 From the Antique: no classical source for this piece has been discovered; the title may have been devised to deflect personal application, or suggest an age-old plaint.

p. 37 Three Stages: Part 1, dated 14 February 1848, has a MS note 'In memory of Schiller's 'Der Pilgrim'.

1. l.2 hope deferred: phrase taken by CGR as a personal motto, designating disappointments large and small, from Proverbs 13:12, 'Hope deferred maketh the heart sick'.
   l.6 object: these verses describe the experience of unfulfilled longing, not desire for any specific item.
2. ll.9–10 I must pull down my palace . . .: cf. Tennyson's 'Palace of Art'.
3. l.10 This sand is slow . . .: time imaged as sand falling through the neck of an hour-glass.

p. 40 Listening: traditionally taken to have been inspired by Elizabeth Siddal, with whom DGR was currently in love.

p. 41 My Dream: a favourite with CGR and her family, leading to long-running jokes about her predilection for crocodiles. Later, she made a MS note 'Not a real dream' but for literary antecedents see Thomas de Quincey's crocodile-infested dreams in *Confessions of an Opium-Eater* (1822) and Thomas Beddoes grotesque 'Song by Isbrand' in *Death's Jest Book* (1850), a Rossettian favourite, also his *The Crocodile* (1851).

l.48 appropriate: 'crocodile tears' are those shed hypocritically, to simulate grief (from the archaic belief that the crocodile wept to allure its victim).

p. 43 **An Afterthought**: the first of CGR's writings on Eve whose 'disobedience' and expulsion from Eden she pondered repeatedly and resistantly. For the theme, see not only Genesis 3, but also Milton's *Paradise Lost* (1667) and EBB's *A Drama of Exile* (1844).

l.31 fiery messenger: archangel Gabriel.
l.34 the flaming sword: see Genesis 3:24.
l.46 Rachel: wife of Jacob, see Genesis 30.

p. 45 **Shut Out**: MS title 'What Happened to me'; thematically linked with 'An Afterthought' (above).

p. 46 **By the water**: was published by WMR (PW 321) with an additional stanza taken from CGR's notebook.

p. 46 **A Chilly Night**: partly inspired by Border Ballads involving ghostly encounters; cf. 'The Hour and the Ghost' (below).

p. 48 **The Hour and the Ghost**: see 'A Chilly Night' (above).

l.62 toss and howl and spin: cf. Dante's *Inferno*, canto v, where the lovers Paolo and Francesca are seen tossing in the winds of eternity. In autumn 1855 DGR produced a watercolour drawing of this subject, which CGR may have seen.

p. 50 **A Triad**: published 1862 but afterwards omitted by CGR from her collections, perhaps owing to adverse comments on its treatment of contemporary womanhood. The three types characterised are, respectively, a 'kept woman' or mistress, a conventional wife, and a spinster.

p. 51 **Love from the North**: MS title 'In the Days of the Sea-Kings' in reference to contemporary interest in Nordic legends and Viking themes, as well as Border Ballads such as 'The Gypsy Rover'.

p. 52 **In an Artist's Studio**: believed to be based on a visit to DGR's studio, and his many portraits of Elizabeth Siddal. In 1854 Ford Madox Brown remarked on the many 'wonderful and lovely' drawings of Siddal by DGR. At the date of this poem she was wintering in the south of France for health reasons.

p. 52 **A Better Resurrection**
l.6 everlasting hills: a Christian emblem of hope; see Anglican Prayer-book, Psalm 121: 'I will lift up mine eyes unto the hills: from whence cometh my help.'

p. 53 **'The heart knoweth its own bitterness'**: title (used more than once by CGR) from Proverbs 14:10, 'The heart knoweth his own bitterness; and a stranger doth not intermeddle with his joy'; cf. 'Books in the Running Brooks' (above).

l.33 You: the final words of this stanza indicate that 'you' is plural.
l.44 fountain sealed: a favourite motif of CGR, from Song of Solomon 4:12, 'A garden inclosed is my sister, my spouse; a spring shut up, a fountain sealed.'
l.51 Eye hath not seen: another favourite phrase, from Revelation, indicating the unknowable ideality of heaven.

p. 55 **Day-Dreams**: this is the original title; a second MS version bears the title 'Reflection', which happens to have been a Portfolio Society theme.

l.53 alabaster: commonly used for memorial effigies.

p. 57 **In the Round Tower at Jhansi**: a topical poem prompted by an incident reported to have taken place at Jhansi in India on 8 June 1857 (news of which reached Britain towards the end of August) where the commanding officer Captain Skene was said to have shot his wife and himself rather than be killed by insurgents. This incident was never confirmed and in later editions CGR appended a note: 'I retain this little poem, not as historically accurate, but as written and published before I heard the supposed facts of its first verse contradicted.' Its feeling reflects the national wave of angry distress that swept Britain as reports of mutinous insurrection by Indian troops – and more especially the killing of British wives and families resident with officers in India – began to reach London; cf. in this respect, Tennyson's *The Charge of the Light Brigade* (1854) and also his *Lucknow* (1860). Four stanzas of 'Jhansi' were published in a magazine in 1859, the central stanza being added on re-publication in 1862, apparently in deference to the religious prohibition on suicide, and perhaps to indicate the action more clearly.

p. 57 **A Nightmare**: also known as 'A Coast – Nightmare' from a MS copy, made by CGR for circulation to the Portfolio Society *c.* 1863–4, probably when the set theme was 'A Coast'. The Portfolio version has 'friend' for 'love' (l.1) and 'hunts' for 'rides' (l.37), but the retention of 'lover' (l.27) is consistent with the original MS text. One of a number of pieces written at this period referring to keeping secrets.

p. 61 **An Apple-Gathering**: first published in *Macmillan's Magazine* (1861).

p. 62 **Winter: My Secret**: MS title 'Nonsense'.

p. 63 **Maude Clare**: first published in *Once a Week* (1859), illustrated by J. E. Millais and drastically reduced in length from the MS version. For a discussion of this revision, see Antony H. Harrison, *Christina Rossetti in Context*, 1988, pp. 4–8.

l.24 beck: dialect term for brook taken from the Border balladry whose form is borrowed here.

p. 65 Up-hill: 'the first poem by Christina which excited marked attention' (PW, p. 481).

p. 66 Old and New Year Ditties: three poems marking the end and beginning of the year, given an unfortunately whimsical title when jointly printed in 1862.

3. l.5 laurel nor bay: classical symbols of renown, from the wreaths awarded for outstanding achievement; cf. the 'sprig of bay' in *Maude* (see note to p. 255, below) suggesting CGR saw this as an image of the literary recognition she craved. See also Introduction.

p. 68 L.E.L.: first published in *Victoria Magazine* (1863). MS title 'Spring', with note: '"L.E.L." by E.B.B', referring to EBB's poem 'L.E.L.'s Last Question', on the words of poet Letitia E. Landon in her last letter to friends, 'Do you think of me as I think of you?' CGR's epigraph echoes EBB's description of Landon as 'one thirsty for a little love'. Other poems indirectly alluded to here in CGR's acknowledgement of her poetic foremothers include Landon's 'Night at Sea' and Felicia Hemans's 'A Parting Song'. For a discussion of this sequence, see Angela Leighton, *Writing Against the Heart*, 1992, pp. 72–6.

l.1 I laugh . . .: cf. EBB's 'The Mask': 'I have a smiling face, she said, I have a jest for all I meet . . .'
l.36 scathe: injury (archaic even in 1850s but lingering in 'unscathed' etc.).

p. 70 'Then they that feared the Lord spake often one to another': a variation on Matthew: 19–21, 'Lay not up for yourselves treasures upon earth, where moth and rust doth corrupt, and where thieves break through and steal', one of CGR's favourite texts.

p. 70 Cousin Kate: MS title 'Up and Down', referring to social mobility and the wheel of fortune. The subject may perhaps be linked with CGR's work at the Penitentiary for Fallen Women. First published in 1862, the poem was later suppressed by CGR, presumably because of its endorsement of single motherhood.

p. 72 Noble Sisters

l.59 shame: is the first sister married, as the second claims to have told her lover? She says she has 'none other love'; but if unmarried, what is the reason for the second sister's curse? This deliberate obscurity in a ballad-style setting may be compared with narratives in William Morris's *The Defence of Guenevere* (1858).

p. 73 Sister Maude: first published 1862 but afterwards suppressed by CGR.

p. 74 'No, Thank You, John': the title echoes the traditional English song 'O, No, John', and the poem is said by WMR to refer to the painter

John Brett, who had been 'somewhat smitten' by CGR; if so, this must have occurred in 1857–8 when Brett painted the unfinished portrait of CGR which appears on the jacket of this book. Few details are known, but it is unlikely that Brett proposed to CGR in the manner here described; later she told DGR (who feared the poem would be taken as autobiographical) that 'no such person' as John existed; in 1890, however, she added a MS note: 'The original John was obnoxious, because he never gave scope for "No, thank you"' (PW, p. 483) – thus adding to the mystery.

p. 75 Mirage

ll.5–6 I hang my harp . . .: traditional emblem of the lyric voice silenced through grief.

p. 75 Promises like Piecrust: 'Promises and pie-crust are made to be broken', Jonathan Swift, *Polite Conversation* (1738).

p. 77 Good Friday: first published in a religious anthology in 1864.

l.5 those women: present at the Crucifixion – see Mark 15:40
l.11 darkness at broad noon: see Mark 15:33.

p. 77 On the Wing: first published 1866, under the title 'A Dream'.

p. 78 The Queen of Hearts: first published *Macmillan's Magazine* (1863).

p. 79 Helen Grey: published in *Macmillan's Magazine* (1866), but not afterwards reprinted by CGR.

p. 79 A Bird's-Eye View: first published *Macmillan's Magazine* (1863). The title may have been one set for the Portfolio Society. The ballad text has echoes of Edgar Allan Poe, *Sir Patrick Spens* and *The Two Corbies*.

p. 82 A Dumb Friend: again, the title may derive from a Portfolio Society theme.

p. 83 Consider: a verbal variation on Matthew 6:28; first published *Macmillan's Magazine* (1866).

p. 83 The Lowest Place: in some sense, a 'signature poem' of CGR's, occupying final position in her collected edition of 1875.

p. 85 The Ghost's Petition: MS title 'A Return'.

l.31 Robin: familiar diminutive of 'Robert', much used in Border Ballads.

p. 89 Bird or Beast?: a reprise of 'An Afterthought' (see above); see also 'Eve' (below).

p. 89 Eve: a continuation of Eve's story; see Genesis 4 for the murder of Abel by his brother Cain, both sons of Adam and Eve.

p. 91 A Sketch: according to WMR (PW, p. 484), these affectionately teasing verses were addressed to Charles Cayley, towards whom CGR evinced a *tendresse* at this date – it would seem without his awareness.

p. 92 If I had Words

l.3 speechless herds: i.e. animals.
l.7 brazen: bronze.

p. 93 *Amor Si sveglia?*: Is Love awakening?

With a new spring
  The old spirit is reborn;
Love whispers to you 'Hope'—
  Still I'll not say it.

If Love bids you 'Love',
  If he emboldens you, my friend,
Swearing 'That heart is yours'—
  Still I'll not say it.

And in truth who can say
  If that heart is worth a fig?
I believe, or I hope, so:
  Yet still not say it.

The second of nineteen pieces written in Italian 1864–7, collected together by CGR under the title '*Il Rosseggiar dell' Oriente*' (The Reddening East), apparently inspired by Charles Cayley and never published by CGR.

p. 93 '*Lassù fia caro il riverderci*': 'It will be sweet to meet again above.'

Sweet heart, lost to me and yet not lost,
  My sweet life, that leavest me in death
  Friend and more than friend, I greet thee.
Remember me; for blind and brief
  Were all my hopes, though they were of thee:
  Do not contemn me for so hard a fate.
Let me say 'His hopes
  Like mine languish in this winter cold'—
  Yet I will be resigned, that what was, was.
Let me say once more 'With him I see
  Day rising from this frosty night,
  Eternal heaven beyond this passing hell,
Beyond this winter, spring.'

The fifth of the *Il Rosseggiar* sequence.

p. 93 Jessie Cameron

l.53 grandam: archaism for 'grandmother' in keeping with the ballad mode.

l.55 unked: dismal (dialect).

p. 99 ***Amor Mundi***: written during the completion of 'The Prince's Progress', and first published in a magazine in 1865. The title means 'Love of the World' and in her 1875 collection CGR paired this with 'Up-hill'.

p. 99 Maggie A Lady: written shortly before 'The Iniquity of the Fathers' and, as CGR acknowledged, influenced by EBB's 'Lady Geraldine's Courtship', on the theme of social mobility.

p. 101 ***En Route***: written during CGR's visit to Italy; see also 'An "Immurata' Sister" (below).

p. 101 Enrica: inspired by a family friend named Enrica Filopanti; first published in an anthology (1865).

p. 102 A Daughter of Eve: all women are daughters of Eve.

p. 102 Mother Country: first published in *Macmillan's Magazine* (1868). Not, as is first thought, another piece inspired by Italy, but another meditation on paradise.

p. 104 'Cannot sweeten': title from *Macbeth*, V.i.

From this date CGR gave up the habit of dating the completion of each poem.

p. 106 An Echo from Willowwood: a poetic response to DGR's triple sonnet sequence *Willow-wood* (1870) from which the epigraph is taken. It may be that CGR's lines refer indirectly to DGR's passion for the already-married Jane Morris, which dominated his emotional life at this date.

p. 106 The German-French Campaign 1870–1: written at two dates, in response to the Franco-Prussian War, declared in July 1870 and ending with the defeat of France on 28 January 1871. CGR was more naturally sympathetic to the French nation, but deplored all forms of military aggression; this is essentially an anti-war poem.

p. 106 'Thy Brother's Blood crieth': see Jeremiah 25, which foretells the overthrow of nations.

l.25 thou King: probably a reference to Napoleon III, self-styled Emperor of France; normally CGR's capitalisation refers to God, but the absence of such in 'thy past' (l.26) suggests an earthly king is meant here.
l.27 King of Sheshach: a figure for Babylon or evil; see Jeremiah 25:26 and 51:41ff. in which the destruction of Babylon is foretold.

p. 107 'Today for Me'

l.63 One abides: Christ.

p. 108 A Christmas Carol: first published in *Scribner's Monthly* (New York) January 1872; now among the best-known of CGR's works, having been memorably set to music by Gustav Holst.

p. 109 A Rose Plant in Jericho: first published in a religious anthology (1875).

p. 110 *'Italia, Io Ti Saluto!'*: thematically, this belongs with 'En Route' and 'Enrica'. Translated, the title is 'Italy, I Salute Thee!'

p. 112 Untitled: composed for the feast-day of St John the Baptist; one of several pieces included in *Called to be Saints* (completed 1875 but published 1881).

l.2 Jordan: river of baptism, also standing as figure for death.
l.6 stand up: see Exodus 14.
l.30–32 Thy rod: for Aaron's rod see Numbers 17:8.

p. 113 A Life's Parallels: probably written in mourning for MFR, who died November 1876.

p. 113 *De Profundis*: 'From the depths of sorrow': see Psalm 130.

p. 114 An October Garden: first published Athenaeum (1877) and probably written while staying with DGR near Herne Bay in Kent.

p. 114 'Summer is Ended': see Jeremiah 8:20.

p. 115 *Soeur Louise de la Miséricorde*: the eponymous Soeur Louise was formerly la Duchesse de la Vallière, mistress of Louis XIV, who retired to a Carmelite convent in 1674.

p. 117 An 'Immurata' Sister: a revised portion of a longer piece, from which 'En Route' (see above) was also taken, written during CGR's visit to Italy with FLR and WMR, and given a different cast when published in 1881. An 'immurata' sister is an immured nun, belonging to a strictly enclosed order.

p. 118 Freaks of Fashion: first published in a girls' annual and apparently written on request.

p. 120 Brother Bruin: written in response to a newspaper article. CGR was a longtime opponent of cruelty to animals.

p. 122 Untitled: first published in *Time Flies* (1885).

l.12 or . . . or: either . . . or.

p. 123 Rogationtide: the period before the feast of the Ascension in the Anglican calendar.

p. 124 Untitled (Where shall I find a white rose blowing?): written as a donation for a boys' home or orphanage.

p. 124 Untitled (Roses on a brier)

l.8 no more sea: allusion to the End of Time, 'when there shall be no more sea'.

p. 126 Doeth well . . . doeth better: the title refers to a Pauline text commending celibacy over matrimony, and may also be a tribute to MFR, CGR's 'beloved sister and friend'.

p. 127 'Son, remember': based on the parable of Lazarus the beggar (Luke 16: 19–25) who ate crumbs from the rich man's table and whose sores were licked by dogs.

p. 129 'A Helpmeet for Him': this piece, echoing God's words regarding Eve, was first published in a church magazine, *New and Old*, in January 1888.

p. 130 Untitled: a tour de force on a single rhyme, but also bidding farewell to the desire for literary fame, in the final stanza, 'Does thou covet bay?'

p. 132 These two poems constitute CGR's own epitaph.

SingSong

Early in 1870 CGR completed a collection of poems for young children – her own Nursery Rhymes – which she submitted to DGR's publisher F. S. Ellis as 'a marketable proposition', with thumbnail sketches for each piece indicating how she conceived the volume. Her illness and Ellis's inexperience led to trouble and delay, and in 1871 CGR negotiated a new contract with the Dalziel Bros, who produced *SingSong* (title suggested by FLR) for George Routledge. Arthur Hughes made attractive and much-praised illustrations – CGR particularly liked his image of a black crow turning grey in the wash – and the book was published for Christmas 1871. It is carefully structured, from waking rhymes at the beginning to bedtime rhymes at the end, and includes over 120 separate poems; many, as WMR noted, 'are perfectly suited for figuring among her verse for adults, and even for taking an honoured place as such' (PW, p. 490). In 1878, hearing her cousin Teodorico Pietrocola Rossetti was aiming to translate the text into Italian, CGR made her own attempts at thirty-three of the rhymes, which figure among her most accomplished and witty Italian poems. Not all critics have shared WMR's assessment; according to the Pelican Guide to English Literature (1958, vol. 6, p. 89), *SingSong* 'contains too much talk of death and transience to be useful in the nursery'; but poet Fredegond Shove, writing in 1931, 'well remembered the pale silky green cover, veined like a young beech leaf', and the contents:

> There was something about the drawings and poems together which partook,

> if not of fairyland, but of the enchantment of life itself – indescribable as a sea of changing colours touching all the shores of possibility. In this sea one paddled comfortably and easily, as one learnt by heart the phrases in *Sing Song*, aware all the time that whilst one was never out of one's depth, that was not because there were no depths, no soundless mystery of poetic wonder in which to bathe if one wished to do so, later on, in the distant grown-up days. Now, in my grown-up days, I have come to the conclusion that these artless poems of childhood and for childhood do indeed evince a sort of immensity of vision and a reality in poetry pure and simple which make them, if not mysterious, at least marvellous . . . They are as tiny as a grasshopper's little thin treble in the grass, yet each one is so perfect that whoever reads it must exclaim over it, 'Oh, if I could have written that!' (Fredegond Shove, *Christina Rossetti: A Study*, Cambridge, 1931, pp. 54–6)

Individual items hardly need annotation, but it is worth knowing that 'Kookoorookoo!' is based on a memory of the cockadoodle-doo noise CGR's father made to wake his children, and that 'Dead in the cold' retains an echo of the elegy for a thrush composed by MFR at the age of ten.

Narrative and Longer Poems

p. 138 The Dead City: first printed in *Verses* (1847). MS title 'The City of Statues', betraying influence of Tennyson's 'The Day-Dream' (*Poems*, 1842). Note also the opening echo of Dante, the anticipations of 'Goblin Market' and the moral lesson that sensual indulgence leads to spiritual petrifaction.

p. 146 Look on this Picture: never published by CGR; printed by WMR in 1896 with half its forty-six stanzas omitted on grounds of repetitiveness, but also because, were it not for the name Eva, he would have been 'embarrassed to guess what could have directed my sister's pen to so singular a subject and treatment' (PW, p. 480), presumably owing to the comparable state of DGR's feelings towards Elizabeth Siddal at the time of composition. Title taken from *Hamlet* where Hamlet forces on his mother a comparison of her two husbands; but the source of CGR's emotional triangle and hectic tone would seem to be the hero's conflicting desire for two different women (one of whom is named Eva) in Maturin's *Women*, one of CGR's favourite novels.

l.31 break not bend: the Rossetti family motto, adopted by DGR, '*frangas non flectas*'.
l.53 tiring: attiring.
l.53 Bridegroom: Christ.
l.102 kill: from this point Eva appears to die in her faithless lover's arms, raising the possibility that he has literally killed her.

p. 150 The lowest Room: first published in 1875, after DGR successfully argued against its inclusion in earlier volumes, but sneakily printed by

CGR in *Macmillan's Magazine* (1864) under the title 'Sit Down in the Lowest Room'. MS title 'An Argument over the Body of Homer'. The subject of the sisters' debate derives in part from MFR's lifelong enthusiasm for the Homeric heroes, especially Achilles, despite her moral disapproval of his conduct. Other influences include Carlyle's *On Heroes and Hero-Worship* (1841), and, indirectly, Tennyson's *The Princess* (1847), another debate on femininity. The MS text is longer by fourteen stanzas, including an opening pair which, with the conclusion, originally 'framed' the poem. A dialogue in ballad form, 'The Lowest Room' enacts a proto-feminist protest against exclusion from the public world, such as was being articulated by the emergent women's movement, and by EBB's *Aurora Leigh,* coincidentally published shortly after CGR's poem was written.

l.23 Aeacides: patronymic of the descendants of Aeacus, such as Achilles who killed Hector.
l.54 would not bend: from the Rossetti family motto '*frangas non flectas*'.
l.63 a slave: a double reference, to Achilles' love for the captive Briseis, a central element in the action of the *Iliad*, and to the legal doctrine of coverture in English law, withholding legal status for married women, a focus of feminist debate at this time; cf. J. S. Mill's *Subjection of Women* (1867).
l.77 Dian: the moon, tutelary goddess of unmarried women.
l.80 waste of white: satiric stab at the endless needlework undertaken by Victorian women.
l.101ff: cf. a similar passage in *Aurora Leigh*, Book 5, 149–200.
l.124 Diomed: Greek hero in Homer, Dante, Shakespeare.
ll.174 wisest man: Solomon was reputedly author of Ecclesiastes, from whose opening verses comes the phrase 'vanity of vanities'.
l.250 like a vine: a favourite Victorian image of wifehood, entwined and dependent on the stronger spouse.
l.280 And many last be first: in context, a subversive final line, despite the ostensible submission. The text comes from Luke 14: 10, Jesus's parable in the house of the chief Pharisee, with its implied continuation that 'when he that bade thee cometh, he may say unto thee, Friend, go up higher . . . For whosoever exalted himself shall be abased: and he that humbleth himself shall be exalted.'

p. 158 The Convent Threshold: a dramatic monologue in which a penitent woman on the verge of entering a convent after an apparently illicit love affair, urges her lover to repent also. Partly based on the story of Heloise and Abelard, which CGR would have known in Pope's 'Eloisa to Abelard' (1717), it was the poem in her first volume that spoke most powerfully to the young Gerard Manley Hopkins, who conceived of his 'Against the World' as a response.

l.13 sea of glass and fire: see Revelation 15:2.

p. 162 Goblin Market: MS title 'A Peep at the Goblins', derived from a book of Devon folktales written for children by FLR's cousin in 1854; retitled by DGR for publication. Inscribed to MFR in MS, but no specific reason for this is known. CGR 'more than once' denied that the poem was intended as allegory, but it is certainly a deliberate moral tale of temptation, resistance, remorse and redemption. John Ruskin complained of the metrical irregularity, but the varied pace and fluid rhyme scheme gives the narrative its irresistible and innovative quality. In late twentieth-century criticism, it has become CGR's most discussed work.

l.27 barberries: berberis.
l.76 ratel: burrowing animal native to Africa and India.
l.120 furze: gorse.
ll.125 golden curl: cf. Pope's *Rape of the Lock* (1714) where a similar exchange takes place.
l.147 Jeanie: pronounced to rhyme with 'many' and thus homonymically linked to the fallen woman in DGR's 'Jenny', written 1858–9.
l.408 White and golden: emblematic of the Virgin Mary.
l.471 Eat me, drink me: cf. the Last Supper and the Christian Eucharist. Lewis Carroll parodied this in *Alice through the Looking Glass* (1865), a story first told very shortly after Carroll read and admired 'Goblin Market'.

p. 176 A Royal Princess: first published in a fund-raising anthology for workers in the Lancashire cotton industries laid off owing to the American Civil War, and therefore an appropriate protest against tyranny, though there is no evidence that CGR had American slavery in mind at the time of writing (though she was a confirmed opponent of the Confederate cause on this account); the poem is more comfortably read as a protest against patriarchy, in strongly accented triplets, with pulsing rhythm and vivid imagery of famine, vultures and violence. In revising the text for publication, CGR deleted the Princess's desire for love as an escape route, thus strengthening the political element. Among the lines later deleted are:

> I was weak, tears gathered, while a something in me stirred,
> Struggling blind and dumb, yet crying an inarticulate cry.

l.31 Some to work: cf. Keat's *Isabella or the Pot of Basil,* which also features tyrannical menfolk.
l.63 families out grazing: during the Irish Famine of 1847–8 there were reports of the starving peasantry being reduced to eating grass.
l.76 the deluge: attributed to Madame de Pompadour (d. 1764) but also conflated with Marie Antoinette's 'Let them eat cake'.
l.93 yell for fire: in 1865, in response to criticism from DGR regarding the violence of this poem, CGR wrote: 'I do not fight for the R.P's

heroism; though it seems to me that the royal soldiers might yet have succeeded in averting roasting. A yell is one thing, and a *fait accompli* quite another.' (*Rossetti Papers 1862–1870*, p. 99)
l.104 if I perish: the words of Queen Esther, defying King Ashasuerus; cf. Sonnet 8 of *Monna Innominata*.

p. 180 **Maiden-Song**: one of CGR's own favourites, though rather insipid for modern taste. Inspired by the 'triple wooing' theme of traditional tales, but also unappealing to modern tastes in its endorsement of female rivalry and the traditional pairing of fairest maiden with richest suitor.

p. 186 **The Prince's Progress**: published as lead poem in CGR's second collection (1866) and written specifically for this purpose over the winter of 1864–5, to a suggestion by DGR that an existing 'dirge' entitled 'The Prince who arrived too Late' (the last six stanzas of the present text) be extended into a full narrative. This accounts for the change of metre and rhyme at the conclusion. For the remainder, CGR chose a demanding rhyme scheme, with each short sixth line, uncommon in the narrative genre. More specifically than 'Goblin Market', this is a moral allegory on a folkloric base, borrowing from both Perrault's *Sleeping Beauty* and Bunyan's *Pilgrim's Progress*, two of the Victorian age's most popular texts. On 3 March 1855 CGR told DGR that 'the plot is now obvious to mean capacities, without further development or addition', and defending various phrases as giving 'a subtle hint (by symbol)' of her intended meaning. In deference to DGR's objection, she deleted a reference to the Prince smoking a pipe, though when he failed to give the Prince a curly black beard in his design for the frontispiece, she joked that she would not alter the text to describe the waste of time in shaving. She also refused DGR's suggestion that the episode with the Alchemist be replaced by a Tournament, citing Tennyson's intimidating account of at least two tournaments in *Idylls of the King* (1859); she also explained the six-part structure of her poem: prelude, sojourn with beguiling milkmaid; trial of 'barren boredom'; 'the social element again'; more barren boredom; conclusion (see *Rossetti Papers*, p. 78). This itself is not pellucid, however, and readers must interpret the sequence for themselves; my best guess is that by delays and diversions the Prince neglects his immortal soul until it is too late, but the 'subtext' of Romantic love and procrastination which is the ostensible story also resonates in terms of the Victorian practice of delayed marriage.

l.15 staff and hat: traditional attributes of the pilgrim.
l.17 moon's at full: 'happily suggestive of the Prince's character', according to CGR.
l.33 hairy: CGR resisted DGR's view that this adjective was coarse, saying it precisely described poppy buds. White poppies are emblematic of death.

l.47 Strong of limb: a certain unconscious resemblance in the dilatory Prince to DGR may be noted; 'toil tomorrow' (l.359) might have been his motto.
l.94 serpent-coils: a figure of alluring evil, akin to the snake in the Garden of Eden.
l.100 mavis and merle: thrush and blackbird.
l.181 atomy: skeleton.
l.203 Elixir of Life: the Alchemist offers the Prince a false promise of immortality.
l.291 aftermath: 'left for various reasons; the most patient I need scarcely give', according to CGR; the aftermath is the second growth on a mown meadow.
l.430 opal stone: several attributes of this final landscape are those of paradise.

p. 200 'The Iniquity of the Fathers upon the Children': written at speed expressly to fill space in CGR's second collection, which she was preparing for the press. Originally called 'Under the Rose', with the present title (from the second commandment, Genesis 20:5) as epigraph. 'Under the rose' refers to the phrase *sub rosa* to denote illegitimacy. 'The Iniquity of the Fathers' increases the strong element of social and moral commination of the menfolk in the poem, which in general terms exonerates the speaker from shame (commonly imposed on those of irregular parentage), forgives the mother for her 'mistake', and roundly blames the absent father for all subsequent ills. According to CGR, the plot was 'all fancy', but similar accounts were popular in melodramatic narratives, and influences include Dickens's *Bleak House* (1852–3) and George Crabbe's poems, which CGR admired. The plain speech mode (almost doggerel) adopted, with little use of imagery or verbal pleasure, is one CGR rarely deployed and which frequently falls flat; it may derive from her recent re-reading of EBB (see 'Maggie a Lady'). The poem's social satire may be compared with that of *Family Correspondence*, while the outspoken moral lesson is less heavily occluded than that in 'An Apple-Gathering'. But the lack of a denouement to the tale (apart from Margaret's resolve to keep her mother's secret and never marry) makes the story rather slack, and the pious final lines seem perfunctory.

p. 214 A Ballad of Boding: stylistically, a return to the fluid forms of 'Goblin Market' but more allegorically explicit than either this or 'Prince's Progress'. Influenced and perhaps inspired by Edmund Spenser, whose *Faerie Queene* CGR had recently studied to identify Petrarchan borrowings for a scholarly edition, and also by Petrarch himself, whose *Rime* had recently been translated by Charles Cayley and were well-known to CGR. Note again the popular shipwreck motif.

ll.3–4 my window: see *The Visions of Petrarch*, translated by Spenser, for a similar opening.

l.20 a Love with wings: Cupid.
l.21 Worm: serpent representing Satan.
l.22 Lily tangled to Rose: Christian emblems.
l.137 Monster: this horned, hoofed figure also features in 'The World'.
l.215 the bar: literally a sandbank at the entrance to a harbour; figuratively the passage of death into the safe haven of Christian salvation; cf. Tennyson's 'Crossing the Bar' (1881), where the symbolic voyager faces the opposite way, moving out to sea.

p. 220 **An Old-World Thicket**: probably the last-written of all CGR's moral allegories, returning in part to the themes of 'From House to Home', but exploring the depths of spiritual despair, and perhaps influenced by grief at MFR's death and DGR's inexorable physical and mental decline in the years before his death in 1882. The title remains partly obscure: 'Old-World' refers to the Covenant of the Old Law, before the coming of Christ, while the thicket is a reference to the story of Abraham and Isaac ('the ram caught in the thicket', Genesis 23:13) as a type of Christ's sacrifice. The text, however, describes the poet's travail through the dark night of the soul, characterised by anguish, impotent rage, emptiness, in a mode reminiscent of Donne and Hopkins, followed by a redeeming, epiphanic vision of Christ the Saviour as a ram leading his flock towards spiritual solace. As an expression of grief, it also has affinities with Milton's *Lycidas* and Tennyson's *In Memoriam*, though 'An Old-World Thicket' articulates spiritual despair rather than emotional loss. Elsewhere in CGR's work such moods are characterised by guilt; but here the despair seems to lie deeper than self-blame.

una selva oscura: a dark wood, from the opening of Dante's *Inferno*.
l.55 its jubilee: contesting the Romantic view of Nature as a solace to human woes which, by this date, had become for many Victorians a sort of spongy substitute for religious belief.
l.75 pain or fear: cf. Satan's words in *Paradise Lost*, IV, 73–7:

> Me miserable! which way shall I fly
> Infinite wrath and infinite despair?
> Which way I fly is Hell; myself am Hell;
> And in the lowest deep a lower deep
> Still threatening to devour me opens wide . . .

l.95 without an ark: this is close to a confession of unbelief.
l.109 haply: perhaps.
l.131 creature of the wood: here the poet employs the pathetic fallacy to convey her inward state.

Sonnet Sequences

These sonnet sequences are printed together, in order of composition. CGR objected to single sonnets being extracted from sequences for quotation or anthology, believing that the meaning was dependent on the whole sequence being read together.

p. 225 'They desire a better country': first published in *Macmillan's Magazine* (1869).

l.14 Follow me: echoes Christ's message when raising Lazarus from the dead.

p. 226 By Way of Remembrance: never published by CGR and thought to be related to '*Il Rosseggiar*'.

2. l.1 Will you be there?: Isidora's final words to Melmoth in Maturin's novel.

p. 228 The Thread of Life: related in mood to 'An Old-World Thicket' and similarly taking issue with the idea of Nature as spiritual solace.

p. 229 *Monna Innominata*: 'a sonnet of sonnets', i.e. a sequence of fourteen sonnets mirroring the fourteen lines of a single sonnet, comparable to Italian poetic devices such as a *corona* or crown of twelve sonnets. Written, like 'Later Life' in the context of a revival of poetic interest in the sonnet form around 1880, with numerous anthologies being compiled and composed, and more significantly in the context of CGR's study of Dante at University College London 1878–80, and her work on Petrarch during Cayley's translation and her own Spenserian research (see 'A Ballad of Boding'). Both DGR and WMR produced large-scale sonnet sequences (*House of Life* and *Democratic Sonnets*, respectively). See also Introduction. '*Monna Innominata*' means, literally, 'My "Nameless" or unknown Lady'.

Preface

'altissimo poeta . . . cotanto amante': the greatest poet, who loved so greatly, i.e. Dante.

great tho' inferior bard: Petrarch.

'donne innominate': nameless ladies.

school of less conspicuous poets: Troubadours.

that land and that period: Provence in the days of the Troubadours.

Great Poetess of our own day: EBB, whose *Sonnets from the Portuguese* were camouflaged by a deliberately misleading title.

According to WMR, the sequence is 'an intensely personal one', and the preface 'a blind – not an untruthful blind, for it alleges nothing that is not reasonable and on the surface correct, but still a blind interposed to draw off attention from the writer in her proper person' (PW, p. 462); 'it is indisputable that the real veritable speaker is Christina herself, giving expression to her love for Charles Cayley' (*Family Letters*, p. 97). I do not believe this to be the case, except insofar as a poet draws on their own experience and emotions, if only because, as with the 'dark lady' of

Shakespeare's sonnets, the meagre details of the beloved given here do not fit with what is known of Cayley's relationship with CGR. She was, I believe, experimenting with a new genre – the love sonnet spoken by a woman to an unattainable man – and deploying a historical fiction (or semi-historical fact, given that the work of some fourteen 'female troubadours' was known in this period) to express a modern version of unfulfilled but dignified passion; hence the allusion to EBB and her sonnets of fulfilled love. The idea seems to have prompted the composition rather than being used to camouflage personal application. 'I rather wonder that no one (so far as I know) ever hit on my semi-historical argument before for such treatment – it seems to me so full of poetic suggestiveness,' CGR told DGR in 1881 (*Family Letters*, 1908, p. 98). For a detailed analysis of *Monna Innominata*'s structure see William Whitla, 'Questioning the Convention', in *The Achievement of Christina Rossetti*, ed. David A. Kent, Cornell University, 1987, pp. 82–131.

WMR's translations of each epigraph, comprising paired quotations from Dante and Petrarch, which add to each poem another layer of allusion, are as follows:

1. The day that they have said adieu to their sweet friends.
   Love, with how great a stress dost thou vanquish me today!
2. It was already the hour which turns back the desire.
   I recur to the time when I first saw thee.
3. Oh shades, empty save in semblances!
   An imaginary guide conducts her.
4. A small spark fosters a great flame.
   Every other thing, every other thought, goes off, and love alone remains there with you.
5. Love, who exempts no loved one from loving.
   Love led me into such joyous hope.

   l.3 leal: loyal.
6. Now canst thou comprehend the quantity of the love which glows in me towards thee
   I do not choose that Love should release me from such a lie.
   l.4 Lot's wife: see Genesis 10:26.
7. Here always Spring and every fruit.
   Conversing with me, and I with him.
8. As if he were to say to God, 'I care for nought else'.
   I hope to find pity and not only pardon.

This, the sonnet in the sequence that represents the *volta* or eighth line on which the sonnet conventionally 'turns' between octave and sestet, is the only one with a dramatic subject, that of Esther, who saved her people (see Esther 4–5).

9. O dignified and pure conscience!
   Spirit more lit with burning virtues.

10. With better course and not with better star.
Life flees, and stays not an hour.
11. Come after me, and leave folk to talk.
Relating the casualties of our life.
12. Love, who speaks within my mind.
Loves comes in the beautiful face of this woman.
13. And we will direct our eyes to the primal Love.
But I find a burden to which my arms suffice not.
14. And His will is our peace.
Only with these thoughts, with different locks.

p. 237 **Later Life: A Double Sonnet of Sonnets**: a more ambitious sequence of twenty-eight sonnets and therefore probably composed after *Monna Innominata*, in which the poet speaks in *propria persona*, without a dramatic pretext (though not necessarily autobiographically). The title refers to the theme: in 1880 CGR passed her fiftieth birthday, and *Later Life* is a poetic retrospective.

4. l.13 Thief in Paradise: see the story of Christ's Passion and the Thief crucified alongside Jesus.
13. l.4 bruit: noise, sound.
l.11 cautery: surgical instrument for searing or cauterising tissue.
20. l.2 solitary bird: nightingale.
21 and 22: based directly on CGR's visit to Switzerland and Italy in summer 1865.

FICTION

Maude: A Story for Girls

p. 252 **commonplace-book, album**: a commonplace book was for the copying out of striking or edifying passages from one's reading, or other observations; an album was generally for friends and relatives to inscribe appropriate lines accompanying their photographs, together with pressed flowers and similar souvenirs of friendship.

p. 255 **bay**: emblem of fame, in recognition of Maude's poetic attainment.

p. 255 ***bonbonnière***: a small decorated box to hold sweets.

p. 258 **Bason . . . in St James's Park**: ornamental water in the public gardens close to Buckingham Palace.

p. 259 **wine and soup**: fortified wine was used as medicinal tonic in sickness owing to the presence of iron.

p. 260 **Cross and Crown of Thorns**: sacred symbols newly in vogue for High Anglican church embroideries and vestments.

p. 261 **sleeping together**: it was still common practice for sisters and female relatives to share a bed as well as a room.

p. 261 **not proper clothes on their beds**: the austerity of life in the newly founded Anglican orders was a matter for criticism and concern.

p. 262 **Mr Paulson offered me a district**: 'district visiting', whereby female parishioners took a poor area under their jurisdiction, was an early form of welfare work promoted by the Church. Rev. Paulson's name alludes to his calling, as one of the spiritual heirs of St Paul.

p. 262 **need not dress**: i.e. dress up.

p. 262 **St Andrew's**: St Andrews, Wells Street, in central London, was one of the first High Anglican churches to reintroduce the sung liturgy, and other choral music.

p. 263 **a subject had to be started**: the rules of politeness decreed that conversation be maintained, if it showed signs of flagging or discord, by the introduction of new, uncontroversial topics.

p. 263 **we never go to the play**: theatre-going was frowned upon by many pious and respectable families, owing to the presence of prostitutes in the foyers, and the often indelicate nature of the dramas; shortly before writing *Maude*, CGR resolved to stop going to the theatre and opera (see *Hero*) for this reason.

p. 266 **I shall not receive tomorrow**: receive Holy Communion, the central Anglican rite, the Blessed Sacrament.

p. 269 **lock of her beautiful hair**: postulants' hair was commonly cut, if not completely shorn, to symbolise their withdrawal from the world.

p. 273 **Fade, tender lily**: the two final poems from Maude Foster's remains represent the two main strands in CGR's verse – lyric and devotional.

Family Correspondence

p. 276 **Gertrude Orme**: Gertrude was the name of Aunt Charlotte's pupil at Longleat; Orme was the name of some family friends of the Rossettis, whose daughters Helen and Rosalind were a little younger than CGR. In her text she used the Italian form, Geltrude.

p. 277 **Duchess of Bridport**: a fictional title.

p. 277 **rice-straw**: fine straw for hat-making.

p. 277 **jessamine**: poetic for jasmine.

p. 278 **netting**: form of crochet work.

p. 279 **oratory**: private chapel.

p. 280 I should be honoured to receive a letter: in this communication, Angela-Maria employs the polite forms deemed appropriate for formal correspondence, congratulations and condolence, in contrast to the more informal style commonly used between girls.

p. 280 Mr Foster: it was also correct to use formal modes of address when referring to a prospective spouse, until after the marriage had taken place (see also 'Mr Herbert' in *Maude*).

p. 281 conversazione: a soirée or evening party for polite and cultured conversation rather than dining or dancing.

p. 281 Countess of Crawley: fictional title.

p. 281 album: see note to p. 252, above.

p. 281 the Season: the London 'Season' of aristocratic entertaining, roughly from Easter through to July.

p. 283 Miss Edgeworth: Maria Edgeworth (1768–1849), author of popular and improving tales for the young, much admired by CGR's mother and partly imitated here.

Nick

p. 286 The idea of this tale, though traditional, may be compared with Charlotte Perkins Gilman's *When I was a Witch* (1910).

p. 287 Hodge: archetypal name for agricultural workers in English literature.

p. 287 marvellous array of barrels: marvellous indeed, for a revolver, unlike a shotgun, has only one barrel.

p. 288 fatal cry: identifying a rabid dog, to be caught and destroyed.

p. 289 ham: a cured (but not smoked) side of ham or bacon commonly hung in a cottage kitchen.

p. 290 turnpike: toll gate. In this and other details CGR is consciously harking back to an earlier age, as (perhaps) portrayed in the work of Goldsmith and Crabbe.

p. 291 to bury him: this is a finely comic version of CGR's characteristic poetic fancy of being buried alive.

Hero

p. 292 epigraph: see Robert Burns's 'To a Louse'.

p. 293 carbuncle: semi-precious stone.

p. 293 Hero: in classical mythology, the priestess of Aphrodite whose lover Leander swam the Hellespont; in Shakespeare the falsely accused cousin of Beatrice in *Much Ado About Nothing*.

p. 293 **Forss**: a name derived from the Nordic tales that partly inspire this story.

p. 295 **lieges**: vassals, subjects.

p. 297 **a world's wonder**: the great Koh-i-noor diamond had been displayed at the 1851 Great Exhibition before being set into the British Crown Jewels.

p. 301 **commeline**: semi-precious stone.

p. 301 **unnamed alien seed**: this whole episode refers to the passion for rare plants that, like the earlier tulip-mania, occupied Victorian botanists. Uncle Treeh is thus a precursor of the Alchemist in *The Prince's Progress*.

p. 303 **succous**: juicy.

The Lost Titian

p. 305 **cymbals . . . panther**: these details suggest Titian's *Bacchus and Ariadne* in the National Gallery, London, which contains a cymbal-clashing bacchante and a pair of leopards. CGR's story also brings to mind the biography of Titian in Vasari's *Lives of the Artists* (1568) the first full translation of which was published in English in 1850. There is, however, no firm evidence that CGR read Vasari in either English or Italian before writing her story.

p. 306 ***colorito***: palette.

p. 306 **sunset-coloured tresses**: 'Titian' is a term for glowing auburn hair, after the examples in his art.

p. 306 **bloomed and tempted**: the senses of touch, sight, taste and smell are invoked in the preceding description of artistic mimesis. According to Vasari, Titian completed a work for Giovanni Bellini, showing a river flowing with red wine, drunken musicians, and a nude woman asleep 'so beautiful that she seems alive'.

p. 307 **bumpers**: large, full wineglasses.

p. 307 ***evviva!***: hurrah!/cheers!

p. 307 **Argus-eyed**: watchful, after the hundred-eyed giant in Greek mythology.

p. 307 **evil eye**: the merest hint, here, that the story has a double meaning.

p. 307 ***solitario passero***: solitary bird, by which CGR appears to mean the lark.

p. 308 ***amico mio***: my friend.

p. 308 **cogged dice**: loaded.

p. 309 **yet moist surface**: as Titian had only just completed his masterpiece, the oil paint would not yet have hardened.

p. 310 ***casa***: house.

p. 310 **taste was unimpeachable**: here, CGR anticipates the Aesthetes and the attitudes of, say, Whistler or Wilde.

p. 311 **Florentine goldsmith**: Benvenuto Cellini.

p. 311 **quaintly allusive**: *benvenuto* means 'welcome'.

p. 311 **Giorgione . . . Tintoret**: Venetian artists, the latter now usually known as Tintoretto, who claimed to be the pupil of Titian, while Giorgione was his mentor.

p. 311 **Signori miei**: 'Gentlemen—'.

p. 311 **Bevilacqua Mangiaruva**: a satirical name for a landlord, signifying 'drink water, eat coarse fare'.

p. 311 **Lupo Vorace**: 'hungry wolf'.

p. 311 ***Orco decapitato***: headless ogre, the name of Lupo's inn.

p. 312 **Dr Landau**: fictional, like the other proper names in this paragraph satirising the pursuit of valuable artworks.

p. 313 **Andromeda**: heroine of Greek mythology, rescued by Perseus from a great sea-dragon, and a favourite subject for artists, including (as it happens) Titian.

p. 313 **a world**: a final hint of the 'worldliness' theme; in CGR's philosophy, there was more than one world.

Vanna's Twins

p. 315 **forty-five**: at the time of writing CGR was approaching forty.

p. 315 **fly**: light horse-drawn cab.

p. 315 **three eggs**: presumably boiled.

p. 316 **ex-kingdom**: the former kingdom of Naples was by 1870 incorporated into the unified Italy.

p. 316 **marine curiosities**: Victorian holidaymakers liked to buy stones, seaweeds and live or dead sea-creatures as souvenirs, which Cola sells as a sideline.

p. 316 **magic-lantern**: an early projector, for magnifying images.

p. 316 ***la Signora***: the lady, or Madam.

p. 316 ***per noi due e per li piccini***: for us and the babies.

p. 317 ***due maccheroni***: macaroni, or pasta.

p. 317 ***calamarello***: cuttlefish or squid, not generally eaten in England at this date.

p. 317 **Felice**: happy.

p. 317 **Gioconda**: joyful.

p. 317 **scurf**: cradle-cap.

p. 317 ***paese***: country, homeland.

p. 317–18 ***E che male . . .***: 'and what harm could there possibly be? I see no crocodiles.'

p. 318 **small competence**: savings or inherited wealth.

p. 318 **marine oddities:** see above p.316; the skate would have been dried specimens, decorated to resemble a group of figures.

p. 318 ***Nossignore***: Our Lord.

p. 319 **St L—**: St Leonards is the neighbouring, and adjoining town to Hastings.

p. 319 ***proprio maravigliosi***: really marvellous.

p. 319 ***Non c'è male . . .***: 'not bad, neither he nor she.'

p. 319 **Holy Innocents' Day**: 28 December – in the Church calendar commemorating the slaughter of male children by Herod, an appropriate feast-day for Vanna's twins.

p. 320 **Twelfth Day**: 6 January.

p. 320 **E—**: probably Eastbourne.

p. 320 **Tu scendi dalle stelle . . .**: this Italian carol appears to be CGR's own composition. It is similar in treatment to 'In the bleak mid-winter', and translates thus:

> Thou camest down from the stars, O King of Heaven
> Into a cold and chilly cave
> O Holy Babe
> I would love Thee for ever!
> O blessed Lord
> How much it has cost you to love me

p. 320 ***Non hanno padre***: they have no father.

p. 320 **charing**: rough housework, especially scrubbing floors.

p. 321 **charity-purse**: containing money set aside for charitable giving.

p. 321 ***Mamma sì***: Mamma yes.

p. 321 ***Nossignore avrà cura . . .***: 'God will take care of them.'

p. 322 ***Non son che piccini . . .***: 'They're only babies, poor little babies, my poor little babies.'

p. 322 ***Vanna, Vanna mia! . . .***: 'Vanna, my Vanna, where are you? answer me: children: answer me.'

p. 322 ***Dio mio . . .***: 'My God, my God, have pity on us.'

p. 323 ***Sì Vanna mia . . .***: 'Yes, my Vanna, we will return; God forbid I should lose you as well.'

p. 323 ***Nossignore è buono . . .***: 'God is good, and will certainly bless them.'

Speaking Likenesses

FLORA

p. 325 The first part of this text, Flora's story, is also reprinted in the *Oxford Book of Children's Stories*, edited by Jan Mark, 1994. It is, however, unfortunately detached from the rest of the text, and in addition most of the interpolated questions and answers have been omitted.

p. 328 **Apple of Discord**: classical symbol of strife and conflict.

p. 329 **the frog did not know . . .**: he will be met again, in Edith's story.

p. 329 **footstools glided about**: cf. the moving furniture in *Alice Through the Looking-Glass*.

p. 332 **Lord Nelson**: British Admiral at the Battle of Trafalgar and national hero.

p. 333 **Les Grâces**: a children's game with hoops.

p. 333 **Hunt the Pincushion**: this, of course, is a horrific imaginary game, whose name suggests something far more benign along the lines of hunt the thimble; its various 'pins' represent the anger and hostility that cause quarrelling, discord and injury, to victims and perpetrators.

p. 334 **Self Help**: presumably a glancing satire on Victorian counsels of self-interest is intended here, to be 'resolved' by Maggie's selflessness in Part Three.

p. 339 **too many poor friends**: Victorian women commonly undertook sewing (always known as 'work') as a charitable activity, making layettes and household items for the deserving poor.

p. 340 **lunns**: currant buns or tea cakes

p. 341 **lucifers**: matches.

p. 341 **purple grapes**: see Aesop's fable *The Fox and the Grapes*. Edith's story contains several references to such fables.

p. 342 **fagot**: bundle of firewood.

p. 344 **foxes always carried about a brush**: 'brush' is a fox's tail.

p. 345 **fire-wheels**: for striking a spark.

p. 346 **Arabian Nights**: *The Thousand and One Nights*, which enjoyed immense popularity in the nineteenth century and is, of course, based on a framework of continuous story-telling partly imitated here.

p. 347 **tapers**: wax candles.

p. 349 **I mustn't stop to play**: by resisting successive temptations during her journey, Maggie redeems the failures of Flora and Edith. The boisterous children, Mouth Boy and sleeping figures are all symbolic personages.

p. 352 **flashed with glittering gold**: Maggie's devotion to duty is reward by a brief epiphany. At a well-concealed level, *Speaking Likenesses* describes the religious journey through the trials of life towards a paradise of blissful rest.

Commonplace

p. 354 **Bradshaw**: ubiquitous Victorian railway guide. Brompton-on-Sea is thus a fictional place, though Brompton is the name of a fashionable London district, and the town is loosely based on south-coast seaside resorts like Brighton and Eastbourne.

p. 355 **cap**: the custom for women over a certain age to wear a pleated or lace cap indoors was being phased out at this period.

p. 355 **'Times' Supplement**: *The Times* was the major daily paper carrying such announcements.

p. 356 **Indian army-surgeon**: a surgeon to the British Army in India, not an Indian national.

p. 357 **general practice**: as a family physician.

p. 357 royal duke: Brighton was popularised by the Prince Regent, later George IV.

p. 361 formally come out: marking the transition from childhood to adulthood in social terms.

p. 361 prospects: of marriage.

p. 362 self-chaperoning: in keeping with her slightly old-fashioned ways, Catherine insists on her sisters being chaperoned to social gatherings.

p. 362 succeeded his father: inherited house and income.

p. 364 Notting Hill: residential district in west London.

p. 364 petted each other: indulge, treat affectionately.

p. 366 hood: carriage-cover, as on a convertible.

p. 367 ***Se non è vero è ben trovato***: If not true, it is apt (well found).

p. 368 pines: pineapples.

p. 369 Newcastle-upon-Tyne: by this date an industrial city.

p. 370 her Grace: formal mode of address for dukes and duchesses.

p. 373 an M.D.: doctor of medicine.

p. 373 French assistant: employed as a teacher in Miss Drum's school.

p. 374 quoted Hone: *Hone's Every Day Book* (1826–7), a favourite in the Rossetti household, contained traditional rhymes and sayings.

p. 375 ***tableaux vivants***: mute and motionless representation of a painting or scene by persons in costume, a form of non-dramatic acting (literally, living pictures).

p. 376 charades: semi-theatrical acting game, with dialogue. The dispute is resolved, in Chapter X, by combining *tableaux* and charades.

p. 376 Crystal Palace: erected for the Great Exhibition of 1851 and removed to a site in south London, where it hosted concerts, exhibitions, etc.

p. 376 toilettes: ladies' fashions.

p. 377 Jenny: diminutive of Jane.

p. 379 the East: anywhere east of Greece; in this case, apparently Turkey, from the reference to the Bosphorus.

p. 379 been called to the bar: qualified as an advocate.

p. 382 Love-apple: archaic name for tomato.

p. 382 **little boys**: traditionally, Love is represented by Cupid.

p. 382 **Paris**: the proposed scene is based on the Judgement of Paris.

p. 383 **English-Grecian maidens**: young Englishwomen in classical-style costume.

p. 384 **Athenian owl**: the emblem of Minerva/Athena, goddess of wisdom, and tutelary deity of the city of Athens.

p. 385 ***corps dramatique***: cast.

p. 388 **county family**: from landed or titled ancestry.

p. 389 **own absolute disposal**: the details of Jane's proposed marriage settlement indicate that she would retain her personal inheritance, at a time when under English law a husband acquired all his wife's property unless a separate legal settlement were made.

p. 389 **set as a copy**: for handwriting practice.

p. 392 **Mr Durham might object**: to his fiancée attending such a social gathering. It is, of course, Catherine who objects to this breach of etiquette.

p. 396 **Cooee**: the long-distance call used as a signal by native Australians, and adopted by British settlers.

p. 398 ***vis-à-vis***: seated opposite, in improper proximity.

p. 398 **Gateshead**: industrial city in north-east England.

p. 399 **tatting**: a form of crochet-work.

p. 401 **flinging shoes**: popular custom following a wedding ceremony, as bride and groom depart, to bring luck.

p. 401 **bagatelle**: a drawing-room game played on a board, somewhat like billiards.

p. 401 **turnip-ghost**: Hallowe'en lantern made from hollowed-out turnip.

p. 401 **the Lakes**: the Lake District.

p. 402 ***Quel che piace giova***: that which pleases is beneficial.

p. 402 **all seeing Naples**: an allusion to the saying 'see Naples and die'.

p. 402 **over at thirty**: traditionally, women were accustomed to regard themselves as 'old maids' if unmarried at age thirty, though in fact many Victorian women married at a later age owing to family responsibilities and prudential concerns.

p. 404 **East-end poor**: poverty and poor housing were concentrated in the working-class East End of London, in contrast with the fashionable and wealthy West End.

ROSSETTI AND HER CRITICS

Athenaeum, 26 April 1862, pp. 557–8

This review of CGR's first book was typical of those in the leading periodicals of the day, where most reviews were unsigned.

Goblin Market and Other Poems
These lays by Miss Rossetti have the charm of a welcome surprise. They are no mere reflections and echoes of previous beauty and music, but, whatever their faults, express both in essence and form the individuality of the writer. To read these poems after the laboured and skilful, but not original, verse which has been issued of late, is like passing from a picture gallery, with its well-figured semblance of nature, to the real nature out-of-doors, which greets us with the waving grass and the pleasant shock of the breeze.

'Goblin Market', the most important of Miss Rossetti's poems, has true dramatic character, life and picture for those who read it simply as a legend, while it has an inner meaning for all who can discern it. Like many of its companions it is suggestive and symbolical without the stiffness of set allegory . . .

In other cases, both thought and expression are so delicate that the full meaning can only be discerned by a poetic eye. The reader, for instance, must himself bring imagination to the poem called 'An Apple Gathering', or he will lose much of its significance . . . The sweetness of [the] lines lingers on the ear, and makes us regret that Miss Rossetti who is, when she chooses, a mistress of verbal harmony, should at times employ discords with a frequency which aims at variety but results in harshness . . . Miss Rossetti's poems are not all of equal merit, and there is more than one from the teaching of which we dissent; but the entire series displays imagination and beauty which are both undeniable and unborrowed.

Fraser's Magazine, July 1864, p. 204

Our Camp in the Woodland: A Day with the Gentle Poets
In Miss Rossetti's poems we do not remark that peculiar perfection of form which we find in Miss Ingelow's; but she shows, I think, a more entire and racy individuality. She is the slave neither of forms

nor of ideas. She is bold, vigorous, peculiar, daring. Speaking generally, her feelings are strong and in command; she does not weep openly; though at times a touch of careless sadness wanders across the strings . . .

Saturday Review, 23 June 1866, pp. 761–2

The Prince's Progress and Other Poems

There is a lightly tuneful meditativeness about most of Miss Rossetti's verses which in a manner stamps them . . . as records of the best moments of one of the happiest minds.[1] They have the delicious and truly poetic effect of striking us as things overheard, as if they were the unconscious outcome of the most harmonious moods, in which a hearer is neither suspected nor wished . . . There is not much thinking in them, not much high or deep feeling, no passion, and no sense of the vast blank space which a great poet always finds encompassing the ideas of life and nature and human circumstance. But they are melodious and sweet, and marked with that peculiar calm which lay at the root of Shelley's notion of happiness as an essential condition of poetry . . .

Neither the 'Prince's Progress', nor the shorter poems that follow can be said to open up veins of thought and feeling that are new, but there is a certain quaint originality both in the versification and the concrete style in which the writer delights to treat all her fancies . . . All her visions of social and moral truths seem to come to her through pictures, and to stay in her mind in the pictorial shape. Instead of analysing her ideas, she embodies and dramatises them . . . It is this vivid and picturesque way of moulding her subjects which compensates for Miss Rossetti's want of strong grasp and expansiveness. Nearly every stanza presents a picture full of colour and movement and redolent of a peculiarly purified sensuousness.

The Examiner, 18 December 1875, p. 1418

This review marked the appearance of CGR's *Poems* (1875) a re-issue of her two previous collections in one volume, with some additional pieces. For E. W. Gosse, see Prose Extracts, Letter to Edmund Gosse, page 421.

Miss Rossetti's Poems reviewed by E. W. G[osse]

It is natural to compare her with the one other poetess of the first rank which England has possessed, Elizabeth Browning, but it is this accidental analogy alone which unites their names. Beyond the tie of

[1] from Shelley's definition of poetry as 'the record of the best and happiest moments of the best and happiest minds'.

sex, there is hardly any link between them. The one was eager for objective successes, full of rhetorical ardour, wide dramatic sympathy, and irrepressible vivacity of intellect; the other is subdued, restrained, withdrawn, rippling over with faultless music in a low key, introspective, melancholy, pensive. In Mrs Browning the fiery, almost volcanic torrent of thought rent and scarred the inadequate channel of the form; in Miss Rossetti an intense thread of imagination flows onwards in the close control of a most artistic style. The two poets are as nearly allied to one another as Dryden to Gray, as Byron to Coleridge. In the isolation of the living poetess it is perhaps to Coleridge more than to any other writer to whom we must look for a kindred genius. Her occasional assimilation of style to that of her brother, her rare adoption of Tennysonian mannerisms, are accidental and exterior; but the resemblance to Coleridge is more essential. There is in them both the same struggle between a direct didactic purpose and a purely romantic inspiration, the same tendency to darken poetic thought with pietistic or transcendental transports, the same occasional gift of unsurpassed melody. With special regard to this last quality it appears to us that there are and have been singers amongst us whose fulness [sic] of voice, whose range of notes, whose sonorousness of organ far exceeded these two; but that in subtlety and magic of music there have been none that have surpassed Coleridge and Christina Rossetti at their highest.

The Academy, 27 August 1881, p. 152

Thomas Hall Caine (1853–1931) was an aspiring novelist who had befriended DGR and edited *Sonnets of Three Centuries* (1882) to which CGR contributed. His observations reflect the status commonly accorded in this period to 'nature poetry' as a quasi-substitute for religious faith.

A Pageant, and other Poems reviewed by T. Hall Caine
As to Miss Rossetti's especial vocation for depicting Nature's changeful aspects, it must be said . . . that she is never so happy as when realising the gentler side of Nature's temper – her stillness, which the rippling of rivers or twittering of birds makes yet more still, her cloudlessness, her hopefulness and peace. With Nature's less tractable moods of mist and wind, and with her sterner heights of hill and fell, the poet displays less sympathy, and it may be doubted if, together with her love of loveliness, she could possess the gift that compasses them. This point is the worthier of remark from the clear tendency Miss Rossetti has shown, more than ever in recent years, to drop into a despondent personal tone, which, though

wholly natural and unforced, is clearly somewhat pampered, even in the face of robuster promptings. Such a tone as I speak of finds vent in the admirable 'Ballad of Boding' (a poem full of symbol, and surpassed for truth and fervour by nothing in this volume).

The Letters of Sir Walter Raleigh, ed. Lady Raleigh, 2 vols., 1926, p. 164

Walter Raleigh (1861–1922) became in 1904 the first Professor of English Literature at Oxford.

11 January 1892

Three or four of her poems . . . make a cheap fool of Browning – and leave E. B. B. barely human. I think she is the best poet alive. You read *Wife to Husband* and then try to read *Any Wife to Any Husband* – it is like going out of Heaven on a visit to a monkey house . . . read *Twice*, and *A Green Cornfield* and *They desire a better country* and *The Hour and the Ghost* and *From House to Home* (the framework is vague but the end is marvellous) and *Old and New Year Ditties*; and then say how R. B. can be a poet. He is an educated, interesting, progressive pig . . .

New Poems by Christina Rossetti, ed. William Michael Rossetti, 1896, pp. xii–xiii

[preface] Christina's habits of composing were eminently of the spontaneous kind. I question her having ever once deliberated with herself whether or not she would write out something or other, and then, after thinking out a subject, having proceeded to treat it in regular spells of work. Instead of this, something impelled her feelings, or 'came into her head', and her hand obeyed the dictation. I suppose she scribbled the lines off rapidly enough, and afterwards took whatever amount of pains she deemed requisite for keeping them right in form and expression – for she was quite conscious that a poem demands to be good in execution, as well as genuine in impulse; but (strange as it seems to say so of a sister who, up to the year 1876, was almost constantly in the same house as me) I cannot remember ever seeing her in the act of composition (I take no count here of the *bouts-rimés* sonnets of 1848). She consulted nobody, and solicited no advice; though it is true that with regard to her published volumes – or at any rate the first two of them – my brother volunteered to point out what seemed well adapted for insertion, and what the reverse, and he found her a very willing recipient of his monitions.

The Swinburne Letters, ed. C. Y. Lang, 7 vols., Yale University Press, 1962, vol. 6, p. 176

A. C. Swinburne (1837–1909), whose *Poems and Ballads* (1866) caused a storm of protest against their blasphemy and indecency, was otherwise a warm admirer of CGR, in personal and literary terms. According to Edmund Gosse (*The Life of Algernon Charles Swinburne*, 1917, p. 137) in poetic matters 'Swinburne never failed to recognise the priority of Christina; he used to call her the Jael who led their host to victory'.

To W. M. Rossetti, 25 January 1904, on the publication of *The Poetical Works of Christina Rossetti*, edited by William Michael Rossetti, 1904

> The book, in the monumental phrase of Blessed Sarah Gamp, is indeed 'rich in beauty': but, good Satan! what a fearful warning against the criminal lunacy of theolatry! It is horrible to think of such a woman – and of so many otherwise noble and beautiful natures – spiritually infected and envenomed by the infernal and putrefying genius of the Galilean serpent [i.e. Christ].

A. C. Benson, *Rossetti*, Macmillan (English Men of Letters Series), 1904, pp. 142–3

> In one important direction did [Dante Gabriel Rossetti] and his sister Christina and Mr Swinburne . . . modify the literary art of the time. They effected a reformation in language. Poetry had fallen under the influence of Tennyson in an almost helpless fashion . . . Rossetti, Christina Rossetti, and Mr Swinburne struck boldly across the path, leaving a trail of fire. They were not so much rebellious, but they did again what Tennyson had done in his early prime. They dared to use simple and direct words, which they infused with new and audacious charm. There was nothing didactic about them; they went straight to the source of pure beauty; they recharged, so to speak, homely and direct expressions with the very element of poetical vigour. Even Christina Rossetti, deeply religious as she is, had little ethical about her. She enjoyed her faith, if I may use the expression, with all the rapture of a medieval saint. She visualized her dreams without timidity, and spoke her thoughts, not because they were improving, but because they were beautiful.

Arthur Symons, 'Christina Rossetti', *Poets and the Poetry of the Nineteenth Century*, vol. 9, ed. Alfred H. Miles, 1907, pp. 7–8

Arthur Symons (1865–1945) was a leading figure in the Decadent movement, best known for his critical book *The Symbolist Movement in Literature* (1899).

Miss Rossetti's genius was essentially sombre, or it wrote itself at least on a dark background of gloom. The thought of death had a constant fascination for her, almost such a fascination as it had for Leopardi or Baudelaire; only it was not the fascination of attraction, as with the one, nor of repulsion, as with the other, but of interest, sad but scarcely unquiet interest in what the dead are doing underground, in their memories – if memory they have – of the world they have left; a singular whimsical sympathy with the poor dead, like that expressed in two famous lines of the 'Fleurs du Mal'.

These strange little poems, with their sombre and fantastic colouring – the picturesque outcome of deep and curious pondering on things unseen – lead easily, by an obvious transition, to the poems of spiritual life, in the customary or religious sense of the term. Miss Rossetti's devotional poetry is quite unlike most other poetry of the devotional sort. It is intensely devout, sometimes almost liturgical in character; surcharged with personal emotion, a cry of the heart, an ecstasy of the soul's grief or joy; it is never didactic, or concerned with purposes of edification. She does not preach; she prays. We are allowed to overhear a dialogue of the soul with God. Her intensity of religious feeling touches almost, on the ecstasy of Jacopone da Todi, but without his delirium. It is usually a tragic ecstasy. In such a poem as 'Despised and Rejected', one of the most marvellous religious poems in the language, the reality of the externalised emotion is almost awful: it is scarcely to be read without a shudder.

The Diary of Virginia Woolf, vol. 1, ed. Anne Olivier Bell, Hogarth Press, London, 1977, pp. 178–9

Virginia Woolf (1882–1941) novelist and critic, had previously reviewed CGR's letters in the *Times Literary Supplement*. It is suggested that Woolf had been reading the 1904 edition of Christina Rossetti's *Poetical Works*, but her remarks do not relate closely to the biographical preface of that volume. For a longer appreciation of Christina Rossetti by Virginia Woolf, see Virginia Woolf, 'I Am Christina Rossetti', *The Common Reader*, [below].

Monday 4 August 1918

While waiting to buy a book in which to record my impressions first of Christina Rossetti, then of Byron, I had better write them here . . . Christina has the great distinction of being a born poet, as she seems to have known very well herself. But if I were bringing a case against God she is one of the first witnesses I should call. It is melancholy reading. First she starved herself of love, which meant also life; then of poetry in deference to what she thought her religion demanded . . . Poetry was castrated too. She would set herself to do the psalms into verse; & to make all her poetry subservient to the Christian doctrines. Consequently, as I think, she starved into austere emaciation a very fine original gift, which only wanted licence to take to itself a far finer form than, shall we say, Mrs Browning's. She wrote very easily; in a spontaneous childlike kind of way one imagines, as is the case generally with a true gift; still undeveloped. She has the natural singing power. She thinks, too. She has fancy. She could, one is profane enough to guess, have been ribald & witty. And, as a reward for all her sacrifices, she died in terror, uncertain of salvation.

Dorothy Margaret Stuart, *Christina Rossetti*, Macmillan (English Men of Letters Series, edited by J. C. Squire), 1930, pp. v and 175–6

Stuart's views are typical of the slightly defensive tone adopted by Rossetti's admirers in the wake of Modernism ('the storm of literary Bolshevism'). Despite Stuart's claims, Rossetti's reputation did suffer a subsequent eclipse, even greater than that suffered by Victorian poetry in general, from which it only began to recover in the 1960s.

It is a happy chance that Christina Rossetti should be admitted to the English Men of Letters Series in the centenary year of her birth. During the thirty-six years that have passed since her death her fame has been quietly and steadily growing, and few will now be found to question her claim to a niche in that illustrious company . . .

In the matter of sincerity there is nothing to choose between these two true-hearted and single-minded ladies [Elizabeth Barrett Browning and Christina Rossetti]; in the matter of mental equipment Mrs Browning was perhaps the more fortunate, though too much has been made of Miss Rossetti's lack of mere 'book-learning' . . .

They both wrote too much, and preserved too much of what they had written; and if the sum total of their poetry were weighed in the balance it might be found that the elder lady's general level of attainment was at least as high as the younger lady's, and that she achieved a rather more even distribution of ore and dross. But if we make a small bouquet of Christina Rossetti's most beautiful songs and sonnets we shall be constrained to acknowledge that within her limits no woman-poet of the modern world can be found to equal her, and not an overwhelming number of men . . .

Christina Rossetti was not an imitator; nor, although she evolved from her instincts and experiences a style inalienably hers, can she be called an innovator. She left no successors, she founded no school . . . Her fame has suffered no fluctuations. Aestheticism did not bring it forward. Neo-Georgianism has not driven it back. She has weathered the storm of literary Bolshevism which broke after the Great War, and it is difficult to conceive what consequence yet hanging in the stars could throw her back into complete eclipse . . . Her candour, her emotional depth, her felicity of phrase, and intensity of vision, are strangely congenial to a world which has moved so far away both from her moral code and from her religious creed.

Virginia Woolf, 'I Am Christina Rossetti', *The Common Reader*, Second Series, 1932, pp. 237–44.

Virginia Woolf wrote this in 1930 after reading Margaret Sandars's biography; the title refers to an incident related by Sanders, not to any claim made by Woolf.

Your poems are full of gold dust and 'sweet geraniums' varied brightness; your eye noted incessantly how rushes are 'velvet-headed', and lizards have a 'strange metallic mail' – your eye, indeed, observed with a sensual pre-Raphaelite intensity that must have surprised Christina the Anglo-Catholic. But to her perhaps you owed the fixity and sadness of your muse . . . your God was a harsh God, your heavenly crown was set with thorns. No sooner have you feasted on beauty with your eyes than your mind tells you that beauty is vain and beauty passes. Death, oblivion and rest lap round your songs with their dark wave. And then, incongruously, a sound of scurrying and laughter is heard. There is the patter of animals' feet and the odd gutteral noises of rooks and the snufflings of obtuse furry animals grunting and nosing. For you were not a pure saint by any means. You pulled legs; you tweaked noses. You were at war with all humbug and pretence. Modest as you were, still you were drastic, sure of your gift, convinced of your vision. A firm hand pruned your lines; a sharp ear tested their music. Nothing soft, otiose, irrelevant cumbered your pages. In a word, you were an artist.

The Pelican Guide to English Literature, vol. 6, ed. Boris Ford, Penguin, 1958, pp. 364–6

At the time of writing, Robson was lecturer in English Literature at Oxford University. Few critics would agree that *Spring Quiet* represents a high point in CGR's writing.

> 'Pre-Raphaelite Poetry' by W. W. Robson
> . . . negation, denial, deprivation are the characteristic notes of Christina's religious poetry: and it must be admitted that an extensive reading of it is depressing. The sadness, often morbidity, which is felt even in her delightful poetry for children, even in Goblin Market . . . the felt absence of any outlet for aggressive impulses, deepening into depression or resignation; the compensating yearning for death imagined as an anodyne, an eternal anaesthetic – these are familiar to every reader of her poetry. And it is difficult to find many poems in which she either transcends them or turns them into the conditions for major creation.
>
> . . . a comparison of her better known *Spring Quiet* with Hopkins' early *Heaven Haven* brings out a certain community of temperament . . . but it reminds us that *Heaven Haven*, unlike *Spring Quiet*, by no means represents a high point of its author's achievement.

David Daiches, *A Critical History of English Literature*, 2 vols., Ronald Press, 1960, pp. 1021–2

A respected British scholar, Daiches was professor of English Literature at the University of Sussex.

> The series of sonnets *Monna Innominata* are of more biographical than poetic interest (Christina Rossetti rejected two offers of marriage on religious grounds, and the latter particularly left a sense of loss): all except the final sonnet in the sequence have a thinness that is the most conspicuous fault of her weaker poetry.

Stuart Curran, 'The Lyric Voice of Christina Rossetti', *Victorian Poetry*, vol. 9, 1971, pp. 287ff

At the time of writing, Stuart Curran was Associate Professor at the University of Wisconsin. His views are typical of the meagre, qualified recognition CGR received in this period.

> *Goblin Market*, remarkable as it is, cannot sustain itself, though not through any lack in the poet's technique. Indeed, it is a technical tour-de-force, but the mind behind the poem is implacably shallow . . .
>
> But a great poet cannot be unpretentious: he dares and questions; he attempts to answer, not only in the matter of the human being and his universe but in the less glamorous matters of diction and meter, of dramatic imagery and formal necessities, of all the mundane materials out of which great poetry is forged. Christina Rossetti's

> universe was settled before she came of age, and it neither changed nor developed . . . Her poetry is largely devoid of sharp observation, whether intellectual or imaginative . . . She falls back on pretty language, the bane of so many women poets. Whereas Emily Dickinson can sustain a totally feminine tone without sacrificing a crystalline perception and subtle imagination, this woman's tone is too often merely effeminate, weak and nebulous. She is a good poet, an able poet, but not a great one.

Germaine Greer, introduction to *Goblin Market*, 1975, pp. xvi and xxxvi. Reprinted in Germaine Greer, *Essays on Women and Literature*, (forthcoming).

Germaine Greer is a leading feminist writer, author of *The Female Eunuch* (1971); her interpretation of *Goblin Market* is in keeping with other contemporary critics who find the poem expressive of sexual arousal and link this to infantine experiences and desires.

> Christina Rossetti was not simply a Victorian, who had sucked guilt with her mother's milk and could not refer to her own body without embarrassment; she was also a woman. Her sensuality was unknown to her: the more it loomed vast and polymorphous in her dreams, the less able she was to confront it in any recognizable form. What was called innocence in women like Christina Rossetti was in fact agonized self-consciousness. Appalled by the uncontrollable violence of her own nature, Rossetti resolved to stifle herself, no matter what the cost, even though she could not conjure up what her reward for such relentless self-abuse might be . . .
>
> *Goblin Market* is a deeply perverse poem which will like Christina Rossetti herself keep its secret forever. It stirs in each reader the depths of half-remembered infantile experience only to baffle him by withholding the means of verbalizing and externalizing the memories that are printed on his flesh . . . Homosexuals may make superficially convincing cases that the poem is about the great virtue of physical love between sisters, and those who believe that heterosex is fundamentally distorted and sadistic will want to agree with them. All of us, however, have grown up with the unexpressed incest taboo which regulated the degree of physical contact we think appropriate between brothers and sisters, and all of us have somehow violated it. The poem it seems is about guilt, and the pleasure of guilt. However we reduce the poem to expound our own philosophies, we are left with the overriding fact of its subtle perversity and our own complicity.

Sandra Gilbert and Susan Gubar, *The Madwoman in the Attic*, 1979, pp. 566–7

'Goblin Market' seems to have a tantalizing number of other levels of meaning – meaning about and for women in particular so that it has recently begun to be something of a textual crux for feminist critics. To such readers, certainly, the indomitable Lizzie, standing like a lily, a rock, a beacon . . . may well seem almost a Victorian Amazon, a nineteenth century reminder that 'sisterhood is powerful'. Certainly, too, from, one feminist perspective, 'Goblin Market', with its evil and mercantile little men and its innocent, highminded women, suggests that men *hurt* while women redeem. Significantly, there are no men in the poem other than the unpleasant goblins . . . Rossetti does, then, seem to be dreamily positing an effectively matrilineal and matriarchal world, perhaps, even considering the strikingly sexual redemption scene between the sisters, a covertly (if ambivalently) lesbian world.

Dolores Rosenblum, 'Christina Rossetti: the Inward Pose', *Shakespeare's Sisters*, eds Sandra Gilbert and Susan Gubar, 1979, pp. 83–98

Both *The Madwoman in the Attic* and *Shakespeare's Sisters* represent key texts in the early feminist project of identifying the patriarchal nature of literary culture and women writers' struggle within or against it. Dolores Rosenblum went on to write *Christina Rossetti: the Poetry of Endurance* (1986); Simone de Beauvoir (1906–1986), French novelist and critic, was author of *The Second Sex* (trans. 1953).

Like most Victorian poets, Rossetti is sensitive to the disjunction between surface and depths, between appearances and the buried life. More than others, however, she is concerned with the point of juncture, literally the face that is looked at and the eyes that look out from it. Her poems are full of references to faces, masks, veils, shrouds and, less frequently, bodies fixed in an attitude – all surfaces to be regarded. This preoccupation with being looked at is not surprising in a woman poet. As Simone de Beauvoir has pointed out, in a patriarchal culture woman inevitably experiences herself as object and and other . . .

Perhaps Rossetti shrank from all the implications of woman's mask; she certainly did not flinch from anatomizing her own passion however, and she kept on protesting all her life. Hedged round by all kinds of prohibitions, struggling with 'fightings without and fears within' ('The Offering of the New Law') she remained resolutely her own person. Nothing ever really changed for her. The situation of being looked at – as a woman who was either marriageable or not, as an artist's model, and finally as a rather odd celebrity: a swarthy, dour, dumpy Victorian-woman-poet – was simply a prevailing condition of her life. Out of it and against it she wrote poetry moving from self absorption to self possession. Possessing her own soul comes down to lines like

> Thus am I mine own prison . . .
> I am not what I have, nor what I do;
> But what I was I am, I am even I.

G. B. Tennyson, *Victorian Devotional Poetry: The Tractarian Mode*, Harvard, 1981, pp. 198–202

In this book G. B. Tennyson, Professor of English at the University of California, Los Angeles (UCLA), discusses CGR in the context of work by John Keble, John Henry Newman, Isaac Williams and Charlotte Yonge.

Christina Rossetti is the true inheritor of the Tracterian devotional mode in poetry . . . Except for an occasional Christopher Smart or an occasional ordering of a few hymns along the lines of the Church year, devotional poetry as the Tractarians understood it had not been seen in England since the seventeenth century. When one comes upon Christina Rossetti without awareness of the intervention of the Tractarians, one is inclined to think she has sprung full grown from the brow of George Herbert; yet when one comes upon her poetry from an encounter with the Tractarians, one can see that her genesis is of a more conventional kind . . .

Christina Rossetti's most Tractarian element is her very approach to poetry itself as a way of seeking the Deity. Keble's bedrock principle that poetry is the expression of intense religious longing finds no more complete exemplification than in the poetry of Christina Rossetti. The biographical approach to her poetry, the strange, modern view that all longing must be sexual, especially if it is the longing of an umarried Victorian woman, has shrouded the extent to which Christina Rossetti's poetry illustrates not Freud's theory but Keble's. Much has been made of Christina Rossetti's yearnings in psychological terms, but not enough has been made of them in religious terms. Put in the context of Tractarian poetics, however, her yearnings are the material from which poetry and art proceeds.

Isobel Armstrong, 'Christina Rossetti: A Reading Diary', *Women Reading Women's Writing*, ed. Sue Roe, Harvester Wheatsheaf, 1987, pp. 117–37

At the time of writing, Isobel Armstrong was Professor of English Literature at the University of Southampton, and author of *Language as Living Form in Nineteenth Century Poetry* (1982). Her quotation from Julia Kristeva is taken from *Oxford Literary Review*, vol. 5, 1982, p. 128.

During public examinations and throughout my undergraduate career no single poem by Christina Rossetti was put before us for close reading. No essays were set on her work. Or, if poems of hers were discussed, I forgot them, which is equally significant. It was as if she and real poetry had never been . . . T. S. Eliot, I. A. Richards, William Empson, F. R. Leavis, these were the people I learned from . . .

Though it seems to me that the poem ['Winter Rain'] understands oppression in language very well, I do not want to settle for the politically dangerous notion of a female language which circumvents phallocentrism by separatism. The strength of the poem is that it negotiates directly with the power of repressive language, using pastoral in a way which recognises that pastoral conventions can be both liberating and coercive. Again, for the first time in my criticism I have talked of deconstruction. It seems to me that wrongful Derridean readings revolve on their own axis round the perpetual abstract sameness of the nature of the sign, of absence and presence, just as the Lacanian postulates of lack can be abstracted. Christina Rossetti's opening up of endless and very particular interrogations is not like this at all. The poem has a deconstructive movement because it reveals contradictions by putting pressure on its own logic . . .

I am still struggling with Kristeva's work on abjection and with layers of reading, or changed reading, of 'Winter Rain'. Kristeva's exploration of abjection as 'the recognition of the fundamental *lack* of all being, meaning, language and desire' as a constant dissolution and creation of limits which must therefore provoke a 'narcissistic crisis' because it disrupts the self-sufficient order of self-reflection, must bear upon this poem and [its] doubled but non-existent lilies. Her association of the incommensurable of abjection with religious constructions may well be a way into Christina Rossetti's religious poetry and back from that to the other poems. It is not proper to sever her religious poems from the rest of the work . . . And yet I am worried by Kristeva because the notion of abjection does without history . . . The same worry pursues Derrida's cunning conceptualisation of woman in terms of disruption through suspension of decidable oppositions. And I still wonder if you can say this only if you are a man.

D. M. R. Bentley, 'The Meretricious and the Meritorious in Goblin Market', *The Achievement of Christina Rossetti*, ed. David A. Kent, Cornell University Press, 1987, pp. 63–4

In this essay David Bentley, of the University of Western Ontario, proposed the conjecture that *Goblin Market* was written for the penitents and staff (Sisters) at the St Mary Magdalene Home. Subsequent research shows that Rossetti began work there sometime in 1859, around the time the poem was written.

> Corresponding to the educated and by definition literate 'readers' of the poem [*Goblin Market*] is Lizzie, the sister (Sister) whose moral reason enables her to interpret accurately such things as the goblins' fruit and her sister's illness, and who moreover cautions Laura with the exemplary tale of Jeanie, a simulacrum within *Goblin Market* of the poem itself and its didactic purpose . . . Rescued from the fate of Jeanie by a sister's love and acquainted with deep remorse, a spiritually and physically regenerated Laura becomes at the conclusion a wife, a mother and (in another simulacrum of the poem's didactic aim) a teller of exemplary tales – a model of aspiration, that is, for anyone with a desire to change for the better and the belief that, with the help of 'a sister' and the grace of God, good can be brought out of evil . . .
>
> If it was not read at the St Mary Magdalene Home [for Fallen Women] one cannot help think that it should have been.

Anthony H. Harrison, *Christina Rossetti in Context*, 1988, p. 63

Harrison's is the first full-length critical study of Rossetti in recent years; as well as intertextuality it discusses her sense of poetic vocation and the aesthetics of conciseness and renunciation in her work. Further discussion followed in Antony H. Harrison, *Victorian Poets and Romantic Poems: Intertextuality and Ideology* (1990); and in the special edition of *Victorian Poetry* devoted to Rossetti (1994).

> Recent studies of Rossetti have begun to expose the full extent to which her art depends upon literary models. Despite the ostensibly personal and sincere voice that speaks from many of her lyrics of disappointed love as well as from almost all of her devotional poetry, her work is as genuinely intertextual in its extrapolation of particular models as any poetry written by Swinburne or Morris or her brother . . . While treating such traditional topics as erotic and spiritual love, mutability, the quest for salvation, and the beauty of nature, however, Rossetti self-consciously imitated and revised tradition or diverged from it in an avant-garde pursuit of appropriate, if not ideal, forms and prosodic modes. Thus her concerns

(and her poetry) are at once traditional and radically innovative, sincere and artificial, self-effacing and self-promoting, self-expressive and parodic. Because of these features of her poetry Rossetti stands out (perhaps in greater relief than any of her contemporaries) as a pivotal figure in some of the most important cultural transitions that took place between 1850 and 1900.

Angela Leighton, *Victorian Women Poets: Writing Against the Heart*, 1992, p. 158

In *Writing Against the Heart*, Angela Leighton, lecturer in English at the University of Hull, places CGR midway in the tradition of female writing running from Felicia Hemans, L.E.L., Elizabeth Barrett Browning, Augusta Webster, Michael Field, Alice Meynell and Charlotte Mew.

> In the end, the secret itself [in *Winter: My Secret*] may be only another device of 'fun'. By implication, the idea of some inherent, unlockable meaning at the heart of poetry may be only another of its enticing lies; another of the supplementary 'flaming dragons', debarring the way to the true original. 'The Lost Titian' is about secrets, both the secret of Titian's subject matter and the secret of the painting's whereabouts. Both of those, however, are permanently lost references, like so many of the secrets in Rossetti's poetry. All that remains in this seductively self-deconstructing story is the difference, never to be resolved but always felt, between the lying decoy and the nostalgically desired authenticity of the lost work, like the difference between the man's interpretation and the woman's dream [in *Reflection*], the lilies on the surface and the dark pool below [in *Echo from Willowwood*]. Secrets, for Rossetti, are a figure for that game of reference which, true to the mood of many of her poems, is both a haunting loss and a teasing strategy of 'fun'.

Isobel Armstrong, *Victorian Poetry: Poetry, poetics and politics*, 1993, p. 257

This extract is from '"A Music of Thine Own": Women's Poetry', a chapter in a magisterial re-reading of Victorian poetry in terms of self-conscious post-Romantic responses to the modern world. At the time of writing, Armstrong was Professor of English at Birkbeck College, London, and a leading British critic in the re-evaluation of Rossetti's work.

> Christina Rossetti does not write with the heat and prolixity which the expressive lyric seems to imply for her contemporaries. Her lyrics do negotiate with the terms of expressive theory but not in terms of the *obstruction* to expression to be seen in the work of so many women poets of this time. The insight of *Goblin Market*, that

overflow and resistance, expression and repression, create one another, leads her to exploit the barrier ambiguously. It restricts and creates possibility. It invites and refuses transgression. This may be why in her hands the 'conventional' religious lyric is more unorthodox than any other religious poetry by women at this time.

The cool discipline with which the struggle for the smallest space goes on, the nakedness and reserve, passion and restraint, the aggression and rigour of so much of Rossetti's work, creates both the moments of lyric exhilaration and the resilient and savage wit in her poems. In 'A Birthday' – 'My heart is like a singing bird' – the release of exuberant passion is celebrated characteristically with a ritual of artifice. In 'My Dream' a lascivious and bloated crocodile works destruction, crunching and sucking his victims, until it is time for it to conform to convention: his tumescent size diminishes . . . In 'Eve' 'Huge camels knelt/As if in deprecation' of her grief. Only the serpent grins, truthful to a world of nature in which animals and human beings cannot exist in mutual sympathy.

'Winter: My Secret' is a poem in which the wit and lyric energy of Rossetti's work came together. It is a poem about secrecy and reserve, prohibition, taboo, revealing and concealing, and is almost a summa of her work. Provocative and flirtatious and yet deeply reticent, it turns on the refusal of expression. It is about and is itself a barrier.

CHECKLIST OF BOOKS BY CHRISTINA ROSSETTI

Verses: dedicated to Her Mother, privately printed by G. Polidori, 1847
Goblin Market and Other Poems, Macmillan, 1862 (issued as *Poems*, Roberts Bros, 1866)
The Prince's Progress and Other Poems, Macmillan, 1866
Commonplace, and Other Short Stories, F. S. Ellis and Roberts Bros, 1870
SingSong: a Nursery Rhyme Book, George Routledge and Roberts Bros, 1872, re-issued 1893
Speaking Likenesses, Macmillan, 1874
Annus Domini: A Prayer for Each Day of the Year, James Parker & Co, 1874
Goblin Market, The Prince's Progress and Other Poems, Macmillan, 1875 (issued as *Poems*, Roberts Bros, 1876)
Seek and Find: A Double Series of Short Studies of the Benedicite, SPCK, 1879
A Pageant and Other Poems, Macmillan and Roberts Bros, 1881
Called to be Saints: the Minor Festivals Devotionally Studied, SPCK and E. & J. B. Young, 1881
Letter and Spirit: Notes on the Commandments, SPCK, 1883
Time Flies: A Reading Diary, SPCK, 1885, and Roberts Bros, 1886
Poems: New and Enlarged Edition, Macmillan, 1890
The Face of the Deep: a Devotional Commentary on the Apocalypse, SPCK and E. & J. B. Young, 1892
Verses: reprinted from 'Called to be Saints', 'Time Flies' and 'The Face of the Deep', SPCK and E. & J. B. Young, 1893
New Poems, hitherto Unpublished or Uncollected, ed. W. M. Rossetti, Macmillan, 1896
Maude: A Story for Girls, ed. W. M. Rossetti, James Bowden and Herbert S. Stone, 1897
The Poetical Works of Christina Rossetti, with Memoir and Notes, ed. W. M. Rossetti, Macmillan, 1904

SUGGESTIONS FOR FURTHER READING

Armstrong, Isobel, *Victorian Poetry: Poetry, poetics and politics*, Routledge, 1993.

Battersby, Christine, *Gender and Genius: Towards a Feminist Aesthetics*, The Women's Press, 1989.

Bell, Mackenzie, *Christina Rossetti, A Biographical and Critical Study*, Hurst and Blackett, 1898.

Blake, Kathleen, *Love and the Woman Question: the Art of Self-Postponement*, Barnes & Noble, 1982.

Bornand, Odette (ed.) *The Diary of William Michael Rossetti*, Clarendon Press, 1977.

Chapman, Raymond, *Faith and Revolt: Studies in the Literary Influence of the Oxford Movement*, Weidenfeld & Nicolson, 1970.

Clarke, Norma, *Ambitious Heights: Writing, Friendship, Love*, Routledge, 1990.

Crump, R. W. (ed.), *The Complete Poems of Christine Rossetti: A Variorum Edition*, 3 vols, Louisiana State University Press, 1979–90.

Daly, Gay, *The Pre-Raphaelites in Love*, Ticknor & Fields/Constable, 1989.

Doughty, O. and Wahl, J. R. (eds), *The Letters of Dante Gabriel Rossetti*, 4 vols, Clarendon Press, 1965.

Faxon, Alicia C., *Dante Gabriel Rossetti*, Phaidon, 1989.

Fredeman, W. E., *Pre-Raphaelitism: A Bibliocritical Study*, Harvard University Press/OUP, 1965.

The Germ: the Literary Magazine of the Pre-Raphaelites, facsimile reprint by Ashmolean Museum/Birmingham Museums and Art Gallery, 1979.

Gilbert, Sandra, and Gubar, Susan, *The Madwoman in the Attic: The Woman Writer and the Nineteenth-Century Literary Imagination*, Yale University Press, 1979.

Gilbert, Sandra and Gubar, Susan (eds), *Shakespeare's Sisters*, Yale University Press, 1979.

Harrison, Antony H., *Christina Rossetti in Context*, University of North Carolina Press/Harvester, 1988.

Harrison, Antony H., *Victorian Poets and Romantic Poems*, University Press of Virginia, 1990.

Harrison, Antony H. (ed.), *The Collected Letters of Christina Rossetti*, 3 vols., University Press of Virginia, 1995–.

Hunt, John Dixon, *The Pre-Raphaelite Imagination 1848–1900*, Routledge, 1968.

Jones, Kathleen, *Learning not to be First: the Life of Christina Rossetti*, Windrush Press/Oxford Paperbacks, 1991.

Kent, David A. (ed.), *The Achievement of Christina Rossetti*, Cornell University Press, 1987.

Landow, George, *Victorian Types: Biblical Typology in Victorian Literature, Art and Thought*, Routledge, 1980.

Leighton, Angela, *Victorian Women Poets: Writing Against the Heart*, Harvester/University Press of Virginia, 1992.

Marsh, Jan, *Christina Rossetti: a Literary Biography*, Cape/Viking, 1994.

Moers, Ellen, *Literary Women*, Women's Press, 1978.

Packer, Lona Mosk, *Christina Rossetti*, CUP/University of California Press, 1963.

Packer, L. M. (ed.), *The Rossetti-Macmillan Letters*, CUP, 1963.

Paulin, Tom, 'Overthrowing the Fathers', *Minotaur*, Faber, 1992.

Peattie, R. W. (ed.), *Selected Letters of William Michael Rossetti*, Pennsylvania University Press, 1990.

Ricks, Christopher (ed.), *The Poems of Tennyson*, Longmans, 1969.

Ricks, Christopher (ed.), *The New Oxford Book of Victorian Verse*, OUP, 1987.

Rosenblum, Dolores, *Christina Rossetti: the Poetry of Endurance*, Southern Illinois University Press, 1986.

Rossetti, W. M. (ed.), *The Political Works of Dante Gabriel Rossetti*, Ellis & Elvey, 1891.

Rossetti, W. M. (ed.), *Rossetti Papers 1862 to 1870*, Sands & Co, 1903.

Rossetti, W. M. (ed.), *The Family Letters of Christina Rossetti*, Brown & Langham, 1908.

Rossetti, W. M., *Some Reminiscences*, Brown & Langham, 1906.

Sandars, Mary, *The Life of Christina Rossetti*, Hutchinson, 1930.

Sawtell, Margaret, *Christina Rossetti, her Life and Religion*, Mowbray, 1955.

Showalter, Elaine (ed.), *Maude: a Story for Girls*, Pickering and Chatto, 1993.

Sisson, C. H. (ed.) *Christina Rossetti: Selected Poems*, Carcanet, 1984.

Tennyson, G. B., *Victorian Devotional Poetry*, Harvard University Press, 1981.

Thomas, Eleanor W., *Christina Georgina Rossetti*, Columbia University Press, 1931.

Thomas, Frances, *Christina Rossetti*, Virago Press, 1994.

Todd, Janet (ed.), *Dictionary of British Women Writers*, Routledge, 1989.

Waller, R. D., *The Rossetti Family 1824–1854*, Manchester University Press, 1932.

Weintraub, Stanley, *Four Rossettis*, W. H. Allen, 1978.

INDEX OF TITLES AND FIRST LINES